𝔄𝔲𝔱𝔬𝔠𝔯𝔞𝔱 𝔈𝔡𝔦𝔱𝔦𝔬𝔫

THE COMPLETE WRITINGS OF OLIVER WENDELL HOLMES

WITH PORTRAITS, ILLUSTRATIONS, AND FACSIMILES

IN THIRTEEN VOLUMES

VOLUME XI

Dr. Holmes in the Study of his Boston House

RALPH WALDO EMERSON
JOHN LOTHROP MOTLEY

TWO MEMOIRS

BY

OLIVER WENDELL HOLMES

BOSTON AND NEW YORK
HOUGHTON, MIFFLIN AND COMPANY
The Riverside Press, Cambridge
1904

The Riverside Press, Cambridge, Mass., U. S. A.
Electrotyped and Printed by H. O. Houghton & Company.

CONTENTS.

RALPH WALDO EMERSON.

His Patience and Amiability. — Feeling with
which he was regarded. — Emerson and Burns.
— His Religious Belief. — His Relations with
Clergymen. — Future of his Reputation. — His
Life judged by the Ideal Standard.

JOHN LOTHROP MOTLEY.

LIST OF ILLUSTRATIONS

RALPH WALDO EMERSON.

" Thou wert the morning star among the living,
   Ere thy fair light had fled :
Now, having died, thou art as Hesperus, giving
   New splendor to the dead "

NOTE.

My thanks are due to the members of Mr. Emerson's family, and the other friends who kindly assisted me by lending interesting letters and furnishing valuable information.

OLIVER WENDELL HOLMES.

Boston, *November* 25, 1884.

1859.

RALPH WALDO EMERSON.

INTRODUCTION.

"I HAVE the feeling that every man's biography is at his own expense. He furnishes not only the facts, but the report. I mean that all biography is autobiography. It is only what he tells of himself that comes to be known and believed."

So writes the man whose life we are to pass in review, and it is certainly as true of him as of any author we could name. He delineates himself so perfectly in his various writings that the careful reader sees his nature just as it was in all its essentials, and has little more to learn than those human accidents which individualize him in space and time. About all these accidents we have a natural and pardonable curiosity. We wish to know of what race he came, what were the conditions into which he was born, what educational and social influences helped to mould his character, and what new elements Nature added to make him Ralph Waldo Emerson.

He himself believes in the hereditary transmission of certain characteristics. Though Nature appears capricious, he says, "Some qualities she carefully fixes and transmits, but some, and those the finer, she exhales with the breath of the individual, as too costly to perpetuate. But I notice also that they may become fixed and permanent in any stock, by painting

and repainting them on every individual, until at last
Nature adopts them and bakes them in her porcelain."

We have in New England a certain number of fam-
ilies who constitute what may be called the Academic
Races.   Their names have been on college catalogues
for generation after generation.   They have filled the
learned professions, more especially the ministry, from
the old colonial days to our own time.   If aptitudes
for the acquisition of knowledge can be bred into
a family as the qualities the sportsman wants in his
dog are developed in pointers and setters, we know
what we may expect of a descendant of one of the
Academic Races.   Other things being equal, he will
take more naturally, more easily, to his books.   His
features will be more pliable, his voice will be more
flexible, his whole nature more plastic than those of
the youth with less favoring antecedents.   The gift of
genius is never to be reckoned upon beforehand, any
more than a choice new variety of pear or peach in a
seedling; it is always a surprise, but it is born with
great advantages when the stock from which it springs
has been long under cultivation.

These thoughts suggest themselves in looking back
at the striking record of the family made historic by
the birth of Ralph Waldo Emerson.   It was remarkable for the long succession of clergymen in its gene-
alogy, and for the large number of college graduates
it counted on its rolls.

A genealogical table is very apt to illustrate the
"survival of the fittest," — in the estimate of the
descendants.   It is inclined to remember and record
those ancestors who do most honor to the living heirs

of the family name and traditions. As every man may count two grandfathers, four great-grandfathers, eight great-great-grandfathers, and so on, a few generations give him a good chance for selection. If he adds his distinguished grandmothers, he may double the number of personages to choose from. The great-grandfathers of Mr. Emerson at the sixth remove were thirty-two in number, unless the list was shortened by intermarriage of relatives. One of these, from whom the name descended, was Thomas Emerson of Ipswich, who furnished the staff of life to the people of that wonderfully interesting old town and its neighborhood.

His son, the Reverend Joseph Emerson, minister of the town of Mendon, Massachusetts, married Elizabeth, daughter of the Reverend Edward Bulkeley, who succeeded his father, the Reverend Peter Bulkeley, as minister of Concord, Massachusetts.

Peter Bulkeley was therefore one of Emerson's sixty-four grandfathers at the seventh remove. We know the tenacity of certain family characteristics through long lines of descent, and it is not impossible that any one of a hundred and twenty-eight grandparents, if indeed the full number existed in spite of family admixtures, may have transmitted his or her distinguishing traits through a series of lives that cover more than two centuries, to our own contemporary. Inherited qualities move along their several paths not unlike the pieces in the game of chess. Sometimes the character of the son can be traced directly to that of the father or of the mother, as the pawn's move carries him from one square to the next. Sometimes a series of distinguished fathers follows in a line, or a succession of superior mothers, as the black or white bishop sweeps the board on his own color. Sometimes the distinguishing characters pass from one sex to the other indifferently, as the castle strides over the black and white squares. Sometimes an uncle or aunt lives over again in a nephew or niece, as if the knight's move were repeated on the squares of human individuality. It is not impossible, then, that some of the qualities we mark in Emerson may have come from the remote ancestor whose name figures with distinction in the early history of New England.

The Reverend Peter Bulkeley is honorably commemorated among the worthies consigned to immortality in that precious and entertaining medley of fact and fancy, enlivened by a wilderness of quotations at first or second hand, the "Magnalia Christi Americana," of the Reverend Cotton Mather. The old chronicler tells his story so much better than any one can tell it for him that he must be allowed to speak for himself in a few extracts, transferred with all their typographical idiosyncrasies from the London-printed folio of 1702.

"He was descended of an Honourable Family in *Bedfordshire*. — He was born at *Woodhil* (or *Odel*) in *Bedfordshire*, *January* 31st, 1582.

"His *Education* was answerable unto his *Original*; it was *Learned*, it was *Genteel*, and, which was the top of all, it was very *Pious*: At length it made him *Batchellor* of *Divinity*, and a Fellow of Saint *Johns* Colledge, in Cambridge.——

"When he came abroad into the World, a good benefice befel him, added unto the estate of a Gentleman, left him by his Father; whom he succeeded in his Ministry, at the place of his Nativity: Which one would imagine *Temptations* enough to keep him out of a *Wilderness*."

But he could not conscientiously conform to the ceremonies of the English Church, and so, —

"When Sir *Nathaniel Brent* was Arch-Bishop *Laud's* General, as Arch-Bishop *Laud* was *another's*, Complaints were made against Mr. *Bulkly*, for his Non-Conformity, and he was therefore Silenced.

"To *New-England* he therefore came, in the Year 1635; and there having been for a while, at *Cambridge*, he carried a good Number of Planters with him, up further into the *Woods*, where they gathered the *Twelfth Church*, then formed in the Colony, and call'd the Town by the Name of *Concord*.

"Here he *buried* a great Estate, while he *raised* one still, for almost every Person whom he employed in the Affairs of his Husbandry. —

"He was a most excellent *Scholar*, a very *well-read* Person, and one, who in his advice to young Students, gave Demonstrations, that he knew what would go to make a *Scholar*.   But it being essential unto a *Scholar* to love a *Scholar*, so did he; and in Token thereof, endowed the Library of *Harvard*-Colledge with no small part of his own.

"And he was therewithal a most exalted *Christian* — "In his Ministry he was another *Farel*, *Quo nemo tonuit fortius* — And the observance which his own People had for him, was also paid him from all sorts of People throughout the Land; but especially from the Ministers of the Country, who would still address him as a *Father*, a *Prophet*, a *Counsellor*, on all occasions."

These extracts may not quite satisfy the exacting reader, who must be referred to the old folio from which they were taken, where he will receive the following counsel: —

"If then any Person would know what Mr. *Peter Bulkly* was, let him read his Judicious and Savory Treatise of the *Gospel Covenant*, which has passed through several

Editions, with much Acceptance among the People of God." It must be added that "he had a competently good Stroke at Latin Poetry; and even in his Old Age, affected sometimes to improve it. Many of his Composure are yet in our Hands."

It is pleasant to believe that some of the qualities of this distinguished scholar and Christian were reproduced in the descendant whose life we are studying. At his death in 1659 he was succeeded, as was mentioned, by his son Edward, whose daughter became the wife of the Reverend Joseph Emerson, the minister of Mendon who, when that village was destroyed by the Indians, removed to Concord, where he died in the year 1680. This is the first connection of the name of Emerson with Concord, with which it has since been so long associated.

Edward Emerson, son of the first and father of the second Reverend Joseph Emerson, though not a minister, was the next thing to being one, for on his gravestone he is thus recorded: "Mr. Edward Emerson, sometime Deacon of the first church in Newbury." He was noted for the virtue of patience, and it is a family tradition that he never complained but once, when he said mildly to his daughter that her dumplings were somewhat harder than needful, — "*but not often.*" This same Edward was the only break in the line of ministers who descended from Thomas of Ipswich. He is remembered in the family as having been "a merchant in Charlestown."

Their son, the second Reverend Joseph Emerson, minister of Malden for nearly half a century, married Mary, the daughter of the Reverend Samuel Moody, — Father Moody, — of York, Maine. Three of his sons were ministers, and one of these, William, was pastor of the church at Concord at the period of the outbreak of the Revolutionary War.

As the successive generations narrow down towards the individual whose life we are recalling, the character of his progenitors becomes more and more important and interesting to the biographer. The Reverend William Emerson, grandfather of Ralph Waldo, was an excellent and popular preacher and an ardent and devoted patriot. He preached resistance to tyrants from the pulpit, he encouraged his townsmen and their allies to make a stand against the soldiers who had marched upon their peaceful village, and would have taken a part in the Fight at the Bridge, which he saw from his own house, had not the friends around him prevented his quitting his doorstep. He left Concord in 1776 to join the army at Ticonderoga, was taken with fever, was advised to return to Concord and set out on the journey, but died on his way. His wife was the daughter of the Reverend Daniel Bliss, his predecessor in the pulpit at Concord. This was another very noticeable personage in the line of Emerson's ancestors. His merits and abilities are described at great length on his tombstone in the Concord burial-ground. There is no reason to doubt that his epitaph was composed by one who knew him well. But the slabs which record the excellences of our New England clergymen of the past generations are so crowded with virtues that the reader can hardly help inquiring whether a sharp bargain was not driven with the stonecutter, like that which the good Vicar of Wakefield arranged with the portrait-painter. He was to represent Sophia as a shepherdess, it will be remembered, with as many sheep as he could afford to put in for nothing.

William Emerson left four children, a son bearing the same name, and three daughters, one of whom, Mary Moody Emerson, is well remembered as pictured for us by her nephew, Ralph Waldo. His widow became the wife of the Reverend Ezra Ripley, Doctor of Divinity, and his successor as minister at Concord.

The Reverend William Emerson, the second of that name and profession, and the father of Ralph Waldo Emerson, was born in the year 1769, and graduated at Harvard College in 1789. He was settled as minister in the town of Harvard in the year 1792, and in 1799 became minister of the First Church in Boston. In 1796 he married Ruth Haskins of Boston. He died in 1811, leaving five sons, of whom Ralph Waldo was the second.

The interest which attaches itself to the immediate parentage of a man like Emerson leads us to inquire particularly about the characteristics of the Reverend William Emerson so far as we can learn them from his own writings and from the record of his contemporaries.

The Reverend Dr. Sprague's valuable and well-known work, "Annals of the American Pulpit," contains three letters from which we learn some of his leading characteristics. Dr. Pierce of Brookline, the faithful chronicler of his time, speaks of his pulpit talents as extraordinary, but thinks there was not a perfect sympathy between him and the people of the quiet little town of Harvard, while he was highly acceptable in the pulpits of the metropolis. In personal appearance he was attractive; his voice was melodious, his utterance distinct, his manner agreeable. " He was a faithful and generous friend and

the reader to the article mentioned. Her character and intellectual traits are what we are most concerned with. "Her early reading was Milton, Young, Akenside, Samuel Clarke, Jonathan Edwards, and always the Bible. Later, Plato, Plotinus, Marcus Antoninus, Stewart, Coleridge, Herder, Locke, Madam De Staël, Channing, Mackintosh, Byron. Nobody can read in her manuscript, or recall the conversation of old-school people, without seeing that Milton and Young had a religious authority in their minds, and nowise the slight merely entertaining quality of modern bards. And Plato, Aristotle, Plotinus, — how venerable and organic as Nature they are in her mind!"

There are many sentences cited by Mr. Emerson which remind us very strongly of his own writings. Such a passage as the following might have come from his essay, "Nature," but it was written when her nephew was only four years old.

"Malden, 1807, September. — The rapture of feeling I would part from for days devoted to higher discipline. But when Nature beams with such excess of beauty, when the heart thrills with hope in its Author, — feels it is related to Him more than by any ties of creation, — it exults, too fondly, perhaps, for a state of trial. But in dead of night, nearer morning, when the eastern stars glow, or appear to glow, with more indescribable lustre, a lustre which penetrates the spirits with wonder and curiosity, — then, however awed, who can fear?" — "A few pulsations of created beings, a few successions of acts, a few lamps held out in the firmament, enable us to talk of Time, make epochs, write histories, — to do more, — to date the revelations of God to man. But these lamps are held to measure out some of the moments of eternity, to divide the history of God's operations in the birth and death of nations, of worlds. It is a goodly name for our notions of breathing, suffering, enjoying, acting. We personify it. We call it by every name of fleeting, dreaming, vaporing imagery. Yet it is nothing. We exist in eternity. Dissolve the body and the night is gone; the stars are extinguished, and we measure duration by the number of our thoughts, by the activity of reason, the discovery of truths, the acquirement of virtue, the approval of God."

Miss Mary Emerson showed something of the same feeling towards natural science which may be noted in her nephews Waldo and Charles. After speaking of "the poor old earth's chaotic state, brought so near in its long and gloomy transmutings by the geologist," she says: —

"Yet its youthful charms, as decked by the hand of Moses' Cosmogony, will linger about the heart, while Poetry succumbs to science." — "And the bare bones of this poor embryo earth may give the idea of the Infinite, far, far better than when dignified with arts and industry; its oceans, when beating the symbols of countless ages, than when covered with cargoes of war and oppression. How grand its preparation for souls, souls who were to feel the Divinity, before Science had dissected the emotions and applied its steely analysis to that state of being which recognizes neither psychology nor element." — "Usefulness, if it requires action, seems less like existence than the desire of being absorbed in God, retaining consciousness. . . . Scorn trifles, lift your aims; do what you are afraid to do. Sublimity of character must come from sublimity of motive."

So far as hereditary and family influences can account for the character and intellect of Ralph Waldo Emerson, we could hardly ask for a better inborn inheritance, or better counsels and examples.

Having traced some of the distinguishing traits which belong by descent to Mr. Emerson to those who were before him, it is interesting to note how far they showed themselves in those of his own generation, his brothers. Of these I will mention two, one of whom I knew personally.

Edward Bliss Emerson, who graduated at Harvard College in 1824, three years after Ralph Waldo, held the first place in his class. He began the study of the law with Daniel Webster, but overworked himself and suffered a temporary disturbance of his reason. After this he made another attempt, but found his health unequal to the task and exiled himself to Porto Rico, where, in 1834, he died. Two poems preserve his memory, one that of Ralph Waldo, in which he addresses his memory, —

" Ah, brother of the brief but blazing star,"

the other his own "Last Farewell," written in 1832, whilst sailing out of Boston Harbor. The lines are unaffected and very touching, full of that deep affection which united the brothers in the closest intimacy, and of the tenderest love for the mother whom he was leaving to see no more.

I had in my early youth a key furnished me to some of the leading traits which were in due time to develop themselves in Emerson's character and intelligence. As on the wall of some great artist's studio one may find unfinished sketches which he recognizes as the first growing conceptions of pictures painted in after years, so we see that Nature often sketches, as it were, a living portrait, which she leaves in its rudimentary condition, perhaps for the reason that earth has no colors which can worthily fill in an outline too perfect for humanity. The sketch is left in its consummate incompleteness because this mortal life is not rich enough to carry out the Divine idea.

Such an unfinished but unmatched outline is that which I find in the long portrait-gallery of memory, recalled by the name of Charles Chauncy Emerson. Save for a few brief glimpses of another, almost lost among my life's early shadows, this youth was the most angelic adolescent my eyes ever beheld. Remembering what well-filtered blood it was that ran in the veins of the race from which he was descended, those who knew him in life might well say with Dryden, —

> "If by traduction came thy mind
> Our wonder is the less to find
> A soul so charming from a stock so good."

His image is with me in its immortal youth as when, almost fifty years ago, I spoke of him in these lines, which I may venture to quote from myself, since others have quoted them before me : —

> Thou calm, chaste scholar ! I can see thee now,
> The first young laurels on thy pallid brow,
> O'er thy slight figure floating lightly down
> In graceful folds the academic gown,
> On thy curled lip the classic lines that taught
> How nice the mind that sculptured them with thought,
> And triumph glistening in the clear blue eye,
> Too bright to live, — but oh, too fair to die.

Being about seven years younger than Waldo, he must have received much of his intellectual and moral guidance at his elder brother's hands. I told the story at a meeting of our Historical Society of Charles Emerson's coming into my study, — this was probably in 1826 or 1827, — taking up Hazlitt's "British

Poets" and turning at once to a poem of Marvell's, which he read with his entrancing voice and manner. The influence of this poet is plain to every reader in some of Emerson's poems, and Charles' liking for him was very probably caught from Waldo.

When Charles was nearly through college, a periodical called "The Harvard Register" was published by students and recent graduates. Three articles were contributed by him to this periodical. Two of them have the titles "Conversation," "Friendship." His quotations are from Horace and Juvenal, Plato, Plutarch, Bacon, Jeremy Taylor, Shakespeare, and Scott. There are passages in these essays which remind one strongly of his brother, the lecturer of twenty-five or thirty years later. Take this as an example: —

"Men and mind are my studies. I need no observatory high in air to aid my perceptions or enlarge my prospect. I do not want a costly apparatus to give pomp to my pursuit or to disguise its inutility. I do not desire to travel and see foreign lands and learn all knowledge and speak with all tongues, before I am prepared for my employment. I have merely to go out of my door; nay, I may stay at home at my chambers, and I shall have enough to do and enjoy."

The feeling of this sentence shows itself constantly in Emerson's poems. He finds his inspiration in the objects about him, — the forest in which he walks; the sheet of water which the hermit of a couple of seasons made famous; the lazy Musketaquid; the titmouse that mocked his weakness in the bitter cold winter's day; the mountain that rose in the horizon; the lofty pines; the lowly flowers. All talked with him as brothers and sisters, and he with them as of his own household.

The same lofty idea of friendship which we find in the man in his maturity, we recognize in one of the essays of the youth.

"All men of gifted intellect and fine genius," says Charles Emerson, "must entertain a noble idea of friendship. Our reverence we are constrained to yield where it is due, — to rank, merit, talents. But our affections we give not thus easily.

> 'The hand of Douglas is his own.'"

— "I am willing to lose an hour in gossip with persons whom good men hold cheap. All this I will do out of regard to the decent conventions of polite life. But my friends I must know, and, knowing, I must love. There must be a daily beauty in their life that shall secure my constant attachment. I cannot stand upon the footing of ordinary acquaintance. Friendship is aristocratical — the affections which are prostituted to every suitor I will not accept."

Here are glimpses of what the youth was to be, of what the man who long outlived him became. Here is the dignity which commands reverence, — a dignity which, with all Ralph Waldo Emerson's sweetness of manner and expression, rose almost to majesty in his serene presence. There was something about Charles Emerson which lifted those he was with into a lofty and pure region of thought and feeling. A vulgar soul stood abashed in his presence. I could never think of him in the presence of such, listening to a paltry sentiment or witnessing a mean action, without recalling Milton's line,

> "Back stepped those two fair angels half amazed,"

and thinking how he might well have been taken for a celestial messenger.

No doubt there is something of idealization in all

these reminiscences, and of that exaggeration which belongs to the *laudator temporis acti.* But Charles Emerson was idolized in his own time by many in college and out of college. George Stillman Hillard was his rival. Neck and neck they ran the race for the enviable position of first scholar in the class of 1828, and when Hillard was announced as having the first part assigned to him, the excitement within the college walls, and to some extent outside of them, was like that when the telegraph proclaims the result of a presidential election, — or the winner of the Derby. But Hillard honestly admired his brilliant rival. "Who has a part with . . . at this next exhibition?" I asked him one day, as I met him in the college yard. " . . . the Post," answered Hillard. "Why call him *the Post?*" said I. "He is a wooden creature," said Hillard. "Hear him and Charles Emerson translating from the Latin *Domus tota inflammata erat.* The Post will render the words, 'The whole house was on fire.' Charles Emerson will translate the sentence, 'The entire edifice was wrapped in flames.'" It was natural enough that a young admirer should prefer the Bernini drapery of Charles Emerson's version to the simple nudity of "the Post's" rendering.

The nest is made ready long beforehand for the bird which is to be bred in it and to fly from it. The intellectual atmosphere into which a scholar is born, and from which he draws the breath of his early mental life, must be studied if we would hope to understand him thoroughly.

When the present century began, the elements, thrown into confusion by the long struggle for Inde-

pendence, had not had time to arrange themselves in
new combinations.   The active intellects of the country had found enough to keep them busy in creating
and organizing a new order of political and social
life.   Whatever purely literary talent existed was as
yet in the nebular condition, a diffused luminous
spot here and there, waiting to form centres of condensation.

Such a nebular spot had been brightening in and
about Boston for a number of years, when, in the
year 1804, a small cluster of names became visible as
representing a modest constellation of literary lumina-
ries: John Thornton Kirkland, afterwards President
of Harvard University; Joseph Stevens Buckminster;
John Sylvester John Gardiner; William Tudor;
Samuel Cooper Thacher; William Emerson.   These
were the chief stars of the new cluster, and their light
reached the world, or a small part of it, as reflected
from the pages of "The Monthly Anthology," which
very soon came under the editorship of the Reverend
William Emerson.

The father of Ralph Waldo Emerson may be judged
of in good measure by the associates with whom he
was thus connected.   A brief sketch of these friends
and fellow-workers of his may not be out of place, for
these men made the local sphere of thought into which
Ralph Waldo Emerson was born.

John Thornton Kirkland should have been seen and
heard as he is remembered by old graduates of Harvard, sitting in the ancient presidential chair, on
Commencement Day, and calling in his penetrating
but musical accents : "*Expectatur oratio in lingua
Latina,*" or "*vernacula*" if the "First Scholar" was
about to deliver the English oration.   It was a pres-

ence not to be forgotten. His "shining morning face" was round as a baby's, and talked as pleasantly as his voice did, with smiles for accents and dimples for punctuation. Mr. Ticknor speaks of his sermons as "full of intellectual wealth and practical wisdom, with sometimes a quaintness that bordered on humor." It was of him that the story was always told, — it may be as old as the invention of printing, — that he threw his sermons into a barrel, where they went to pieces and got mixed up, and that when he was going to preach he fished out what he thought would be about enough for a sermon, and patched the leaves together as he best might. The Reverend Dr. Lowell says: "He always found the right piece, and that was better than almost any of his brethren could have found in what they had written with twice the labor." Mr. Cabot, who knew all Emerson's literary habits, says he used to fish out the number of leaves he wanted for a lecture in somewhat the same way. Emerson's father, however, was very methodical, according to Dr. Lowell, and had "a place for everything, and everything in its place." Dr. Kirkland left little to be remembered by, and like many of the most interesting personalities we have met with, has become a very thin ghost to the grandchildren of his contemporaries.

Joseph Stevens Buckminster was the pulpit darling of his day, in Boston. The beauty of his person, the perfection of his oratory, the finish of his style, added to the sweetness of his character, made him one of those living idols which seem to be as necessary to Protestantism as images and pictures are to Romanism.

John Sylvester John Gardiner, once a pupil of the

famous Dr. Parr, was then the leading Episcopal clergyman of Boston. Him I reconstruct from scattered hints I have met with as a scholarly, social man, with a sanguine temperament and the cheerful ways of a wholesome English parson, blest with a good constitution and a comfortable benefice. Mild Orthodoxy, ripened in Unitarian sunshine, is a very agreeable aspect of Christianity, and none was readier than Dr. Gardiner, if the voice of tradition may be trusted, to fraternize with his brothers of the liberal persuasion, and to make common cause with them in all that related to the interests of learning.

William Tudor was a chief connecting link between the period of "The Monthly Anthology" and that of "The North American Review," for he was a frequent contributor to the first of these periodicals, and he was the founder of the second. Edward Everett characterizes him, in speaking of his "Letters on the Eastern States," as a scholar and a gentleman, an impartial observer, a temperate champion, a liberal opponent, and a correct writer. Daniel Webster bore similar testimony to his talents and character.

Samuel Cooper Thacher was hardly twenty years old when the "Anthology" was founded, and died when he was only a little more than thirty. He contributed largely to that periodical, besides publishing various controversial sermons, and writing the "Memoir of Buckminster."

There was no more brilliant circle than this in any of our cities. There was none where so much freedom of thought was united to so much scholarship. The "Anthology" was the literary precursor of "The North American Review," and the theological herald

of "The Christian Examiner." Like all first beginnings it showed many marks of immaturity. It mingled extracts and original contributions, theology and
medicine, with all manner of literary chips and shav-
ings. It had magazine ways that smacked of Sylvanus
Urban; leading articles with balanced paragraphs
which recalled the marching tramp of Johnson; translations that might have been signed with the name of
Creech, and Odes to Sensibility, and the like, which
recalled the syrupy sweetness and languid trickle of
Laura Matilda's sentimentalities. It talked about
"the London Reviewers" with a kind of provincial
deference. It printed articles with quite too much
of the license of Swift and Prior for the magazines of
to-day. But it had opinions of its own, and would
compare well enough with "The Gentleman's Magazine," to say nothing of "My Grandmother's Review,
the British." A writer in the third volume (1806)
says: "A taste for the belles lettres is rapidly spread-
ing in our country. I believe that, fifty years ago,
England had never seen a Miscellany or a Review so
well conducted as our 'Anthology,' however superior
such publications may now be in that kingdom."

It is well worth one's while to look over the volumes
of the "Anthology" to see what our fathers and
grandfathers were thinking about, and how they expressed themselves. The stiffness of Puritanism was
pretty well relaxed when a magazine conducted by
clergymen could say that "The child" — meaning
the new periodical — "shall not be destitute of the
manners of a gentleman, nor a stranger to genteel
amusements. He shall attend Theatres, Museums,
Balls, and whatever polite diversions the town shall
furnish." The reader of the "Anthology" will find

for his reward an improving discourse on "Ambition," and a commendable schoolboy's "theme" on "Inebriation." He will learn something which may be for his advantage about the "Anjou Cabbage," and may profit by a "Remedy for Asthma." A controversy respecting the merits of Sir Richard Blackmore may prove too little exciting at the present time, and he can turn for relief to the epistle "Studiosus" addresses to "Alcander." If the lines of "The Minstrel" who hails, like Longfellow in later years, from "The District of Maine," fail to satisfy him, he cannot accuse "R. T. Paine, Jr., Esq.," of tameness when he exclaims:—

> "Rise, Columbia, brave and free,
> Poise the globe and bound the sea!"

But the writers did not confine themselves to native or even to English literature, for there is a distinct mention of "Mr. Goethe's new novel," and an explicit reference to "Dante Aligheri, an Italian bard." But let the smiling reader go a little farther and he will find Mr. Buckminster's most interesting account of the destruction of Goldau. And in one of these same volumes he will find the article, by Dr. Jacob Bigelow, doubtless, which was the first hint of our rural cemeteries, and foreshadowed that new era in our underground civilization which is sweetening our atmospheric existence.

The late President Josiah Quincy, in his "History of the Boston Athenæum," pays a high tribute of respect to the memory and the labors of the gentlemen who founded that institution and conducted the "Anthology." A literary journal had already been published in Boston, but very soon failed for want of patronage. An enterprising firm of publishers, "being desirous that the work should be continued, applied to the Reverend William Emerson, a clergyman of the place, distinguished for energy and literary taste; and by his exertions several gentlemen of Boston and its vicinity, conspicuous for talent and zealous for literature, were induced to engage in conducting the work, and for this purpose they formed themselves into a Society. This Society was not completely organized until the year 1805, when Dr. Gardiner was elected President, and William Emerson Vice-President. The Society thus formed maintained its existence with reputation for about six years, and issued ten octavo volumes from the press, constituting one of the most lasting and honorable monuments of the literature of the period, and may be considered as a true revival of polite learning in this country after that decay and neglect which resulted from the distractions of the Revolutionary War, and as forming an epoch in the intellectual history of the United States. Its records yet remain, an evidence that it was a pleasant, active, high-principled association of literary men, laboring harmoniously to elevate the literary standard of the time, and with a success which may well be regarded as remarkable, considering the little sympathy they received from the community, and the many difficulties with which they had to struggle."

The publication of the "Anthology" began in 1804, when Mr. William Emerson was thirty-four years of age, and it ceased to be published in the year of his death, 1811. Ralph Waldo Emerson was eight years old at that time. His intellectual life began, we may say, while the somewhat obscure afterglow of the "Anthology" was in the western horizon of the New England sky.

The nebula which was to form a cluster about "The North American Review" did not take definite shape until 1815. There is no such memorial of the growth of American literature as is to be found in the first half century of that periodical. It is easy to find fault with it for uniform respectability and occasional dulness. But take the names of its contributors during its first fifty years from the literary record of that period, and we should have but a meagre list of mediocrities, saved from absolute poverty by the genius of two or three writers like Irving and Cooper. Strike out the names of Webster, Everett, Story, Sumner, and Cushing; of Bryant, Dana, Longfellow, and Lowell; of Prescott, Ticknor, Motley, Sparks, and Bancroft; of Verplanck, Hillard, and Whipple; of Stuart and Robinson; of Norton, Palfrey, Peabody, and Bowen; and, lastly, that of Emerson himself, and how much American classic literature would be left for a new edition of "Miller's Retrospect"?

These were the writers who helped to make "The North American Review" what it was during the period of Emerson's youth and early manhood. These, and men like them, gave Boston its intellectual character. We may count as symbols the three hills of "this darling town of ours," as Emerson called it, and say that each had its beacon. Civil liberty lighted the torch on one summit, religious freedom caught the flame and shone from the second, and the lamp of the scholar has burned steadily on the third from the days when John Cotton preached his first sermon to those in which we are living.

The social religious influences of the first part of the century must not be forgotten. The two high-caste religions of that day were white-handed Unitarianism and ruffled-shirt Episcopalianism. What called itself "society" was chiefly distributed between them. Within less than fifty years a social revolution has taken place which has somewhat changed the relation between these and other worshipping bodies. This movement is the general withdrawal of the native New Englanders of both sexes from domestic service. A large part of the "hired help" — for the word servant was commonly repudiated — worshipped, not with their employers, but at churches where few or no well-appointed carriages stood at the doors. The congregations that went chiefly from the drawing-room and those which were largely made up of dwellers in the culinary studio were naturally separated by a very distinct line of social cleavage. A certain exclusiveness and fastidiousness, not reminding us exactly of primitive Christianity, was the inevitable result. This must always be remembered in judging the men and women of that day and their immediate descendants, as much as the surviving prejudices of those whose parents were born subjects of King George in the days when loyalty to the crown was a virtue. The line of social separation was more marked, probably, in Boston, the headquarters of Unitarianism, than in the other large cities; and even at the present day our Jerusalem and Samaria, though they by no means refuse dealing with each other, do not exchange so many cards as they do checks and dollars. The exodus of those children of Israel from the house of bondage, as they chose to consider it, and their fusion with the mass of independent citizens, got rid of a class distinction which was felt even in the sanctuary. True religious equality is harder to establish than civil liberty. No man has done more for spiritual republicanism

than Emerson, though he came from the daintiest sectarian circle of the time in the whole country.

Such were Emerson's intellectual and moral parentage, nurture, and environment; such was the atmosphere in which he grew up from youth to manhood.

CHAPTER I.

1803–1823.   To Æt. 20.

Birthplace. — Boyhood. — College Life.

RALPH WALDO EMERSON was born in Boston, Massachusetts, on the 25th of May, 1803.

He was the second of five sons; William, R. W., Edward Bliss, Robert Bulkeley, and Charles Chauncy.

His birthplace and that of our other illustrious Bostonian, Benjamin Franklin, were within a kite-string's distance of each other. When the baby philosopher of the last century was carried from Milk Street through the narrow passage long known as Bishop's Alley, now Hawley Street, he came out in Summer Street, very nearly opposite the spot where, at the beginning of this century, stood the parsonage of the First Church, the home of the Reverend William Emerson, its pastor, and the birthplace of his son, Ralph Waldo. The oblong quadrangle between Newbury, now Washington Street, Pond, now Bedford Street, Summer Street, and the open space called Church Green, where the New South Church was afterwards erected, is represented on Bonner's maps of 1722 and 1769 as an almost blank area, not crossed or penetrated by a single passageway.

Even so late as less than half a century ago this region was still a most attractive little *rus in urbe*. The sunny gardens of the late Judge Charles Jackson and the late Mr. S. P. Gardner opened their flowers and ripened their fruits in the places now occupied by great warehouses and other massive edifices. The most aristocratic pears, the "Saint Michael," the "Brown Bury," found their natural homes in these sheltered enclosures. The fine old mansion of Judge William Prescott looked out upon these gardens. Some of us can well remember the window of his son's, the historian's, study, the light from which used every evening to glimmer through the leaves of the pear-trees while "The Conquest of Mexico" was achieving itself under difficulties hardly less formidable than those encountered by Cortes. It was a charmed region in which Emerson first drew his breath, and I am fortunate in having a communication from one who knew it and him longer than almost any other living person.

Mr. John Lowell Gardner, a college classmate and life-long friend of Mr. Emerson, has favored me with a letter which contains matters of interest concerning him never before given to the public. With his kind permission I have made some extracts and borrowed such facts as seemed especially worthy of note from his letter.

"I may be said to have known Emerson from the very beginning. A very low fence divided my father's estate in Summer Street from the field in which I remember the old wooden parsonage to have existed, — but this field, when we were very young, was to be covered by Chauncy Place Church and by the brick houses on Summer Street. Where the family removed to I do not remember, but I always knew the boys, William, Ralph, and perhaps Edward, and I again associated with Ralph at the Latin School, where we were instructed by Master Gould from 1815 to 1817, entering college in the latter year.

. . . "I have no recollection of his relative rank as a scholar, but it was undoubtedly high, though not the highest. He never was idle or a lounger, nor did he ever engage in frivolous pursuits. I should say that his conduct was absolutely faultless. It was impossible that there should be any feeling about him but of regard and affection. He had then the same manner and courtly hesitation in addressing you that you have known in him since. Still, he was not prominent in the class, and, but for what all the world has since known of him, his would not have been a conspicuous figure to his classmates in recalling college days.

"The fact that we were almost the only Latin School fellows in the class, and the circumstance that he was slow during the Freshman year to form new acquaintances, brought us much together, and an intimacy arose which continued through our college life. We were in the habit of taking long strolls together, often stopping for repose at distant points, as at Mount Auburn, etc. . . . Emerson was not talkative; he never spoke for effect; his utterances were well weighed and very deliberately made, but there was a certain flash when he uttered anything that was more than usually worthy to be remembered. He was so universally amiable and complying that my evil spirit would sometimes instigate me to take advantage of his gentleness and forbearance, but nothing could disturb his equanimity. All that was wanting to render him an almost perfect character was a few harsher traits and perhaps more masculine vigor.

"On leaving college our paths in life were so remote from each other that we met very infrequently. He soon became, as it were, public property, and I was engrossed for many years in my commercial undertakings. All his course of life is known to many survivors. I am inclined to believe he had a most liberal spirit. I remember that some years since, when it was known that our classmate —— was reduced almost to absolute want by the war, in which he lost his two sons, Emerson exerted himself to raise a fund among his classmates for his relief, and, there being very few possible subscribers, made what I considered a noble contribution, and this you may be sure was not

from any Southern sentiment on the part of Emerson.   I
send you herewith the two youthful productions of Emerson of which I spoke to you some time since."

The first of these is a prose essay of four pages,
written for a discussion in which the professions of
divinity, medicine, and law were to be weighed
against each other.   Emerson had the lawyer's side
to advocate.   It is a fair and sensible paper, not of
special originality or brilliancy.   His opening paragraph is worth citing, as showing the same instinct for
truth which displayed itself in all his after writings
and the conduct of his life.

"It is usual in advocating a favorite subject to appropriate all possible excellence, and endeavor to concentrate
every doubtful auxiliary, that we may fortify to the utmost the theme of our attention.   Such a design should be
utterly disdained, except as far as is consistent with fairness; and the sophistry of weak arguments being abandoned, a bold appeal should be made to the heart, for the
tribute of honest conviction, with regard to the merits of
the subject."

From many boys this might sound like well-meaning commonplace, but in the history of Mr. Emerson's
life that "bold appeal to the heart," that "tribute of
honest conviction," were made eloquent and real.
The boy meant it when he said it.   To carry out his
law of sincerity and self-trust the man had to sacrifice
much that was dear to him, but he did not flinch from
his early principles.

It must not be supposed that the blameless youth
was an ascetic in his college days.   The other old
manuscript Mr. Gardner sends me is marked " 'Song
for Knights of Square Table,' R. W. E."

There are twelve verses of this song, with a chorus

of two lines. The Muses and all the deities, not forgetting Bacchus, were duly invited to the festival.

> " Let the doors of Olympus be open for all
>   To descend and make merry in Chivalry's hall."
>   . . . .

Mr. Sanborn has kindly related to me several circumstances told him by Emerson about his early years.

The parsonage was situated at the corner of Summer and what is now Chauncy streets. It had a yard, and an orchard which Emerson said was as large as Dr. Ripley's, which might have been some two or three acres. Afterwards there was a brick house looking on Summer Street, in which Emerson the father lived. It was separated, Emerson said, by a brick wall from a garden in which *pears grew* (a fact a boy is likely to remember). Master Ralph Waldo used to *sit on this wall*, — but we cannot believe he ever got off it on the wrong side, unless politely asked to do so. On the occasion of some alarm the little boy was carried in his nightgown to a neighboring house.

After Reverend William Emerson's death Mrs. Emerson removed to a house in Beacon Street, where the Athenæum building now stands. She kept some boarders, — among them Lemuel Shaw, afterwards Chief Justice of the State of Massachusetts. It was but a short distance to the Common, and Waldo and Charles used to drive their mother's cow there to pasture.

The Reverend Doctor Rufus Ellis, the much respected living successor of William Emerson as minister of the First Church, says that R. W. Emerson

must have been born in the old parsonage, as his father (who died when he was eight years old) lived but
a very short time in "the new parsonage," which was,
doubtless, the "brick house" above referred to.

We get a few glimpses of the boy from other
sources.   Mr. Cooke tells us that he entered the public grammar school at the age of eight years, and soon
afterwards the Latin School.   At the age of eleven
he was turning Virgil into very readable English he-
roics.   He loved the study of Greek; was fond of
reading history and given to the frequent writing of
verses.   But he thinks "the idle books under the
bench at the Latin School" were as profitable to him
as his regular studies.

Another glimpse of him is that given us by Mr.
Ireland from the "Boyhood Memories" of Rufus
Dawes.   His old schoolmate speaks of him as "a
spiritual-looking boy in blue nankeen, who seems to
be about ten years old, — whose image more than any
other is still deeply stamped upon my mind, as I
then saw him and loved him, I knew not why, and
thought him so angelic and remarkable."   That "blue
nankeen" sounds strangely, it may be, to the readers
of this later generation, but in the first quarter of the
century blue and yellow or buff-colored cotton from
China were a common summer clothing of children.
The places where the factories and streets of the cities
of Lowell and Lawrence were to rise were then open
fields and farms.   My recollection is that we did not
think very highly of ourselves when we were in blue
nankeen, — a dull-colored fabric, too nearly of the
complexion of the slates on which we did our cipher-
ing.

Emerson was not particularly distinguished in college. Having a near connection in the same class as he, and being, as a Cambridge boy, generally familiar with the names of the more noted young men in college from the year when George Bancroft, Caleb Cushing, and Francis William Winthrop graduated until after I myself left college, I might have expected to hear something of a young man who afterwards became one of the great writers of his time. I do not recollect hearing of him except as keeping school for a short time in Cambridge, before he settled as a minister. His classmate, Mr. Josiah Quincy, writes thus of his college days: —

"Two only of my classmates can be fairly said to have got into history, although one of them, Charles W. Upham [the connection of mine referred to above], has written history very acceptably. Ralph Waldo Emerson and Robert W. Barnwell, for widely different reasons, have caused their names to be known to well-informed Americans. Of Emerson, I regret to say, there are few notices in my journals. Here is the sort of way in which I speak of the man who was to make so profound an impression upon the thought of his time. 'I went to the chapel to hear Emerson's dissertation; a very good one, but rather too long to give much pleasure to the hearers.' The fault, I suspect, was in the hearers; and another fact which I have mentioned goes to confirm this belief. It seems that Emerson accepted the duty of delivering the Poem on Class Day, after seven others had been asked who positively refused. So it appears that, in the opinion of this critical class, the author of the 'Woodnotes' and the 'Humble Bee' ranked about eighth in poetical ability. It can only be because the works of the other five [seven] have been 'heroically unwritten' that a different impression has come to prevail in the outside world. But if, according to the measurement of undergraduates, Emerson's ability as a poet was not conspicuous, it must also be admitted that, in the judgment of persons old enough to know better, he was not credited with that mastery of weighty prose which the world has since accorded him. In our senior year the higher classes competed for the Boylston prizes for English composition. Emerson and I sent in our essays with the rest and were fortunate enough to take the two prizes; but — Alas for the infallibility of academic decisions! — Emerson received the second prize. I was of course much pleased with the award of this intelligent committee, and should have been still more gratified had they mentioned that the man who was to be the most original and influential writer born in America was my unsuccessful competitor. But Emerson, incubating over deeper matters than were dreamt of in the established philosophy of elegant letters, seems to have given no sign of the power that was fashioning itself for leadership in a new time. He was quiet, unobtrusive, and only a fair scholar according to the standard of the college authorities. And this is really all I have to say about my most distinguished classmate."

Barnwell, the first scholar in the class, delivered the Valedictory Oration, and Emerson the Poem. Neither of these performances was highly spoken of by Mr. Quincy.

I was surprised to find by one of the old catalogues that Emerson roomed during a part of his college course with a young man whom I well remember, J. G. K. Gourdin. The two Gourdins, Robert and John Gaillard Keith, were dashing young fellows as I recollect them, belonging to Charleston, South Carolina. The "Southerners" were the reigning college *elegans* of that time, the *merveilleux*, the *mirliflores*, of their day. Their swallow-tail coats tapered to an arrow-point angle, and the prints of their little delicate calfskin boots in the snow were objects of great admiration to the village boys of the period. I cannot help wondering what brought Emerson and the showy, fascinating John Gourdin together as room-mates.

CHAPTER II.

1823–1828. Æt. 20–25.

Extract from a Letter to a Classmate. — School-Teaching. —
Study of Divinity. — " Approbated " to Preach. — Visit to the
South. — Preaching in Various Places.

WE get a few brief glimpses of Emerson during
the years following his graduation. He writes in
1823 to a classmate who had gone from Harvard to
Andover: —

"I am delighted to hear there is such a profound
studying of German and Hebrew, Parkhurst and Jahn,
and such other names as the memory aches to think of, on
foot at Andover. Meantime, Unitarianism will not hide
her honors; as many hard names are taken, and as much
theological mischief planned, at Cambridge as at Andover.
By the time this generation gets upon the stage, if the
controversy will not have ceased, it will run such a tide
that we shall hardly be able to speak to one another, and
there will be a Guelf and Ghibelline quarrel, which cannot tell where the differences lie."

"You can form no conception how much one grovelling
in the city needs the excitement and impulse of literary
example. The sight of broad vellum-bound quartos, the
very mention of Greek and German names, the glimpse of
a dusty, tugging scholar, will wake you up to emulation
for a month."

After leaving college, and while studying divinity, Emerson employed a part of his time in giving
instruction in several places successively.

Emerson's older brother William was teaching in Boston, and Ralph Waldo, after graduating, joined him in that occupation. In the year 1825 or 1826, he taught school also in Chelmsford, a town of Middlesex County, Massachusetts, a part of which helped to constitute the city of Lowell. One of his pupils in that school, the Honorable Josiah Gardiner Abbott, has favored me with the following account of his recollections: —

The school of which Mr. Emerson had the charge was an old-fashioned country "Academy." Mr. Emerson was probably studying for the ministry while teaching there. Judge Abbott remembers the impression he made on the boys. He was very grave, quiet, and very impressive in his appearance. There was something engaging, almost fascinating, about him; he was never harsh or severe, always perfectly self-controlled, never punished except with words, but exercised complete command over the boys. His old pupil recalls the stately, measured way in which, for some offence the little boy had committed, he turned on him, saying only these two words: "Oh, sad!" That was enough, for he had the faculty of making the boys love him. One of his modes of instruction was to give the boys a piece of reading to carry home with them, — from some book like Plutarch's Lives, — and the next day to examine them and find out how much they retained from their reading. Judge Abbott remembers a peculiar look in his eyes, as if he saw something beyond what seemed to be in the field of vision. The whole impression left on this pupil's mind was such as no other teacher had ever produced upon him.

Mr. Emerson also kept a school for a short time at

Cambridge, and among his pupils was Mr. John Holmes. His impressions seem to be very much like those of Judge Abbott.

My brother speaks of Mr. Emerson thus: —

"Calm, as not doubting the virtue residing in his scep-tre. Rather stern in his very infrequent rebukes. Not inclined to win boys by a surface amiability, but kindly in explanation or advice. Every inch a king in his domin-ion. Looking back, he seems to me rather like a captive philosopher set to tending flocks; resigned to his destiny, but not amused with its incongruities. He once rec-ommended the use of rhyme as a cohesive for historical items."

In 1823, two years after graduating, Emerson be-gan studying for the ministry. He studied under the direction of Dr. Channing, attending some of the lec-tures in the divinity school at Cambridge, though not enrolled as one of its regular students.

The teachings of that day were such as would now be called "old-fashioned Unitarianism." But no creed can be held to be a finality. From Edwards to Mayhew, from Mayhew to Channing, from Channing to Emerson, the passage is like that which leads from the highest lock of a canal to the ocean level. It is impossible for human nature to remain permanently shut up in the highest lock of Calvinism. If the gates are not opened, the mere leakage of belief or unbelief will before long fill the next compartment, and the freight of doctrine finds itself on the lower level of Arminianism, or Pelagianism, or even subsides to Arianism. From this level to that of Unitarianism the outlet is freer, and the subsidence more rapid. And from Unitarianism to Christian Theism, the passage is largely open for such as cannot accept the evidence of the supernatural in the history of the church.

There were many shades of belief in the liberal churches. If De Tocqueville's account of Unitarian preaching in Boston at the time of his visit is true, the Savoyard vicar of Rousseau would have preached acceptably in some of our pulpits. In fact, the good vicar might have been thought too conservative by some of our unharnessed theologians.

At the period when Emerson reached manhood, Unitarianism was the dominating form of belief in the more highly educated classes of both of the two great New England centres, the town of Boston and the university at Cambridge. President Kirkland was at the head of the college, Henry Ware was professor of theology, Andrews Norton of sacred literature, followed in 1830 by John Gorham Palfrey in the same office. James Freeman, Charles Lowell, and William Ellery Channing were preaching in Boston. I have mentioned already as a simple fact of local history, that the more exclusive social circles of Boston and Cambridge were chiefly connected with the Unitarian or Episcopalian churches. A Cambridge graduate of ambition and ability found an opening far from undesirable in a worldly point of view, in a profession which he was led to choose by higher motives. It was in the Unitarian pulpit that the brilliant talents of Buckminster and Everett had found a noble eminence from which their light could shine before men.

Descended from a long line of ministers, a man of spiritual nature, a reader of Plato, of Augustine, of Jeremy Taylor, full of hope for his fellow-men, and longing to be of use to them, conscious, undoubtedly,

of a growing power of thought, it was natural that
Emerson should turn from the task of a school-master
to the higher office of a preacher. It is hard to conceive of Emerson in either of the other so-called
learned professions. His devotion to truth for its
own sake and his feeling about science would have
kept him out of both those dusty highways. His
brother William had previously begun the study of
divinity, but found his mind beset with doubts and
difficulties, and had taken to the profession of law.
It is not unlikely that Mr. Emerson was more or less
exercised with the same questionings. He has said,
speaking of his instructors: "If they had examined
me, they probably would not have let me preach at
all." His eyes had given him trouble, so that he had
not taken notes of the lectures which he heard in the
divinity school, which accounted for his being excused from examination. In 1826, after three years'
study, he was "approbated to preach" by the Middlesex Association of Ministers. His health obliging
him to seek a southern climate, he went in the following winter to South Carolina and Florida. During
this absence he preached several times in Charleston
and other places. On his return from the South he
preached in New Bedford, in Northampton, in Concord, and in Boston. His attractiveness as a preacher,
of which we shall have sufficient evidence in a following chapter, led to his being invited to share the duties
of a much esteemed and honored city clergyman, and
the next position in which we find him is that of a settled minister in Boston.

CHAPTER III.

1828–1833.   ÆT. 25–30.

Settled as Colleague of Rev. Henry Ware. — Married to Ellen
Louisa Tucker. — Sermon at the Ordination of Rev. H. B.
Goodwin. — His Pastoral and Other Labors. — Emerson and
Father Taylor. — Death of Mrs. Emerson. — Difference of
Opinion with some of his Parishioners. — Sermon Explaining
his Views. — Resignation of his Pastorate.

ON the 11th of March, 1829, Emerson was or-
dained as colleague with the Reverend Henry Ware,
minister of the Second Church in Boston. In September of the same year he was married to Miss Ellen
Louisa Tucker. The resignation of his colleague
soon after his settlement threw all the pastoral duties
upon the young minister, who seems to have performed
them diligently and acceptably. Mr. Conway gives
the following brief account of his labors, and tells in
the same connection a story of Father Taylor too good
not to be repeated : —

"Emerson took an active interest in the public affairs of
Boston. He was on its school board, and was chosen
chaplain of the state senate. He invited the anti-slavery
lecturers into his church, and helped philanthropists of
other denominations in their work. Father Taylor [the
Methodist preacher to the sailors], to whom Dickens gave
an English fame, found in him his most important sup-
porter when establishing the Seaman's Mission in Boston.
This was told me by Father Taylor himself in his old age.
I happened to be in his company once, when he spoke

rather sternly about my leaving the Methodist Church; but when I spoke of the part Emerson had in it, he softened at once, and spoke with emotion of his great friend. I have no doubt that if the good Father of Boston Seamen was proud of any personal thing, it was of the excellent answer he is said to have given to some Methodists who objected to his friendship for Emerson. Being a Unitarian, they insisted that he must go to " — [the place which a divine of Charles the Second's day said it was not good manners to mention in church]. — "'It does look so,' said Father Taylor, 'but I am sure of one thing: if Emerson goes to' " — [that place] — "'he will change the climate there, and emigration will set that way.' "

In 1830, Emerson took part in the services at the ordination of the Reverend H. B. Goodwin as Dr. Ripley's colleague. His address on giving the right hand of fellowship was printed, but is not included among his collected works.

The fair prospects with which Emerson began his life as a settled minister were too soon darkened. In February, 1832, the wife of his youth, who had been for some time in failing health, died of consumption.

He had become troubled with doubts respecting a portion of his duties, and it was not in his nature to conceal these doubts from his people. On the 9th of September, 1832, he preached a sermon on the Lord's Supper, in which he announced unreservedly his conscientious scruples against administering that ordinance, and the grounds upon which those scruples were founded. This discourse, as his only printed sermon, and as one which heralded a movement in New England theology which has never stopped from that day to this, deserves some special notice. The sermon is in no sense "Emersonian" except in its directness, its sweet temper, and its outspoken honesty.

He argues from his comparison of texts in a perfectly
sober, old - fashioned way, as his ancestor Peter
Bulkeley might have done. It happened to that
worthy forefather of Emerson that upon his "press-
ing a piece of *Charity* disagreeable to the will of the
Ruling Elder, there was occasioned an unhappy *Discord* in the Church of *Concord;* which yet was at last
healed, by their calling in the help of a *Council* and
the *Ruling Elder's* Abdication." So says Cotton
Mather. Whether zeal had grown cooler or charity
grown warmer in Emerson's days we need not try to
determine. The sermon was only a more formal declaration of views respecting the Lord's Supper, which
he had previously made known in a conference with
some of the most active members of his church. As
a committee of the parish reported resolutions radically
differing from his opinion on the subject, he preached
this sermon and at the same time resigned his office.
There was no "discord," there was no need of a "council." Nothing could be more friendly, more truly
Christian, than the manner in which Mr. Emerson
expressed himself in this parting discourse. All the
kindness of his nature warms it throughout. He details the differences of opinion which have existed in
the church with regard to the ordinance. He then
argues from the language of the Evangelists that it
was not intended to be a permanent institution. He
takes up the statement of Paul in the Epistle to the
Corinthians, which he thinks, all things considered,
ought not to alter our opinion derived from the Evangelists. He does not think that we are to rely upon
the opinions and practices of the primitive church. If
that church believed the institution to be permanent,
their belief does not settle the question for us. On

every other subject, succeeding times have learned to form a judgment more in accordance with the spirit of Christianity than was the practice of the early ages.

"But, it is said, 'Admit that the rite was not designed to be perpetual.' What harm doth it?"

He proceeds to give reasons which show it to be inexpedient to continue the observance of the rite. It was treating that as authoritative which, as he believed that he had shown from Scripture, was not so. It confused the idea of God by transferring the worship of Him to Christ. Christ is the Mediator only as the instructor of man. In the least petition to God "the soul stands alone with God, and Jesus is no more present to your mind than your brother or child." Again: —

"The use of the elements, however suitable to the people and the modes of thought in the East, where it originated, is foreign and unsuited to affect us. The day of formal religion is past, and we are to seek our well-being in the formation of the soul. The Jewish was a religion of forms; it was all body, it had no life, and the Almighty God was pleased to qualify and send forth a man to teach men that they must serve him with the heart; that only that life was religious which was thoroughly good; that sacrifice was smoke and forms were shadows. This man lived and died true to that purpose; and with his blessed word and life before us, Christians must contend that it is a matter of vital importance, — really a duty to commemorate him by a certain form, whether that form be acceptable to their understanding or not. Is not this to make vain the gift of God? Is not this to turn back the hand on the dial?"

To these objections he adds the practical consideration that it brings those who do not partake of the communion service into an unfavorable relation with those who do.

The beautiful spirit of the man shows itself in all its noble sincerity in these words at the close of his argument: —

"Having said this, I have said all. I have no hostility to this institution; I am only stating my want of sympathy with it. Neither should I ever have obtruded this opinion upon other people, had I not been called by my office to administer it. That is the end of my opposition, that I am not interested in it. I am content that it stand to the end of the world if it please men and please Heaven, and I shall rejoice in all the good it produces."

He then announces that, as it is the prevailing opinion and feeling in our religious community that it is a part of a pastor's duties to administer this rite, he is about to resign the office which had been confided to him.

This is the only sermon of Mr. Emerson's ever published. It was impossible to hear or to read it without honoring the preacher for his truthfulness, and recognizing the force of his statement and reasoning. It was equally impossible that he could continue his ministrations over a congregation which held to the ordinance he wished to give up entirely. And thus it was, that with the most friendly feelings on both sides, Mr. Emerson left the pulpit of the Second Church and found himself obliged to make a beginning in a new career.

CHAPTER IV.

1833–1838.   ÆT. 30–35.

§ 1. IN the year 1833 Mr. Emerson visited Europe for the first time. A great change had come over his life, and he needed the relief which a corresponding change of outward circumstances might afford him. A brief account of this visit is prefixed to the volume entitled "English Traits." He took a short tour, in which he visited Sicily, Italy, and France, and, crossing from Boulogne, landed at the Tower Stairs in London. He finds nothing in his diary to publish concerning visits to places. But he saw a number of distinguished persons, of whom he gives pleasant accounts, so singularly different in tone from the rough caricatures in which Carlyle vented his spleen and caprice, that one marvels how the two men could have talked ten minutes together, or would wonder, had not one been as imperturbable as the other was explosive. Horatio Greenough and Walter Savage Landor are the chief persons he speaks of as having met upon the Continent. Of these he reports various opinions as delivered in conversation. He mentions incidentally that he visited Professor Amici, who showed him his microscopes "magnifying (it was said) two thousand diameters." Emerson hardly knew his privilege; he may have been the first American to look through an immersion lens with the famous Modena professor. Mr. Emerson says that his narrow and desultory reading had inspired him with the wish to see the faces of three or four writers, Coleridge, Wordsworth, Landor, De Quincey, Carlyle. His accounts of his interviews with these distinguished persons are too condensed to admit of further abbreviation. Goethe and Scott, whom he would have liked to look upon, were dead; Wellington he saw at Westminster Abbey, at the funeral of Wilberforce. His impressions of each of the distinguished persons whom he visited should be looked at in the light of the general remark which follows: —

"The young scholar fancies it happiness enough to live with people who can give an inside to the world; without reflecting that they are prisoners, too, of their own thought, and cannot apply themselves to yours. The conditions of literary success are almost destructive of the best social power, as they do not have that frolic liberty which only can encounter a companion on the best terms. It is probable you left some obscure comrade at a tavern, or in the farms, with right mother-wit, and equality to life, when you crossed sea and land to play bo-peep with celebrated scribes. I have, however, found writers superior to their books, and I cling to my first belief that a strong head will dispose fast enough of these impediments, and give one the satisfaction of reality, the sense of having been met, and a larger horizon."

Emerson carried a letter of introduction to a gentleman in Edinburgh, who, being unable to pay him all the desired attention, handed him over to Mr. Alexander Ireland, who has given a most interesting account of him as he appeared during that first visit to Europe. Mr. Ireland's presentation of Emerson as he heard him in the Scotch pulpit shows that he was not less impressive and attractive before an audience of strangers than among his own countrymen and countrywomen: —

"On Sunday, the 18th of August, 1833, I heard him deliver a discourse in the Unitarian Chapel, Young Street, Edinburgh, and I remember distinctly the effect which it produced on his hearers. It is almost needless to say that nothing like it had ever been heard by them before, and many of them did not know what to make of it. The originality of his thoughts, the consummate beauty of the language in which they were clothed, the calm dignity of his bearing, the absence of all oratorical effort, and the singular directness and simplicity of his manner, free from the least shadow of dogmatic assumption, made a deep impression on me. Not long before this I had listened to a wonderful sermon by Dr. Chalmers, whose force, and energy, and vehement, but rather turgid eloquence carried, for the moment, all before them, — his audience becoming like clay in the hands of the potter. But I must confess that the pregnant thoughts and serene self-possession of the young Boston minister had a greater charm for me than all the rhetorical splendors of Chalmers. His voice

was the sweetest, the most winning and penetrating, of
any I ever heard; nothing like it have I listened to since.

> ' That music in our hearts we bore
> Long after it was heard no more.' "

Mr. George Gilfillan speaks of "the solemnity of
his manner, and the earnest thought pervading his
discourse."

As to the effect of his preaching on his American
audiences, I find the following evidence in Mr.
Cooke's diligently gathered collections. Mr. Sanborn says: —

"His pulpit eloquence was singularly attractive, though
by no means equally so to all persons. In 1829, before
the two friends had met, Bronson Alcott heard him preach
in Dr. Channing's church on 'The Universality of the
Moral Sentiment,' and was struck, as he said, with the
youth of the preacher, the beauty of his elocution, and
the direct and sincere manner in which he addressed his
hearers."

Mr. Charles Congdon, of New Bedford, well known
as a popular writer, gives the following account of
Emerson's preaching in his "Reminiscences." I borrow the quotation from Mr. Conway: —

"One day there came into our pulpit the most gracious
of mortals with a face all benignity, who gave out the
first hymn and made the first prayer as an angel might
have read and prayed. Our choir was a pretty good one,
but its best was coarse and discordant after Emerson's
voice. I remember of the sermon only that it had an indefinite charm of simplicity and wisdom, with occasional
illustrations from nature, which were about the most delicate and dainty things of the kind which I had ever
heard. I could understand them, if not the fresh philosophical novelties of the discourse."

Everywhere Emerson seems to have pleased his audiences. The Reverend Dr. Morison, formerly the much respected Unitarian minister of New Bedford, writes to me as follows: —

"After Dr. Dewey left New Bedford, Mr. Emerson preached there several months, greatly to the satisfaction and delight of those who heard him. The society would have been glad to settle him as their minister, and he would have accepted a call, had it not been for some difference of opinion, I think, in regard to the communion service. Judge Warren, who was particularly his friend, and had at that time a leading influence in the parish, with all his admiration for Mr. Emerson, did not think he could well be the pastor of a Christian church, and so the matter was settled between him and his friend, without any action by the society."

All this shows well enough that his preaching was eminently acceptable. But every one who has heard him lecture can form an idea of what he must have been as a preacher. In fact, we have all listened, probably, to many a passage from old sermons of his, — for he tells us he borrowed from those old sermons for his lectures, — without ever thinking of the pulpit from which they were first heard.

Among the stray glimpses we get of Emerson between the time when he quitted the pulpit of his church and that when he came before the public as a lecturer is this, which I owe to the kindness of Hon. Alexander H. Rice. In 1832 or 1833, probably the latter year, he, then a boy, with another boy, Thomas R. Gould, afterwards well known as a sculptor, being at the Episcopal church in Newton, found that Mr. Emerson was sitting in the pew behind them. Gould knew Mr. Emerson, and introduced young Rice to him, and they walked down the street together. As they went along, Emerson burst into a rhapsody over the Psalms of David, the sublimity of thought, and the poetic beauty of expression of which they are full, and spoke also with enthusiasm of the Te Deum as that grand old hymn which had come down through the ages, voicing the praises of generation after generation.

When they parted at the house of young Rice's father, Emerson invited the boys to come and see him at the Allen farm, in the afternoon. They came to a piece of woods, and, as they entered it, took their hats off. "Boys," said Emerson, "here we recognize the presence of the Universal Spirit. The breeze says to us in its own language, How d' ye do? How d' ye do? and we have already taken our hats off and are answering it with our own How d' ye do? How d' ye do? And all the waving branches of the trees, and all the flowers, and the field of corn yonder, and the singing brook, and the insect and the bird, — every living thing and things we call inanimate feel the same divine universal impulse while they join with us, and we with them, in the greeting which is the salutation of the Universal Spirit."

We perceive the same feeling which pervades many of Emerson's earlier essays and much of his verse, in these long-treasured reminiscences of the poetical improvisation with which the two boys were thus unexpectedly favored. Governor Rice continues: —

"You know what a captivating charm there always was in Emerson's presence, but I can never tell you how this line of thought then impressed a country boy. I do not remember anything about the remainder of that walk, nor of the after-incidents of that day, — I only remember that I went home wondering about that mystical dream of the Universal Spirit, and about what manner of man he was under whose influence I had for the first time come. . . .

"The interview left impressions that led me into new channels of thought which have been a life-long pleasure to me, and, I doubt not, taught me somewhat how to distinguish between mere theological dogma and genuine religion in the soul."

In the summer of 1834 Emerson became a resident of Concord, Massachusetts, the town of his forefathers, and the place destined to be his home for life. He first lived with his venerable connection, Dr. Ripley, in the dwelling made famous by Hawthorne as the "Old Manse." It is an old-fashioned gambrel-roofed house, standing close to the scene of the Fight on the banks of the river. It was built for the Reverend William Emerson, his grandfather. In one of the rooms of this house Emerson wrote "Nature," and in the same room, some years later, Hawthorne wrote "Mosses from an Old Manse."

The place in which Emerson passed the greater part of his life well deserves a special notice. Concord might sit for its portrait as an ideal New England town. If wanting in the variety of surface which many other towns can boast of, it has at least a vision of the distant summits of Monadnock and Wachusett. It has fine old woods, and noble elms to give dignity to its open spaces. Beautiful ponds, as they modestly call themselves, — one of which, Walden, is as well known in our literature as Windermere in that of Old England, — lie quietly in their clean basins. And through the green meadows runs, or rather lounges, a gentle, unsalted stream, like an English river, lick-

ing its grassy margin with a sort of bovine placidity
and contentment. This is the Musketaquid, or
Meadow River, which, after being joined by the more
restless Assabet, still keeps its temper and flows peace-
fully along by and through other towns, to lose itself
in the broad Merrimac. The names of these rivers
tell us that Concord has an Indian history, and there
is evidence that it was a favorite residence of the race
which preceded our own. The native tribes knew as
well as the white settlers where were pleasant streams
and sweet springs, where corn grew tall in the meadows and fish bred fast in the unpolluted waters.

The place thus favored by nature can show a record
worthy of its physical attractions. Its settlement
under the lead of Emerson's ancestor, Peter Bulkeley,
was effected in the midst of many difficulties, which
the enterprise and self-sacrifice of that noble leader
were successful in overcoming. On the banks of the
Musketaquid was fired the first fatal shot of the
"rebel" farmers. Emerson appeals to the records
of the town for two hundred years as illustrating the
working of our American institutions and the character of the men of Concord: —

"If the good counsel prevailed, the sneaking counsel
did not fail to be suggested; freedom and virtue, if they
triumphed, triumphed in a fair field. And so be it an
everlasting testimony for them, and so much ground of
assurance of man's capacity for self-government."

What names that plain New England town reckons
in the roll of its inhabitants! Stout Major Buttrick
and his fellow-soldiers in the war of Independence,
and their worthy successors in the war of Freedom;
lawyers and statesmen like Samuel Hoar and his
descendants; ministers like Peter Bulkeley, Daniel

Bliss, and William Emerson; and men of genius such as the idealist and poet whose inspiration has kindled so many souls; as the romancer who has given an atmosphere to the hard outlines of our stern New England; as that unique individual, half college-graduate and half Algonquin, the Robinson Crusoe of Walden Pond, who carried out a school-boy whim to its full proportions, and told the story of Nature in undress as only one who had hidden in her bed-room could have told it. I need not lengthen the catalogue by speaking of the living, or mentioning the women whose names have added to its distinction. It has long been an intellectual centre such as no other country town of our own land, if of any other, could boast. Its groves, its streams, its houses, are haunted by undying memories, and its hillsides and hollows are made holy by the dust that is covered by their turf.

Such was the place which the advent of Emerson made the Delphi of New England and the resort of many pilgrims from far-off regions.

On his return from Europe in the winter of 1833–34, Mr. Emerson began to appear before the public as a lecturer. His first subjects, "Water," and the "Relation of Man to the Globe," were hardly such as we should have expected from a scholar who had but a limited acquaintance with physical and physiological science. They were probably chosen as of a popular character, easily treated in such a way as to be intelligible and entertaining, and thus answering the purpose of introducing him pleasantly to the new career he was contemplating. These lectures are not included in his published works, nor were they ever published, so far as I know. He gave three lectures during the same winter, relating the experiences of his recent tour in Europe. Having made himself at home on the platform, he ventured upon subjects more congenial to his taste and habits of thought than some of those earlier topics. In 1834 he lectured on Michael Angelo, Milton, Luther, George Fox, and Edmund Burke. The first two of these lectures, though not included in his collected works, may be found in "The North American Review" for 1837 and 1838. The germ of many of the thoughts which he has expanded in prose and verse may be found in these essays.

The *Cosmos* of the Ancient Greeks, the *piu nel' uno*, "The Many in One," appear in the essay on Michael Angelo as they also appear in his "Nature." The last thought takes wings to itself and rises in the little poem entitled "Each and All." The "Rhodora," another brief poem, finds itself foreshadowed in the inquiry, "What is Beauty?" and its answer, "This great Whole the understanding cannot embrace. Beauty may be felt. It may be produced. But it cannot be defined." And throughout this essay the feeling that truth and beauty and virtue are one, and that Nature is the symbol which typifies it to the soul, is the inspiring sentiment. *Noscitur a sociis* applies as well to a man's dead as to his living companions. A young friend of mine in his college days wrote an essay on Plato. When he mentioned his subject to Mr. Emerson, he got the caution, long remembered, "When you strike at a *King*, you must kill him." He himself knew well with what kings of thought to measure his own intelligence. What was grandest, loftiest, purest, in human character chiefly interested him. He rarely meddles with what is petty or ignoble. Like his "Humble Bee," the "yellow-breeched philosopher," whom he speaks of as

> "Wiser far than human seer,"

and says of him,

> "Aught unsavory or unclean
> Hath my insect never seen,"

he goes through the world where coarser minds find so much that is repulsive to dwell upon,

> "Seeing only what is fair,
> Sipping only what is sweet."

Why Emerson selected Michael Angelo as the subject of one of his earliest lectures is shown clearly enough by the last sentence as printed in the essay.

"He was not a citizen of any country; he belonged to the human race; he was a brother and a friend to all who acknowledged the beauty that beams in universal nature, and who seek by labor and self-denial to approach its source in perfect goodness."

Consciously or unconsciously men describe themselves in the characters they draw. One must have the mordant in his own personality or he will not take the color of his subject. He may force himself to picture that which he dislikes or even detests; but when he loves the character he delineates, it is his own, in some measure, at least, or one of which he feels that its possibilities and tendencies belong to himself. Let us try Emerson by this test in his essay on Milton: —

"It is the prerogative of this great man to stand at this hour foremost of all men in literary history, and so (shall we not say?) of all men, in the power to *inspire*. Virtue goes out of him into others." . . . "He is identified in the mind with all select and holy images, with the supreme interests of the human race." — "Better than any other he has discharged the office of every great man, namely, to raise the idea of Man in the minds of his contemporaries and of posterity, — to draw after nature a life of man, exhibiting such a composition of grace, of strength, and of virtue as poet had not described nor hero lived. Human nature in these ages is indebted to him for its best portrait. Many philosophers in England, France, and Germany, have formally dedicated their study to this problem; and we think it impossible to recall one in those countries who communicates the same vibration of hope, of self-reverence, of piety, of delight in beauty, which the name of Milton awakes."

Emerson had the same lofty aim as Milton, "To raise the idea of man;" he had "the power *to inspire*" in a preëminent degree. If ever a man communicated those *vibrations* he speaks of as characteristic of Milton, it was Emerson. In elevation, purity, nobility of nature, he is worthy to stand with the great poet and patriot, who began like him as a schoolmaster, and ended as the teacher in a school-house which had for its walls the horizons of every region where English is spoken. The similarity of their characters might be followed by the curious into their fortunes. Both were turned away from the clerical office by a revolt of conscience against the beliefs required of them; both lost very dear objects of affection in early manhood, and mourned for them in tender and mellifluous threnodies. It would be easy to trace many parallelisms in their prose and poetry, but to have dared to name any man whom we have known in our common life with the seraphic singer of the Nativity and of Paradise is a tribute which seems to savor of audacity. It is hard to conceive of Emerson as "an expert swordsman" like Milton. It is impossible to think of him as an abusive controversialist as Milton was in his controversy with Salmasius. But though Emerson never betrayed it to the offence of others, he must have been conscious, like Milton, of "a certain niceness of nature, an honest haughtiness," which was as a shield about his inner nature. Charles Emerson, the younger brother, who was of the same type, expresses the feeling in his college essay on Friendship, where it is all summed up in the line he quotes: —

> "The hand of Douglas is his own."

It must be that in writing this essay on Milton Emerson felt that he was listening in his own soul to whispers that seemed like echoes from that of the divine singer.

My friend, the Rev. James Freeman Clarke, a life-long friend of Emerson, who understood him from the first, and was himself a great part in the movement of which Emerson, more than any other man, was the leader, has kindly allowed me to make use of the following letters: —

TO REV. JAMES F. CLARKE, LOUISVILLE, KY.

PLYMOUTH, MASS., *March* 12, 1834.

MY DEAR SIR, — As the day approaches when Mr. Lewis should leave Boston, I seize a few moments in a friendly house in the first of towns, to thank you heartily for your kindness in lending me the valued manuscripts which I return. The translations excited me much, and who can estimate the value of a good thought? I trust I am to learn much more from you hereafter of your German studies, and much I hope of your own. You asked in your note concerning Carlyle. My recollections of him are most pleasant, and I feel great confidence in his character. He understands and recognizes his mission. He is perfectly simple and affectionate in his manner, and frank, as he can well afford to be, in his communications. He expressed some impatience of his total solitude, and talked of Paris as a residence. I told him I hoped not; for I should always remember him with respect, meditating in the mountains of Nithsdale. He was cheered, as he ought to be, by learning that his papers were read with interest by young men unknown to him in this continent; and when I specified a piece which had attracted warm commendation from the New Jerusalem people here, his wife said that is always the way; whatever he has writ that he thinks has fallen dead, he hears of two or three years afterward. — He has many, many tokens of Goethe's regard, miniatures, medals, and many letters. If you should go to Scotland one day, you would gratify him, yourself, and me, by your visit to Craigenputtock, in the parish of Dunscore, near Dumfries. He told me he had a book which he thought to publish, but was in the purpose of dividing into a series of articles for "Fraser's Magazine." I therefore subscribed for that book, which he calls the "Mud Magazine," but have seen nothing of his workmanship in the two last numbers. The mail is going, so I shall finish my letter another time.

Your obliged friend and servant,

R. WALDO EMERSON.

CONCORD, MASS., *November 25, 1834.*

MY DEAR SIR, — Miss Peabody has kindly sent me your manuscript piece on Goethe and Carlyle. I have read it with great pleasure and a feeling of gratitude, at the same time with a serious regret that it was not published. I have forgotten what reason you assigned for not printing it; I cannot think of any sufficient one. Is it too late now? Why not change its form a little and annex to it some account of Carlyle's later pieces, to wit: "Diderot," and "Sartor Resartus"? The last is complete, and he has sent it to me in a stitched pamphlet.   Whilst I see its vices (relatively to the reading public) of style, I cannot but esteem it a noble philosophical poem, reflecting the ideas, institutions, men of this very hour.   And it seems to me that it has so much wit and other secondary graces as must strike a class who would not care for its primary merit, that of being a sincere exhortation to seekers of truth.   If you still retain your interest in his genius (as I see not how you can avoid, having understood it and coöperated with it so truly), you will be glad to know that he values his American readers very highly; that he does not defend this offensive style of his, but calls it questionable tentative; that he is trying other modes, and is about publishing a historical piece called "The Diamond Necklace," as a part of a great work which he meditates on the subject of the French Revolution.   He says it is part of his creed that history is poetry, could we tell it right.   He adds, moreover, in a letter I have recently received from him, that it has been an odd dream that he might end in the western woods.   Shall we not bid him come, and be Poet and Teacher of a most scattered flock wanting a shepherd?   Or, as I sometimes think, would it not be a new and worse chagrin to become acquainted with the extreme deadness of our community to spiritual influences of the higher kind?   Have you read Sampson Reed's "Growth of the Mind"?   I rejoice to be contemporary with that man, and cannot wholly despair of the society in which he lives; there must be some oxygen yet, and La Fayette is only just dead.

Your friend,   R. WALDO EMERSON.

It occurs to me that 't is unfit to send any white paper so far as to your house, so you shall have a sentence from Carlyle's letter.

[This may be found in Carlyle's first letter, dated 12th August, 1834.]

Dr. Le Baron Russell, an intimate friend of Emerson for the greater part of his life, gives me some particulars with reference to the publication of "Sartor Resartus," which I will repeat in his own words: —

"It was just before the time of which I am speaking [that of Emerson's marriage] that the 'Sartor Resartus' appeared in 'Fraser.' Emerson lent the numbers, or the collected sheets of 'Fraser,' to Miss Jackson, and we all had the reading of them. The excitement which the book caused among young persons interested in the literature of the day at that time you probably remember. I was quite carried away by it, and so anxious to own a copy, that I determined to publish an American edition. I consulted James Munroe & Co. on the subject. Munroe advised me to obtain a subscription to a sufficient number of copies to secure the cost of the publication. This, with the aid of some friends, particularly of my classmate, William Silsbee, I readily succeeded in doing. When this was accomplished, I wrote to Emerson, who up to this time had taken no part in the enterprise, asking him to write a preface. (This is the Preface which appears in the American edition, James Munroe & Co., 1836. It was omitted in the third American from the second London edition,[1] by the same publishers, 1840.) Before the first edition appeared, and after the subscription had been secured, Munroe & Co. offered to assume the whole responsibility of the publication, and to this I assented.

"This American edition of 1836 was the first appearance of the 'Sartor' in either country, as a distinct edition. Some copies of the sheets from 'Fraser,' it appears, were stitched together and sent to a few persons, but Carlyle could find no English publisher willing to take the responsibility of printing the book. This shows, I think, how much more interest was taken in Carlyle's writings in this country than in England."

On the 14th of May, 1834, Emerson wrote to Carlyle the first letter of that correspondence which has since been given to the world under the careful editor-

---

[1] Revised and corrected by the author.

ship of Mr. Charles Norton. This correspondence
lasted from the date mentioned to the 2d of April, 1872,
when Carlyle wrote his last letter to Emerson. The
two writers reveal themselves as being in strong sympathy with each other, in spite of a radical difference
of temperament and entirely opposite views of life.
The hatred of unreality was uppermost with Carlyle ;
the love of what is real and genuine with Emerson.
Those old moralists, the weeping and the laughing
philosophers, find their counterparts in every thinking
community. Carlyle did not weep, but he scolded;
Emerson did not laugh, but in his gravest moments
there was a smile waiting for the cloud to pass from his
forehead. The Duet they chanted was a Miserere
with a Te Deum for its Antiphon; a *De Profundis*
answered by a *Sursum Corda*. "The ground of my
existence is black as death," says Carlyle. "Come
and live with me a year," says Emerson, "and if you
do not like New England well enough to stay, one of
these years (when the 'History' has passed its ten editions, and been translated into as many languages) I
will come and dwell with you."

§ 2. In September, 1835, Emerson was married to
Miss Lydia Jackson, of Plymouth, Massachusetts.
The wedding took place in the fine old mansion known
as the Winslow House, Dr. Le Baron Russell and his
sister standing up with the bridegroom and his bride.
After their marriage, Mr. and Mrs. Emerson went to
reside in the house in which he passed the rest of his
life, and in which Mrs. Emerson and their daughter
still reside. This is the "plain, square, wooden
house," with horse-chestnut trees in the front yard,
and evergreens around it, which has been so often

described and figured.   It is without pretensions, but
not without an air of quiet dignity.   A full and well-
illustrated account of it and its arrangements and surroundings is given in "Poets' Homes," by Arthur
Gilman and others, published by D. Lothrop & Company in 1879.

On the 12th of September, 1835, Emerson delivered an "Historical Discourse, at Concord, on the
Second Centennial Anniversary of the Incorporation
of the Town."   There is no "mysticism," no "transcendentalism" in this plain, straightforward address.
The facts are collected and related with the patience
and sobriety which became the writer as one of the
Dryasdusts of our very diligent, very useful, very
matter-of-fact, and for the most part judiciously unimaginative Massachusetts Historical Society.   It
looks unlike anything else Emerson ever wrote, in
being provided with abundant foot-notes and an appendix.   One would almost as soon have expected to
see Emerson equipped with a musket and a knapsack
as to find a discourse of his clogged with annotations,
and trailing a supplement after it.   Oracles are brief
and final in their utterances.   Delphi and Cumæ are
not expected to explain what they say.

It is the habit of our New England towns to celebrate their own worthies and their own deeds on occasions like this, with more or less of rhetorical gratitude and self-felicitation.   The discourses delivered
on these occasions are commonly worth reading, for
there was never a clearing made in the forest that did
not let in the light on heroes and heroines.   Concord
is on the whole the most interesting of all the inland
towns of New England.   Emerson has told its story
in as painstaking, faithful a way as if he had been by

nature an annalist. But with this fidelity, we find
also those bold generalizations and sharp picturesque
touches which reveal the poetic philosopher.

"I have read with care," he says, "the town records
themselves. They exhibit a pleasing picture of a community almost exclusively agricultural, where no man has
much time for words, in his search after things; of a
community of great simplicity of manners, and of a manifest love of justice. I find our annals marked with a
uniform good sense. — The tone of the record rises with
the dignity of the event. These soiled and musty books
are luminous and electric within. The old town clerks
did not spell very correctly, but they contrive to make intelligible the will of a free and just community." . . .
"The matters there debated (in town meetings) are such
as to invite very small consideration. The ill-spelled
pages of the town records contain the result. I shall be
excused for confessing that I have set a value upon any
symptom of meanness and private pique which I have met
with in these antique books, as proof that justice was
done; that if the results of our history are approved as
wise and good, it was yet a free strife; if the good counsel prevailed, the sneaking counsel did not fail to be
suggested; freedom and virtue, if they triumphed, triumphed in a fair field. And so be it an everlasting testimony for them, and so much ground of assurance of man's
capacity for self-government."

There was nothing in this address which the plainest of Concord's citizens could not read understand-
ingly and with pleasure. In fact Mr. Emerson himself, besides being a poet and a philosopher, was also
a plain Concord citizen. His son tells me that he was
a faithful attendant upon town meetings and, though
he never spoke, was an interested and careful listener
to the debates on town matters. That respect for
"mother-wit" and for all the wholesome human quali-

ties which reveals itself all through his writings was
bred from this kind of intercourse with men of sense
who had no pretensions to learning, and in whom,
for that very reason, the native qualities came out
with less disguise in their expression. He was surrounded by men who ran to extremes in their idiosyncrasies: Alcott in speculations, which often led him
into the fourth dimension of mental space; Hawthorne,
who brooded himself into a dream-peopled solitude;
Thoreau, the nullifier of civilization, who insisted on
nibbling his asparagus at the wrong end, to say nothing of idolaters and echoes. He kept his balance
among them all. It would be hard to find a more
candid and sober record of the result of self-government in a small community than is contained in this
simple discourse, patient in detail, large in treatment,
more effective than any unsupported generalities about
the natural rights of man, which amount to very little
unless men earn the right of asserting them by attending fairly to their natural duties. So admirably is the
working of a town government, as it goes on in a well-
disposed community, displayed in the history of Concord's two hundred years of village life, that one of
its wisest citizens had portions of the address printed
for distribution, as an illustration of the American
principle of self-government.

After settling in Concord, Emerson delivered
courses of lectures in Boston during several successive winters; in 1835, ten lectures on English Literature; in 1836, twelve lectures on the Philosophy of
History; in 1837, ten lectures on Human Culture.
Some of these lectures may have appeared in print
under their original titles; all of them probably contributed to the essays and discourses which we find
in his published volumes.

On the 19th of April, 1836, a meeting was held to celebrate the completion of the monument raised in commemoration of the Concord Fight. For this occasion Emerson wrote the hymn made ever memorable by the lines: —

> " Here once the embattled farmers stood,
>   And fired the shot heard round the world."

The last line of this hymn quickens the heart-beats of every American, and the whole hymn is admirable in thought and expression.

Until the autumn of 1838, Emerson preached twice on Sundays to the church at East Lexington, which desired him to become its pastor. Mr. Cooke says that when a lady of the society was asked why they did not settle a friend of Emerson's whom he had urged them to invite to their pulpit, she replied: "We are a very simple people, and can understand no one but Mr. Emerson." He said of himself: "My pulpit is the lyceum platform." Knowing that he made his sermons contribute to his lectures, we need not mourn over their not being reported.

In March, 1837, Emerson delivered in Boston a lecture on War, afterwards published in Miss Peabody's "Æsthetic Papers." He recognizes war as one of the temporary necessities of a developing civilization, to disappear with the advance of mankind: —

"At a certain stage of his progress the man fights, if he be of a sound body and mind. At a certain high stage he makes no offensive demonstrations, but is alert to repel injury, and of an unconquerable heart. At a still higher stage he comes into the region of holiness; passion has passed away from him; his warlike nature is all converted into an active medicinal principle; he sacrifices himself, and accepts with alacrity wearisome tasks of de-

nial and charity; but being attacked, he bears it, and
turns the other cheek, as one engaged, throughout his being, no longer to the service of an individual, but to the
common good of all men."

In 1834 Emerson's brother Edward died, as already mentioned, in the West India island where he
had gone for his health. In his letter to Carlyle, of
November 12th of the same year, Emerson says:
"Your letter, which I received last week, made a
bright light in a solitary and saddened place. I had
quite recently received the news of the death of a
brother in the island of Porto Rico, whose loss to me
will be a life-long sorrow." It was of him that Emerson wrote the lines "In Memoriam," in which he
says, —

> "There is no record left on earth
> Save on tablets of the heart,
> Of the rich, inherent worth,
> Of the grace that on him shone
> Of eloquent lips, of joyful wit ;
> He could not frame a word unfit,
> An act unworthy to be done."

Another bereavement was too soon to be recorded.
On the 7th of October, 1835, he says in a letter to
Carlyle: —

"I was very glad to hear of the brother you describe,
for I have one too, and know what it is to have presence
in two places. Charles Chauncy Emerson is a lawyer now
settled in this town, and, as I believe, no better Lord
Hamlet was ever. He is our doctor on all questions of
taste, manners, or action. And one of the pure pleasures
I promise myself in the months to come is to make you
two gentlemen know each other."

Alas for human hopes and prospects! In less than

a year from the date of that letter, on the 17th of September, 1836, he writes to Carlyle:—

"Your last letter, dated in April, found me a mourner, as did your first. I have lost out of this world my brother Charles, of whom I have spoken to you, — the friend and companion of many years, the inmate of my house, a man of a beautiful genius, born to speak well, and whose conversation for these last years has treated every grave question of humanity, and has been my daily bread. I have put so much dependence on his gifts, that we made but one man together; for I needed never to do what he could do by noble nature, much better than I. He was to have been married in this month, and at the time of his sickness and sudden death, I was adding apartments to my house for his permanent accommodation. I wish that you could have known him. At twenty-seven years the best life is only preparation. He built his foundation so large that it needed the full age of man to make evident the plan and proportions of his character. He postponed always a particular to a final and absolute success, so that his life was a silent appeal to the great and generous. But some time I shall see you and speak of him."

§ 3. In the year 1836 there was published in Boston a little book of less than a hundred very small pages, entitled "Nature." It bore no name on its title-page, but was at once attributed to its real author, Ralph Waldo Emerson.

The Emersonian adept will pardon me for burdening this beautiful essay with a commentary which is worse than superfluous for him. For it has proved for many, — I will not say a *pons asinorum*, — but a very narrow bridge, which it made their heads swim to attempt crossing, and yet they must cross it, or one domain of Emerson's intellect will not be reached.

It differed in some respects from anything he had

hitherto written. It talked a strange sort of philosophy in the language of poetry. Beginning simply enough, it took more and more the character of a rhapsody, until, as if lifted off his feet by the deepened and stronger undercurrent of his thought, the writer dropped his personality and repeated the words which "a certain poet sang" to him.

This little book met with a very unemotional reception. Its style was peculiar, — almost as unlike that of his essays as that of Carlyle's "Sartor Resartus" was unlike the style of his "Life of Schiller." It was vague, mystic, incomprehensible, to most of those who call themselves common-sense people. Some of its expressions lent themselves easily to travesty and ridicule. But the laugh could not be very loud or very long, since it took twelve years, as Mr. Higginson tells us, to sell five hundred copies. It was a good deal like Keats's

> " doubtful tale from fairy-land
> Hard for the non-elect to understand."

The same experience had been gone through by Wordsworth.

"Whatever is too original," says De Quincey, "will be hated at the first. It must slowly mould a public for itself; and the resistance of the early thoughtless judgments must be overcome by a counter-resistance to itself, in a better audience slowly mustering against the first. Forty and seven years it is since William Wordsworth first appeared as an author. Twenty of these years he was the scoff of the world, and his poetry a by-word of scorn. Since then, and more than once, senates have rung with acclamations to the echo of his name."

No writer is more deeply imbued with the spirit of Wordsworth than Emerson, as we cannot fail to see in turning the pages of "Nature," his first thoroughly characteristic essay. There is the same thought in the Preface to "The Excursion" that we find in the Introduction to "Nature."

"The foregoing generations beheld God and nature face to face; we, through their eyes. Why should not we also enjoy an original relation to the universe? Why should not we have a poetry and philosophy of insight and not of tradition, and a religion by revelation to us, and not the history of theirs?"

> "Paradise, and groves
> Elysian, Fortunate Fields, — like those of old
> Sought in the Atlantic Main, — why should they be
> A history only of departed things,
> Or a mere fiction of what never was?"

"Nature" is a reflective prose poem. It is divided into eight chapters, which might almost as well have been called cantos.

Never before had Mr. Emerson given free utterance to the passion with which the aspects of nature inspired him. He had recently for the first time been at once master of himself and in free communion with all the planetary influences above, beneath, around him. The air of the country intoxicated him. There are sentences in "Nature" which are as exalted as the language of one who is just coming to himself after having been etherized. Some of these expressions sounded to a considerable part of his early readers like the vagaries of delirium. Yet underlying these excited outbursts there was a general tone of serenity which reassured the anxious. The gust passed over, the ripples smoothed themselves, and the stars shone again in quiet reflection.

After a passionate outbreak, in which he sees all, is nothing, loses himself in nature, in Universal Being,

becomes "part or particle of God," he considers
briefly, in the chapter entitled "Commodity," the
ministry of nature to the senses. A few picturesque
glimpses in pleasing and poetical phrases, with a touch
of archaism, and reminiscences of Hamlet and Jeremy Taylor, "the Shakspeare of divines," as he has
called him, are what we find in this chapter on Commodity, or natural conveniences.

But "a nobler want of man is served by Nature,
namely, the love of Beauty," which is his next subject. There are some touches of description here,
vivid, high-colored, not so much pictures as hints and
impressions for pictures.

Many of the thoughts which run through all his
prose and poetry may be found here. Analogy is seen
everywhere in the works of Nature. "What is common to them all, — that perfectness and harmony, is
beauty." "Nothing is quite beautiful alone: nothing
but is beautiful in the whole." "No reason can be
asked or given why the soul seeks beauty." How
easily these same ideas took on the robe of verse may
be seen in the poems, "Each and All," and "The
Rhodora." A good deal of his philosophy comes out in
these concluding sentences of the chapter : —

"Beauty in its largest and profoundest sense is one expression for the universe. God is the all-fair. Truth
and goodness and beauty are but different faces of the
same All. But beauty in Nature is not ultimate. It is
the herald of inward and eternal beauty, and is not alone
a solid and satisfactory good. It must therefore stand as
a part and not as yet the highest expression of the final
cause of Nature."

In "The Rhodora" the flower is made to answer that
"Beauty is its own excuse for being."

In this essay the beauty of the flower is not enough, but it must excuse itself for being, mainly as the symbol of something higher and deeper than itself.

He passes next to a consideration of Language. Words are signs of natural facts, particular material facts are symbols of particular spiritual facts, and Nature is the symbol of spirit. Without going very profoundly into the subject, he gives some hints as to the mode in which languages are formed, — whence words are derived, how they become transformed and worn out. But they come at first fresh from Nature.

"A man conversing in earnest, if he watch his intellectual processes, will find that always a material image, more or less luminous, arises in his mind, contemporaneous with every thought, which furnishes the vestment of the thought. Hence good writing and brilliant discourse are perpetual allegories."

From this he argues that country life is a great advantage to a powerful mind, inasmuch as it furnishes a greater number of these material images. They cannot be summoned at will, but they present themselves when great exigencies call for them.

"The poet, the orator, bred in the woods, whose senses have been nourished by their fair and appeasing changes, year after year, without design and without heed, — shall not lose their lesson altogether, in the roar of cities or the broil of politics. Long hereafter, amidst agitations and terror in national councils, — in the hour of revolution, — these solemn images shall reappear in their morning lustre, as fit symbols and words of the thought which the passing events shall awaken. At the call of a noble sentiment, again the woods wave, the pines murmur, the river rolls and shines, and the cattle low upon the mountains, as he saw and heard them in his infancy. And with these forms the spells of persuasion, the keys of power, are put into his hands."

It is doing no wrong to this very eloquent and beautiful passage to say that it reminds us of certain lines
in one of the best known poems of Wordsworth: —

> "These beauteous forms,
> Through a long absence, have not been to me
> As is a landscape to a blind man's eye ;
> But oft, in lonely rooms, and mid the din
> Of towns and cities, I have owed to them
> In hours of weariness sensations sweet
> Felt in the blood and felt along the heart."

It is needless to quote the whole passage. The
poetry of Wordsworth may have suggested the prose
of Emerson, but the prose loses nothing by the comparison.

In "Discipline," which is his next subject, he treats
of the influence of Nature in educating the intellect,
the moral sense, and the will. Man is enlarged and
the universe lessened and brought within his grasp,
because

"Time and space relations vanish as laws are known."
"The moral law lies at the centre of Nature and radiates to the circumference." "All things with which we
deal preach to us. What is a farm but a mute gospel?"
"From the child's successive possession of his several
senses up to the hour when he sayeth, 'Thy will be done!'
he is learning the secret that he can reduce under his will,
not only particular events, but great classes, nay, the
whole series of events, and so conform all facts to his
character."

The unity in variety which meets us everywhere is
again referred to. He alludes to the ministry of our
friendships to our education. When a friend has done
for our education in the way of filling our minds with
sweet and solid wisdom "it is a sign to us that his
office is closing, and he is commonly withdrawn from

our sight in a short time." This thought was probably suggested by the death of his brother Charles, which occurred a few months before "Nature" was published. He had already spoken in the first chapter of this little book as if from some recent experience of his own, doubtless the same bereavement. "To a man laboring under calamity, the heat of his own fire hath sadness in it. Then there is a kind of contempt of the landscape felt by him who has just lost by death a dear friend. The sky is less grand as it shuts down over less worth in the population." This was the first effect of the loss; but after a time he recognizes a superintending power which orders events for us in wisdom which we could not see at first.

The chapter on "Idealism" must be read by all who believe themselves capable of abstract thought, if they would not fall under the judgment of Turgot, which Emerson quotes: "He that has never doubted the existence of matter may be assured he has no aptitude for metaphysical inquiries." The most essential statement is this: —

"It is a sufficient account of that Appearance we call the World, that God will teach a human mind, and so makes it the receiver of a certain number of congruent sensations, which we call sun and moon, man and woman, house and trade. In my utter impotence to test the authenticity of the report of my senses, to know whether the impressions they make on me correspond with outlying objects, what difference does it make, whether Orion is up there in heaven, or some god paints the image in the firmament of the soul?"

We need not follow the thought through the argument from illusions, like that when we look at the shore from a moving ship, and others which cheat the senses by false appearances.

The poet animates Nature with his own thoughts, perceives the affinities between Nature and the soul, with Beauty as his main end. The philosopher pursues Truth, but, "not less than the poet, postpones the apparent order and relation of things to the empire of thought." Religion and ethics agree with all lower culture in degrading Nature and suggesting its dependence on Spirit. "The devotee flouts Nature." "Plotinus was ashamed of his body." "Michael Angelo said of external beauty, 'It is the frail and weary weed, in which God dresses the soul which He has called into time.'". Emerson would not undervalue Nature as looked at through the senses and "the unrenewed understanding." "I have no hostility to Nature," he says, "but a child's love of it. I expand and live in the warm day like corn and melons." But, "seen in the light of thought, the world always is phenomenal; and virtue subordinates it to the mind. Idealism sees the world in God," — as one vast picture, which God paints on the instant eternity, for the contemplation of the soul.

The unimaginative reader is likely to find himself off soundings in the next chapter, which has for its title "Spirit."

Idealism only denies the existence of matter; it does not satisfy the demands of the spirit. "It leaves God out of me." Of these three questions, What is matter? Whence is it? Whereto? the ideal theory answers the first only. The reply is that matter is a phenomenon, not a substance.

"But when we come to inquire Whence is matter? and Whereto? many truths arise to us out of the recesses of consciousness. We learn that the highest is present to the soul of man; that the dread universal essence, which is not wisdom, or love, or beauty, or power, but all in one, and each entirely, is that for which all things exist, and that by which they are; that spirit creates; that behind nature, throughout nature, spirit is present; that spirit is one and not compound; that spirit does not act upon us from without, that is, in space and time, but spiritually, or through ourselves." "As a plant upon the earth, so a man rests upon the bosom of God; he is nourished by unfailing fountains, and draws, at his need, inexhaustible power."

Man may have access to the entire mind of the Creator, himself become a "creator in the finite."

"As we degenerate, the contrast between us and our house is more evident. We are as much strangers in nature as we are aliens from God. We do not understand the notes of birds. The fox and the deer run away from us; the bear and the tiger rend us."

All this has an Old Testament sound as of a lost Paradise. In the next chapter he dreams of Paradise regained.

This next and last chapter is entitled "Prospects." He begins with a bold claim for the province of intuition as against induction, undervaluing the "half sight of science" as against the "untaught sallies of the spirit," the surmises and vaticinations of the mind, — the "imperfect theories, and sentences which contain glimpses of truth." In a word, he would have us leave the laboratory and its crucibles for the sibyl's cave and its tripod. We can all — or most of us, certainly — recognize something of truth, much of imagination, and more of danger in speculations of this sort. They belong to visionaries and to poets. Emerson feels distinctly enough that he is getting into the realm of poetry. He quotes five beautiful verses from George Herbert's poem on Man. Presently he is himself taken off his feet into the air of song, and finishes his essay with "some traditions of man and nature which a certain poet sang to me." "A man is a god in ruins." "Man is the dwarf of himself. Once he was permeated and dissolved by spirit. He filled nature with his overflowing currents. Out from him sprang the sun and moon; from man the sun, from woman the moon." But he no longer fills the mere shell he had made for himself; "he is shrunk to a drop." Still something of elemental power remains to him. "It is instinct." Such teachings he got from his "poet." It is a kind of New England Genesis in place of the Old Testament one. We read in the Sermon on the Mount: "Be ye therefore perfect, as your Father in heaven is perfect." The discourse which comes to us from the Trimount oracle commands us, "Build, therefore, your own world. As fast as you conform your life to the pure idea in your mind, that will unfold its great proportions." The seer of Patmos foretells a heavenly Jerusalem, of which he says, "There shall in no wise enter into it anything that defileth." The sage of Concord foresees a new heaven on earth. "A correspondent revolution in things will attend the influx of the spirit. So fast will disagreeable appearances, swine, spiders, snakes, pests, mad-houses, prisons, enemies, vanish; they are temporary and shall be no more seen."

It may be remembered that Calvin, in his Commentary on the New Testament, stopped when he came to the Book of the Revelation. He found it full of difficulties which he did not care to encounter. Yet, considered only as a poem, the vision of St. John is full of noble imagery and wonderful beauty. "Nature" is the Book of Revelation of our Saint Radulphus. It has its obscurities, its extravagances, but as a poem it is noble and inspiring. It was objected to on the score of its pantheistic character, as Wordsworth's "Lines composed near Tintern Abbey" had been long before. But here and there it found devout readers who were captivated by its spiritual elevation and great poetical beauty, among them one who wrote of it in "The Democratic Review" in terms of enthusiastic admiration.

Mr. Bowen, the Professor of Natural Theology and Moral Philosophy in Harvard University, treated this singular semi-philosophical, semi-poetical little book in a long article in "The Christian Examiner," headed "Transcendentalism," and published in the January number for 1837. The acute and learned professor meant to deal fairly with his subject. But if one has ever seen a sagacious pointer making the acquaintance of a box-tortoise, he will have an idea of the relations between the reviewer and the reviewed as they appear in this article. The professor turns the book over and over, — inspects it from plastron to carapace, so to speak, and looks for openings everywhere, sometimes successfully, sometimes in vain. He finds good writing and sound philosophy, passages of great force and beauty of expression, marred by obscurity, under assumptions and faults of style. He was not, any more than the rest of us, acclimated to the Emersonian atmosphere, and after some not unjust or unkind comments with which many readers will heartily agree, confesses his bewilderment, saying: —

"On reviewing what we have already said of this singular work, the criticism seems to be couched in contradictory terms; we can only allege in excuse the fact that the book is a contradiction in itself."

Carlyle says in his letter of February 13, 1837: —

"Your little azure-colored 'Nature' gave me true satisfaction. I read it, and then lent it about to all my acquaintance that had a sense for such things; from whom a similar verdict always came back. You say it is the first chapter of something greater. I call it rather the Foundation and Ground-plan on which you may build whatsoever of great and true has been given you to build. It is the true Apocalypse, this when the 'Open Secret' becomes revealed to a man. I rejoice much in the glad serenity of soul with which you look out on this wondrous Dwelling-place of yours and mine, — with an ear for the *Ewigen Melodien*, which pipe in the winds round us, and utter themselves forth in all sounds and sights and things; *not* to be written down by gamut-machinery; but which all right writing is a kind of attempt to write down."

The first edition of "Nature" had prefixed to it the following words from Plotinus: "Nature is but an image or imitation of wisdom, the last thing of the soul; Nature being a thing which doth only do, but not know." This is omitted in after editions, and in its place we read: —

> "A subtle chain of countless rings
> The next unto the farthest brings;
> The eye reads omens where it goes,
> And speaks all languages the rose;
> And, striving to be man, the worm
> Mounts through all the spires of form."

The copy of "Nature" from which I take these lines, his own, of course, like so many others which he prefixed to his different essays, was printed in the year 1849, ten years before the publication of Darwin's "Origin of Species," twenty years and more before the publication of "The Descent of Man." But the "Vestiges of Creation," published in 1844, had already popularized the resuscitated theories of Lamarck. It seems as if Emerson had a warning from the poetic instinct which, when it does not precede the movement of the scientific intellect, is the first to catch the hint of its discoveries. There is nothing more audacious in the poet's conception of the worm looking up towards humanity, than the naturalist's theory that the progenitor of the human race was an acephalous mollusk. "I will not be sworn," says Benedick, "but love may transform me to an oyster." For "love" read "science."

Unity in variety, "*il piu nell uno*," symbolism of Nature and its teachings, generation of phenomena — appearances — from spirit, to which they correspond and which they obey; evolution of the best and elimination of the worst as the law of being; all this and much more may be found in the poetic utterances of this slender essay. It fell like an aerolite, unasked for, unaccounted for, unexpected, almost unwelcome, — a stumbling-block to be got out of the well-trodden highway of New England scholastic intelligence. But here and there it found a reader to whom it was, to borrow, with slight changes, its own quotation, —

" The golden key
Which opes the palace of eternity,"

inasmuch as it carried upon its face the highest certificate of truth, because it animated them to create a new world for themselves through the purification of their own souls.

Next to "Nature" in the series of his collected publications comes "The American Scholar. An Oration delivered before the Phi Beta Kappa Society at Cambridge, August 31, 1837."

The society known by these three letters, long a mystery to the uninitiated, but which, filled out and interpreted, signify that philosophy is the guide of life, is one of long standing, the annual meetings of which have called forth the best efforts of many distinguished scholars and thinkers. Rarely has any one of the annual addresses been listened to with such profound attention and interest. Mr. Lowell says of it, that its delivery "was an event without any former parallel in our literary annals, a scene to be always treasured in the memory for its picturesqueness and its inspiration. What crowded and breathless aisles, what windows clustering with eager heads, what enthusiasm of approval, what grim silence of foregone dissent!"

Mr. Cooke says truly of this oration, that nearly all his leading ideas found expression in it. This was to be expected in an address delivered before such an audience. Every real thinker's world of thought has its centre in a few formulæ, about which they revolve as the planets circle round the sun which cast them off. But those who lost themselves now and then in the pages of "Nature" will find their way clearly enough through those of "The American Scholar." It is a plea for generous culture; for the development of all the faculties, many of which tend to become atrophied by the exclusive pursuit of single objects of thought. It begins with a note like a trumpet call.

"Thus far," he says, "our holiday has been simply a friendly sign of the survival of the love of letters amongst a people too busy to give to letters any more. As such it is precious as the sign of an indestructible instinct. Perhaps the time is already come when it ought to be, and will be, something else; when the sluggard intellect of this continent will look from under its iron lids and fill the postponed expectations of the world with something better than the exertions of mechanical skill. Our day of dependence, our long apprenticeship to the learning of other lands, draws to a close. The millions that around us are rushing into life cannot always be fed on the sere remains of foreign harvests. Events, actions arise, that must be sung, that will sing themselves. Who can doubt that poetry will revive and lead in a new age, as the star in the constellation Harp, which now flames in our zenith, astronomers announce shall one day be the pole-star for a thousand years?"

Emerson finds his text in the old fable which tells that Man, as he was in the beginning, was divided into men, as the hand was divided into fingers, the better to answer the end of his being. The fable covers the doctrine that there is One Man; present to individuals only in a partial manner; and that we must take the whole of society to find the whole man. Unfortunately the unit has been too minutely subdivided, and many faculties are practically lost for want of use.

"The state of society is one in which the members have suffered amputation from the trunk, and strut about so many walking monsters, — a good finger, a neck, a stomach, an elbow, but never a man. Man is thus metamorphosed into a thing, into many things. . . . The priest becomes a form; the attorney a statute book; the mechanic a machine; the sailor a rope of the ship."

This complaint is by no means a new one. Scaliger says, as quoted by omnivorous old Burton: "*Nequaquam nos homines sumus sed partes hominis.*" The old illustration of this used to be found in pin-making. It took twenty different workmen to make a pin, beginning with drawing the wire and ending with sticking in the paper. Each expert, skilled in one small performance only, was reduced to a minute fraction of a fraction of humanity. If the complaint was legitimate in Scaliger's time, it was better founded half a century ago when Mr. Emerson found cause for it. It has still more serious significance to-day, when in every profession, in every branch of human knowledge, special acquirements, special skill have greatly tended to limit the range of men's thoughts and working faculties.

"In this distribution of functions the scholar is the delegated intellect. In the right state he is *Man thinking*. In the degenerate state, when the victim of society, he tends to become a mere thinker, or still worse, the parrot of other men's thinking. In this view of him, as Man thinking, the theory of his office is contained. Him Nature solicits with all her placid, all her monitory pictures; him the past instructs; him the future invites."

Emerson proceeds to describe and illustrate the influences of nature upon the mind, returning to the strain of thought with which his previous essay has made us familiar. He next considers the influence of the past, and especially of books as the best type of that influence. "Books are the best of things well used; abused among the worst." It is hard to distil what is already a quintessence without loss of what is just as good as the product of our labor. A sentence or two may serve to give an impression of the epigrammatic wisdom of his counsel.

"Each age must write its own books, or rather, each generation for the next succeeding. The books of an older period will not fit this."

When a book has gained a certain hold on the mind, it is liable to become an object of idolatrous regard.

"Instantly the book becomes noxious: the guide is a tyrant. The sluggish and perverted mind of the multitude, slow to open to the incursions of reason, having once so opened, having received this book, stands upon it and makes an outcry if it is disparaged. Colleges are built on it. Books are written on it by thinkers, not by Man thinking; by men of talent, that is, who start wrong, who set out from accepted dogmas, not from their own sight of principles. Meek young men grow up in libraries, believing it their duty to accept the views which Cicero, which Locke, which Bacon have given; forgetful that Cicero, Locke, and Bacon were only young men in libraries when they wrote these books. . . . One must be an inventor to read well. As the proverb says, 'He that would bring home the wealth of the Indies must carry out the wealth of the Indies.' . . . When the mind is braced by labor and invention, the page of whatever book we read becomes luminous with manifold allusion. Every sentence is doubly significant, and the sense of our author is as broad as the world."

It is not enough that the scholar should be a student of nature and of books. He must take a part in the affairs of the world about him.

"Action is with the scholar subordinate, but it is essential. Without it he is not yet man. Without it thought can never ripen into truth. . . . The true scholar grudges every opportunity of action past by, as a loss of power. It is the raw material out of which the intellect moulds her splendid products. A strange process, too, this by which experience is converted into thought, as a mulberry leaf is converted into satin. The manufacture goes forward at all hours."

Emerson does not use the words "unconscious cerebration," but these last words describe the process

in an unmistakable way.   The beautiful paragraph in
which he pictures the transformation, the transfiguration of experience, closes with a sentence so thoroughly
characteristic, so Emersonially Emersonian, that I
fear some readers who thought they were his disciples
when they came to it went back and walked no more
with him, at least through the pages of this discourse.
The reader shall have the preceding sentence to prepare him for the one referred to.

"There is no fact, no event in our private history,
which shall not, sooner or later, lose its adhesive, inert
form, and astonish us by soaring from our body into the
empyrean.

"Cradle and infancy, school and playground, the fear
of boys, and dogs, and ferules, the love of little maids
and berries, and many another fact that once filled the
whole sky, are gone already; friend and relative, profession and party, town and country, nation and world, must
also soar and sing."

Having spoken of the education of the scholar by
nature, by books, by action, he speaks of the scholar's
duties.   "They may all," he says, "be comprised in
self-trust."   We have to remember that the *self* he
means is the highest self, that consciousness which he
looks upon as open to the influx of the divine essence
from which it came, and towards which all its upward
tendencies lead, always aspiring, never resting; as he
sings in "The Sphinx:" —

> " The heavens that now draw him
>   With sweetness untold,
>   Once found, — for new heavens
>   He spurneth the old."

"First one, then another, we drain all cisterns, and
waxing greater by all these supplies, we crave a better and

more abundant food. The man has never lived that can feed us ever. The human mind cannot be enshrined in a person who shall set a barrier on any one side to this unbounded, unboundable empire. It is one central fire, which, flaming now out of the lips of Etna, lightens the capes of Sicily, and now out of the throat of Vesuvius, illuminates the towers and vineyards of Naples. It is one light which beams out of a thousand stars. It is one soul which animates all men."

And so he comes to the special application of the principles he has laid down to the American scholar of to-day. He does not spare his censure; he is full of noble trust and manly courage. Very refreshing it is to remember in this day of specialists, when the walking fraction of humanity he speaks of would hardly include a whole finger, but rather confine itself to the single joint of the finger, such words as these: —

"The scholar is that man who must take up into himself all the ability of the time, all the contributions of the past, all the hopes of the future. He must be a university of knowledges. . . . We have listened too long to the courtly muses of Europe. The spirit of the American freeman is already suspected to be timid, imitative, tame. . . . The scholar is decent, indolent, complaisant. . . . The mind of this country, taught to aim at low objects, eats upon itself. There is no work for any but the decorous and the complaisant."

The young men of promise are discouraged and disgusted.

"What is the remedy? They did not yet see, and thousands of young men as hopeful now crowding to the barriers for the career do not yet see, that if the single man plant himself indomitably on his instincts, and there abide, the huge world will come round to him."

Each man must be a unit, — must yield that peculiar fruit which he was created to bear.

"We will walk on our own feet; we will work with our own hands; we will speak our own minds. . . . A nation of men will for the first time exist, because each believes himself inspired by the Divine Soul which also inspires all men."

This grand oration was our intellectual Declaration of Independence. Nothing like it had been heard in the halls of Harvard since Samuel Adams supported the affirmative of the question, "Whether it be lawful to resist the chief magistrate, if the commonwealth cannot otherwise be preserved." It was easy to find fault with an expression here and there. The dignity, not to say the formality, of an Academic assembly was startled by the realism that looked for the infinite in "the meal in the firkin, the milk in the pan." They could understand the deep thoughts suggested by "the meanest flower that blows," but these domestic illustrations had a kind of nursery homeliness about them which the grave professors and sedate clergymen were unused to expect on so stately an occasion. But the young men went out from it as if a prophet had been proclaiming to them "Thus saith the Lord." No listener ever forgot that address, and among all the noble utterances of the speaker it may be questioned if one ever contained more truth in language more like that of immediate inspiration.

CHAPTER V.

1838–1843.   Æt. 35–40.

§ 1. On Sunday evening, July 15, 1838, Emerson delivered an address before the senior class in Divinity College, Cambridge, which caused a profound sensation in religious circles, and led to a controversy, in which Emerson had little more than the part of Patroclus when the Greeks and Trojans fought over his body. In its simplest and broadest statement this discourse was a plea for the individual consciousness as against all historical creeds, bibles, churches; for the soul as the supreme judge in spiritual matters.

He begins with a beautiful picture which must be transferred without the change of an expression : —

"In this refulgent summer, it has been a luxury to draw the breath of life. The grass grows, the buds burst, the meadow is spotted with fire and gold in the tint of flowers. The air is full of birds, and sweet with the breath of the pine, the balm of Gilead, and the new hay. Night brings no gloom to the heart with its welcome shade. Through the transparent darkness the stars pour their almost spiritual rays. Man under them seems a young child, and his huge globe a toy. The cool night bathes the world as with a river, and prepares his eyes again for the crimson dawn."

How softly the phrases of the gentle iconoclast steal upon the ear, and how they must have hushed the questioning audience into pleased attention! The "Song of Songs, which is Solomon's," could not have wooed the listener more sweetly. "Thy lips drop as the honeycomb: honey and milk are under thy tongue, and the smell of thy garments is like the smell of Lebanon." And this was the prelude of a discourse which, when it came to be printed, fared at the hands of many a theologian, who did not think himself a bigot, as the roll which Baruch wrote with ink from the words of Jeremiah fared at the hands of Jehoia-kim, the King of Judah. He listened while Jehudi read the opening passages. But "when Jehudi had read three or four leaves he cut it with the penknife, and cast it into the fire that was on the hearth, until all the roll was consumed in the fire that was on the hearth." Such was probably the fate of many a copy of this famous discourse.

It is reverential, but it is also revolutionary. The file-leaders of Unitarianism drew back in dismay, and the ill names which had often been applied to them were now heard from their own lips as befitting this new heresy; if so mild a reproach as that of heresy belonged to this alarming manifesto. And yet, so changed is the whole aspect of the theological world since the time when that discourse was delivered that it is read as calmly to-day as a common "election sermon," if such are ever read at all. A few extracts, abstracts, and comments may give the reader who has not the address before him some idea of its contents and its tendencies.

The material universe, which he has just pictured in its summer beauty, deserves our admiration. But when the mind opens and reveals the laws which govern the world of phenomena, it shrinks into a mere fable and illustration of this mind. What am I? What is? — are questions always asked, never fully answered. We would study and admire forever.

But above intellectual curiosity, there is the sentiment of virtue. Man is born for the good, for the perfect, low as he now lies in evil and weakness.

"The sentiment of virtue is a reverence and delight in the presence of certain divine laws. . . . These laws refuse to be adequately stated. . . . They elude our persevering thought; yet we read them hourly in each other's faces, in each other's actions, in our own remorse. . . . The intuition of the moral sentiment is an insight of the perfection of the laws of the soul. These laws execute themselves. . . . As we are, so we associate. The good, by affinity, seek the good; the vile, by affinity, the vile. Thus, of their own volition, souls proceed into heaven, into hell."

These facts, Emerson says, have always suggested to man that the world is the product not of manifold power, but of one will, of one mind, — that one mind is everywhere active. "All things proceed out of the same spirit, and all things conspire with it." While a man seeks good ends, nature helps him; when he seeks other ends, his being shrinks, "he becomes

less and less, a mote, a point, until absolute badness
is absolute death." "When he says 'I ought;' when
love warms him; when he chooses, warned from on
high, the good and great deed; then deep melodies
wander through his soul from Supreme Wisdom."

"This sentiment lies at the foundation of society and
successively creates all forms of worship. . . . This thought
dwelled always deepest in the minds of men in the devout
and contemplative East; not alone in Palestine, where it
reached its purest expression, but in Egypt, in Persia, in
India, in China. Europe has always owed to Oriental
genius its divine impulses. What these holy bards said,
all sane men found agreeable and true. And the unique
impression of Jesus upon mankind, whose name is not so
much written as ploughed into the history of this world,
is proof of the subtle virtue of this infusion."

But this truth cannot be received at second hand;
it is an intuition. What another announces, I must
find true in myself, or I must reject it. If the word
of another is taken instead of this primary faith, the
church, the state, art, letters, life, all suffer degrada-
tion, — "the doctrine of inspiration is lost; the base
doctrine of the majority of voices usurps the place of
the doctrine of the soul."

The following extract will show the view that he
takes of Christianity and its Founder, and sufficiently
explain the antagonism called forth by the discourse:

"Jesus Christ belonged to the true race of prophets.
He saw with open eye the mystery of the soul. Drawn
by its severe harmony, ravished with its beauty, he lived
in it, and had his being there. Alone in all history he
estimated the greatness of man. One man was true to
what is in you and me. He saw that God incarnates himself in man, and evermore goes forth anew to take possession of his World. He said, in this jubilee of sublime

emotion, 'I am divine. Through me God acts; through me, speaks. Would you see God, see me; or see thee, when thou also thinkest as I now think.' But what a distortion did his doctrine and memory suffer in the same, in the next, and the following ages! There is no doctrine of the Reason which will bear to be taught by the Understanding. The understanding caught this high chant from the poet's lips, and said, in the next age, 'This was Jehovah come down out of heaven. I will kill you if you say he was a man.' The idioms of his language and the figures of his rhetoric have usurped the place of his truth; and churches are not built on his principles, but on his tropes. Christianity became a Mythus, as the poetic teaching of Greece and of Egypt, before. He spoke of miracles; for he felt that man's life was a miracle, and all that man doth, and he knew that this miracle shines as the character ascends. But the word Miracle, as pronounced by Christian churches, gives a false impression; it is Monster. It is not one with the blowing clover and the falling rain."

He proceeds to point out what he considers the great defects of historical Christianity. It has exaggerated the personal, the positive, the ritual. It has wronged mankind by monopolizing all virtues for the Christian name. It is only by his holy thoughts that Jesus serves us. "To aim to convert a man by miracles is a profanation of the soul." The preachers do a wrong to Jesus by removing him from our human sympathies; they should not degrade his life and dialogues by insulation and peculiarity.

Another defect of the traditional and limited way of using the mind of Christ is that the Moral Nature — the Law of Laws — is not explored as the fountain of the established teaching in society.

" Men have come to speak of the revelation as somewhat long ago given and done, as if God were dead. . . .

The soul is not preached. The church seems to totter to its fall, almost all life extinct. . . . The stationariness of religion; the assumption that the age of inspiration is past, that the Bible is closed; the fear of degrading the character of Jesus by representing him as a man; indicate with sufficient clearness the falsehood of our theology. It is the office of a true teacher to show us that God is, not was; that he speaketh, not spake. The true Christianity — a faith like Christ's in the infinitude of man — is lost."

When Emerson came to what his earlier ancestors would have called the "practical application," some of his young hearers must have been startled at the style of his address.

"Yourself a new-born bard of the Holy Ghost, cast behind you all conformity, and acquaint men at first hand with Deity. Look to it first and only, that fashion, custom, authority, pleasure, and money are nothing to you, — are not bandages over your eyes, that you cannot see, — but live with the privilege of the immeasurable mind."

Emerson recognized two inestimable advantages as the gift of Christianity: first the Sabbath, — hardly a Christian institution, — and secondly the institution of preaching. He spoke not only eloquently, but with every evidence of deep sincerity and conviction. He had sacrificed an enviable position to that inner voice of duty which he now proclaimed as the sovereign law over all written or spoken words. But he was assailing the cherished beliefs of those before him, and of Christendom generally; not with hard or bitter words, not with sarcasm or levity, rather as one who felt himself charged with a message from the same divinity who had inspired the prophets and evangelists of old with whatever truth was in their messages. He might be wrong, but his words carried the evidence of his own serene, unshaken confidence that the spirit of all truth was with him. Some of his audience, at least, must have felt the contrast between his utterances and the formal discourses they had so long listened to, and said to themselves, "He speaks 'as one having authority, and not as the scribes.'"

Such teaching, however, could not be suffered to go unchallenged. Its doctrines were repudiated in "The Christian Examiner," the leading organ of the Unitarian denomination. The Rev. Henry Ware, greatly esteemed and honored, whose colleague he had been, addressed a letter to him, in which he expressed the feeling that some of the statements of Emerson's discourse would tend to overthrow the authority and influence of Christianity. To this note Emerson returned the following answer: —

"What you say about the discourse at Divinity College is just what I might expect from your truth and charity, combined with your known opinions. I am not a stick or a stone, as one said in the old time, and could not but feel pain in saying some things in that place and presence which I supposed would meet with dissent, I may say, of dear friends and benefactors of mine. Yet, as my conviction is perfect in the substantial truth of the doctrines of this discourse, and is not very new, you will see at once that it must appear very important that it be spoken; and I thought I could not pay the nobleness of my friends so mean a compliment as to suppress my opposition to their supposed views, out of fear of offense. I would rather say to them, these things look thus to me, to you otherwise. Let us say our uttermost word, and let the all-pervading truth, as it surely will, judge between us. Either of us would, I doubt not, be willingly apprised of his error. Meantime, I shall be admonished by this expression of your thought, to revise with greater care the address, before it is printed (for the use of the class): and I heartily thank you for this expression of your tried toleration and love."

Dr. Ware followed up his note with a sermon, preached on the 23d of September, in which he dwells especially on the necessity of adding the idea of personality to the abstractions of Emerson's philosophy, and sent it to him with a letter, the kindness and true Christian spirit of which were only what were inseparable from all the thoughts and feelings of that most excellent and truly apostolic man.

To this letter Emerson sent the following reply:—

CONCORD, *October* 8, 1838.

MY DEAR SIR, — I ought sooner to have acknowledged your kind letter of last week, and the sermon it accompanied. The letter was right manly and noble. The sermon, too, I have read with attention. If it assails any doctrine of mine, — perhaps I am not so quick to see it as writers generally, — certainly I did not feel any disposition to depart from my habitual contentment, that you should say your thought, whilst I say mine. I believe I must tell you what I think of my new position. It strikes me very oddly that good and wise men at Cambridge and Boston should think of raising me into an object of criticism. I have always been — from my very incapacity of methodical writing — a "chartered libertine," free to worship and free to rail, — lucky when I could make myself understood, but never esteemed near enough to the institutions and mind of society to deserve the notice of the masters of literature and religion. I have appreciated fully the advantages of my position, for I well know there is no scholar less willing or less able than myself to be a polemic. I could not give an account of myself, if challenged. I could not possibly give you one of the "arguments" you cruelly hint at, on which any doctrine of mine stands; for I do not know what arguments are in reference to any expression of a thought. I delight in telling what I think; but if you ask me how I dare say so, or why it is so, I am the most helpless of mortal men. I do not even see that either of these questions admits of an answer. So that in the present droll posture of my affairs, when I see myself suddenly raised to the importance of a heretic, I am very uneasy when I advert to the supposed duties of such a personage, who is to make good his thesis against all comers. I certainly shall do no such thing. I shall read what you and other good men write, as I have always done, glad when you speak my thoughts, and skipping the page that has nothing for me. I shall go on just as before, seeing whatever I can, and telling what I see; and, I suppose, with the same fortune that has hitherto attended me, — the joy of finding that my able and better brothers, who work with the sympathy of society, loving and beloved, do now and then unexpectedly confirm my conceptions, and find my nonsense is only their own thought in motley, — and so I am your affectionate servant, etc.

The controversy which followed is a thing of the past; Emerson took no part in it, and we need not return to the discussion. He knew his office and has defined it in the clearest manner in the letter just given, — "seeing whatever I can, and telling what I see." But among his listeners and readers was a man of very different mental constitution, not more independent or fearless, but louder and more combative, whose voice soon became heard and whose strength soon began to be felt in the long battle between the traditional and immanent inspiration, — Theodore Parker. If Emerson was the moving spirit, he was the right arm in the conflict, which in one form or another has been waged up to the present day.

In the winter of 1838–39 Emerson delivered his usual winter course of lectures. He names them in a letter to Carlyle as follows: "Ten Lectures: I. The Doctrine of the Soul; II. Home; III. The School; IV. Love; V. Genius; VI. The Protest; VII. Tragedy; VIII. Comedy; IX. Duty; X. Demonology. I designed to add two more, but my lungs played me false with unseasonable inflammation, so I discoursed no more on Human Life." Two or three of these titles only are prefixed to his published lectures or essays: Love, in the first volume of "Essays;" "Demonology," in "Lectures and Biographical Sketches;" and "The Comic," in "Letters and Social Aims."

I owe the privilege of making use of the two following letters to my kind and honored friend, James Freeman Clarke.

The first letter was accompanied by the poem "The Humble-Bee," which was first published by Mr. Clarke in "The Western Messenger," from the autograph copy, which begins "Fine humble-bee! fine humble-bee!" and has a number of other variations from the poem as printed in his collected works.

CONCORD, *December* 7, 1838.

MY DEAR SIR, — Here are the verses. They have pleased some of my friends, and so may please some of your readers, and you asked me in the spring if I had n't somewhat to contribute to your journal. I remember in your letter you mentioned the remark of some friend of yours that the verses, "Take, O take those lips away," were not Shakespeare's; I think they are. Beaumont, nor Fletcher, nor both together, were ever, I think, visited by such a starry gleam as that stanza. I know it is in "Rollo," but it is in "Measure for Measure" also; and I remember noticing that the Malones, and Stevens, and critical gentry were about evenly divided, these for Shakespeare, and those for Beaumont and Fletcher. But the internal evidence is all for one, none for the other. If he did not write it, they did not, and we shall have some fourth unknown singer. What care we *who* sung this or that. It is we at last who sing.

Your friend and servant,

R. W. EMERSON.

TO JAMES FREEMAN CLARKE.

CONCORD, *February* 27, 1839.

MY DEAR SIR, — I am very sorry to have made you wait so long for an answer to your flattering request for two such little poems. You are quite welcome to the lines "To the Rhodora;" but I think they need the superscription ["Lines on being asked, 'Whence is the Flower?'"]. Of the other verses ["Good-bye, proud world," etc.] I send you a corrected copy, but I wonder so much at your wishing to print them that I think you must read them once again with your critical spectacles before they go further. They were written sixteen years ago, when I kept school in Boston, and lived in a corner of Roxbury called Canterbury. They have a slight misanthropy, a shade deeper than belongs to me; and as it seems nowadays I am a philosopher and am grown to have opinions, I think they must have an apologetic date, though I well know that poetry that needs a date is no poetry, and so you will wiselier suppress them. I heartily wish I had any verses which with a clear mind I could send you in lieu of these juvenilities. It is strange, seeing the delight we take in verses, that we can so seldom write them, and so are not ashamed to lay up old ones, say sixteen years, instead of improvising them as freely as the wind blows, whenever we and our brothers are attuned to music. I have heard of a citizen who made an annual joke. I believe I have in April or May an annual poetic *conatus* rather than *afflatus*, experimenting to the length of thirty lines or so, if I may judge from the dates of the rhythmical scraps I detect among my MSS. I look upon this incontinence as merely the redundancy of a susceptibility to poetry which makes all the bards my daily treasures, and I can well run the risk of being ridiculous once a year for the benefit of happy reading all the other days. In regard to the Providence Discourse, I have no copy of it; and as far as I remember its contents, I have since used whatever is striking in it; but I will get the MS., if Margaret Fuller has it, and you shall have it if it will pass muster. I shall certainly avail myself of the good order you gave me for twelve copies of the "Carlyle Miscellanies," so soon as they appear. He, T. C., writes in excellent spirits of his American friends and readers. . . . A new book, he writes, is growing in him, though not to begin until his spring lectures are over (which begin in May). Your sister Sarah was kind enough to carry me the other day to see some pencil sketches done by Stuart Newton when in the Insane Hospital. They seemed to me to betray the richest invention, so rich as almost to say, Why draw any line, since you can draw all? Genius has given you the freedom of the universe, why then come within any walls? And this seems to be the old moral which we draw from our fable, read it how or where you will, that we cannot make one good stroke until we can make every possible stroke; and when we can one, every one seems superfluous. I heartily thank you for the good wishes you send me to open the year, and I say them back again to you. Your field is a world, and all men are your spectators, and all men respect the true and great-hearted service you render. And yet it is not spectator nor spectacle that concerns either you or me. The whole world is sick of that very ail, of being seen, and of seemliness. It belongs to the brave now to trust themselves infinitely, and to sit and hearken alone. I am glad to see William Channing is one of your coadjutors. Mrs. Jameson's new book, I should think, would bring a caravan of travellers, æsthetic, artistic, and what not, up your mighty stream, or along the lakes to Mackinaw. As I read I almost vowed an exploration, but I doubt if I ever get beyond the Hudson.

Your affectionate servant,
R. W. EMERSON.

On the 24th of July, 1838, a little more than a week after the delivery of the address before the divinity school, Mr. Emerson delivered an oration before the literary societies of Dartmouth College. If any rumor of the former discourse had reached Dartmouth, the audience must have been prepared for a much more startling performance than that to which they listened. The bold avowal which fluttered the dovecotes of Cambridge would have sounded like the crash of doom to the cautious old tenants of the Hanover aviary. If there were any drops of false or questionable doctrine in the silver shower of eloquence under which they had been sitting, the plumage of orthodoxy glistened with unctuous repellents, and a shake or two on coming out of church left the sturdy old dogmatists as dry as ever.

Those who remember the Dartmouth College of that day cannot help smiling at the thought of the contrast in the way of thinking between the speaker and the larger part, or at least the older part, of his audience. President Lord was well known as the scriptural defender of the institution of slavery. Not long before a controversy had arisen, provoked by the setting up of the Episcopal form of worship by one of the professors, the most estimable and scholarly Dr. Daniel Oliver. Perhaps, however, the extreme difference between the fundamental conceptions of Mr. Emerson and the endemic orthodoxy of that place and time was too great for any hostile feeling to be awakened by the sweet-voiced and peaceful-mannered speaker. There is a kind of harmony between boldly contrasted beliefs like that between complementary colors. It is when two shades of the same color are brought side by side that comparison makes them odious to each

other. Mr. Emerson could go anywhere and find
willing listeners among those farthest in their belief
from the views he held. Such was his simplicity of
speech and manner, such his transparent sincerity,
that it was next to impossible to quarrel with the gentle image-breaker.

The subject of Mr. Emerson's Address is "Literary
Ethics." It is on the same lofty plane of sentiment
and in the same exalted tone of eloquence as the Phi
Beta Kappa address. The word "impassioned" would
seem misplaced, if applied to any of Mr. Emerson's
orations. But these discourses were both written and
delivered in the freshness of his complete manhood.
They were produced at a time when his mind had
learned its powers and the work to which it was called,
in the struggle which freed him from the constraint of
stereotyped confessions of faith and all peremptory
external authority. It is not strange, therefore, to
find some of his paragraphs glowing with heat and
sparkling with imaginative illustration.

"Neither years nor books," he says, "have yet
availed to extirpate a prejudice rooted in me, that a
scholar is the favorite of Heaven and earth, the excel-
lency of his country, the happiest of men." And yet,
he confesses that the scholars of this country have
not fulfilled the reasonable expectation of mankind.
"Men here, as elsewhere, are indisposed to innova-
tion, and prefer any antiquity, any usage, any livery
productive of ease or profit, to the unproductive service of thought." For all this he offers those correc-
tives which in various forms underlie all his teachings.
"The resources of the scholar are proportioned to his
confidence in the attributes of the Intellect." New
lessons of spiritual independence, fresh examples and

illustrations, are drawn from history and biography. There is a passage here so true to nature that it permits a half page of quotation and a line or two of comment: —

"An intimation of these broad rights is familiar in the sense of injury which men feel in the assumption of any man to limit their possible progress. We resent all criticism which denies us anything that lies in our line of advance. Say to the man of letters that he cannot paint a Transfiguration, or build a steamboat, or be a grand-marshal, and he will not seem to himself depreciated. But deny to him any quality of literary or metaphysical power, and he is piqued. Concede to him genius, which is a sort of Stoical *plenum* annulling the comparative, and he is content; but concede him talents never so rare, denying him genius, and he is aggrieved."

But it ought to be added that if the pleasure of denying the genius of their betters were denied to the mediocrities, their happiness would be forever blighted.

From the resources of the American scholar Mr. Emerson passes to his tasks. Nature, as it seems to him, has never yet been truly studied. "Poetry has scarce chanted its first song. The perpetual admonition of Nature to us is, 'The world is new, untried. Do not believe the past. I give you the universe a virgin to-day.'" And in the same way he would have the scholar look at history, at philosophy. The world belongs to the student, but he must put himself into harmony with the constitution of things. "He must embrace solitude as a bride." Not superstitiously, but after having found out, as a little experience will teach him, all that society can do for him with its foolish routine. I have spoken of the exalted strain into which Mr. Emerson sometimes rises in the midst of his general serenity. Here is an instance of it: —

"You will hear every day the maxims of a low prudence. You will hear that the first duty is to get land and money, place and name. 'What is this truth you seek? What is this beauty?' men will ask, with derision. If, nevertheless, God have called any of you to explore truth and beauty, be bold, be firm, be true. When you shall say, 'As others do, so will I: I renounce, I am sorry for it, my early visions; I must eat the good of the land, and let learning and romantic expectations go, until a more convenient season,'— then dies the man in you; then once more perish the buds of art, and poetry, and science, as they have died already in a thousand thousand men. . . . Bend to the persuasion which is flowing to you from every object in nature, to be its tongue to the heart of man, and to show the besotted world how passing fair is wisdom. . . . Why should you renounce your right to traverse the starlit deserts of truth, for the premature comforts of an acre, house, and barn? Truth also has its roof and bed and board. Make yourself necessary to the world, and mankind will give you bread; and if not store of it, yet such as shall not take away your property in all men's possessions, in all men's affections, in art, in nature, and in hope."

The next address Emerson delivered was "The Method of Nature," before the Society of the Adelphi, in Waterville College, Maine, August 11, 1841.

In writing to Carlyle on the 31st of July, he says: "As usual at this season of the year, I, incorrigible spouting Yankee, am writing an oration to deliver to the boys in one of our little country colleges nine days hence. . . . My whole philosophy — which is very real — teaches acquiescence and optimism. Only when I see how much work is to be done, what room for a poet — for any spiritualist — in this great, intelligent, sensual, and avaricious America, I lament my fumbling fingers and stammering tongue." It may be remembered that Mr. Matthew Arnold quoted the expression about America, which sounded more harshly as pronounced in a public lecture than as read in a private letter.

The oration shows the same vein of thought as the letter. Its title is "The Method of Nature." He begins with congratulations on the enjoyments and promises of this literary anniversary.

"The scholars are the priests of that thought which establishes the foundations of the earth. . . . We hear too much of the results of machinery, commerce, and the useful arts. We are a puny and a fickle folk. Avarice, hesitation, and following are our diseases. The rapid wealth which hundreds in the community acquire in trade, or by the incessant expansions of our population and arts, enchants the eyes of all the rest; the luck of one is the hope of thousands, and the bribe acts like the neighborhood of a gold mine to impoverish the farm, the school, the church, the house, and the very body and feature of man. . . . Whilst the multitude of men degrade each other, and give currency to desponding doctrines, the scholar must be a bringer of hope, and must reinforce man against himself."

I think we may detect more of the manner of Carlyle in this address than in any of those which preceded it.

"Why then goest thou as some Boswell or literary worshipper to this saint or to that? That is the only lese-majesty. Here art thou with whom so long the universe travailed in labor; darest thou think meanly of thyself whom the stalwart Fate brought forth to unite his ragged sides, to shoot the gulf, to reconcile the irreconcilable?"

That there is an "intimate divinity" which is the source of all true wisdom, that the duty of man is to listen to its voice and to follow it, that "the sanity of man needs the poise of this immanent force," that the rule is, "Do what you know, and perception is converted into character," — all this is strongly enforced and richly illustrated in this oration. Just how easily it was followed by the audience, just how far they were satisfied with its large principles wrought into a few broad precepts, it would be easier at this time to ask than to learn. We notice not so much the novelty of the ideas to be found in this discourse on The Method of Nature, as the pictorial beauty of their expression. The deep reverence which underlies all Emerson's speculations is well shown in this paragraph: —

"We ought to celebrate this hour by expressions of manly joy. Not thanks, not prayer seem quite the highest or truest name for our communication with the infinite, — but glad and conspiring reception, — reception that becomes giving in its turn, as the receiver is only the All-Giver in part and in infancy. . . . It is God in us which checks the language of petition by a grander thought. In the bottom of the heart it is said: 'I am, and by me, O child! this fair body and world of thine stands and grows. I am, all things are mine; and all mine are thine.' "

We must not quarrel with his peculiar expressions. He says, in this same paragraph, "I cannot — nor can any man — speak precisely of things so sublime; but it seems to me the wit of man, his strength, his grace, his tendency, his art, is the grace and the presence of God. It is beyond explanation."

"We can point nowhere to anything final; but tendency appears on all hands; planet, system, constellation, total nature is growing like a field of maize in July; is becoming somewhat else; is in rapid metamorphosis. The embryo does not more strive to be man, than yonder burr of light we call a nebula tends to be a ring, a comet, a globe, and parent of new stars. . . . In short, the spirit and peculiarity of that impression nature makes on us is this, that it does not exist to any one or to any number of particular ends, but to numberless and endless benefit; that there is in it no private will, no rebel leaf or limb, but the whole is oppressed by one superincumbent tendency, obeys that redundancy or excess of life which in conscious beings we call ecstasy."

Here is another of those almost lyrical passages which seem too long for the music of rhythm and the resonance of rhyme: —

"The great Pan of old, who was clothed in a leopard skin to signify the beautiful variety of things, and the firmament, his coat of stars, was but the representative of thee, O rich and various Man! thou palace of sight and sound, carrying in thy senses the morning and the night and the unfathomable galaxy; in thy brain the geometry of the City of God; in thy heart the bower of love and the realms of right and wrong."

His feeling about the soul, which has shown itself in many of the extracts already given, is summed up in the following sentence: —

"We cannot describe the natural history of the soul, but we know that it is divine. I cannot tell if these wonderful qualities which house to-day in this mortal frame shall ever reassemble in equal activity in a similar frame, or whether they have before had a natural history like that of this body you see before you; but this one thing I know, that these qualities did not now begin to exist, cannot be sick with my sickness, nor buried in any grave; but that they circulate through the Universe: before the world was, they were."

It is hard to see the distinction between the omnipresent Deity recognized in our formal confessions of faith and the "pantheism" which is the object of dread to many of the faithful. But there are many expressions in this address which must have sounded strangely and vaguely to his Christian audience.

"Are there not moments in the history of heaven when the human race was not counted by individuals, but was only the Influenced; was God in distribution, God rushing into multiform benefit?" It might be feared that the practical philanthropists would feel that they lost by his counsels.

"The reforms whose fame now fills the land with Temperance, Anti-Slavery, Non-Resistance, No Government, Equal Labor, fair and generous as each appears, are poor bitter things when prosecuted for themselves as an end. . . . I say to you plainly there is no end to which your practical faculty can aim so sacred or so large, that, if pursued for itself, will not at last become carrion and an offence to the nostril. The imaginative faculty of the soul must be fed with objects immense and eternal. Your end should be one inapprehensible to the senses; then it will be a god, always approached, — never touched; always giving health."

Nothing is plainer than that it was Emerson's calling to supply impulses and not methods. He was not an organizer, but a power behind many organizers, inspiring them with lofty motive, giving breadth to their views, always tending to become narrow through concentration on their special objects. The oration we have been examining was delivered in the interval between the delivery of two addresses, one called "Man the Reformer," and another called "Lecture on the Times." In the first he preaches the dignity and virtue of manual labor; that "a man should have a farm, or a mechanical craft for his culture;" that he cannot give up labor without suffering some loss of power. "How can the man who has learned but one art procure all the conveniences of life honestly? Shall we say all we think? — Perhaps with his own hands. . . . Let us learn the meaning of economy. . . . Parched corn eaten to-day that I may have roast fowl to my dinner on Sunday is a baseness; but parched corn and a house with one apartment, that I may be free of all perturbations, that I may be serene and docile to what the mind shall speak, and girt and road-ready for the lowest mission of knowledge or goodwill, is frugality for gods and heroes."

This was what Emerson wrote in January, 1841. This "house with one apartment" was what Thoreau built with his own hands in 1845. In April of the former year, he went to live with Mr. Emerson, but had been on intimate terms with him previously to that time. Whether it was from him that Thoreau got the hint of the Walden cabin and the parched corn, or whether this idea was working in Thoreau's mind and was suggested to Emerson by him, is of no great consequence. Emerson, to whom he owed so much, may well have adopted some of those fancies which Thoreau entertained, and afterwards worked out in practice. He was at the philanthropic centre of a good many movements which he watched others carrying out, as a calm and kindly spectator, without losing his common sense for a moment. It would never have occurred to him to leave all the conveniences and comforts of life to go and dwell in a shanty, so as to prove to himself that he could live like a savage, or like his friends "Teague and his jade," as he called the man and brother and sister, more commonly known nowadays as Pat, or Patrick, and his old woman.

"The Americans have many virtues," he says in this address, "but they have not Faith and Hope." Faith and Hope, Enthusiasm and Love, are the burden of this address. But he would regulate these qualities by "a great prospective prudence," which shall mediate between the spiritual and the actual world.

In the "Lecture on the Times" he shows very clearly the effect which a nearer contact with the class of men and women who called themselves Reformers had upon him.

"The Reforms have their high origin in an ideal justice, but they do not retain the purity of an idea. They are quickly organized in some low, inadequate form, and present no more poetic image to the mind than the evil tradition which they reprobated. They mix the fire of the moral sentiment with personal and party heats, with measureless exaggerations, and the blindness that prefers some darling measure to justice and truth. Those who are urging with most ardor what are called the greatest benefits of mankind are narrow, self-pleasing, conceited men, and affect us as the insane do. They bite us, and we run mad also. I think the work of the reformer as innocent as other work that is done around him; but when I have seen it near, I do not like it better. It is done in the same way; it is done profanely, not piously; by management, by tactics and clamor."

All this, and much more like it, would hardly have been listened to by the ardent advocates of the various reforms, if anybody but Mr. Emerson had said it. He undervalued no sincere action except to suggest a wiser and better one. He attacked no motive which had a good aim, except in view of some larger and loftier principle. The charm of his imagination and the music of his words took away all the sting from the thoughts that penetrated to the very marrow of the entranced listeners.   Sometimes it was a splendid hyperbole that illuminated a statement which by the dim light of common speech would have offended or repelled those who sat before him.   He knew the force of *felix audacia* as well as any rhetorician could have taught him.   He addresses the reformer with one of those daring images which defy the critics.

"As the farmer casts into the ground the finest ears of his grain, the time will come when we too shall hold nothing back, but shall eagerly convert more than we possess into means and powers, when we shall be willing to sow the sun and the moon for seeds."

He said hard things to the reformer, especially to the Abolitionist, in his "Lecture on the Times."   It would have taken a long while to get rid of slavery if some of Emerson's teachings in this lecture had been accepted as the true gospel of liberty.   But how much its last sentence covers with its soothing tribute!

"All the newspapers, all the tongues of to-day will of course at first defame what is noble; but you who hold not of to-day, not of the times, but of the Everlasting, are to stand for it; and the highest compliment man ever receives from heaven is the sending to him its disguised and discredited angels."

The lecture called "The Transcendentalist" will naturally be looked at with peculiar interest, inasmuch as this term has been very commonly applied to Emerson, and to many who were considered his disciples. It has a proper philosophical meaning, and it has also a local and accidental application to the individuals of a group which came together very much as any literary club might collect about a teacher.   All this comes out clearly enough in the lecture.   In the first place, Emerson explains that the "*new views*," as they are called, are the oldest of thoughts cast in a new mould.

"What is popularly called Transcendentalism among us is Idealism: Idealism as it appears in 1842. As thinkers, mankind have ever divided into two sects, Materialists and Idealists; the first class founding on experience, the second on consciousness; the first class beginning to think from the data of the senses, the second class perceive that the senses are not final, and say, The senses give us representations of things, but what are the things themselves, they cannot tell. The materialist insists on facts, on history, on the force of circumstances and the animal wants of man; the idealist on the power of Thought and of Will, on inspiration, on miracle, on individual culture. . . .

"The materialist takes his departure from the external world, and esteems a man as one product of that. The idealist takes his departure from his consciousness, and reckons the world an appearance. . . . His thought, that is the Universe."

The association of scholars and thinkers to which the name of "Transcendentalists" was applied, and which made itself an organ in the periodical known as "The Dial," has been written about by many who were in the movement, and others who looked on or got their knowledge of it at second hand. Emerson was closely associated with these same Transcendentalists, and a leading contributor to "The Dial," which was their organ. The movement borrowed its inspiration more from him than from any other source, and the periodical owed more to him than to any other writer. So far as his own relation to the circle of illumination and the dial which they shone upon was concerned, he himself is the best witness.

In his "Historic Notes of Life and Letters in New

England," he sketches in a rapid way the series of intellectual movements which led to the development of the "new views" above mentioned. "There are always two parties," he says, "the party of the Past and the party of the Future; the Establishment and the Movement."

About 1820, and in the twenty years which followed, an era of activity manifested itself in the churches, in politics, in philanthropy, in literature. In our own community the influence of Swedenborg and of the genius and character of Dr. Channing were among the more immediate early causes of the mental agitation. Emerson attributes a great importance to the scholarship, the rhetoric, the eloquence, of Edward Everett, who returned to Boston in 1820, after five years of study in Europe. Edward Everett is already to a great extent a tradition, somewhat as Rufus Choate is, a voice, a fading echo, as must be the memory of every great orator. These wondrous personalities have their truest and warmest life in a few old men's memories. It is therefore with delight that one who remembers Everett in his robes of rhetorical splendor, who recalls his full-blown, high-colored, double-flowered periods, the rich, resonant, grave, far-reaching music of his speech, with just enough of nasal vibration to give the vocal sounding-board its proper value in the harmonies of utterance, — it is with delight that such a one reads the glowing words of Emerson whenever he refers to Edward Everett. It is enough if he himself caught inspiration from those eloquent lips; but many a listener has had his youthful enthusiasm fired by that great master of academic oratory.

Emerson follows out the train of influences which added themselves to the impulse given by Mr. Everett.

German scholarship, the growth of science, the generalizations of Goethe, the idealism of Schelling, the influence of Wordsworth, of Coleridge, of Carlyle, and,
in our immediate community, the writings of Channing, — he left it to others to say of Emerson, — all
had their part in this intellectual or, if we may call it
so, spiritual revival. He describes, with that exquisite
sense of the ridiculous which was a part of his mental
ballast, the first attempt at organizing an association
of cultivated, thoughtful people. They came together,
the cultivated, thoughtful people, at Dr. John Collins
Warren's, — Dr. Channing, the great Dr. Channing,
among the rest, full of the great thoughts he wished
to impart. The preliminaries went on smoothly enough
with the usual small talk, —

"When a side-door opened, the whole company streamed
in to an oyster supper, crowned by excellent wines [this
must have been before Dr. Warren's temperance epoch],
and so ended the first attempt to establish æsthetic society
in Boston.

"Some time afterwards Dr. Channing opened his mind
to Mr. and Mrs. Ripley, and with some care they invited
a limited party of ladies and gentlemen. I had the honor
to be present. Margaret Fuller, George Ripley, Dr.
Convers Francis, Theodore Parker, Dr. Hedge, Mr.
Brownson, James Freeman Clarke, William H. Channing,
and many others gradually drew together, and from time
to time spent an afternoon at each other's houses in a serious conversation."

With them was another, "a pure Idealist, — who
read Plato as an equal, and inspired his companions
only in proportion as they were intellectual." He
refers, of course, to Mr. Alcott. Emerson goes on to
say : —

"I think there prevailed at that time a general belief

in Boston that there was some concert of *doctrinaires* to establish certain opinions, and inaugurate some movement in literature, philosophy, and religion, of which design the supposed conspirators were quite innocent; for there was no concert, and only here and there two or three men and women who read and wrote, each alone, with unusual vivacity. Perhaps they only agreed in having fallen upon Coleridge and Wordsworth and Goethe, then on Carlyle, with pleasure and sympathy. Otherwise their education and reading were not marked, but had the American superficialness, and their studies were solitary. I suppose all of them were surprised at this rumor of a school or sect, and certainly at the name of Transcendentalism, given, nobody knows by whom, or when it was applied."

Emerson's picture of some of these friends of his is so peculiar as to suggest certain obvious and not too flattering comments.

"In like manner, if there is anything grand and daring in human thought or virtue; any reliance on the vast, the unknown; any presentiment; any extravagance of faith, the spiritualist adopts it as most in nature. The Oriental mind has always tended to this largeness. Buddhism is an expression of it. The Buddhist who thanks no man, who says, 'Do not flatter your benefactors,' but who, in his conviction that every good deed can by no possibility escape its reward, will not deceive the benefactor by pretending that he has done more than he should, is a Transcendentalist."

"These exacting children advertise us of our wants. There is no compliment, no smooth speech with them; they pay you only this one compliment, of insatiable expectation; they aspire, they severely exact, and if they only stand fast in this watch-tower, and persist in demanding unto the end, and without end, then are they terrible friends, whereof poet and priest cannot choose but stand in awe; and what if they eat clouds, and drink wind, they have not been without service to the race of man."

The person who adopts "any presentiment, any extravagance as most in nature," is not commonly called a Transcendentalist, but is known colloquially as a "crank." The person who does not thank, by word or look, the friend or stranger who has pulled him out of the fire or water, is fortunate if he gets off with no harder name than that of a churl.

Nothing was farther from Emerson himself than whimsical eccentricity or churlish austerity. But there was occasionally an air of bravado in some of his followers, as if they had taken out a patent for some knowing machine which was to give them a monopoly of its products. They claimed more for each other than was reasonable, — so much occasionally that their pretensions became ridiculous. One was tempted to ask: "What forlorn hope have you led? What immortal book have you written? What great discovery have you made? What heroic task of any kind have you performed?" There was too much talk about earnestness and too little real work done. Aspiration too frequently got as far as the alpenstock and the brandy flask, but crossed no dangerous crevasse, and scaled no arduous summit. In short, there was a kind of "Transcendentalist" dilettanteism, which betrayed itself by a phraseology as distinctive as that of the Della Cruscans of an earlier time.

In reading the following description of the "intelligent and religious persons" who belonged to the "Transcendentalist" communion, the reader must remember that it is Emerson who draws the portrait, — a friend and not a scoffer: —

"They are not good citizens, not good members of society: unwillingly they bear their part of the public and private burdens; they do not willingly share in the public charities, in the public religious rites, in the enterprises of education, of missions foreign and domestic, in the abolition of the slave-trade or in the temperance society. They do not even like to vote."

After arraigning the representatives of Transcendental or spiritual beliefs in this way, he summons them to plead for themselves, and this is what they have to say : —

"'New, we confess, and by no means happy, is our condition : if you want the aid of our labor, we ourselves stand in greater want of the labor. We are miserable with inaction. We perish of rest and rust : but we do not like your work.'

"'Then,' says the world, 'show me your own.'

"'We have none.'

"'What will you do, then?' cries the world.

"'We will wait.'

"'How long?'

"'Until the Universe beckons and calls us to work.'

"'But whilst you wait you grow old and useless.'

"'Be it so : I can sit in a corner and *perish* (as you call it), but I will not move until I have the highest command.'"

And so the dissatisfied tenant of this unhappy creation goes on with his reasons for doing nothing.

It is easy to stay away from church and from town-meetings. It is easy to keep out of the way of the contribution box and to let the subscription paper go by us to the next door. The common duties of life and the good offices society asks of us may be left to take care of themselves while we contemplate the infinite. There is no safer fortress for indolence than "the Everlasting No." The chimney-corner is the true arena for this class of philosophers, and the pipe and mug furnish their all-sufficient panoply. Emerson undoubtedly met with some of them among his disciples. His wise counsel did not always find listeners in a fitting condition to receive it. He was a sower who went forth to sow. Some of the good seed fell among the thorns of criticism. Some fell on the rocks of hardened conservatism. Some fell by the wayside and was picked up by the idlers who went to the lecture-room to get rid of themselves. But when it fell upon the right soil it bore a growth of thought which ripened into a harvest of large and noble lives.

Emerson shows up the weakness of his young enthusiasts with that delicate wit which warns its objects rather than wounds them. But he makes it all up with the dreamers before he can let them go.

"Society also has its duties in reference to this class, and must behold them with what charity it can. Possibly some benefit may yet accrue from them to the state. Besides our coarse implements, there must be some few finer instruments, — rain-gauges, thermometers, and telescopes; and in society, besides farmers, sailors, and weavers, there must be a few persons of purer fire kept specially as gauges and meters of character; persons of a fine, detecting instinct, who note the smallest accumulations of wit and feeling in the bystander. Perhaps too there might be room for the exciters and monitors; collectors of the heavenly spark, with power to convey the electricity to others. Or, as the storm-tossed vessel at sea speaks the frigate or 'line-packet' to learn its longitude, so it may not be without its advantage that we should now and then encounter rare and gifted men, to compare the points of our spiritual compass, and verify our bearings from superior chronometers."

It must be confessed that it is not a very captivating picture which Emerson draws of some of his Transcendental friends. Their faults were naturally still more obvious to those outside of their charmed circle, and some prejudice, very possibly, mingled with their critical judgments. On the other hand we have the evidence of a visitor who knew a good deal of the world as to the impression they produced upon him : —

"There has sprung up in Boston," says Dickens, in his "American Notes," "a sect of philosophers known as Transcendentalists. On inquiring what this appellation might be supposed to signify, I was given to understand that whatever was unintelligible would be certainly Transcendental. Not deriving much comfort from this elucidation, I pursued the inquiry still further, and found that the Transcendentalists are followers of my friend Mr. Carlyle, or, I should rather say, of a follower of his, Mr. Ralph Waldo Emerson. This gentleman has written a volume of Essays, in which, among much that is dreamy and fanciful (if he will pardon me for saying so), there is much more that is true and manly, honest and bold. Transcendentalism has its occasional vagaries (what school has not?), but it has good healthful qualities in spite of them; not least among the number a hearty disgust of Cant, and an aptitude to detect her in all the million varieties of her everlasting wardrobe. And therefore, if I were a Bostonian, I think I would be a Transcendentalist."

In December, 1841, Emerson delivered a lecture entitled "The Conservative." It was a time of great excitement among the members of that circle of which he was the spiritual leader. Never did Emerson show the perfect sanity which characterized his practical judgment more beautifully than in this lecture and in his whole course with reference to the intellectual agitation of the period. He is as fair to the conservative as to the reformer. He sees the fanaticism of the one as well as that of the other. "Conservatism tends to

universal seeming and treachery; believes in a negative fate; believes that men's temper governs them;
that for me it avails not to trust in principles, they
will fail me, I must bend a little; it distrusts Nature;
it thinks there is a general law without a particular
application, — law for all that does not include any
one.   Reform in its antagonism inclines to asinine
resistance, to kick with hoofs; it runs to egotism and
bloated self-conceit; it runs to a bodiless pretension,
to unnatural refining and elevation, which ends in
hypocrisy and sensual reaction.   And so, whilst we
do not go beyond general statements, it may be safely
affirmed of these two metaphysical antagonists that
each is a good half, but an impossible whole."

He has his beliefs, and, if you will, his prejudices,
but he loves fair play, and though he sides with the
party of the future, he will not be unjust to the present or the past.

We read in a letter from Emerson to Carlyle, dated
March 12, 1835, that Dr. Channing "lay awake all
night, he told my friend last week, because he had
learned in the evening that some young men proposed
to issue a journal, to be called 'The Transcendentalist,' as the organ of a spiritual philosophy."   Again
on the 30th of April of the same year, in a letter in
which he lays out a plan for a visit of Carlyle to this
country, Emerson says: —

"It was suggested that if Mr. C. would undertake a
journal of which we have talked much, but which we have
never yet produced, he would do us great service, and we
feel some confidence that it could be made to secure him
a support.   It is that project which I mentioned to you
in a letter by Mr. Barnard, — a book to be called 'The

Transcendentalist;' or, 'The Spiritual Inquirer,' or the like. . . . Those who are most interested in it designed to make gratuitous contribution to its pages, until its success could be assured."

The idea of the grim Scotchman as editor of what we came in due time to know as "The Dial"! A concert of singing mice with a savage and hungry old grimalkin as leader of the orchestra! It was much safer to be content with Carlyle's purring from his own side of the water, as thus: —

" 'The Boston Transcendentalist,' whatever the fate or merit of it may prove to be, is surely an interesting symptom. There must be things not dreamt of over in that *Transoceanic* parish! I shall certainly wish well to this thing; and hail it as the sure forerunner of things better."

There were two notable products of the intellectual ferment of the Transcendental period which deserve an incidental notice here, from the close connection which Emerson had with one of them and the interest which he took in the other, in which many of his friends were more deeply concerned. These were the periodical just spoken of as a possibility realized, and the industrial community known as Brook Farm. They were to a certain extent synchronous, — the magazine beginning in July, 1840, and expiring in April, 1844; Brook Farm being organized in 1841, and breaking up in 1847.

"The Dial" was edited at first by Margaret Fuller, afterwards by Emerson, who contributed more than forty articles in prose and verse, among them, "The Conservative," "The Transcendentalist," "Chardon Street and Bible Convention," and some of his best and best-known poems, "The Problem," "Woodnotes," "The Sphinx," "Fate." The other principal writers were Margaret Fuller, A. Bronson Alcott, George Ripley, James Freeman Clarke, Theodore Parker, William H. Channing, Henry Thoreau, Eliot Cabot, John S. Dwight, C. P. Cranch, William Ellery Channing, Mrs. Ellen Hooper, and her sister Mrs. Caroline Tappan. Unequal as the contributions are in merit, the periodical is of singular interest. It was conceived and carried on in a spirit of boundless hope and enthusiasm. Time and a narrowing subscription list proved too hard a trial, and its four volumes remain stranded, like some rare and curiously patterned shell which a storm of yesterday has left beyond the reach of the receding waves. Thoreau wrote for nearly every number. Margaret Fuller, less attractive in print than in conversation, did her part as a contributor as well as editor. Theodore Parker came down with his "trip-hammer" in its pages. Mrs. Ellen Hooper published a few poems in its columns which remain, always beautiful, in many memories. Others, whose literary lives have fulfilled their earlier promise, and who are still with us, helped forward the new enterprise with their frequent contributions. It is a pleasure to turn back to "The Dial" with all its crudities. It should be looked through by the side of "The Anthology." Both were April buds, opening before the frosts were over, but with the pledge of a better season.

We get various hints touching the new magazine in the correspondence between Emerson and Carlyle. Emerson tells Carlyle, a few months before the first number appeared, that it will give him a better knowledge of our *young people* than any he has had. It is true that unfledged writers found a place to try their wings in it, and that makes it more interesting. This was the time above all others when out of the mouth of babes and sucklings was to come forth strength. The feeling that intuition was discovering a new heaven and a new earth was the inspiration of these "young people" to whom Emerson refers. He has to apologize for the first number. "It is not yet much," he says; "indeed, though no copy has come to me, I know it is far short of what it should be, for they have suffered puffs and dulness to creep in for the sake of the complement of pages, but it is better than anything we had. — The Address of the Editors to the Readers is all the prose that is mine, and whether they have printed a few verses for me I do not know." They did print " The Problem." There were also some fragments of criticism from the writings of his brother Charles, and the poem called "The Last Farewell," by his brother Edward, which is to be found in Emerson's "May-Day and other Pieces."

On the 30th of August, after the periodical had been published a couple of months, Emerson writes: —

"Our community begin to stand in some terror of Transcendentalism; and 'The Dial,' poor little thing, whose first number contains scarce anything considerable or even visible, is just now honored by attacks from almost every newspaper and magazine; which at least betrays the irritability and the instincts of the good public."

Carlyle finds the second number of "The Dial" better than the first, and tosses his charitable recognition, as if into an alms-basket, with his usual air of superiority. He distinguishes what is Emerson's readily, — the rest he speaks of as the work of οἱ πολλοί for the most part. "But it is all good and very good as a *soul;* wants only a body, which want means a great deal." And again, "'The Dial,' too, it is all spirit-like, aeriform, aurora-borealis like. Will no *Angel* body himself out of that; no stalwart Yankee *man*, with color in the cheeks of him and a coat on his back?"

Emerson, writing to Carlyle in March, 1842, speaks of the "dubious approbation on the part of you and other men," notwithstanding which he found it with "a certain class of men and women, though few, an object of tenderness and religion." So, when Margaret Fuller gave it up, at the end of the second volume, Emerson consented to become its editor. "I cannot bid you quit 'The Dial,'" says Carlyle, "though it, too, alas, is Antinomian somewhat! *Perge, perge*, nevertheless."

In the next letter he says: —

"I love your 'Dial,' and yet it is with a kind of shudder. You seem to me in danger of dividing yourselves from the Fact of this present Universe, in which alone, ugly as it is, can I find any anchorage, and soaring away after Ideas, Beliefs, Revelations, and such like, — into perilous altitudes, as I think; beyond the curve of perpetual frost, for one thing. I know not how to utter what impression you give me; take the above as some stamping of the fore-hoof."

A curious way of characterizing himself as a critic, — but he was not always as well-mannered as the Houyhnhnms.

To all Carlyle's complaints of "The Dial's" shortcomings Emerson did not pretend to give any satisfactory answer, but his plea of guilty, with extenuating circumstances, is very honest and definite.

"For 'The Dial' and its sins, I have no defence to set up. We write as we can, and we know very little about it.

If the direction of these speculations is to be deplored, it is yet a fact for literary history that all the bright boys and girls in New England, quite ignorant of each other, take the world so, and come and make confession to fathers and mothers, — the boys, that they do not wish to go into trade, the girls, that they do not like morning calls and evening parties. They are all religious, but hate the churches; they reject all the ways of living of other men, but have none to offer in their stead. Perhaps one of these days a great Yankee shall come, who will easily do the unknown deed."

"All the bright boys and girls in New England," and " 'The Dial' dying of inanition!"

In October, 1840, Emerson writes to Carlyle: —

"We are all a little wild here with numberless projects of social reform. Not a reading man but has a draft of a new community in his waistcoat pocket. I am gently mad myself, and am resolved to live cleanly. George Ripley is talking up a colony of agriculturists and scholars, with whom he threatens to take the field and the book. One man renounces the use of animal food; and another of coin; and another of domestic hired service; and another of the state; and on the whole we have a commendable share of reason and hope."

Mr. Ripley's project took shape in the West Roxbury Association, better known under the name of Brook Farm. Emerson was not involved in this undertaking. He looked upon it with curiosity and interest, as he would have looked at a chemical experiment, but he seems to have had only a moderate degree of faith in its practical working. "It was a noble and generous movement in the projectors to try an experiment of better living. . . . One would say that impulse was the rule in the society, without centripetal balance; perhaps it would not be severe to say, intellectual sans-culottism, an impatience of the formal routinary character of our educational, religious, social, and economical life in Massachusetts."

The reader will find a full detailed account of the Brook Farm experiment in Mr. Frothingham's Life of George Ripley, its founder, and the first president of the association. Emerson had only tangential relations with the experiment, and tells its story in his "Historic Notes" very kindly and respectfully, but with that sense of the ridiculous in the aspect of some of its conditions which belongs to the sagacious common-sense side of his nature. The married women, he says, were against the community. "It was to them like the brassy and lacquered life in hotels. The common school was well enough, but to the common nursery they had grave objections. Eggs might be hatched in ovens, but the hen on her own account much preferred the old way. A hen without her chickens was but half a hen." Is not the inaudible, inward laughter of Emerson more refreshing than the explosions of our noisiest humorists?

This is his benevolent summing up: —

"The founders of Brook Farm should have this praise, that they made what all people try to make, an agreeable place to live in. All comers, even the most fastidious, found it the pleasantest of residences. It is certain that freedom from household routine, variety of character and talent, variety of work, variety of means of thought and instruction, art, music, poetry, reading, masquerade, did not permit sluggishness or despondency; broke up routine. There is agreement in the testimony that it was, to most of the associates, education; to many, the most important period of their life, the birth of valued friendships, their first acquaintance with the riches of conversation, their training in behavior. The art of letter-writing, it is said, was immensely cultivated. Letters were always flying, not only from house to house, but from room to room. It was a perpetual picnic, a French Revolution in small, an Age of Reason in a patty-pan."

The public edifice called the "Phalanstery" was destroyed by fire in 1846. The association never recovered from this blow, and soon afterwards it was dissolved.

§ 2. Emerson's first volume of his collected Essays was published in 1841. In the reprint it contains the following essays: History; Self - Reliance; Compensation; Spiritual Laws; Love; Friendship; Prudence; Heroism; The Over-Soul; Circles; Intellect; Art.

Once accustomed to Emerson's larger formulæ we can to a certain extent project from our own minds his treatment of special subjects. But we cannot anticipate the daring imagination, the subtle wit, the curious illustrations, the felicitous language, which make the lecture or the essay captivating as read, and almost entrancing as listened to by the teachable disciple. The reader must be prepared for occasional extravagances. Take the essay on History, in the first series of Essays, for instance. "Let it suffice that in the light of these two facts, namely, that the mind is One, and that nature is its correlative, history is to be read and written." When we come to the application, in the same essay, almost on the same page, what can we make of such discourse as this? The sentences I quote do not follow immediately, one upon the other, but their sense is continuous.

" I hold our actual knowledge very cheap. Hear the rats in the wall, see the lizard on the fence, the fungus

under foot, the lichen on the log.   What do I know sympathetically, morally, of either of these worlds of life?
. . . How many times we must say Rome, and Paris, and Constantinople!   What does Rome know of rat and lizard?   What are Olympiads and Consulates to these neighboring systems of being?   Nay, what food or experience or succor have they for the Esquimau seal-hunter, for the Kanàka in his canoe, for the fisherman, the stevedore, the porter? "

The connection of ideas is not obvious.   One can hardly help being reminded of a certain great man's Rochester speech as commonly reported by the storyteller.   "Rome in her proudest days never had a waterfall a hundred and fifty feet high!   Greece in her palmiest days never had a waterfall a hundred and fifty feet high !   Men of Rochester, go on!   No people ever lost their liberty who had a waterfall a hundred and fifty feet high! "

We cannot help smiling, perhaps laughing, at the odd mixture of Rome and rats, of Olympiads and Esquimaux.   But the underlying idea of the interdependence of all that exists in nature is far from ridiculous.   Emerson says, not absurdly or extravagantly, that "every history should be written in a wisdom which divined the range of our affinities and looked at facts as symbols."

We have become familiar with his doctrine of "Self-Reliance," which is the subject of the second lecture of the series.   We know that he always and everywhere recognized that the divine voice which speaks authoritatively in the soul of man is the source of all our wisdom.   It is a man's true self, so that it follows that absolute, supreme self-reliance is the law of his being.   But see how he guards his proclamation of self-reliance as the guide of mankind : —

"Truly it demands something godlike in him who has cast off the common motives of humanity and has ventured to trust himself for a taskmaster. High be his heart, faithful his will, clear his sight, that he may in good earnest be doctrine, society, law, to himself, that a simple purpose may be to him as strong as iron necessity is to others!"

"Compensation" might be preached in a synagogue, and the rabbi would be praised for his performance. Emerson had been listening to a sermon from a preacher esteemed for his orthodoxy, in which it was assumed that judgment is not executed in this world, that the wicked are successful, and the good are miserable. This last proposition agrees with John Bunyan's view: —

> "A Christian man is never long at ease,
> When one fright's gone, another doth him seize."

Emerson shows up the "success" of the bad man and the failures and trials of the good man in their true spiritual characters, with a noble scorn of the preacher's low standard of happiness and misery, which would have made him throw his sermon into the fire.

The essay on Spiritual Laws is full of pithy sayings: —

"As much virtue as there is, so much appears; as much goodness as there is, so much reverence it commands. All the devils respect virtue. . . . A man passes for that he is worth. . . . The ancestor of every action is a thought. . . . To think is to act. . . . Let a man believe in God, and not in names and places and persons. Let the great soul incarnated in some woman's form, poor and sad and single, in some Dolly or Joan, go out to service and sweep chambers and scour floors, and its effulgent day-beams cannot be hid, but to sweep and scour will instantly appear supreme and beautiful actions, the top and radiance of human life, and all people will get mops and brooms; until, lo! suddenly the great soul has enshrined itself in some other form and done some other deed, and that is now the flower and head of all living nature."

This is not any the worse for being the flowering out of a poetical bud of George Herbert's. The essay on Love is poetical, but the three poems, "Initial, Dæmonic, and Celestial Love," are more nearly equal to his subject than his prose.

There is a passage in the lecture on Friendship which suggests some personal relation of Emerson's about which we cannot help being inquisitive: —

"It has seemed to me lately more possible than I knew, to carry a friendship greatly, on one side, without due correspondence on the other. Why should I cumber myself with regrets that the receiver is not capacious? It never troubles the sun that some of his rays fall wide and vain into ungrateful space, and only a small part on the reflecting planet. Let your greatness educate the crude and cold companion. . . . Yet these things may hardly be said without a sort of treachery to the relation. The essence of friendship is entireness, a total magnanimity and trust. It must not surmise or provide for infirmity. It treats its object as a god, that it may deify both."

Was he thinking of his relations with Carlyle? It is a curious subject of speculation what would have been the issue if Carlyle had come to Concord and taken up his abode under Emerson's most hospitable roof. "You shall not come nearer a man by getting into his house." How could they have got on together? Emerson was well-bred, and Carlyle was wanting in the social graces. "Come rest in this bosom" is a sweet air, heard in the distance, too apt to be followed, after a protracted season of close proximity, by that other strain, —

> " No, fly me, fly me, far as pole from pole !
> Rise Alps between us and whole oceans roll ! "

But Emerson may have been thinking of some very different person, perhaps some "crude and cold companion" among his disciples, who was not equal to the demands of friendly intercourse.

He discourses wisely on Prudence, a virtue which he does not claim for himself, and nobly on Heroism, which was a shining part of his own moral and intellectual being.

The points which will be most likely to draw the reader's attention are the remarks on the literature of heroism; the claim for our own America, for Massachusetts and Connecticut River and Boston Bay, in spite of our love for the names of foreign and classic topography ; and most of all one sentence which, coming from an optimist like Emerson, has a sound of sad sincerity painful to recognize : —

"Who that sees the meanness of our politics but inly congratulates Washington that he is long already wrapped in his shroud, and forever safe; that he was laid sweet in his grave, the hope of humanity not yet subjugated in him. Who does not sometimes envy the good and brave who are no more to suffer from the tumults of the natural world, and await with curious complacency the speedy term of his own conversation with finite nature? And yet the love that will be annihilated sooner than treacherous has already made death impossible, and affirms itself no mortal, but a native of the deeps of absolute and inextinguishable being."

In the following essay, "The Over-Soul," Emerson has attempted the impossible. He is as fully conscious of this fact as the reader of his rhapsody, — nay, he is more profoundly penetrated with it than any of his readers. In speaking of the exalted condition the soul is capable of reaching, he says, —

"Every man's words, who speaks from that life, must sound vain to those who do not dwell in the same thought on their own part. I dare not speak for it. My words do not carry its august sense; they fall short and cold. Only itself can inspire whom it will, and behold! their speech shall be lyrical and sweet, and universal as the rising of the wind. Yet I desire, even by profane words, if I may not use sacred, to indicate the heaven of this deity, and to report what hints I have collected of the transcendent simplicity and energy of the Highest Law."

"The Over-Soul" might almost be called the over-*flow* of a spiritual imagination. We cannot help thinking of the "pious, virtuous, God-intoxicated" Spinoza. When one talks of the infinite in terms borrowed from the finite, when one attempts to deal with the absolute in the language of the relative, his words are not symbols, like those applied to the objects of experience, but the shadows of symbols, varying with the position and intensity of the light of the individual intelligence. It is a curious amusement to trace many of these thoughts and expressions to Plato, or Plotinus, or Proclus, or Porphyry, to Spinoza or Schelling, but the same tune is a different thing according to the instrument on which it is played. There are songs without words, and there are states in which, in place of the trains of thought moving in endless procession with ever-varying figures along the highway of consciousness, the soul is possessed by a single all-absorbing idea, which, in the highest state of spiritual exaltation, becomes a vision. Both Plotinus and Porphyry believed they were privileged to look upon Him whom "no man can see and live."

But Emerson states his own position so frankly in his essay entitled "Circles," that the reader cannot take issue with him as against utterances which he will not defend. There can be no doubt that he would have confessed as much with reference to "The Over-Soul" as he has confessed with regard to "Circles," the essay which follows "The Over-Soul."

"I am not careful to justify myself. . . . But lest I should mislead any when I have my own head and obey my whims, let me remind the reader that I am only an experimenter. Do not set the least value on what I do, or the least discredit on what I do not, as if I pretended to settle anything as true or false. I unsettle all things. No facts are to me sacred; none are profane; I simply experiment, an endless seeker, with no Past at my back."

Perhaps, after reading these transcendental essays of Emerson, we might borrow Goethe's language about Spinoza, as expressing the feeling with which we are left.

"I am reading Spinoza with Frau von Stein. I feel myself very near to him, though his soul is much deeper and purer than mine.

"I cannot say that I ever read Spinoza straight through, that at any time the complete architecture of his intellectual system has stood clear in view before me. But when I look into him I seem to understand him, — that is, he always appears to me consistent with himself, and I can always gather from him very salutary influences for my own way of feeling and acting."

Emerson would not have pretended that he was always "consistent with himself," but these "salutary influences," restoring, enkindling, vivifying, are felt

by many of his readers who would have to confess,
like Dr. Walter Channing, that these thoughts, or
thoughts like these, as he listened to them in a lecture,
"made his head ache."

The three essays which follow "The Over-Soul,"
"Circles," "Intellect," "Art," would furnish us a
harvest of good sayings, some of which we should
recognize as parts of our own (borrowed) axiomatic
wisdom.

"Beware when the great God lets loose a thinker on
this planet. Then all things are at risk."

"God enters by a private door into every individual."

"God offers to every mind its choice between truth and
repose. Take which you please, — you can never have
both."

"Though we travel the world over to find the beautiful,
we must carry it with us, or we find it not."

But we cannot reconstruct the Hanging Gardens
with a few bricks from Babylon.

Emerson describes his mode of life in these years in
a letter to Carlyle, dated May 10, 1838.

"I occupy, or improve, as we Yankees say, two acres
only of God's earth; on which is my house, my kitchen-
garden, my orchard of thirty young trees, my empty barn.
My house is now a very good one for comfort, and
abounding in room. Besides my house, I have, I believe,
$22,000, whose income in ordinary years is six per cent.
I have no other tithe or glebe except the income of my
winter lectures, which was last winter $800. Well, with
this income, here at home, I am a rich man. I stay at
home and go abroad at my own instance. I have food,
warmth, leisure, books, friends. Go away from home, I
am rich no longer. I never have a dollar to spend on a
fancy. As no wise man, I suppose, ever was rich in the

Yours always
T. Carlyle

Engraved by H.W.Smith,
from an original likeness in the possesion of R.W. Emerson Esq.

sense of freedom to spend, because of the inundation of claims, so neither am I, who am not wise. But at home, I am rich, — rich enough for ten brothers. My wife Lidian is an incarnation of Christianity, — I call her Asia, — and keeps my philosophy from Antinomianism; my mother, whitest, mildest, most conservative of ladies, whose only exception to her universal preference for old things is her son; my boy, a piece of love and sunshine, well worth my watching from morning to night; — these, and three domestic women, who cook, and sew, and run for us, make all my household. Here I sit and read and write, with very little system, and, as far as regards composition, with the most fragmentary result: paragraphs incompressible, each sentence an infinitely repellent particle."

A great sorrow visited Emerson and his household at this period of his life. On the 30th of October, 1841, he wrote to Carlyle: "My little boy is five years old to-day, and almost old enough to send you his love."

Four months later, on the 28th of February, 1842, he writes once more: —

"My dear friend, you should have had this letter and these messages by the last steamer; but when it sailed, my son, a perfect little boy of five years and three months, had ended his earthly life. You can never sympathize with me; you can never know how much of me such a young child can take away. A few weeks ago I accounted myself a very rich man, and now the poorest of all. What would it avail to tell you anecdotes of a sweet and wonderful boy, such as we solace and sadden ourselves with at home every morning and evening? From a perfect health and as happy a life and as happy influences as ever child enjoyed, he was hurried out of my arms in three short days by scarlatina. We have two babes yet, one girl of three years, and one girl of three months and a week, but a promise like that Boy's I shall never see. How often I have pleased myself that one day I should send to you this Morning Star of mine, and stay at home so gladly behind such a representative. I dare not fathom the Invisible and Untold to inquire what relations to my Departed ones I yet sustain."

This was the boy whose memory lives in the tenderest and most pathetic of Emerson's poems, the "Threnody," — a lament not unworthy of comparison with "Lycidas" for dignity, but full of the simple pathos of Cowper's well-remembered lines on the receipt of his mother's picture, in the place of Milton's sonorous academic phrases.

EMERSON was American in aspect, temperament,
way of thinking, and feeling; American, with an atmosphere of Oriental idealism; American, so far as he
belonged to any limited part of the universe.   He believed in American institutions, he trusted the future
of the American race.   In the address first mentioned
in the contents of this chapter, delivered February
7, 1844, he claims for this country all that the most
ardent patriot could ask.   Not a few of his fellow-
countrymen will feel the significance of the following
contrast : —

"The English have many virtues, many advantages, and
the proudest history in the world; but they need all and
more than all the resources of the past to indemnify a heroic gentleman in that country for the mortifications prepared for him by the system of society, and which seem to

[1] These two addresses are to be found in the first and eleventh
volumes, respectively, of the last collective edition of Emerson's works, namely, *Nature, Addresses, and Lectures*, and *Miscellanies*.

impose the alternative to resist or to avoid it. . . . It is for Englishmen to consider, not for us; we only say, Let us live in America, too thankful for our want of feudal institutions. . . . If only the men are employed in conspiring with the designs of the Spirit who led us hither, and is leading us still, we shall quickly enough advance out of all hearing of others' censures, out of all regrets of our own, into a new and more excellent social state than history has recorded."

Thirty years have passed since the lecture from which these passages are taken was delivered. The "Young American" of that day is the more than middle-aged American of the present. The intellectual independence of our country is far more solidly established than when this lecture was written. But the social alliance between certain classes of Americans and English is more and more closely cemented from year to year, as the wealth of the new world burrows its way among the privileged classes of the old world. It is a poor ambition for the possessor of suddenly acquired wealth to have it appropriated as a feeder of the impaired fortunes of a deteriorated household, with a family record of which its representatives are unworthy. The plain and wholesome language of Emerson is on the whole more needed now than it was when spoken. His words have often been extolled for their stimulating quality; following the same analogy, they are, as in this address, in a high degree tonic, bracing, strengthening to the American, who requires to be reminded of his privileges that he may know and find himself equal to his duties.

On the first day of August, 1844, Emerson delivered in Concord an address on the Anniversary of the

Emancipation of the Negroes in the British West India Islands. This discourse would not have satisfied the Abolitionists. It was too general in its propositions, full of humane and generous sentiments, but not looking to their extreme and immediate method of action.

Emerson's second series of Essays was published in 1844. There are many sayings in the essay called "The Poet," which are meant for the initiated, rather than for him who runs, to read: —

"All that we call sacred history attests that the birth of a poet is the principal event in chronology."

Does this sound wild and extravagant? What were the political ups and downs of the Hebrews, — what were the squabbles of the tribes with each other, or with their neighbors, compared to the birth of that poet to whom we owe the Psalms, — the sweet singer whose voice is still the dearest of all that ever sang to the heart of mankind?

The poet finds his materials everywhere, as Emerson tells him in this eloquent apostrophe: —

"Thou true land-lord! sea-lord! air-lord! Wherever snow falls, or water flows, or birds fly, wherever day and night meet in twilight, wherever the blue heaven is hung by clouds or sown with stars, wherever are forms with transparent boundaries, wherever are outlets into celestial space, wherever is danger and awe and love, — there is Beauty, plenteous as rain, shed for thee, and though thou shouldst walk the world over, thou shalt not be able to find a condition inopportune or ignoble."

"Experience" is, as he says himself, but a fragment. It bears marks of having been written in a less tranquil state of mind than the other essays. His most important confession is this:—

"All writing comes by the grace of God, and all doing and having. I would gladly be moral and keep due metes and bounds, which I dearly love, and allow the most to the will of man; but I have set my heart on honesty in this chapter, and I can see nothing at last, in success or failure, than more or less of vital force supplied from the Eternal."

The essay on Character requires no difficult study, but is well worth the trouble of reading. A few sentences from it show the prevailing tone and doctrine.

"Character is nature in the highest form. It is of no use to ape it, or to contend with it. Somewhat is possible of resistance and of persistence and of creation to this power, which will foil all emulation. . . .

"There is a class of men, individuals of which appear at long intervals, so eminently endowed with insight and virtue that they have been unanimously saluted as *divine*, and who seem to be an accumulation of that power we consider. . . .

"The history of those gods and saints which the world has written, and then worshipped, are documents of character. The ages have exulted in the manners of a youth who owed nothing to fortune, and who was hanged at the Tyburn of his nation, who, by the pure quality of his nature, shed an epic splendor around the facts of his death which has transfigured every particular into an universal symbol for the eyes of mankind. This great defeat is hitherto our highest fact."

In his essay on Manners, Emerson gives us his ideas of a gentleman:—

"The gentleman is a man of truth, lord of his own actions and expressing that lordship in his behavior, not in any manner dependent and servile either on persons or opinions or possessions. Beyond this fact of truth and real force, the word denotes good-nature or benevolence: manhood first, and then gentleness. . . . Power first, or no leading class. . . . God knows that all sorts of gentlemen knock at the door; but whenever used in strictness, and with any emphasis, the name will be found to point at original energy. . . . The famous gentlemen of Asia and Europe have been of this strong type: Saladin, Sapor, the Cid, Julius Cæsar, Scipio, Alexander, Pericles, and the lordliest personages. They sat very carelessly in their chairs, and were too excellent themselves to value any condition at a high rate. . . . I could better eat with one who did not respect the truth or the laws than with a sloven and unpresentable person. . . . The person who screams, or uses the superlative degree, or converses with heat, puts whole drawing-rooms to flight. . . . I esteem it a chief felicity of this country that it excels in women."

So writes Emerson, and proceeds to speak of woman in language which seems almost to pant for rhythm and rhyme.

This essay is plain enough for the least "transcendental" reader. Franklin would have approved it, and was himself a happy illustration of many of the qualities which go to the Emersonian ideal of good manners, a typical American, equal to his position, always as much so in the palaces and salons of Paris as in the Continental Congress, or the society of Philadelphia.

"Gifts" is a dainty little essay with some nice distinctions and some hints which may help to give form to a generous impulse: —

"The only gift is a portion of thyself. Thou must bleed for me. Therefore the poet brings his poem; the shepherd, his lamb; the farmer, corn; the miner, a gem; the sailor, coral and shells; the painter, his picture; the girl, a handkerchief of her own sewing."

"Flowers and fruits are always fit presents; flowers, because they are a proud assertion that a ray of beauty outvalues all the utilities of the world. . . . Fruits are acceptable gifts, because they are the flower of commodities, and admit of fantastic values being attached to them."

"It is a great happiness to get off without injury and heart-burning from one who has had the ill-luck to be served by you. It is a very onerous business, this of being served, and the debtor naturally wishes to give you a slap."

Emerson hates the superlative, but he does unquestionably love the tingling effect of a witty over-statement.

We have recognized most of the thoughts in the essay entitled "Nature," in the previous essay by the same name, and others which we have passed in review. But there are poetical passages which will give new pleasure.

Here is a variation of the formula with which we are familiar: —

"Nature is the incarnation of a thought, and turns to a thought again, as ice becomes water and gas. The world is mind precipitated, and the volatile essence is forever escaping again into the state of free thought."

And here is a quaint sentence with which we may take leave of this essay: —

"They say that by electro-magnetism your salad shall be grown from the seed whilst your fowl is roasting for dinner; it is a symbol of our modern aims and endeavors, of our condensation and acceleration of objects; — but nothing is gained; nature cannot be cheated; man's life is but seventy salads long, grow they swift or grow they slow."

This is pretty and pleasant, but as to the literal value of the prediction, M. Jules Verne would be the best authority to consult. Poets are fond of that branch of science which, if the imaginative Frenchman gave it a name, he would probably call *Onditologie*.

It is not to be supposed that the most sanguine optimist could be satisfied with the condition of the American political world at the present time, or when the essay on Politics was written, some years before the great war which changed the aspects of the country in so many respects, still leaving the same party names, and many of the characters of the old parties unchanged. This is Emerson's view of them as they then were: —

"Of the two great parties which at this hour almost share the nation between them, I should say that one has the best cause, and the other contains the best men. The philosopher, the poet, or the religious man will of course wish to cast his vote with the democrat, for free trade, for wide suffrage, for the abolition of legal cruelties in the penal code, and for facilitating in every manner the access of the young and the poor to the sources of wealth and power. But he can rarely accept the persons whom the so-called popular party propose to him as representatives of these liberalities. They have not at heart the ends which give to the name of democracy what hope and virtue are in it. The spirit of our American radicalism is destructive and aimless; it is not loving; it has no ulterior and divine ends; but is destructive only out of hatred and selfishness. On the other side, the conservative party, composed of the most moderate, able, and cultivated part of the population, is timid, and merely defensive of property. It vindicates no right, it aspires to no real good, it brands no crime, it proposes no generous policy; it does not build, nor write, nor cherish the arts, nor foster religion, nor establish schools, nor encourage science, nor emancipate the slave, nor befriend the poor, or the Indian, or the immigrant. From neither party, when in power, has the world any benefit to expect in science, art, or humanity, at all commensurate with the resources of the nation."

The metaphysician who looks for a closely reasoned argument on the famous old question which so divided the schoolmen of old will find a very moderate satisfaction in the essay entitled "Nominalist and Realist." But there are many discursive remarks in it worth gathering and considering. We have the complaint of the Cambridge Phi Beta Kappa oration, reiterated, that there is no complete man, but only a collection of fragmentary men.

As a Platonist and a poet there could not be any doubt on which side were all his prejudices; but he takes his ground cautiously.

"In the famous dispute with the Nominalists, the Realists had a good deal of reason. General ideas are essences. They are our gods: they round and ennoble the most partial and sordid way of living. . . .

"Though the uninspired man certainly finds persons a conveniency in household matters, the divine man does not respect them: he sees them as a rack of clouds, or a fleet of ripples which the wind drives over the surface of the water. But this is flat rebellion. Nature will not be Buddhist: she resents generalizing, and insults the philosopher in every moment with a million of fresh particulars."

New England Reformers. — Would any one venture to guess how Emerson would treat this subject? With his unsparing, though amiable radicalism, his excellent common sense, his delicate appreciation of the ridiculous, too deep for laughter, as Wordsworth's thoughts were too deep for tears, in the midst of a band of enthusiasts and not very remote from a throng of fanatics, what are we to look for from our philosopher who unites many characteristics of Berkeley and of Franklin?

We must remember when this lecture was written, for it was delivered on a Sunday in the year 1844. The Brook Farm experiment was an index of the state of mind among one section of the reformers of whom he was writing. To remodel society and the world into a "happy family" was the aim of these enthusiasts. Some attacked one part of the old system, some another; some would build a new temple, some would rebuild the old church, some would worship in the fields and woods, if at all; one was for a phalanstery, where all should live in common, and another was meditating the plan and place of the wigwam where he was to dwell apart in the proud independence of the woodchuck and the musquash. Emerson had the largest and kindliest sympathy with their ideals and aims, but he was too clear-eyed not to see through the whims and extravagances of the unpractical experimenters who would construct a working world with the lay figures they had put together, instead of flesh and blood men and women and children with all their congenital and acquired perversities. He describes these reformers in his own good-naturedly half-satirical way: —

"They defied each other like a congress of kings, each of whom had a realm to rule, and a way of his own that made concert unprofitable. What a fertility of projects for the salvation of the world! One apostle thought all men should go to farming; and another that no man should buy or sell, that the use of money was the cardinal evil; another that the mischief was in our diet, that we eat and drink damnation. These made unleavened bread, and were foes to the death to fermentation. It was in vain urged by the housewife that God made yeast as well as dough, and loves fermentation just as dearly as he loves vegetation; that fermentation develops the saccharine element in the grain, and makes it more palatable and more digestible. No, they wish the pure wheat, and will die but it shall not ferment. Stop, dear nature, these incessant advances of thine; let us scotch these ever-rolling wheels! Others attacked the system of agriculture, the use of animal manures in farming, and the tyranny of man over brute nature; these abuses polluted his food. The ox must be taken from the plough and the horse from the cart, the hundred acres of the farm must be spaded, and the man must walk wherever boats and locomotives will not carry him. Even the insect world was to be defended, — that had been too long neglected, and a society for the protection of ground-worms, slugs, and mosquitoes was to be incorporated without delay. With these appeared the adepts of homœopathy, of hydropathy, of mesmerism, of phrenology, and their wonderful theories of the Christian miracles! "

We have already seen the issue of the famous Brook Farm experiment, which was a practical outcome of the reforming agitation.

Emerson has had the name of being a leader in many movements in which he had very limited confidence, this among others to which the idealizing impulse derived from him lent its force, but for the organization of which he was in no sense responsible.

He says in the lecture we are considering: —

"These new associations are composed of men and women of superior talents and sentiments; yet it may easily be questioned whether such a community will draw, except in its beginnings, the able and the good; whether those who have energy will not prefer their chance of superiority and power in the world to the humble certainties of the association; whether such a retreat does not promise to become an asylum to those who have tried and failed, rather than a field to the strong; and whether the members will not necessarily be fractions of men, because each finds that he cannot enter into it without some compromise."

His sympathies were not allowed to mislead him; he knew human nature too well to believe in a Noah's ark full of idealists.

All this time he was lecturing for his support, giving courses of lectures in Boston and other cities, and before the country lyceums in and out of New England.

His letters to Carlyle show how painstaking, how methodical, how punctual he was in the business which interested his distant friend. He was not fond of figures, and it must have cost him a great effort to play the part of an accountant.

He speaks also of receiving a good deal of company in the summer, and that some of this company exacted much time and attention — more than he could spare — is made evident by his gentle complaints, especially in his poems, which sometimes let out a truth he would hardly have uttered in prose.

In 1846 Emerson's first volume of poems was published. Many of the poems had been long before the public — some of the best, as we have seen, having been printed in "The Dial." It is only their being brought together for the first time which belongs especially to this period, and we can leave them for the

present, to be looked over by and by in connection
with a second volume of poems published in 1867,
under the title, "May-Day and Other Pieces."

In October, 1847, he left Concord on a second visit
to England, which will be spoken of in the following
chapter.

A NEW periodical publication was begun in Boston
in 1847, under the name of "The Massachusetts Quarterly Review."   Emerson wrote the "Editor's Address," but took no further active part in it, Theodore
Parker being the real editor.   The last line of this
address is characteristic: "We rely on the truth for
aid against ourselves."

On the 5th of October, 1847, Emerson sailed for
Europe on his second visit, reaching Liverpool on the
22d of that month.   Many of his admirers were desirous that he should visit England and deliver some
courses of lectures.   Mr. Alexander Ireland, who had
paid him friendly attentions during his earlier visit,
and whose impressions of him in the pulpit have been
given on a previous page, urged his coming.   Mr.
Conway quotes passages from a letter of Emerson's
which show that he had some hesitation in accepting
the invitation, not unmingled with a wish to be heard
by the English audiences favorably disposed towards
him.

"I feel no call," he said, "to make a visit of literary propagandism in England. All my impulses to work of that kind would rather employ me at home." He does not like the idea of "coaxing" or advertising to get him an audience. He would like to read lectures before institutions or friendly persons who sympathize with his studies. He has had a good many decisive tokens of interest from British men and women, but he doubts whether he is much and favorably known in any one city, except perhaps in London. It proved, however, that there was a very widespread desire to hear him, and applications for lectures flowed in from all parts of the kingdom.

From Liverpool he proceeded immediately to Manchester, where Mr. Ireland received him at the Victoria station. After spending a few hours with him, he went to Chelsea to visit Carlyle, and at the end of a week returned to Manchester to begin the series of lecturing engagements which had been arranged for him. Mr. Ireland's account of Emerson's visits and the interviews between him and many distinguished persons is full of interest, but the interest largely relates to the persons visited by Emerson. He lectured at Edinburgh, where his liberal way of thinking and talking made a great sensation in orthodox circles. But he did not fail to find enthusiastic listeners. A young student, Mr. George Cupples, wrote an article on these lectures from which, as quoted by Mr. Ireland, I borrow a single sentence, — one only, but what could a critic say more?

Speaking of his personal character, as revealed through his writings, he says: "In this respect, I take leave to think that Emerson is the most mark-worthy, the loftiest, and most heroic mere man that ever appeared." Emerson has a lecture on the superlative, to which he himself was never addicted. But what would youth be without its extravagances, — its pre-terpluperfect in the shape of adjectives, its unmeasured and unstinted admiration?

I need not enumerate the celebrated literary person-ages and other notabilities whom Emerson met in England and Scotland. He thought "the two finest mannered literary men he met in England were Leigh Hunt and De Quincey." His diary might tell us more of the impressions made upon him by the distinguished people he met, but it is impossible to believe that he ever passed such inhuman judgments on the least desirable of his new acquaintances as his friend Carlyle has left as a bitter legacy behind him. Carlyle's merciless discourse about Coleridge and Charles Lamb, and Swinburne's carnivorous lines, which take a barbarous vengeance on him for his offence, are on the level of political rhetoric rather than of scholarly criticism or characterization. Emerson never forgot that he was dealing with human beings. He could not have long endured the asperities of Carlyle, and that "loud shout of laughter," which Mr. Ireland speaks of as one of his customary explosions, would have been discordant to Emerson's ears, which were offended by such noisy manifestations.

During this visit Emerson made an excursion to Paris, which furnished him materials for a lecture on France delivered in Boston, in 1856, but never printed.

From the lectures delivered in England he selected a certain number for publication. These make up the volume entitled "Representative Men," which was published in 1850. I will give very briefly an account of its contents. The title was a happy one, and has passed into literature and conversation as an accepted and convenient phrase. It would teach us a good deal merely to consider the names he has selected as typical, and the ground of their selection. We get his classification of men considered as leaders in thought and in action. He shows his own affinities and repulsions, and, as everywhere, writes his own biography, no matter about whom or what he is talking. There is hardly any book of his better worth study by those who wish to understand, not Plato, not Plutarch, not Napoleon, but Emerson himself. All his great men interest us for their own sake; but we know a good deal about most of them, and Emerson holds the mirror up to them at just such an angle that we see his own face as well as that of his hero, unintentionally, unconsciously, no doubt, but by a necessity which he would be the first to recognize.

Emerson swears by no master. He admires, but always with a reservation. Plato comes nearest to being his idol, Shakespeare next. But he says of all great men: "The power which they communicate is not theirs. When we are exalted by ideas, we do not owe this to Plato, but to the idea, to which also Plato was debtor."

Emerson loves power as much as Carlyle does; he likes "rough and smooth," "scourges of God," and "darlings of the human race." He likes Julius Cæsar, Charles the Fifth, of Spain, Charles the Twelfth, of Sweden, Richard Plantagenet, and Bonaparte.

"I applaud," he says, "a sufficient man, an officer equal to his office; captains, ministers, senators. I like a master standing firm on legs of iron, well born, rich, handsome, eloquent, loaded with advantages, drawing all men by fascination into tributaries and supporters of his power. Sword and staff, or talents sword-like or staff-like, carry on the work of the world. But I find him greater when he can abolish himself and all heroes by letting in this element of reason, irrespective of persons, this subtilizer and irresistible upward force, into our thought, destroying individualism; the power so great that the potentate is nothing. . . .

"The genius of humanity is the right point of view of history. The qualities abide; the men who exhibit them have now more, now less, and pass away; the qualities remain on another brow. . . . All that respects the individual is temporary and prospective, like the individual himself, who is ascending out of his limits into a catholic existence."

No man can be an idol for one who looks in this way at all men. But Plato takes the first place in Emerson's gallery of six great personages whose portraits he has sketched. And of him he says: —

"Among secular books Plato only is entitled to Omar's fanatical compliment to the Koran, when he said, 'Burn the libraries; for their value is in this book.' . . . Out of Plato come all things that are still written and debated among men of thought. . . . In proportion to the culture of men they become his scholars. . . . How many great men Nature is incessantly sending up out of night to be *his men!* . . . His contemporaries tax him with plagiarism. But the inventor only knows how to borrow. . . . When we are praising Plato, it seems we are praising quotations from Solon and Sophron and Philolaus. Be it so. Every book is a quotation; and every house is a quotation out of all forests and mines and stone quarries; and every man is a quotation from all his ancestors."

The reader will, I hope, remember this last gen-

eral statement when he learns from what wide fields
of authorship Emerson filled his storehouses.

A few sentences from Emerson will show us the
probable source of some of the deepest thought of
Plato and his disciples.

The conception of the fundamental Unity, he says,
finds its highest expression in the religious writings of
the East, especially in the Indian Scriptures.

" ' The whole world is but a manifestation of Vishnu,
who is identical with all things, and is to be regarded by
the wise as not differing from, but as the same as themselves. I neither am going nor coming; nor is my dwelling in any one place; nor art thou, thou; nor are others,
others; nor am I, I.' As if he had said, 'All is for the
soul, and the soul is Vishnu; and animals and stars are
transient paintings; and light is whitewash; and dura-
tions are deceptive; and form is imprisonment; and
heaven itself a decoy.' "

All of which we see reproduced in Emerson's poem
"Brahma."

"The country of unity, of immovable institutions, the
seat of a philosophy delighting in abstractions, of men
faithful in doctrine and in practice to the idea of a deaf,
unimplorable, immense fate, is Asia; and it realizes this
faith in the social institution of caste. On the other side,
the genius of Europe is active and creative: it resists
caste by culture; its philosophy was a discipline; it is a
land of arts, inventions, trade, freedom." "Plato came
to join, and by contact to enhance, the energy of each."

But Emerson says, — and some will smile at hearing him say it of another, — "The acutest German,
the lovingest disciple, could never tell what Platonism
was; indeed, admirable texts can be quoted on both
sides of every great question from him."

The transcendent intellectual and moral superior-

ities of this "Euclid of holiness," as Emerson calls
him, with his "soliform eye and his boniform soul,"
— the two quaint adjectives being from the mint of
Cudworth, — are fully dilated upon in the addition
to the original article called "Plato: New Readings."

Few readers will be satisfied with the essay entitled "Swedenborg; or, The Mystic." The believers
in his special communion as a revealer of divine truth
will find him reduced to the level of other seers. The
believers of the different creeds of Christianity will
take offence at the statement that "Swedenborg and
Behmen both failed by attaching themselves to the
Christian symbol, instead of to the moral sentiment,
which carries innumerable christianities, humanities,
divinities in its bosom." The men of science will
smile at the exorbitant claims put forward in behalf
of Swedenborg as a scientific discoverer. "Philosophers" will not be pleased to be reminded that Swedenborg called them "cockatrices," "asps," or "flying serpents;" "literary men" will not agree that they
are "conjurers and charlatans," and will not listen
with patience to the praises of a man who so called
them. As for the poets, they can take their choice of
Emerson's poetical or prose estimate of the great
Mystic, but they cannot very well accept both. In
"The Test," the Muse says: —

> "I hung my verses in the wind,
>   Time and tide their faults may find ;
>   All were winnowed through and through,
>   Five lines lasted sound and true. . . .
>   Sunshine cannot bleach the snow,
>   Nor time unmake what poets know.
>   Have you eyes to find the five
>   Which five hundred did survive ? "

In the verses which follow we learn that the five immortal poets referred to are Homer, Dante, Shakespeare, *Swedenborg*, and Goethe.

And now, in the essay we have just been looking
at, I find that "his books have no melody, no emotion, no humor, no relief to the dead prosaic level.
We wander forlorn in a lack-lustre landscape. No
bird ever sang in these gardens of the dead. The entire want of poetry in so transcendent a mind betokens
the disease, and, like a hoarse voice in a beautiful person, is a kind of warning." Yet Emerson says of
him that "he lived to purpose: he gave a verdict.
He elected goodness as the clue to which the soul must
cling in this labyrinth of nature."

Emerson seems to have admired Swedenborg at a
distance, but seen nearer, he liked Jacob Behmen a
great deal better.

"Montaigne; or, The Skeptic," is easier reading
than the last-mentioned essay. Emerson accounts for
the personal regard which he has for Montaigne by the
story of his first acquaintance with him. But no other
reason was needed than that Montaigne was just what
Emerson describes him as being.

"There have been men with deeper insight; but, one
would say, never a man with such abundance of thought:
he is never dull, never insincere, and has the genius to
make the reader care for all that he cares for.

"The sincerity and marrow of the man reaches to his
sentences. I know not anywhere the book that seems less
written. It is the language of conversation transferred
to a book. Cut these words and they would bleed; they
are vascular and alive. . . .

"Montaigne talks with shrewdness, knows the world and
books and himself, and uses the positive degree; never

shrieks, or protests, or prays; no weakness, no convulsion, no superlative; does not wish to jump out of his skin, or play any antics, or annihilate space or time, but is stout and solid; tastes every moment of the day; likes pain because it makes him feel himself and realize things; as we pinch ourselves to know that we are awake. He keeps the plain; he rarely mounts or sinks; likes to feel solid ground and the stones underneath. His writing has no enthusiasms, no aspiration; contented, self-respecting, and keeping the middle of the road. There is but one exception, — in his love for Socrates. In speaking of him, for once his cheek flushes and his style rises to passion."

The writer who draws this portrait must have many of the same characteristics. Much as Emerson loved his dreams and his dreamers, he must have found a great relief in getting into "the middle of the road" with Montaigne, after wandering in difficult by-paths which too often led him round to the point from which he started.

As to his exposition of the true relations of skepticism to affirmative and negative belief, the philosophical reader must be referred to the essay itself.

In writing of "Shakespeare; or, The Poet," Emerson naturally gives expression to his leading ideas about the office of the poet and of poetry.

"Great men are more distinguished by range and extent than by originality." A poet has "a heart in unison with his time and country." "There is nothing whimsical and fantastic in his production, but sweet and sad earnest, freighted with the weightiest convictions, and pointed with the most determined aim which any man or class knows of in his times."

When Shakespeare was in his youth the drama was the popular means of amusement. It was "ballad, epic, newspaper, caucus, lecture, Punch, and library, at the same time. . . . The best proof of its vitality is the crowd of writers which suddenly broke into this field." Shakespeare found a great mass of old plays existing in manuscript and reproduced from time to time on the stage. He borrowed in all directions: "A great poet who appears in illiterate times absorbs into his sphere all the light which is anywhere radiating." Homer, Chaucer, Saadi, felt that all wit was their wit. "Chaucer is a huge borrower." Emerson gives a list of authors from whom he drew. This list is in many particulars erroneous, as I have learned from a letter of Professor Lounsbury's which I have had the privilege of reading, but this is a detail which need not delay us.

The reason why Emerson has so much to say on this subject of borrowing, especially when treating of Plato and of Shakespeare, is obvious enough. He was arguing in his own cause, — not defending himself, as if there were some charge of plagiarism to be met, but making the proud claim of eminent domain in behalf of the masters who knew how to use their acquisitions.

"Shakespeare is the only biographer of Shakespeare; and even he can tell nothing except to the Shakespeare in us. . . . Shakespeare is as much out of the category of eminent authors as he is out of the crowd. . . . A good reader can in a sort nestle into Plato's brain and think from thence; but not into Shakespeare's. We are still out of doors."

After all the homage which Emerson pays to the intellect of Shakespeare, he weighs him with the rest of mankind, and finds that he shares "the halfness and imperfection of humanity."

"He converted the elements which waited on his command into entertainment. He was master of the revels to mankind."

And so, after this solemn verdict on Shakespeare, after looking at the forlorn conclusions of our old and modern oracles, priest and prophet, Israelite, German, and Swede, he says: "It must be conceded that these are half views of half men. The world still wants its poet-priest, who shall not trifle, with Shakespeare the player, nor shall grope in graves, with Swedenborg the mourner; but who shall see, speak, and act with equal inspiration."

It is not to be expected that Emerson should have much that is new to say about "Napoleon; or, The Man of the World."

The stepping-stones of this essay are easy to find: —

"The instinct of active, brave, able men, throughout the middle class everywhere, has pointed out Napoleon as the incarnate democrat. . . .

"Napoleon is thoroughly modern, and, at the highest point of his fortunes, has the very spirit of the newspapers."

As Plato borrowed, as Shakespeare borrowed, as Mirabeau "plagiarized every good thought, every good word that was spoken in France," so Napoleon is not merely "representative, but a monopolizer and usurper of other minds."

He was "a man of stone and iron," — equipped for his work by nature as Sallust describes Catiline as being.

"He had a directness of action never before combined with so much comprehension. . . . Here was a man who in each moment and emergency knew what to do next. . . . He saw only the object; the obstacle must give way. . . .

"When a natural king becomes a titular king, everybody is pleased and satisfied. . . .

"I call Napoleon the agent or attorney of the middle class of modern society. . . . He was the agitator, the destroyer of prescription, the internal improver, the liberal, the radical, the inventor of means, the opener of doors and markets, the subverter of monopoly and abuse."

But he was without generous sentiments, "a boundless liar," and finishing in high colors the outline of his moral deformities, Emerson gives us a climax in two sentences which render further condemnation superfluous : —

"In short, when you have penetrated through all the circles of power and splendor, you were not dealing with a gentleman, at last, but with an impostor and a rogue; and he fully deserves the epithet of Jupiter Scapin, or a sort of Scamp Jupiter. . . .

"So this exorbitant egotist narrowed, impoverished, and absorbed the power and existence of those who served him; and the universal cry of France and of Europe in 1814 was, Enough of him : '*Assez de Bonaparte.*' "

It was to this feeling that the French poet Barbier, whose death we have but lately seen announced, gave expression in the terrible satire in which he pictured France as a fiery courser bestridden by her spurred rider, who drove her in a mad career over heaps of rocks and ruins.

But after all, Carlyle's "*carrière ouverte aux talens*," is the expression for Napoleon's great message to mankind.

"Goethe; or, The Writer," is the last of the Representative Men who are the subjects of this book of essays. Emerson says he had read the fifty-five volumes of Goethe, but no other German writers, at least

in the original.   It must have been in fulfilment of
some pious vow that he did this.   After all that Carlyle had written about Goethe, he could hardly help
studying him.   But this essay looks to me as if he
had found the reading of Goethe hard work.   It flows
rather languidly, toys with side issues as a stream loiters round a nook in its margin, and finds an excuse
for play in every pebble.   Still, he has praise enough
for his author.

"He has clothed our modern existence with poetry.
. . . He has said the best things about nature that ever
were said. . . . He flung into literature, in his Mephistopheles, the first organic figure that has been added for
some ages, and which will remain as long as the Prome-
theus. . . . He is the type of culture, the amateur of
all arts and sciences and events; artistic but not artist;
spiritual, but not spiritualist. . . . I join Napoleon with
him, as being both representatives of the impatience and
reaction of nature against the morgue of conventions, —
two stern realists, who, with their scholars, have severally set the axe at the root of the tree of cant and seeming, for this time and for all time."

This must serve as an *ex pede* guide to reconstruct
the essay which finishes the volume.

In 1852 there was published a Memoir of Margaret
Fuller Ossoli, in which Emerson, James Freeman
Clarke, and William Henry Channing each took a
part.   Emerson's account of her conversation and extracts from her letters and diaries, with his running
commentaries and his interpretation of her mind and
character, are a most faithful and vivid portraiture of
a woman who is likely to live longer by what is written of her than by anything she ever wrote herself.

CHAPTER VIII.

1853–1858.   ÆT. 50–55.

AFTER Emerson's return from Europe he delivered lectures to different audiences, — one on Poetry, afterwards published in "Letters and Social Aims," a course of lectures in Freeman Place Chapel, Boston, some of which have been published, one on the Anglo-Saxon Race, and many others. In January, 1855, he gave one of the lectures in a course of Anti-Slavery Addresses delivered in Tremont Temple, Boston. In the same year he delivered an address before the Anti-Slavery party of New York. His plan for the extirpation of slavery was to buy the slaves from the planters, not conceding their right to ownership, but because " it is the only practical course, and is innocent." It would cost two thousand millions, he says, according to the present estimate, but "was there ever any contribution that was so enthusiastically paid as this would be? "

His optimism flowers out in all its innocent luxuriance in the paragraph from which this is quoted. Of course with notions like these he could not be hand in hand with the Abolitionists. He was classed with the

Free Soilers, but he seems to have formed a party by himself in his project for buying up the negroes. He looked at the matter somewhat otherwise in 1863, when the settlement was taking place in a different currency, — in steel and not in gold: —

> "Pay ransom to the owner,
>   And fill the bag to the brim.
> Who is the owner?   The slave is owner,
>   And ever was.   Pay him."

His sympathies were all and always with freedom. He spoke with indignation of the outrage on Sumner; he took part in the meeting at Concord expressive of sympathy with John Brown. But he was never in the front rank of the aggressive Anti-Slavery men. In his singular "Ode inscribed to W. H. Channing" there is a hint of a possible solution of the slavery problem which implies a doubt as to the permanence of the cause of all the trouble: —

> "The over-god
>   Who marries Right to Might,
>   Who peoples, unpeoples, —
> He who exterminates
>   Races by stronger races,
>   Black by white faces, —
> Knows to bring honey
>   Out of the lion."

Some doubts of this kind helped Emerson to justify himself when he refused to leave his "honeyed thought" for the busy world where

> "Things are of the snake."

The time came when he could no longer sit quietly in his study, and, to borrow Mr. Cooke's words, "As the agitation proceeded, and brave men took part in it, and it rose to a spirit of moral grandeur, he gave a heartier assent to the outward methods adopted."

No woman could doubt the reverence of Emerson for womanhood. In a lecture read to the Woman's Rights Convention in 1855, he takes bold, and what would then have been considered somewhat advanced, ground in the controversy then and since dividing the community. This is the way in which he expresses himself : —

"I do not think it yet appears that women wish this equal share in public affairs. But it is they and not we that are to determine it. Let the laws be purged of every barbarous remainder, every barbarous impediment to women. Let the public donations for education be equally shared by them, let them enter a school as freely as a church, let them have and hold and give their property as men do theirs ; — and in a few years it will easily appear whether they wish a voice in making the laws that are to govern them. If you do refuse them a vote, you will also refuse to tax them, — according to our Teutonic principle, No representation, no tax. . . . The new movement is only a tide shared by the spirits of man and woman ; and you may proceed in the faith that whatever the woman's heart is prompted to desire, the man's mind is simultaneously prompted to accomplish."

Emerson was fortunate enough to have had for many years as a neighbor that true New England Roman, Samuel Hoar. He spoke of him in Concord before his fellow-citizens, shortly after his death, in 1856. He afterwards prepared a sketch of Mr. Hoar for "Putnam's Magazine," from which I take one prose sentence and the verse with which the sketch concluded : —

"He was a model of those formal but reverend manners

which make what is called a gentleman of the old school, so called under an impression that the style is passing away, but which, I suppose, is an optical illusion, as there are always a few more of the class remaining, and always a few young men to whom these manners are native."

The single verse I quote is compendious enough and descriptive enough for an Elizabethan monumental inscription : —

> " With beams December planets dart
> His cold eye truth and conduct scanned ;
> July was in his sunny heart,
> October in his liberal hand."

Emerson's "English Traits," forming one volume of his works, was published in 1856. It is a thoroughly fresh and original book. It is not a tourist's guide, not a detailed description of sights which tired the traveller in staring at them, and tire the reader who attacks the wearying pages in which they are recorded. Shrewd observation there is indeed, but its strength is in broad generalization and epigrammatic characterizations. They are not to be received as in any sense final; they are not like the verifiable facts of science; they are more or less sagacious, more or less well-founded opinions formed by a fair-minded, sharp-witted, kind-hearted, open-souled philosopher, whose presence made every one well-disposed towards him, and consequently left him well-disposed to all the world.

A glance at the table of contents will give an idea of the objects which Emerson proposed to himself in his tour, and which take up the principal portion of his record. Only one *place* is given as the heading of a chapter, — Stonehenge. The other eighteen chapters have general titles, Land, Race, Ability, Manners, and others of similar character.

He uses plain English in introducing us to the Pil-
grim fathers of the British aristocracy : —

"Twenty thousand thieves landed at Hastings. These
founders of the House of Lords were greedy and ferocious
dragoons, sons of greedy and ferocious pirates. They
were all alike; they took everything they could carry,
they burned, harried, violated, tortured, and killed,
until everything English was brought to the verge of ruin.
Such, however, is the illusion of antiquity and wealth, that
decent and dignified men now existing boast their descent
from these filthy thieves, who showed a far juster conviction of their own merits by assuming for their types the
swine, goat, jackal, leopard, wolf, and snake, which they
severally resembled."

The race preserves some of its better characteristics.

"They have a vigorous health and last well into middle and old age. The old men are as red as roses, and
still handsome. A clear skin, a peach-bloom complexion,
and good teeth are found all over the island."

English "manners" are characterized, according to
Emerson, by pluck, vigor, independence. "Every
one of these islanders is an island himself, safe, tranquil, incommunicable." They are positive, methodical, cleanly, and formal, loving routine and conventional ways; loving truth and religion, to be sure, but
inexorable on points of form.

"They keep their old customs, costumes, and pomps,
their wig and mace, sceptre and crown. . . . A severe
decorum rules the court and the cottage. . . . Pretension and vaporing are once for all distasteful. . . . They
hate nonsense, sentimentalism, and high-flown expressions;
they use a studied plainness. In an aristocratical country
like England, not the Trial by Jury, but the dinner, is
the capital institution."

"They confide in each other, — English believes in English. . . . They require the same adherence, thorough conviction, and reality in public men."

"As compared with the Americans, I think them cheerful and contented. Young people in this country are much more prone to melancholy."

Emerson's observation is in accordance with that of Cotton Mather nearly two hundred years ago.

"*New England*, a country where splenetic Maladies are prevailing and pernicious, perhaps above any other, hath afforded numberless instances, of even pious people, who have contracted those *Melancholy Indispositions*, which have unhinged them from all service or comfort; yea, not a few persons have been hurried thereby to lay *Violent Hands* upon themselves at the last. These are among the *unsearchable Judgments* of God."

If there is a little exaggeration about the following portrait of the Englishman, it has truth enough to excuse its high coloring, and the likeness will be smilingly recognized by every stout Briton.

"They drink brandy like water, cannot expend their quantities of waste strength on riding, hunting, swimming, and fencing, and run into absurd frolics with the gravity of the Eumenides. They stoutly carry into every nook and corner of the earth their turbulent sense; leaving no lie uncontradicted, no pretension unexamined. They chew hasheesh; cut themselves with poisoned creases; swing their hammock in the boughs of the Bohon Upas; taste every poison; buy every secret; at Naples, they put St. Januarius's blood in an alembic; they saw a hole into the head of the 'winking Virgin,' to know why she winks; measure with an English foot-rule every cell of the Inquisition, every Turkish Caaba, every Holy of Holies; translate and send to Bentley the arcanum bribed and bullied away from shuddering Bramins; and measure their own strength by the terror they cause."

This last audacious picture might be hung up as a prose pendant to Marvell's poetical description of Holland and the Dutch.

"A saving stupidity masks and protects their perception as the curtain of the eagle's eye. Our swifter Americans, when they first deal with English, pronounce them stupid; but, later, do them justice as people who wear well, or hide their strength. . . . High and low, they are of an unctuous texture. . . . Their daily feasts argue a savage vigor of body. . . . Half their strength they put not forth. . . . The stability of England is the security of the modern world."

Perhaps nothing in any of his vigorous paragraphs is more striking than the suggestion that "if hereafter the war of races often predicted, and making itself a war of opinions also (a question of despotism and liberty coming from Eastern Europe), should menace the English civilization, these sea-kings may take once again to their floating castles and find a new home and a second millennium of power in their colonies."

In reading some of Emerson's pages it seems as if another Arcadia, or the new Atlantis, had emerged as the fortunate island of Great Britain, or that he had reached a heaven on earth where neither moth nor rust doth corrupt, and where thieves do not break through nor steal, — or if they do, never think of denying that they have done it. But this was a generation ago, when the noun "shoddy," and the verb "to scamp," had not grown such familiar terms to English ears as they are to-day. Emerson saw the country on its best side. Each traveller makes his own England. A Quaker sees chiefly broad brims, and the island looks to him like a field of mushrooms.

The transplanted Church of England is rich and

prosperous and fashionable enough not to be disturbed by Emerson's flashes of light that have not come through its stained windows.

"The religion of England is part of good-breeding. When you see on the Continent the well-dressed English-man come into his ambassador's Chapel, and put his face for silent prayer into his smooth-brushed hat, one cannot help feeling how much national pride prays with him, and the religion of a gentleman. . . .

"The church at this moment is much to be pitied. She has nothing left but possession. If a bishop meets an in-telligent gentleman, and reads fatal interrogations in his eyes, he has no resource but to take wine with him."

Sydney Smith had a great reverence for a bishop, — so great that he told a young lady that he used to roll a crumb of bread in his hand, from nervousness, when he sat next one at a dinner-table, — and if next an archbishop, used to roll crumbs with both hands, — but Sydney Smith would have enjoyed the tingling felicity of this last stinging touch of wit, left as lightly and gracefully as a *banderillero* leaves his little gayly ribboned dart in the shoulders of the bull with whose unwieldy bulk he is playing.

Emerson handles the formalism and the half belief of the Established Church very freely, but he closes his chapter on Religion with soft-spoken words.

"Yet if religion be the doing of all good, and for its sake the suffering of all evil, *souffrir de tout le monde et ne faire souffrir personne*, that divine secret has existed in England from the days of Alfred to those of Romilly, of Clarkson, and of Florence Nightingale, and in thou-sands who have no fame."

"English Traits" closes with Emerson's speech at Manchester, at the annual banquet of the "Free

Trade Athenæum." This was merely an occasional
after-dinner reply to a toast which called him up, but
it had sentences in it which, if we can imagine Milton
to have been called up in the same way, he might well
have spoken and done himself credit in their utterance.

The total impression left by the book is that Emerson was fascinated by the charm of English society,
filled with admiration of the people, tempted to contrast his New Englanders in many respects unfavorably with Old Englanders, mainly in their material
and vital stamina; but with all this not blinded for a
moment to the thoroughly insular limitations of the
phlegmatic islander. He alternates between a turn of
genuine admiration and a smile as at a people that has
not outgrown its playthings. This is in truth the natural and genuine feeling of a self-governing citizen of
a commonwealth where thrones and wigs and mitres
seem like so many pieces of stage property. An
American need not be a philosopher to hold these
things cheap. He cannot help it. Madame Tus-
saud's exhibition, the Lord-Mayor's gilt coach, and
a coronation, if one happens to be in season, are all
sights to be seen by an American traveller, but the
reverence which is born with the British subject went
up with the smoke of the gun that fired the long echo-
ing shot at the little bridge over the sleepy river which
works its way along through the wide-awake town of
Concord.

In November, 1857, a new magazine was established
in Boston, bearing the name of "The Atlantic
Monthly." Professor James Russell Lowell was edi-
tor-in-chief, and Messrs. Phillips and Sampson, who

were the originators of the enterprise, were the publishers. Many of the old contributors to "The Dial" wrote for the new magazine, among them Emerson. He contributed twenty-eight articles in all, more than half of them verse, to different numbers, from the first to the thirty-seventh volume. Among them are several of his best known poems, such as "The Romany Girl," "Days," "Brahma," "Waldeinsamkeit," "The Titmouse," "Boston Hymn," "Saadi," and "Terminus."

At about the same time there grew up in Boston a literary association, which became at last well known as the "Saturday Club," the members dining together on the last Saturday of every month.

The magazine and the club have existed and flourished to the present day. They have often been erroneously thought to have some organic connection, and the "Atlantic Club" has been spoken of as if there was or had been such an institution, but it never existed.

Emerson was a member of the Saturday Club from the first; in reality before it existed as an empirical fact, and when it was only a Platonic idea. The club seems to have shaped itself around him as a nucleus of crystallization, two or three friends of his having first formed the habit of meeting him at dinner at "Parker's," the "Will's Coffee-House" of Boston. This little group gathered others to itself and grew into a club as Rome grew into a city, almost without knowing how. During its first decade the Saturday Club brought together, as members or as visitors, many distinguished persons. At one end of the table sat Longfellow, florid, quiet, benignant, soft-voiced, a most agreeable rather than a brilliant talker, but

a man upon whom it was always pleasant to look, —
whose silence was better than many another man's conversation.   At the other end of the table sat Agassiz,
robust, sanguine, animated, full of talk, boy-like in
his laughter.   The stranger who should have asked
who were the men ranged along the sides of the table
would have heard in answer the names of Hawthorne,
Motley, Dana, Lowell, Whipple, Peirce, the distinguished mathematician, Judge Hoar, eminent at the
bar and in the cabinet, Dwight, the leading musical
critic of Boston for a whole generation, Sumner, the
academic champion of freedom, Andrew, "the great
War Governor" of Massachusetts, Dr. Howe, the
philanthropist, William Hunt, the painter, with others not unworthy of such company.   And with these,
generally near the Longfellow end of the table, sat
Emerson, talking in low tones and carefully measured
utterances to his neighbor, or listening, and recording
on his mental phonograph any stray word worth remembering.   Emerson was a very regular attendant
at the meetings of the Saturday Club, and continued
to dine at its table until within a year or two of his
death.

Unfortunately, the club had no Boswell, and its
golden hours passed unrecorded.

CHAPTER IX.

1858–1863. Æt. 55–60.

Essay on Persian Poetry. — Speech at the Burns Centennial Festival. — Letter from Emerson to a Lady. — Tributes to Theodore Parker and to Thoreau. — Address on the Emancipation Proclamation. — Publication of "The Conduct of Life." Contents : Fate ; Power ; Wealth ; Culture ; Behavior ; Worship ; Considerations by the Way ; Beauty ; Illusions.

THE essay on Persian Poetry, published in "The Atlantic Monthly" in 1858, should be studied by all readers who are curious in tracing the influence of Oriental poetry on Emerson's verse. In many of the shorter poems and fragments published since "May-Day," as well as in the "Quatrains" and others of the later poems in that volume, it is sometimes hard to tell what is from the Persian from what is original.

On the 25th of January, 1859, Emerson attended the Burns Festival, held at the Parker House in Boston, on the centennial anniversary of the poet's birth. He spoke after the dinner to the great audience with such beauty and eloquence that all who listened to him have remembered it as one of the most delightful addresses they ever heard. Among his hearers was Mr. Lowell, who says of it that "every word seemed to have just dropped down to him from the clouds." Judge Hoar, who was another of his hearers, says, that though he has heard many of the chief orators of his time, he never witnessed such an effect of speech upon men. I was myself present on that occasion, and underwent the same fascination that these gentlemen and the varied audience before the speaker experienced. His words had a passion in them not usual in the calm, pure flow most natural to his uttered thoughts; white-hot iron we are familiar with, but white-hot silver is what we do not often look upon, and his inspiring address glowed like silver fresh from the cupel.

I am allowed the privilege of printing the following letter addressed to a lady of high intellectual gifts, who was one of the earliest, most devoted, and most faithful of his intimate friends: —

CONCORD, *May* 13, 1859.

Please, dear C., not to embark for home until I have despatched these lines, which I will hasten to finish. Louis Napoleon will not bayonet you the while, — keep him at the door. So long I have promised to write! so long I have thanked your long suffering! I have let pass the unreturning opportunity your visit to Germany gave to acquaint you with Gisela von Arnim (Bettina's daughter), and Joachim the violinist, and Hermann Grimm the scholar, her friends. Neither has E. — wandering in Europe with hope of meeting you — yet met. This contumacy of mine I shall regret as long as I live. How palsy creeps over us, with gossamer first, and ropes afterwards! and the witch has the prisoner when once she has put her eye on him, as securely as after the bolts are drawn. — Yet I and all my little company watch every token from you, and coax Mrs. H. to read us letters. I learned with satisfaction that you did not like Germany. Where then did Goethe find his lovers? Do all the women have bad noses and bad mouths? And will you stop in England, and bring home the author of "Counterparts"

with you? Or did —— write the novels and send them
to London, as I fancied when I read them? How strange
that you and I alone to this day should have his secret!
I think our people will never allow genius, without it is
alloyed by talent. But —— is paralyzed by his whims,
that I have ceased to hope from him. I could wish your
experience of your friends were more animating than
mine, and that there were any horoscope you could not
cast from the first day. The faults of youth are never
shed, no, nor the merits, and creeping time convinces ever
the more of our impotence, and of the irresistibility of
our bias. Still this is only science, and must remain
science. Our *praxis* is never altered for that. We must
forever hold our companions responsible, or they are not
companions but stall-fed.

I think, as we grow older, we decrease as individuals,
and as if in an immense audience who hear stirring music,
none essays to offer a new stave, but we only join em-
phatically in the chorus. We volunteer no opinion, we
despair of guiding people, but are confirmed in our perception that Nature is all right, and that we have a good understanding with it. We must shine to a few brothers,
as palms or pines or roses among common weeds, not from
greater absolute value, but from a more convenient nature.
But 't is almost chemistry at last, though a meta-chem-
istry. I remember you were such an impatient blas-
phemer, however musically, against the adamantine iden-
tities, in your youth, that you should take your turn of
resignation now, and be a preacher of peace. But there
is a little raising of the eyebrow, now and then, in the
most passive acceptance, — if of an intellectual turn.
Here comes out around me at this moment the new June,
— the leaves say June, though the calendar says May, —
and we must needs hail our young relatives again, though
with something of the gravity of adult sons and daughters
receiving a late-born brother or sister. Nature herself
seems a little ashamed of a law so monstrous, billions of
summers, and now the old game again without a new bract
or sepal. But you will think me incorrigible with my

generalities, and you so near, and will be here again this summer; perhaps with A. W. and the other travellers. My children scan curiously your E.'s drawings, as they have seen them.

The happiest winds fill the sails of you and yours!

R. W. EMERSON.

In the year 1860, Theodore Parker died, and Emerson spoke of his life and labors at the meeting held at the Music Hall to do honor to his memory. Emerson delivered discourses on Sundays and week-days in the Music Hall to Mr. Parker's society after his death. In 1862, he lost his friend Thoreau, at whose funeral he delivered an address which was published in "The Atlantic Monthly" for August of the same year. Thoreau had many rare and admirable qualities, and Thoreau pictured by Emerson is a more living personage than White of Selborne would have been on the canvas of Sir Joshua Reynolds.

The Address on the Emancipation Proclamation was delivered in Boston in September, 1862. The feeling that inspired it may be judged by the following extract: —

"Happy are the young, who find the pestilence cleansed out of the earth, leaving open to them an honest career. Happy the old, who see Nature purified before they depart. Do not let the dying die; hold them back to this world, until you have charged their ear and heart with this message to other spiritual societies, announcing the melioration of our planet: —

"'Incertainties now crown themselves assured,
And Peace proclaims olives of endless age.'"

"The Conduct of Life" was published in 1860. The chapter on Fate might leave the reader with a feeling that what he is to do, as well as what he is to be and to suffer, is so largely predetermined for him, that his will, though formally asserted, has but a questionable fraction in adjusting him to his conditions as a portion of the universe. But let him hold fast to this reassuring statement: —

"If we must accept Fate, we are not less compelled to affirm liberty, the significance of the individual, the grandeur of duty, the power of character. . . . We are sure that, though we know not how, necessity does comport with liberty, the individual with the world, my polarity with the spirit of the times."

But the value of the essay is not so much in any light it throws on the mystery of volition, as in the striking and brilliant way in which the limitations of the individual and the inexplicable rule of law are illustrated.

"Nature is no sentimentalist, — does not cosset or pamper us. We must see that the world is rough and surly, and will not mind drowning a man or a woman; but swallows your ship like a grain of dust. . . . The way of Providence is a little rude. The habit of snake and spider, the snap of the tiger and other leapers and bloody jumpers, the crackle of the bones of his prey in the coil of the anaconda, — these are in the system, and our habits are like theirs. You have just dined, and, however scrupulously the slaughter-house is concealed in the graceful distance of miles, there is complicity, — expensive races, — race living at the expense of race. . . . Let us not deny it up and down. Providence has a wild, rough, incalculable road to its end, and it is of no use to try to whitewash its huge, mixed instrumentalities, or to dress up that terrific benefactor in a clean shirt and white neckcloth of a student in divinity."

Emerson cautions his reader against the danger of the doctrines which he believed in so fully: —

"They who talk much of destiny, their birth-star, etc., are in a lower dangerous plane, and invite the evils they fear."

But certainly no physiologist, no cattle-breeder, no Calvinistic predestinarian could put his view more vigorously than Emerson, who dearly loves a picturesque statement, has given it in these words, which have a dash of science, a flash of imagination, and a hint of the delicate wit that is one of his characteristics: —

"People are born with the moral or with the material bias; — uterine brothers with this diverging destination: and I suppose, with high magnifiers, Mr. Fraunhofer or Dr. Carpenter might come to distinguish in the embryo at the fourth day, this is a whig and that a free-soiler."

Let us see what Emerson has to say of Power: —

"All successful men have agreed in one thing — they were *causationists*. They believed that things went not by luck, but by law; that there was not a weak or a cracked link in the chain that joins the first and the last of things.

"The key to the age may be this, or that, or the other, as the young orators describe; the key to all ages is — Imbecility; imbecility in the vast majority of men at all times, and even in heroes in all but certain eminent moments; victims of gravity, custom, and fear. This gives force to the strong, — that the multitude have no habit of self-reliance or original action. . . .

"We say that success is constitutional; depends on a *plus* condition of mind and body, on power of work, on courage; that it is of main efficacy in carrying on the world, and though rarely found in the right state for an article of commerce, but oftener in the supersaturate or excess, which makes it dangerous and destructive, yet it cannot be spared, and must be had in that form, and absorbents provided to take off its edge."

The "two economics which are the best *succedanea*" for deficiency of temperament are concentration and drill. This he illustrates by example, and he also lays down some good, plain, practical rules which "Poor Richard" would have cheerfully approved. He might have accepted also the essay on Wealth as having a good sense so like his own that he could hardly tell the difference between them.

"Wealth begins in a tight roof that keeps the rain and wind out; in a good pump that yields you plenty of sweet water; in two suits of clothes, so to change your dress when you are wet; in dry sticks to burn; in a good double-wick lamp, and three meals; in a horse or a locomotive to cross the land; in a boat to cross the sea; in tools to work with; in books to read; and so, in giving, on all sides, by tools and auxiliaries, the greatest possible extension to our powers, as if it added feet, and hands, and eyes, and blood, length to the day, and knowledge, and good will. Wealth begins with these articles of necessity. . . .

"To be rich is to have a ticket of admission to the masterworks and chief men of each race. . . .

"The pulpit and the press have many commonplaces denouncing the thirst for wealth; but if men should take these moralists at their word, and leave off aiming to be rich, the moralists would rush to rekindle at all hazards this love of power in the people, lest civilization should be undone."

Who can give better counsels on Culture than Emerson? But we must borrow only a few sentences from his essay on that subject. All kinds of secrets come out as we read these essays of Emerson's. We know something of his friends and disciples who gathered round him and sat at his feet. It is not hard to believe that he was drawing one of those composite portraits Mr. Galton has given us specimens of when he wrote as follows: —

"The pest of society is egotists. . . . This goitre of egotism is so frequent among notable persons that we must infer some strong necessity in nature which it subserves; such as we see in the sexual attraction.   The preservation of the species was a point of such necessity that Nature has secured it at all hazards by immensely overloading the passion, at the risk of perpetual crime and disorder.   So egotism has its root in the cardinal necessity by which each individual persists to be what he is. . . .

"The antidotes against this organic egotism are, the range and variety of attractions, as gained by acquaintance with the world, with men of merit, with classes of society, with travel, with eminent persons, and with the high resources of philosophy, art, and religion: books, travel, society, solitude. . . .

"We can ill spare the commanding social benefits of cities; they must be used; yet cautiously and haughtily, — and will yield their best values to him who can best do without them.   Keep the town for occasions, but the habits should be formed to retirement.   Solitude, the safeguard of mediocrity, is to genius the stern friend, the cold, obscure shelter where moult the wings which will bear it farther than suns and stars."

We must remember, too, that "the calamities are our friends.   Try the rough water as well as the smooth.   Rough water can teach lessons worth knowing.   Don't be so tender at making an enemy now and then.   He who aims high must dread an easy home and popular manners."

Emerson cannot have had many enemies, if any, in his calm and noble career.   He can have cherished no enmity, on personal grounds at least.   But he refused his hand to one who had spoken ill of a friend whom he respected.   It was "the hand of Douglas" again, — the same feeling that Charles Emerson expressed in the youthful essay mentioned in the introduction to this volume.

Here are a few good sayings about Behavior: —

"There is always a best way of doing everything, if it be to boil an egg. Manners are the happy ways of doing things; each once a stroke of genius or of love, — now repeated and hardened into usage."

Thus it is that Mr. Emerson speaks of Manners in his essay under the above title: —

"The basis of good manners is self-reliance. . . . Manners require time, as nothing is more vulgar than haste. . . .

"Men take each other's measure, when they meet for the first time, — and every time they meet. . . .

"It is not what talents or genius a man has, but how he is to his talents, that constitutes friendship and character. The man that stands by himself, the universe stands by him also."

In his Essay on Worship, Emerson ventures the following prediction: —

"The religion which is to guide and fulfil the present and coming ages, whatever else it be, must be intellectual. The scientific mind must have a faith which is science. . . . There will be a new church founded on moral science, at first cold and naked, a babe in a manger again, the algebra and mathematics of ethical law, the church of men to come, without shawms or psaltery or sackbut; but it will have heaven and earth for its beams and rafters; science for symbol and illustration; it will fast enough gather beauty, music, picture, poetry."

It is a bold prophecy, but who can doubt that all improbable and unverifiable traditional knowledge of all kinds will make way for the established facts of science and history when these last reach it in their onward movement? It may be remarked that he now speaks of science more respectfully than of old. I suppose this essay was of later date than "Beauty," or "Illusions." But accidental circumstances made such confusion in the strata of Emerson's published thought that one is often at a loss to know whether a sentence came from the older or the newer layer.

We come to "Considerations by the Way." The common-sense side of Emerson's mind has so much in common with the plain practical intelligence of Franklin that it is a pleasure to find the philosopher of the nineteenth century quoting the philosopher of the eighteenth.

"Franklin said, 'Mankind are very superficial and dastardly: they begin upon a thing, but, meeting with a difficulty, they fly from it discouraged: but they have the means if they would employ them.'"

"Shall we judge a country by the majority, or by the minority? By the minority, surely." Here we have the doctrine of the "saving remnant," which we have since recognized in Mr. Matthew Arnold's well-remembered lecture. Our republican philosopher is clearly enough outspoken on this matter of the *vox populi*.

"Leave this hypocritical prating about the masses. Masses are rude, lame, unmade, pernicious in their demands, and need not to be flattered, but to be schooled. I wish not to concede anything to them, but to tame, drill, divide, and break them up, and draw individuals out of them."

Perè Bouhours asked a question about the Germans which found its answer in due time. After reading what Emerson says about "the masses," one is tempted to ask whether a philosopher can ever have "a constituency" and be elected to Congress? Certainly the essay just quoted from would not make a very promising campaign document.

Perhaps there was no great necessity for Emerson's returning to the subject of Beauty, to which he had devoted a chapter of "Nature," and of which he had so often discoursed incidentally. But he says so many things worth reading in the essay thus entitled in "The Conduct of Life," that we need not trouble ourselves about repetitions. The essay is satirical and poetical rather than philosophical. Satirical when he speaks of science with something of that old feeling betrayed by his brother Charles when he was writing in 1828; poetical in the flight of imagination with which he enlivens, entertains, stimulates, inspires, — or as some may prefer to say, — amuses his listeners and readers.

The reader must decide which of these effects is produced by the following passage: —

"The feat of the imagination is in showing the convertibility of everything into every other thing. Facts which had never before left their stark common-sense suddenly figure as Eleusinian mysteries. My boots and chair and candlestick are fairies in disguise, meteors, and constellations. All the facts in Nature are nouns of the intellect, and make the grammar of the eternal language. Every word has a double, treble, or centuple use and meaning. What! has my stove and pepper-pot a false bottom? I cry you mercy, good shoe-box! I did not know you were a jewel-case. Chaff and dust begin to sparkle, and are clothed about with immortality. And there is a joy in perceiving the representative or symbolic character of a fact, which no bare fact or event can ever give. There are no days so memorable as those which vibrated to some stroke of the imagination."

One is reminded of various things in reading this sentence. An ounce of alcohol, or a few whiffs from an opium-pipe, may easily make a day memorable by bringing on this imaginative delirium, which is apt, if often repeated, to run into visions of rodents and reptiles. A coarser satirist than Emerson indulged his fancy in "Meditations on a Broomstick," which My Lady Berkeley heard seriously and to edification. Meditations on a "Shoe-box" are less promising, but no doubt something could be made of it. A poet must select, and if he stoops too low he cannot lift the object he would fain idealize.

The habitual readers of Emerson do not mind an occasional over-statement, extravagance, paradox, eccentricity; they find them amusing and not misleading. But the accountants, for whom two and two always make four, come upon one of these passages and shut the book up as wanting in sanity. Without a certain sensibility to the humorous, no one should venture upon Emerson. If he had seen the lecturer's smile as he delivered one of his playful statements of a runaway truth, fact unhorsed by imagination, sometimes by wit, or humor, he would have found a meaning in his words which the featureless printed page could never show him.

The essay on Illusions has little which we have not met with, or shall not find repeating itself in the poems.

During this period Emerson contributed many articles in prose and verse to "The Atlantic Monthly," and several to "The Dial," a second periodical of that name, published in Cincinnati. Some of these have been, or will be, elsewhere referred to.

CHAPTER X.

1863–1868. ÆT. 60–65.

"Boston Hymn." — "Voluntaries." — Other Poems. — "May-Day and Other Pieces." — Remarks at the Funeral Services for Abraham Lincoln. — Essay on Persian Poetry. — Remarks at the Organization of the Free Religious Association. — "Progress of Culture." Address before the Phi Beta Kappa Society of Harvard University. — Course of Lectures in Philadelphia. — The Degree of LL. D. conferred upon Emerson by Harvard University. — "Terminus."

THE "Boston Hymn" was read by Emerson in the Music Hall, on the first day of January, 1863. It is a rough piece of verse, but noble from beginning to end. One verse of it, beginning "Pay ransom to the owner," has been already quoted; these are the three that precede it: —

> "I cause from every creature
>   His proper good to flow :
> As much as he is and doeth,
>   So much shall he bestow.

> "But laying hands on another
>   To coin his labor and sweat,
> He goes in pawn to his victim
>   For eternal years in debt.

> "To-day unbind the captive,
>   So only are ye unbound ;
> Lift up a people from the dust,
>   Trump of their rescue, sound ! "

"Voluntaries," published in the same year in "The Atlantic Monthly," is more dithyrambic in its measure and of a more Pindaric elevation than the plain song of the "Boston Hymn."

> " But best befriended of the God
> He who, in evil times,
> Warned by an inward voice,
> Heeds not the darkness and the dread,
> Biding by his rule and choice,
> Feeling only the fiery thread
> Leading over heroic ground,
> Walled with mortal terror round,
> To the aim which him allures,
> And the sweet heaven his deed secures.
> Peril around, all else appalling,
> Cannon in front and leaden rain,
> Him Duty through the clarion calling
> To the van called not in vain."

It is in this poem that we find the lines which, a moment after they were written, seemed as if they had been carved on marble for a thousand years: —

> " So nigh is grandeur to our dust,
> So near is God to man,
> When Duty whispers low, *Thou must*,
> The youth replies, *I can*."

"Saadi " was published in "The Atlantic Monthly " in 1864, "My Garden " in 1866, "Terminus " in 1867. In the same year these last poems with many others were collected in a small volume, entitled "May-Day and Other Pieces." The general headings of these poems are as follows: May-Day; The Adirondacs; Occasional and Miscellaneous Pieces; Nature and Life; Elements; Quatrains; Translations. Some of these poems, which were written at long intervals, have been referred to in previous pages. "The Adirondacs" is a pleasant narrative, but not to be compared for its poetical character with "May-Day," one passage from which, beginning,

"I saw the bud-crowned Spring go forth,"

is surpassingly imaginative and beautiful. In this volume will be found "Brahma," "Days," and others which are well known to all readers of poetry.

Emerson's delineations of character are remarkable for high-relief and sharp-cut lines. In his Remarks at the Funeral Services for Abraham Lincoln, held in Concord, April 19, 1865, he drew the portrait of the homespun-robed chief of the republic with equal breadth and delicacy: —

"Here was place for no holiday magistrate, no fair-weather sailor; the new pilot was hurried to the helm in a tornado. In four years, — four years of battle-days, — his endurance, his fertility of resources, his magnanimity, were sorely tried and never found wanting. There, by his courage, his justice, his even temper, his fertile counsel, his humanity, he stood a heroic figure in the centre of a heroic epoch. He is the true history of the American people in his time. Step by step he walked before them; slow with their slowness, quickening his march by theirs, the true representative of this continent; an entirely public man; father of his country; the pulse of twenty millions throbbing in his heart, the thought of their minds articulated by his tongue."

In his Remarks at the Organization of the Free Religious Association, Emerson stated his leading thought about religion in a very succinct and sufficiently "transcendental" way: intelligibly for those who wish to understand him; mystically to those who do not accept or wish to accept the doctrine shadowed forth in his poem, "The Sphinx."

"As soon as every man is apprised of the Divine Presence within his own mind, — is apprised that the perfect law of duty corresponds with the laws of chemistry, of vegetation, of astronomy, as face to face in a glass; that the basis of duty, the order of society, the power of character, the wealth of culture, the perfection of taste, all draw their essence from this moral sentiment; then we have a religion that exalts, that commands all the social and all the private action."

Nothing could be more wholesome in a meeting of creed-killers than the suggestive remark, —

"What I expected to find here was, some practical suggestions by which we were to reanimate and reorganize for ourselves the true Church, the pure worship. Pure doctrine always bears fruit in pure benefits. It is only by good works, it is only on the basis of active duty, that worship finds expression. . . . The interests that grow out of a meeting like this should bind us with new strength to the old eternal duties."

In a later address before the same association, Emerson says: —

"I object, of course, to the claim of miraculous dispensation, — certainly not to the *doctrine* of Christianity. . . . If you are childish and exhibit your saint as a worker of wonders, a thaumaturgist, I am repelled. That claim takes his teachings out of nature, and permits official and arbitrary senses to be grafted on the teachings."

The "Progress of Culture" was delivered as a Phi Beta Kappa oration just thirty years after his first address before the same society. It is very instructive to compare the two orations written at the interval of a whole generation: one in 1837, at the age of thirty-

four; the other in 1867, at the age of sixty-four.
Both are hopeful, but the second is more sanguine
than the first. He recounts what he considers the
recent gains of the reforming movement: —

"Observe the marked ethical quality of the innovations
urged or adopted. The new claim of woman to a political status is itself an honorable testimony to the civilization which has given her a civil status new in history.
Now that by the increased humanity of law she controls
her property, she inevitably takes the next step to her
share in power."

He enumerates many other gains, from the war or
from the growth of intelligence, — "All, one may say,
in a high degree revolutionary, teaching nations the
taking of governments into their own hands, and
superseding kings."

He repeats some of his fundamental formulæ.

"The foundation of culture, as of character, is at last
the moral sentiment."

"Great men are they who see that spiritual is stronger
than any material force, that thoughts rule the world."

"Periodicity, reaction, are laws of mind as well as of
matter."

And most encouraging it is to read in 1884 what
was written in 1867, — especially in the view of
future possibilities : —

"Bad kings and governors help us, if only they are
bad enough." *Non tali auxilio*, we exclaim, with a
shudder of remembrance, and are very glad to read
these concluding words: "I read the promise of better
times and of greater men."

In the year 1866, Emerson reached the age which
used to be spoken of as the "grand climacteric." In

that year Harvard University conferred upon him the
degree of Doctor of Laws, the highest honor in its gift.

In that same year, having left home on one of his
last lecturing trips, he met his son, Dr. Edward
Waldo Emerson, at the Brevoort House, in New
York. Then, and in that place, he read to his son
the poem afterwards published in "The Atlantic
Monthly," and in his second volume, under the title
"Terminus." This was the first time that Dr. Emerson recognized the fact that his father felt himself
growing old. The thought, which must have been
long shaping itself in the father's mind, had been so
far from betraying itself that it was a shock to the
son to hear it plainly avowed. The poem is one of
his noblest; he could not fold his robes about him
with more of serene dignity than in these solemn lines.
The reader may remember that one passage from it
has been quoted for a particular purpose, but here is
the whole poem: —

TERMINUS.

It is time to be old,
To take in sail: —
The god of bounds,
Who sets to seas a shore,
Came to me in his fatal rounds,
And said : "No more !
No farther shoot
Thy broad ambitious branches, and thy root.
Fancy departs : no more invent ;
Contract thy firmament
To compass of a tent.
There's not enough for this and that,
Make thy option which of two ;
Economize the failing river,
Not the less revere the Giver,

Leave the many and hold the few.
Timely wise accept the terms,
Soften the fall with wary foot ;
A little while
Still plan and smile,
And, — fault of novel germs, —
Mature the unfallen fruit.
Curse, if thou wilt, thy sires,
Bad husbands of their fires,
Who, when they gave thee breath,
Failed to bequeath
The needful sinew stark as once,
The Baresark marrow to thy bones,
But left a legacy of ebbing veins,
Inconstant heat and nerveless reins, —
Amid the Muses, left thee deaf and dumb,
Amid the gladiators, halt and numb."

As the bird trims her to the gale
I trim myself to the storm of time,
I man the rudder, reef the sail,
Obey the voice at eve obeyed at prime :
" Lowly faithful, banish fear,
Right onward drive unharmed ;
The port, well worth the cruise, is near,
And every wave is charmed."

CHAPTER XI.

1868–1873. Æt. 65–70.

DURING three successive years, 1868, 1869, 1870, Emerson delivered a series of lectures at Harvard University on the "Natural History of the Intellect." These lectures, as I am told by Dr. Emerson, cost him a great deal of labor, but I am not aware that they have been collected or reported. They will be referred to in the course of this chapter, in an extract from Professor Thayer's "Western Journey with Mr. Emerson." He is there reported as saying that he cared very little for metaphysics. It is very certain that he makes hardly any use of the ordinary terms employed by metaphysicians. If he does not hold the words "subject" and "object," with their adjectives, in the same contempt that Mr. Ruskin shows for them, he very rarely employs either of these expressions. Once he ventures on the *not me*, but in the main he uses plain English handles for the few metaphysical tools he has occasion to employ.

"Society and Solitude" was published in 1870.

The first essay in the volume bears the same name as the volume itself.

In this first essay, Emerson is very fair to the antagonistic claims of solitary and social life. He recognizes the organic necessity of solitude. We are driven "as with whips into the desert." But there is danger in this seclusion. "Now and then a man exquisitely made can live alone, and must; but coop up most men and you undo them. . . . Here again, as so often, Nature delights to put us between extreme antagonisms, and our safety is in the skill with which we keep the diagonal line. . . . The conditions are met, if we keep our independence, yet do not lose our sympathy."

The essay on Civilization is pleasing, putting familiar facts in a very agreeable way. The framed or stone house in place of the cave or the camp, the building of roads, the change from war, hunting, and pasturage to agriculture, the division of labor, the skilful combinations of civil government, the diffusion of knowledge through the press, are well-worn subjects which he treats agreeably, if not with special brilliancy : —

"Right position of woman in the State is another index. . . . Place the sexes in right relations of mutual respect, and a severe morality gives that essential charm to woman which educates all that is delicate, poetic, and self-sacrificing; breeds courtesy and learning, conversation and wit, in her rough mate; so that I have thought a sufficient measure of civilization is the influence of good women."

My attention was drawn to one paragraph for a reason which my reader will readily understand, and I trust look upon good-naturedly : —

"The ship, in its latest complete equipment, is an abridgment and compend of a nation's arts: the ship steered by compass and chart, longitude reckoned by lunar observation and by chronometer, driven by steam; and in wildest sea-mountains, at vast distances from home, —

> " ' The pulses of her iron heart
>   Go beating through the storm.' "

I cannot be wrong, it seems to me, in supposing those two lines to be an incorrect version of these two from a poem of my own called "The Steamboat:" —

> "The beating of her restless heart
>   Still sounding through the storm."

It is never safe to quote poetry from memory, at least while the writer lives, for he is ready to "cavil on the ninth part of a hair" where his verses are concerned. But extreme accuracy was not one of Emerson's special gifts, and vanity whispers to the misrepresented versifier that

> 't is better to be quoted wrong
> Than to be quoted not at all.

This essay of Emerson's is irradiated by a single precept that is worthy to stand by the side of that which Juvenal says came from heaven. How could the man in whose thought such a meteoric expression suddenly announced itself fail to recognize it as divine? It is not strange that he repeats it on the page next the one where we first see it. Not having any golden letters to print it in, I will underscore it for italics, and doubly underscore it in the second extract for small capitals: —

"Now that is the wisdom of a man, in every instance of his labor, to *hitch his wagon to a star*, and see his chore done by the gods themselves."

"'It was a great instruction,' said a saint in Crom-well's war, 'that the best courages are but beams of the Almighty.' HITCH YOUR WAGON TO A STAR. Let us not fag in paltry works which serve our pot and bag alone. Let us not lie and steal. No god will help. We shall find all their teams going the other way, — Charles's Wain, Great Bear, Orion, Leo, Hercules; every god will leave us. Work rather for those interests which the di-vinities honor and promote, — justice, love, freedom, knowledge, utility."

Charles's Wain and the Great Bear, he should have been reminded, are the same constellation; the *Dip-per* is what our people often call it, and the country folk all know "the pīnters," which guide their eyes to the North Star.

I find in the essay on Art many of the thoughts with which we are familiar in Emerson's poem, "The Problem." It will be enough to cite these passages: —

"We feel in seeing a noble building which rhymes well, as we do in hearing a perfect song, that it is spiritually organic; that is, had a necessity in nature for being; was one of the possible forms in the Divine mind, and is now only discovered and executed by the artist, not arbitrarily composed by him. And so every genuine work of art has as much reason for being as the earth and the sun.

"The Iliad of Homer, the songs of David, the odes of Pindar, the tragedies of Æschylus, the Doric temples, the Gothic cathedrals, the plays of Shakespeare, all and each were made not for sport, but in grave earnest, in tears and smiles of suffering and loving men. . . .

"The Gothic cathedrals were built when the builder and the priest and the people were overpowered by their faith. Love and fear laid every stone. . . .

"Our arts are happy hits. We are like the musician on the lake, whose melody is sweeter than he knows."

The discourse on Eloquence is more systematic,

more professorial, than many of the others. A few brief extracts will give the key to its general purport: —

"Eloquence must be grounded on the plainest narrative. Afterwards, it may warm itself until it exhales symbols of every kind and color, speaks only through the most poetic forms; but, first and last, it must still be at bottom a biblical statement of fact. . . .

"He who will train himself to mastery in this science of persuasion must lay the emphasis of education, not on popular arts, but on character and insight. . . .

"The highest platform of eloquence is the moral sentiment. . . .

"Its great masters . . . were grave men, who preferred their integrity to their talent, and esteemed that object for which they toiled, whether the prosperity of their country, or the laws, or a reformation, or liberty of speech or of the press, or letters, or morals, as above the whole world and themselves also."

"Domestic Life" begins with a picture of childhood so charming that it sweetens all the good counsel which follows like honey round the rim of the goblet which holds some tonic draught: —

"Welcome to the parents the puny struggler, strong in his weakness, his little arms more irresistible than the soldier's, his lips touched with persuasion which Chatham and Pericles in manhood had not. His unaffected lamentations when he lifts up his voice on high, or, more beautiful, the sobbing child, — the face all liquid grief, as he tries to swallow his vexation, — soften all hearts to pity, and to mirthful and clamorous compassion. The small despot asks so little that all reason and all nature are on his side. His ignorance is more charming than all knowledge, and his little sins more bewitching than any virtue. His flesh is angel's flesh, all alive. . . . All day, between his three or four sleeps, he cooes like a pigeon-house, sputters and spurs and puts on his faces of importance; and when he fasts, the little Pharisee fails not to sound his trumpet before him."

Emerson has favored his audiences and readers with what he knew about Farming. Dr. Emerson tells me that this discourse was read as an address before the Middlesex Agricultural Society, and printed in the "Transactions" of that association. He soon found out that the hoe and the spade were not the tools he was meant to work with, but he had some general ideas about farming which he expressed very happily: —

"The farmer's office is precise and important, but you must not try to paint him in rose-color; you cannot make pretty compliments to fate and gravitation, whose minister he is. . . . This hard work will always be done by one kind of man; not by scheming speculators, nor by soldiers, nor professors, nor readers of Tennyson; but by men of endurance, deep-chested, long-winded, tough, slow and sure, and timely."

Emerson's chemistry and physiology are not profound, but they are correct enough to make a fine richly colored poetical picture in his imaginative presentation. He tells the commonest facts so as to make them almost a surprise: —

"By drainage we went down to a subsoil we did not know, and have found there is a Concord under old Concord, which we are now getting the best crops from; a Middlesex under Middlesex; and, in fine, that Massachusetts has a basement story more valuable and that promises to pay a better rent than all the superstructure."

In "Works and Days" there is much good reading, but I will call attention to one or two points only, as having a slight special interest of their own. The

first is the boldness of Emerson's assertions and predictions in matters belonging to science and art.
Thus, he speaks of "the transfusion of the blood, —
which, in Paris, it was claimed, enables a man to
change his blood as often as his linen!" And once
more, —

"We are to have the balloon yet, and the next war will
be fought in the air."

Possibly; but it is perhaps as safe to predict that it
will be fought on wheels; the soldiers on bicycles, the
officers on tricycles.

The other point I have marked is that we find in
this essay a prose version of the fine poem printed in
"May-Day" under the title "Days." I shall refer to
this more particularly hereafter.

It is wronging the essay on Books to make extracts from it. It is all an extract, taken from years
of thought in the lonely study and the public libraries.
If I commit the wrong I have spoken of, it is under
protest against myself. Every word of this essay
deserves careful reading. But here are a few sentences I have selected for the reader's consideration : —

"There are books; and it is practicable to read them
because they are so few. . . .

"I visit occasionally the Cambridge library, and I can
seldom go there without renewing the conviction that the
best of it all is already within the four walls of my study
at home. . . .

"The three practical rules which I have to offer are,
1. Never read any book that is not a year old. 2. Never
read any but famed books. 3. Never read any but what
you like, or, in Shakespeare's phrase, —

"' No profit goes where is no pleasure ta'en ;
    In brief, sir, study what you most affect.' "

Emerson has a good deal to say about conversation in his essay on Clubs, but nothing very notable on the special subject of the essay. Perhaps his diary would have something of interest with reference to the Saturday Club, of which he was a member, which, in fact, formed itself around him as a nucleus, and which he attended very regularly. But he was not given to personalities, and among the men of genius and of talent whom he met there no one was quieter, but none saw and heard and remembered more. He was hardly what Dr. Johnson would have called a "clubable" man, yet he enjoyed the meetings in his still way, or he would never have come from Concord so regularly to attend them. He gives two good reasons for the existence of a club like that of which I have been speaking: —

"I need only hint the value of the club for bringing masters in their several arts to compare and expand their views, to come to an understanding on these points, and so that their united opinion shall have its just influence on public questions of education and politics. . . .

"A principal purpose also is the hospitality of the club, as a means of receiving a worthy foreigner with mutual advantage."

I do not think "public questions of education and politics" were very prominent at the social meetings of the Saturday Club, but "worthy foreigners," and now and then one not so worthy, added variety to the meetings of the company, which included a wide range of talents and callings.

All that Emerson has to say about Courage is worth listening to, for he was a truly brave man in that sphere of action where there are more cowards

than are found in the battle-field.   He spoke his convictions fearlessly; he carried the spear of Ithuriel,
but he wore no breastplate save that which protects
him

> "Whose armor is his honest thought,
> And simple truth his utmost skill."

He mentions three qualities as attracting the wonder
and reverence of mankind: 1. Disinterestedness; 2.
Practical Power; 3. Courage. "I need not show how
much it is esteemed, for the people give it the first
rank.   They forgive everything to it. . . . And any
man who puts his life in peril in a cause which is esteemed becomes the darling of all men."   There are
good and inspiriting lessons for young and old in this
essay or lecture, which closes with the spirited ballad
of "George Nidiver," written "by a lady to whom all
the particulars of the fact are exactly known."

Men will read any essay or listen to any lecture
which has for its subject, like the one now before me,
"Success."   Emerson complains of the same things
in America which Carlyle groaned over in England:

"We countenance each other in this life of show, puf-
fing, advertisement, and manufacture of public opinion;
and excellence is lost sight of in the hunger for sudden
performance and praise. . . .

"Now, though I am by no means sure that the reader
will assent to all my propositions, yet I think we shall
agree in my first rule for success, — that we shall drop the
brag and the advertisement and take Michael Angelo's
course, 'to confide in one's self and be something of worth
and value.' "

Reading about Success is after all very much like
reading in old books of alchemy.   "How not to do
it," is the lesson of all the books and treatises.   Geber
and Albertus Magnus, Roger Bacon and Raymond

Lully, and the whole crew of *pauperes alcumistœ*, all give the most elaborate directions showing their student how to fail in transmuting Saturn into Luna and Sol and making a billionaire of himself. "Success" in its vulgar sense — the gaining of money and position — is not to be reached by following the rules of an instructor. Our "self-made men," who govern the country by their wealth and influence, have found their place by adapting themselves to the particular circumstances in which they were placed, and not by studying the broad maxims of "Poor Richard," or any other moralist or economist. For such as these is meant the cheap cynical saying quoted by Emerson, "*Rien ne réussit mieux que le succès.*"

But this is not the aim and end of Emerson's teaching: —

"I fear the popular notion of success stands in direct opposition in all points to the real and wholesome success. One adores public opinion, the other private opinion; one fame, the other desert; one feats, the other humility; one lucre, the other love; one monopoly, and the other hospitality of mind."

And so, though there is no alchemy in this lecture, it is profitable reading, assigning its true value to the sterling gold of character, the gaining of which is true success, as against the brazen idol of the market-place.

The essay on Old Age has a special value from its containing two personal reminiscences: one of the venerable Josiah Quincy, a brief mention; the other the detailed record of a visit in the year 1825, Emerson being then twenty-two years old, to ex-President John Adams, soon after the election of his son to the Presidency. It is enough to allude to these, which every reader will naturally turn to first of all.

But many thoughts worth gathering are dropped along these pages. He recounts the benefits of age; the perilous capes and shoals it has weathered; the fact that a success more or less signifies little, so that the old man may go below his own mark with impunity; the feeling that he has found expression, — that his condition, in particular and in general, allows the utterance of his mind; the pleasure of completing his secular affairs, leaving all in the best posture for the future: —

"When life has been well spent, age is a loss of what it can well spare, — muscular strength, organic instincts, gross bulk, and works that belong to these. But the central wisdom which was old in infancy is young in fourscore years, and, dropping off obstructions, leaves in happy subjects the mind purified and wise. I have heard that whoever loves is in no condition old. I have heard that whenever the name of man is spoken, the doctrine of immortality is announced; it cleaves to his constitution. The mode of it baffles our wit, and no whisper comes to us from the other side. But the inference from the working of intellect, hiving knowledge, hiving skill, — at the end of life just ready to be born, — affirms the inspirations of affection and of the moral sentiment."

Other literary labors of Emerson during this period were the Introduction to "Plutarch's Morals" in 1870, and a Preface to William Ellery Channing's poem, "The Wanderer," in 1871. He made a speech at Howard University, Washington, in 1872.

In the year 1871, Emerson made a visit to California with a very pleasant company, concerning which Mr. John M. Forbes, one of whose sons married Emerson's daughter Edith, writes to me as follows. Professor James B. Thayer, to whom he refers, has more recently written and published an account of this

trip, from which some extracts will follow Mr.
Forbes's letter : —

Boston, *February* 6, 1884.

My dear Dr., — What little I can give will be of a
very rambling character.

One of the first memories of Emerson which comes up is
my meeting him on the steamboat at returning from De-
troit East.   I persuaded him to stop over at Niagara,
which he had never seen.   We took a carriage and drove
around the circuit.   It was in early summer, perhaps in
1848 or 1849.   When we came to Table Rock on the
British side, our driver took us down on the outer part of
the rock in the carriage.   We passed on by rail, and the
next day's papers brought us the telegraphic news that
Table Rock had fallen over; perhaps we were among the
last persons on it!

About 1871 I made up a party for California, including
Mr. Emerson, his daughter Edith, and a number of gay
young people.   We drove with B——, the famous Ver-
mont coachman, up to the Geysers, and then made the
journey to the Yosemite Valley by wagon and on horseback.   I wish I could give you more than a mere outline
picture of the sage at this time.   With the thermometer
at 100° he would sometimes drive with the buffalo robes
drawn up over his knees, apparently indifferent to the
weather, gazing on the new and grand scenes of mountain
and valley through which we journeyed.   I especially remember once, when riding down the steep side of a mountain, his reins hanging loose, the bit entirely out of the
horse's mouth, without his being aware that this was an
unusual method of riding Pegasus, so fixed was his gaze
into space, and so unconscious was he, at the moment, of
his surroundings.

In San Francisco he visited with us the dens of the
opium smokers, in damp cellars, with rows of shelves
around, on which were deposited the stupefied Mongo-
lians; perhaps the lowest haunts of humanity to be found
in the world.   The contrast between them and the serene

eye and undisturbed brow of the sage was a sight for all beholders.

When we reached Salt Lake City on our way home he made a point of calling on Brigham Young, then at the summit of his power. The Prophet, or whatever he was called, was a burly, bull-necked man of hard sense, really leading a great industrial army. He did not seem to appreciate who his visitor was, at any rate gave no sign of so doing, and the chief interest of the scene was the wide contrast between these leaders of spiritual and of material forces.

I regret not having kept any notes of what was said on this and other occasions, but if by chance you could get hold of Professor J. B. Thayer, who was one of our party, he could no doubt give you some notes that would be valuable.

Perhaps the latest picture that remains in my mind of our friend is his wandering along the beaches and under the trees at Naushon, no doubt carrying home large stealings from my domain there, which lost none of their value from being transferred to his pages. Next to his private readings which he gave us there, the most notable recollection is that of his intense amusement at some comical songs which our young people used to sing, developing a sense of humor which a superficial observer would hardly have discovered, but which you and I know he possessed in a marked degree.

Yours always,
J. M. FORBES.

Professor James B. Thayer's little book, "A Western Journey with Mr. Emerson," is a very entertaining account of the same trip concerning which Mr. Forbes wrote the letter just given. Professor Thayer kindly read many of his notes to me before his account was published, and allows me to make such use of the book as I see fit. Such liberty must not be abused, and I will content myself with a few passages in which

Emerson has a part. No extract will interest the reader more than the following: —

"'How *can* Mr. Emerson,' said one of the younger members of the party to me that day, 'be so agreeable, all the time, without getting tired!' It was the *naïve* expression of what we all had felt.   There was never a more agreeable travelling companion; he was always accessible, cheerful, sympathetic, considerate, tolerant; and there was always that same respectful interest in those with whom he talked, even the humblest, which raised them in their own estimation.   One thing particularly impressed me, — the sense that he seemed to have of a certain great amplitude of time and leisure.   It was the behavior of one who really *believed* in an immortal life, and had adjusted his conduct accordingly; so that, beautiful and grand as the natural objects were, among which our journey lay, they were matched by the sweet elevation of character, and the spiritual charm of our gracious friend. Years afterwards, on that memorable day of his funeral at Concord, I found that a sentence from his own essay on Immortality haunted my mind, and kept repeating itself all the day long; it seemed to point to the sources of his power: 'Meantime the true disciples saw through the letter the doctrine of eternity, which dissolved the poor corpse, and Nature also, and gave grandeur to the passing hour.'"

This extract will be appropriately followed by another alluding to the same subject.

"The next evening, Sunday, the 23d, Mr. Emerson read his address on Immortality, at Dr. Stebbins's church.   It was the first time that he had spoken on the Western coast; never did he speak better.   It was, in the main, the same noble essay that has since been printed.

"At breakfast the next morning we had the newspaper, the 'Alta California.' It gave a meagre outline of the address, but praised it warmly, and closed with the following observations: 'All left the church feeling that an elegant tribute had been paid to the creative genius of the Great First Cause, and that a masterly use of the English language had contributed to that end.'"

The story used to be told that after the Reverend Horace Holley had delivered a prayer on some public occasion, Major Ben. Russell, of ruddy face and ruffled shirt memory, editor of "The Columbian Centinel," spoke of it in his paper the next day as "the most eloquent prayer ever addressed to a Boston audience."

The "Alta California's" "elegant tribute" is not quite up to this rhetorical altitude.

"'The minister,' said he, 'is in no danger of losing his position; he represents the moral sense and the humanities.' He spoke of his own reasons for leaving the pulpit, and added that 'some one had lately come to him whose conscience troubled him about retaining the name of Christian; he had replied that he himself had no difficulty about it. When he was called a Platonist, or a Christian, or a Republican, he welcomed it. It did not bind him to what he did not like. What is the use of going about and setting up a flag of negation?'

"I made bold to ask him what he had in mind in naming his recent course of lectures at Cambridge, 'The Natural History of the Intellect.' This opened a very interesting conversation; but, alas! I could recall but little of it, — little more than the mere hintings of what he said. He cared very little for metaphysics. But he thought that as a man grows he observes certain facts about his own mind, — about memory, for example. These he had set down from time to time. As for making any methodical history, he did not undertake it."

Emerson met Brigham Young at Salt Lake City, as has been mentioned, but neither seems to have made much impression upon the other. Emerson spoke of the Mormons. Some one had said, "They impress the common people, through their imagination, by Bible-names and imagery." "Yes," he said, "it is an after-clap of Puritanism. But one would think that after this Father Abraham could go no further."

The charm of Boswell's Life of Johnson is that it not merely records his admirable conversation, but also gives us many of those lesser peculiarities which are as necessary to a true biography as lights and shades to a portrait on canvas. We are much obliged to Professor Thayer, therefore, for the two following pleasant recollections which he has been good-natured enough to preserve for us, and with which we will take leave of his agreeable little volume: —

"At breakfast we had, among other things, pie. This article at breakfast was one of Mr. Emerson's weaknesses. A pie stood before him now. He offered to help somebody from it, who declined; and then one or two others, who also declined; and then Mr. ——; he too declined. 'But, Mr. ——!' Mr. Emerson remonstrated, with humorous emphasis, thrusting the knife under a piece of the pie, and putting the entire weight of his character into his manner, — 'but, Mr. ——, *what is pie for?*'"

A near friend of mine, a lady, was once in the cars with Emerson, and when they stopped for the refreshment of the passengers he was very desirous of procuring something at the station for her solace. Presently he advanced upon her with a cup of tea in one hand and a wedge of pie in the other, — such a wedge! She could hardly have been more dismayed if one of Cæsar's *cunei*, or wedges of soldiers, had made a charge against her.

Yet let me say here that pie, often foolishly abused, is a good creature, at the right time and in angles of thirty or forty degrees. In semicircles and quadrants it may sometimes prove too much for delicate stomachs. But here was Emerson, a hopelessly confirmed pie-eater, never, so far as I remember, complaining of dyspepsia; and there, on the other side, was Carlyle, feeding largely on wholesome oatmeal, groaning with indigestion all his days, and living with half his self-consciousness habitually centred beneath his diaphragm.

Like his friend Carlyle and like Tennyson, Emerson had a liking for a whiff of tobacco-smoke: —

"When alone," he said, "he rarely cared to finish a whole cigar. But in company it was singular to see how different it was. To one who found it difficult to meet people, as he did, the effect of a cigar was agreeable; one who is smoking may be as silent as he likes, and yet be good company. And so Hawthorne used to say that he found it. On this journey Mr. Emerson generally smoked a single cigar after our mid-day dinner, or after tea, and occasionally after both. This was multiplying, several times over, anything that was usual with him at home."

Professor Thayer adds in a note: —

"Like Milton, Mr. Emerson 'was extraordinary temperate in his Diet,' and he used even less tobacco. Milton's quiet day seems to have closed regularly with a pipe; he 'supped,' we are told, 'upon . . . some light thing; and after a pipe of tobacco and a glass of water went to bed.'"

As Emerson's name has been connected with that of Milton in its nobler aspects, it can do no harm to contemplate him, like Milton, indulging in this semi-philosophical luxury.

One morning in July, 1872, Mr. and Mrs. Emerson woke to find their room filled with smoke and fire coming through the floor of a closet in the room over them. The alarm was given, and the neighbors gathered and did their best to put out the flames, but the upper part of the house was destroyed, and with it were burned many papers of value to Emerson, including his father's sermons. Emerson got wet and chilled, and it seems too probable that the shock hastened that gradual loss of memory which came over his declining years.

His kind neighbors did all they could to save his property and relieve his temporary needs. A study was made ready for him in the old Court House, and the "Old Manse," which had sheltered his grandfather, and others nearest to him, received him once more as its tenant.

On the 15th of October he spoke at a dinner given in New York in honor of James Anthony Froude, the historian, and in the course of this same month he set out on his third visit to Europe, accompanied by his daughter Ellen. We have little to record of this visit, which was suggested as a relief and recreation while his home was being refitted for him. He went to Egypt, but so far as I have learned the Sphinx had no message for him, and in the state of mind in which he found himself upon the mysterious and dream-compelling Nile it may be suspected that the landscape with its palms and pyramids was an unreal vision, — that, as to his humble-bee,

" All was picture as he passed."

But while he was voyaging his friends had not forgotten him. The sympathy with him in his misfortune was general and profound. It did not confine itself to expressions of feeling, but a spontaneous movement organized itself almost without effort. If any such had been needed, the attached friend whose name is appended to the address to the subscribers to the fund for rebuilding Mr. Emerson's house would have been as energetic in this new cause as he had been in the matter of procuring the reprint of "Sartor Resartus." I have his kind permission to publish the whole correspondence relating to the friendly project so happily carried out.

To the Subscribers to the Fund for the Rebuilding of Mr. Emerson's House, after the Fire of July 24, 1872 :

The death of Mr. Emerson has removed any objection which may have before existed to the printing of the following correspondence. I have now caused this to be done, that each subscriber may have the satisfaction of possessing a copy of the touching and affectionate letters in which he expressed his delight in this, to him, most unexpected demonstration of personal regard and attachment, in the offer to restore for him his ruined home.

No enterprise of the kind was ever more fortunate and successful in its purpose and in its results. The prompt and cordial response to the proposed subscription was most gratifying. No contribution was solicited from any one. The simple suggestion to a few friends of Mr. Emerson that an opportunity was now offered to be of service to him was all that was needed. From the first day on which it was made, the day after the fire, letters began to come in, with cheques for large and small amounts, so that in less than three weeks I was enabled to send to Judge Hoar the sum named in his letter as received by him on the 13th of August, and presented by him to Mr. Emerson the next morning, at the Old Manse, with fitting words.

Other subscriptions were afterwards received, increasing the amount on my book to eleven thousand six hundred and twenty dollars. A part of this was handed directly to the builder at Concord. The balance was sent to Mr. Emerson October 7, and acknowledged by him in his letter of October 8, 1872.

All the friends of Mr. Emerson who knew of the plan which was proposed, to rebuild his house, seemed to feel that it was a privilege to be allowed to express in this way the love and veneration with which he was regarded, and the deep debt of gratitude which they owed to him, and there is no doubt that a much larger amount would have been readily and gladly offered, if it had been required, for the object in view.

Those who have had the happiness to join in this friendly "conspiracy" may well take pleasure in the thought that what they have done has had the effect to lighten the load of care and anxiety which the calamity of the fire brought with it to Mr. Emerson, and thus perhaps to prolong for some precious years the serene and noble life that was so dear to all of us.

My thanks are due to the friends who have made me the bearer of this message of good-will.

LE BARON RUSSELL.

BOSTON, *May* 8, 1882.

BOSTON, *August* 13, 1872.

DEAR MR. EMERSON:

It seems to have been the spontaneous desire of your friends, on hearing of the burning of your house, to be allowed the pleasure of rebuilding it.

A few of them have united for this object, and now request your acceptance of the amount which I have to-day deposited to your order at the Concord Bank, through the kindness of our friend, Judge Hoar. They trust that you will receive it as an expression of sincere regard and affection from friends, who will, one and all, esteem it a great privilege to be permitted to assist in the restoration of your home.

And if, in their eagerness to participate in so grateful a work, they may have exceeded the estimate of your ar-

chitect as to what is required for that purpose, they beg
that you will devote the remainder to such other objects
as may be most convenient to you.

        Very sincerely yours,

                LE BARON RUSSELL.

                        CONCORD, *August* 14, 1872.
DR. LE B. RUSSELL:

 Dear Sir, — I received your letters, with the check for
ten thousand dollars enclosed, from Mr. Barrett last evening. This morning I deposited it to Mr. Emerson's
credit in the Concord National Bank, and took a bank
book for him, with his little balance entered at the top,
and this following, and carried it to him with your letter.
I told him, by way of prelude, that some of his friends
had made him treasurer of an association who wished him
to go to England and examine Warwick Castle and other
noted houses that had been recently injured by fire, in
order to get the best ideas possible for restoration, and
then to apply them to a house which the association was
formed to restore in this neighborhood.

 When he understood the thing and had read your letter, he seemed very deeply moved. He said that he had
been allowed so far in life to stand on his own feet, and
that he hardly knew what to say, — that the kindness of
his friends was very great. I said what I thought was
best in reply, and told him that this was the spontaneous
act of friends, who wished the privilege of expressing in
this way their respect and affection, and was done only by
those who thought it a privilege to do so. I mentioned
Hillard as you desired, and also Mrs. Tappan, who, it
seems, had written to him and offered any assistance he
might need, to the extent of five thousand dollars, personally.

 I think it is all right, but he said he must see the list
of contributors, and would then say what he had to say
about it. He told me that Mr. F. C. Lowell, who was
his classmate and old friend, Mr. Bangs, Mrs. Gurney,
and a few other friends, had already sent him five thou-

sand dollars, which he seemed to think was as much as he could bear. This makes the whole a very gratifying result, and perhaps explains the absence of some names on your book.

I am glad that Mr. Emerson, who is feeble and ill, can learn what a debt of obligation his friends feel to him, and thank you heartily for what you have done about it.

Very truly yours,

E. R. HOAR.

CONCORD, *August* 16, 1872.

MY DEAR LE BARON:

I have wondered and melted over your letter and its accompaniments till it is high time that I should reply to it, if I can. My misfortunes, as I have lived along so far in this world, have been so few that I have never needed to ask direct aid of the host of good men and women who have cheered my life, though many a gift has come to me. And this late calamity, however rude and devastating, soon began to look more wonderful in its salvages than in its ruins, so that I can hardly feel any right to this munificent endowment with which you, and my other friends through you, have astonished me. But I cannot read your letter or think of its message without delight, that my companions and friends bear me so noble a good-will, nor without some new aspirations in the old heart toward a better deserving. Judge Hoar has, up to this time, withheld from me the names of my benefactors, but you may be sure that I shall not rest till I have learned them, every one, to repeat to myself at night and at morning.

Your affectionate friend and debtor,

R. W. EMERSON.

DR. LE BARON RUSSELL.

CONCORD, *October* 8, 1872.

MY DEAR DOCTOR LE BARON:

I received last night your two notes, and the cheque, enclosed in one of them, for one thousand and twenty dollars.

Are my friends bent on killing me with kindness? No, you will say, but to make me live longer. I thought myself sufficiently loaded with benefits already, and you add more and more. It appears that you all will rebuild my house and rejuvenate me by sending me in my old days abroad on a young man's excursion.

I am a lover of men, but this recent wonderful experience of their tenderness surprises and occupies my thoughts day by day. Now that I have all or almost all the names of the men and women who have conspired in this kindness to me (some of whom I have never personally known), I please myself with the thought of meeting each and asking, Why have we not met before? Why have you not told me that we thought alike? Life is not so long, nor sympathy of thought so common, that we can spare the society of those with whom we best agree. Well, 't is probably my own fault by sticking ever to my solitude. Perhaps it is not too late to learn of these friends a better lesson.

Thank them for me whenever you meet them, and say to them that I am not wood or stone, if I have not yet trusted myself so far as to go to each one of them directly.

My wife insists that I shall also send her acknowledgments to them and you.

Yours and theirs affectionately,

R. W. EMERSON.

DR. LE BARON RUSSELL.

The following are the names of the subscribers to the fund for rebuilding Mr. Emerson's house: —

Mrs. Anne S. Hooper.
Miss Alice S. Hooper.
Mrs. Caroline Tappan.
Miss Ellen S. Tappan.
Miss Mary A. Tappan.
Mr. T. G. Appleton.
Mrs. Henry Edwards.
Miss Susan E. Dorr.

Misses Wigglesworth.
Mr. Edward Wigglesworth.
Mr. J. Elliot Cabot.
Mrs. Sarah S. Russell.
Friends in New York and Philadelphia, through Mr. Williams.
Mr. William Whiting.

Mr. Frederick Beck.
Mr. H. P. Kidder.
Mrs. Abel Adams.
Mrs. George Faulkner.
Hon. E. R. Hoar.
Mr. James B. Thayer.
Mr. John M. Forbes.
Mr. James H. Beal.
Mrs. Anna C. Lodge.
Mr. H. H. Hunnewell.
Mr. James A. Dupee.
Mrs. M. F. Sayles.
J. R. Osgood & Co.
Mr. Francis Geo. Shaw.

Mr. William P. Mason.
Mr. Sam'l G. Ward.
Mr. Geo. C. Ward.
Mr. John E. Williams.
Mr. T. Jefferson Coolidge.
Mrs. S. Cabot.
Mrs. Anna C. Lowell.
Miss Helen L. Appleton.
Mr. Richard Soule.
Dr. R. W. Hooper.
Mr. William Gray.
Mr. J. I. Bowditch.
Mrs. Lucia J. Briggs.
Dr. Le Baron Russell.

In May, 1873, Emerson returned to Concord. His friends and fellow-citizens received him with every token of affection and reverence. A set of signals was arranged to announce his arrival. Carriages were in readiness for him and his family, a band greeted him with music, and passing under a triumphal arch, he was driven to his renewed old home amidst the welcomes and the blessings of his loving and admiring friends and neighbors.

CHAPTER XII.

1873–1878. ÆT. 70–75.

In December, 1874, Emerson published "Parnassus," a collection of poems by British and American authors. Many readers may like to see his subdivisions and arrangement of the pieces he has brought together. They are as follows: "Nature;" "Human Life;" "Intellectual;" "Contemplative, Moral, Religious;" "Heroic;" "Portraits, Personal, Pictures;" "Narrative Poems and Ballads;" "Songs;" "Dirges and Pathetic Poems;" "Comic and Humorous;" "Poetry of Terror;" "Oracles and Counsels."

I have borrowed so sparingly from the rich mine of Mr. George Willis Cooke's "Ralph Waldo Emerson, His Life, Writings, and Philosophy," that I am pleased to pay him the respectful tribute of taking a leaf from his excellent work.

"This collection," he says, "was the result of his habit, pursued for many years, of copying into his commonplace book any poem which specially pleased him. Many of these favorites had been read to illustrate his

lectures on the English poets. The book has no worth-
less selections, almost everything it contains bearing the
stamp of genius and worth. Yet Emerson's personality
is seen in its many intellectual and serious poems, and
in the small number of its purely religious selections.
With two or three exceptions he copies none of those
devotional poems which have attracted devout souls. . . .
His poetical sympathies are shown in the fact that one
third of the selections are from the seventeenth century.
Shakespeare is drawn on more largely than any other, no
less than eighty-eight selections being made from him.
The names of George Herbert, Herrick, Ben Jonson, and
Milton frequently appear. Wordsworth appears forty-
three times, and stands next to Shakespeare; while Burns,
Byron, Scott, Tennyson, and Chaucer make up the list of
favorites. Many little known pieces are included, and
some whose merit is other than poetical. . . . This selection of poems is eminently that of a poet of keen intellectual tastes. It is not popular in character, omitting many
public favorites, and introducing very much which can
never be acceptable to the general reader. The Preface
is full of interest for its comments on many of the poems
and poets appearing in these selections."

I will only add to Mr. Cooke's criticism these two
remarks: First, that I have found it impossible to
know under which of his divisions to look for many of
the poems I was in search of; and as, in the earlier
copies at least, there was no paged index where each
author's pieces were collected together, one had to
hunt up his fragments with no little loss of time and
patience, under various heads, "imitating the careful
search that Isis made for the mangled body of Osiris."
The other remark is that each one of Emerson's American fellow-poets from whom he has quoted would
gladly have spared almost any of the extracts from the
poems of his brother-bards, if the editor would only

have favored us with some specimens of his own poetry, with a single line of which he has not seen fit to indulge us.

In 1874 Emerson received the nomination by the independent party among the students of Glasgow University for the office of Lord Rector. He received five hundred votes against seven hundred for Disraeli, who was elected. He says in a letter to Dr. J. Hutchinson Sterling: —

"I count that vote as quite the fairest laurel that has ever fallen on me; and I cannot but feel deeply grateful to my young friends in the University, and to yourself, who have been my counsellor and my too partial advocate."

Mr. Cabot informs us in his prefatory Note to "Letters and Social Aims," that the proof sheets of this volume, now forming the eighth of the collected works, showed, even before the burning of his house and the illness which followed from the shock, that his loss of memory and of mental grasp was such as to make it unlikely that he would in any case have been able to accomplish what he had undertaken. Sentences, even whole pages, were repeated, and there was a want of order beyond what even he would have tolerated: —

"There is nothing here that he did not write, and he gave his full approval to whatever was done in the way of selection and arrangement; but I cannot say that he applied his mind very closely to the matter."

This volume contains eleven essays, the subjects of which, as just enumerated, are very various. The longest and most elaborate paper is that entitled "Poetry and Imagination." I have room for little more than the enumeration of the different headings of this long essay. By these it will be seen how wide a ground it covers. They are "Introductory;" "Poetry;" "Imagination;" "Veracity;" "Creation;" "Melody, Rhyme, Form;" "Bards and Trouveurs;" "Morals;" "Transcendency." Many thoughts with which we are familiar are reproduced, expanded, and illustrated in this essay. Unity in multiplicity, the symbolism of nature, and others of his leading ideas appear in new phrases, not unwelcome, for they look fresh in every restatement. It would be easy to select a score of pointed sayings, striking images, large generalizations. Some of these we find repeated in his verse. Thus: —

"Michael Angelo is largely filled with the Creator that made and makes men. How much of the original craft remains in him, and he a mortal man!"

And so in the well-remembered lines of "The Problem:" —

"Himself from God he could not free."

"He knows that he did not make his thought, — no, his thought made him, and made the sun and stars."

"Art might obey but not surpass.
The passive Master lent his hand
To the vast soul that o'er him planned."

Hope is at the bottom of every essay of Emerson's as it was at the bottom of Pandora's box: —

"I doubt never the riches of nature, the gifts of the future, the immense wealth of the mind. O yes, poets we shall have, mythology, symbols, religion, of our own. . . .

"Sooner or later that which is now life shall be poetry, and every fair and manly trait shall add a richer strain to the song."

Under the title "Social Aims" he gives some wise counsel concerning manners and conversation. One of these precepts will serve as a specimen — if we have met with it before it is none the worse for wear:

"Shun the negative side. Never worry people with your contritions, nor with dismal views of politics or society. Never name sickness; even if you could trust yourself on that perilous topic, beware of unmuzzling a valetudinarian, who will soon give you your fill of it."

We have had one essay on Eloquence already. One extract from this new discourse on the same subject must serve our turn: —

"These are ascending stairs, — a good voice, winning manners, plain speech, chastened, however, by the schools into correctness; but we must come to the main matter, of power of statement, — know your fact; hug your fact. For the essential thing is heat, and heat comes of sincerity. Speak what you do know and believe; and are personally in it; and are answerable for every word. Eloquence is *the power to translate a truth into language perfectly intelligible to the person to whom you speak.*"

The italics are Emerson's.

If our learned and excellent John Cotton used to sweeten his mouth before going to bed with a bit of Calvin, we may as wisely sweeten and strengthen our sense of existence with a morsel or two from Emerson's essay on Resources: —

"A Schopenhauer, with logic and learning and wit, teaching pessimism, — teaching that this is the worst of all possible worlds, and inferring that sleep is better than waking, and death than sleep, — all the talent in the world cannot save him from being odious. But if instead of these negatives you give me affirmatives; if you tell me that there is always life for the living; that what man has done man can do; that this world belongs to the energetic; that there is always a way to everything desirable; that every man is provided, in the new bias of his faculty, with a key to nature, and that man only rightly knows himself as far as he has experimented on things, — I am invigorated, put into genial and working temper; the horizon opens, and we are full of good-will and gratitude to the Cause of Causes."

The essay or lecture on "The Comic" may have formed a part of a series he had contemplated on the intellectual processes. Two or three sayings in it will show his view sufficiently: —

"The essence of all jokes, of all comedy, seems to be an honest or well-intended halfness; a non-performance of what is pretended to be performed, at the same time that one is giving loud pledges of performance. . . .

"If the essence of the comic be the contrast in the intellect between the idea and the false performance, there is good reason why we should be affected by the exposure. We have no deeper interest than our integrity, and that we should be made aware by joke and by stroke of any lie we entertain. Besides, a perception of the comic seems to be a balance-wheel in our metaphysical structure. It appears to be an essential element in a fine character. . . . A rogue alive to the ludicrous is still convertible. If that sense is lost, his fellow-men can do little for him."

These and other sayings of like purport are illustrated by well-preserved stories and anecdotes not for the most part of very recent date.

"Quotation and Originality" furnishes the key to Emerson's workshop. He believed in quotation, and borrowed from everybody and every book. Not in any stealthy or shamefaced way, but proudly, royally, as a king borrows from one of his attendants the coin that bears his own image and superscription.

"All minds quote. Old and new make the warp and woof of every moment. There is no thread that is not a twist of these two strands. . . . We quote not only books and proverbs, but arts, sciences, religion, customs, and laws; nay, we quote temples and houses, tables and chairs, by imitation. . . .

"The borrowing is often honest enough, and comes of magnanimity and stoutness. A great man quotes bravely, and will not draw on his invention when his memory serves him with a word as good. . . .

"Next to the originator of a good sentence is the first quoter of it." . . .

The "Progress of Culture," his second Phi Beta Kappa oration, has already been mentioned.

The lesson of self-reliance, which he is never tired of inculcating, is repeated and enforced in the essay on Greatness.

"There are certain points of identity in which these masters agree. Self-respect is the early form in which greatness appears. . . . Stick to your own; don't inculpate yourself in the local, social, or national crime, but follow the path your genius traces like the galaxy of heaven for you to walk in. . . .

"Every mind has a new compass, a new direction of its own, differencing its genius and aim from every other mind. . . . We call this specialty the *bias* of each individual. And none of us will ever accomplish anything excellent or commanding except when he listens to this whisper which is heard by him alone."

If to follow this native bias is the first rule, the second is concentration. To the bias of the individual mind must be added the most catholic receptivity for the genius of others.

"Shall I tell you the secret of the true scholar? It is this: Every man I meet is my master in some point, and in that I learn of him. . . .

"The man whom we have not seen, in whom no regard of self degraded the adorer of the laws, — who by governing himself governed others; sportive in manner, but inexorable in act; who sees longevity in his cause; whose aim is always distinct to him; who is suffered to be himself in society; who carries fate in his eye; — he it is whom we seek, encouraged in every good hour that here or hereafter he shall be found."

What has Emerson to tell us of Inspiration?

"I believe that nothing great and lasting can be done except by inspiration, by leaning on the secret augury. . . .

"How many sources of inspiration can we count? As many as our affinities. But to a practical purpose we may reckon a few of these."

I will enumerate them briefly as he gives them, but not attempting to reproduce his comments on each: —

1. Health. 2. The experience of writing letters. 3. The renewed sensibility which comes after seasons of decay or eclipse of the faculties. 4. The power of the will. 5. Atmospheric causes, especially the influence of morning. 6. Solitary converse with nature. 7. Solitude of itself, like that of a country inn in summer, and of a city hotel in winter. 8. Conversation. 9. New poetry; by which, he says, he means chiefly old poetry that is new to the reader.

"Every book is good to read which sets the reader in a working mood."

What can promise more than an essay by Emerson on Immortality? It is to be feared that many readers will transfer this note of interrogation to the essay itself. What is the definite belief of Emerson as expressed in this discourse, — what does it mean? We must tack together such sentences as we can find that will stand for an answer: —

"I think all sound minds rest on a certain preliminary conviction, namely, that if it be best that conscious personal life shall continue, it will continue; if not best, then it will not; and we, if we saw the whole, should of course see that it was better so."

This is laying the table for a Barmecide feast of nonentity, with the possibility of a real banquet to be provided for us.   But he continues: —

"Schiller said, 'What is so universal as death must be benefit.'"

He tells us what Michael Angelo said, how Plutarch felt, how Montesquieu thought about the question, and then glances off from it to the terror of the child at the thought of life without end, to the story of the two skeptical statesmen whose unsatisfied inquiry through a long course of years he holds to be a better affirmative evidence than their failure to find a confirmation was negative.   He argues from our delight in permanence, from the delicate contrivances and adjustments of created things, that the contriver cannot be forever hidden, and says at last plainly: —

"Everything is prospective, and man is to live hereafter.   That the world is for his education is the only sane solution of the enigma."

But turn over a few pages and we may read: —

"I confess that everything connected with our personality fails.   Nature never spares the individual; we are always balked of a complete success; no prosperity is promised to our self-esteem.   We have our indemnity only in the moral and intellectual reality to which we aspire.   That is immortal, and we only through that.   The soul stipulates for no private good.   That which is private I see not to be good.   'If truth live, I live; if justice live, I live,' said one of the old saints, 'and these by any man's suffering are enlarged and enthroned.' "

Once more we get a dissolving view of Emerson's creed, if such a word applies to a statement like the following : —

"I mean that I am a better believer, and all serious souls are better believers in the immortality than we can give grounds for. The real evidence is too subtle, or is higher than we can write down in propositions, and therefore Wordsworth's 'Ode' is the best modern essay on the subject."

Wordsworth's "Ode" is a noble and beautiful dream; is it anything more? The reader who would finish this essay, which I suspect to belong to an early period of Emerson's development, must be prepared to plunge into mysticism and lose himself at last in an Oriental apologue. The eschatology which rests upon an English poem and an Indian fable belongs to the realm of reverie and of imagination rather than the domain of reason.

On the 19th of April, 1875, the hundredth anniversary of the "Fight at the Bridge," Emerson delivered a short address at the unveiling of the statue of "The Minute-Man," erected at the place of the conflict, to commemorate the event. This is the last address he ever wrote, though he delivered one or more after this date. From the manuscript which lies before me I extract a single passage : —

"In the year 1775 we had many enemies and many friends in England, but our one benefactor was King George the Third. The time had arrived for the political severance of America, that it might play its part in the history of this globe, and the inscrutable divine Providence gave an insane king to England. In the resistance of the Colonies, he alone was immovable on the question of force. England was so dear to us that the Colonies could only be absolutely disunited by violence from England, and only one man could compel the resort to violence. Parliament wavered, Lord North wavered, all the ministers wavered, but the king had the insanity of one idea; he was immovable, he insisted on the impossible, so the army was sent, America was instantly united, and the Nation born."

There is certainly no mark of mental failure in this paragraph, written at a period when he had long ceased almost entirely from his literary labors.

Emerson's collected Poems constitute the ninth volume of the recent collected edition of his works. They will be considered in a following chapter.

CHAPTER XIII.

1878–1882. ÆT. 75–79.

Last Literary Labors. — Addresses and Essays. — "Lectures and
Biographical Sketches." — "Miscellanies."

THE decline of Emerson's working faculties went
on gently and gradually, but he was not condemned to
entire inactivity. His faithful daughter, Ellen, followed him with assiduous, quiet, ever watchful care,
aiding his failing memory, bringing order into the
chaos of his manuscript, an echo before the voice whose
words it was to shape for him when his mind faltered
and needed a momentary impulse.

With her helpful presence and support he ventured
from time to time to read a paper before a select
audience. Thus, March 30, 1878, he delivered a lecture in the Old South Church, — "Fortune of the
Republic." On the 5th of May, 1879, he read a
lecture in the Chapel of Divinity College, Harvard
University, — "The Preacher." In 1881 he read a
paper on Carlyle before the Massachusetts Historical
Society. He also published a paper in "The North
American Review," in 1878, — "The Sovereignty of
Ethics," and one on "Superlatives," in "The Century" for February, 1882.

But in these years he was writing little or nothing.
All these papers were taken from among his manuscripts of different dates. The same thing is true of
the volumes published since his death; they were

only compilations from his stores of unpublished matter, and their arrangement was the work of Mr. Emerson's friend and literary executor, Mr. Cabot. These volumes cannot be considered as belonging to any single period of his literary life.

Mr. Cabot prefixes to the tenth volume of Emerson's collected works, which bears the title, "Lectures and Biographical Sketches," the following "Note : " —

"Of the pieces included in this volume the following, namely, those from 'The Dial,' 'Character,' 'Plutarch,' and the biographical sketches of Dr. Ripley, of Mr. Hoar, and of Henry Thoreau, were printed by Mr. Emerson before I took any part in the arrangement of his papers. The rest, except the sketch of Miss Mary Emerson, I got ready for his use in readings to his friends, or to a limited public. He had given up the regular practice of lecturing, but would sometimes, upon special request, read a paper that had been prepared for him from his manuscripts, in the manner described in the Preface to 'Letters and Social Aims,' — some former lecture serving as a nucleus for the new. Some of these papers he afterwards allowed to be printed; others, namely, 'Aristocracy,' 'Education,' 'The Man of Letters,' 'The Scholar,' 'Historic Notes of Life and Letters in New England,' 'Mary Moody Emerson,' are now published for the first time."

Some of these papers I have already had occasion to refer to. From several of the others I will make one or two extracts, — a difficult task, so closely are the thoughts packed together.

From "Demonology : " —

"I say to the table-rappers

'I well believe
Thou wilt not utter what thou dost not know,
And so far will I trust thee, gentle Kate !'

"Meantime far be from me the impatience which cannot brook the supernatural, the vast; far be from me the lust of explaining away all which appeals to the imagination, and the great presentiments which haunt us. Willingly I too say Hail! to the unknown, awful powers which transcend the ken of the understanding."

I will not quote anything from the essay called "Aristocracy." But let him who wishes to know what the word means to an American whose life has come from New England soil, whose ancestors have breathed New England air for many generations, read it, and he will find a new interpretation of a very old and often greatly wronged appellation.

"Perpetual Forces" is one of those prose poems, — of his earlier epoch, I have no doubt, — in which he plays with the facts of science with singular grace and freedom.

What man could speak more fitly, with more authority, of Character, than Emerson? When he says, "If all things are taken away, I have still all things in my relation to the Eternal," we feel that such an utterance is as natural to his pure spirit as breathing to the frame in which it was imprisoned.

We have had a glimpse of Emerson as a schoolmaster, but behind and far above the teaching drillmaster's desk is the chair from which he speaks to us of Education. Compare the short and easy method of the wise man of old, "He that spareth his rod hateth his son," with this other, "Be the companion of his thought, the friend of his friendship, the lover of his virtue, — but no kinsman of his sin."

"The Superlative" will prove light and pleasant reading after these graver essays. Μηδὲν ἄγαν, — *ne quid nimis*, — nothing in excess, was his precept as to adjectives.

Two sentences from "The Sovereignty of Ethics" will go far towards reconciling elderly readers who have not forgotten the Westminster Assembly's Catechism with this sweet-souled dealer in spiritual dynamite: —

"Luther would cut his hand off sooner than write theses against the pope if he suspected that he was bringing on with all his might the pale negations of Boston Unitarianism. . . .
"If I miss the inspiration of the saints of Calvinism, or of Platonism, or of Buddhism, our times are not up to theirs, or, more truly, have not yet their own legitimate force."

So, too, this from "The Preacher:" —

"All civil mankind have agreed in leaving one day for contemplation against six for practice. I hope that day will keep its honor and its use. . . . The Sabbath changes its forms from age to age, but the substantial benefit endures."

The special interest of the address called "The Man of Letters" is that it was delivered during the war. He was no advocate for peace where great principles were at the bottom of the conflict: —

"War, seeking for the roots of strength, comes upon the moral aspects at once. . . . War ennobles the age. . . . Battle, with the sword, has cut many a Gordian knot in twain which all the wit of East and West, of Northern and Border statesmen could not untie."

"The Scholar" was delivered before two societies at the University of Virginia so late as the year 1876. If I must select any of its wise words, I will choose the questions which he has himself italicized to show his sense of their importance: —

"For all men, all women, Time, your country, your

condition, the invisible world are the interrogators: *Who are you? What do you? Can you obtain what you wish? Is there method in your consciousness? Can you see tendency in your life? Can you help any soul?*

"Can he answer these questions? Can he dispose of them? Happy if you can answer them mutely in the order and disposition of your life! Happy for more than yourself, a benefactor of men, if you can answer them in works of wisdom, art, or poetry; bestowing on the general mind of men organic creations, to be the guidance and delight of all who know them."

The essay on Plutarch has a peculiar value from the fact that Emerson owes more to him than to any other author except Plato, who is one of the only two writers quoted oftener than Plutarch. *Mutato nomine*, the portrait which Emerson draws of the Greek moralist might stand for his own: —

"Whatever is eminent in fact or in fiction, in opinion, in character, in institutions, in science — natural, moral, or metaphysical — or in memorable sayings, drew his attention and came to his pen with more or less fulness of record. . . .

"A poet in verse or prose must have a sensuous eye, but an intellectual co-perception. Plutarch's memory is full and his horizon wide. Nothing touches man but he feels to be his. . . .

"Plutarch had a religion which Montaigne wanted, and which defends him from wantonness; and though Plutarch is as plain-spoken, his moral sentiment is always pure. . . .

"I do not know where to find a book — to borrow a phrase of Ben Jonson's — 'so rammed with life,' and this in chapters chiefly ethical, which are so prone to be heavy and sentimental. . . . His vivacity and abundance never leave him to loiter or pound on an incident. . . .

"In his immense quotation and allusion we quickly cease to discriminate between what he quotes and what he invents. . . . 'T is all Plutarch, by right of eminent domain, and all property vests in this emperor.

"It is in consequence of this poetic trait in his mind, that I confess that, in reading him, I embrace the particulars, and carry a faint memory of the argument or general design of the chapter; but he is not less welcome, and he leaves the reader with a relish and a necessity for completing his studies. . . .

"He is a pronounced idealist, who does not hesitate to say, like another Berkeley, 'Matter is itself privation.' . . .

"Of philosophy he is more interested in the results than in the method. He has a just instinct of the presence of a master, and prefers to sit as a scholar with Plato than as a disputant. . . .

"His natural history is that of a lover and poet, and not of a physicist. . . .

"But though curious in the questions of the schools on the nature and genesis of things, his extreme interest in every trait of character, and his broad humanity, lead him constantly to Morals, to the study of the Beautiful and Good. Hence his love of heroes, his rule of life, and his clear convictions of the high destiny of the soul. La Harpe said that 'Plutarch is the genius the most naturally moral that ever existed.' . . .

"Plutarch thought 'truth to be the greatest good that man can receive, and the goodliest blessing that God can give.' . . .

"All his judgments are noble. He thought with Epicurus that it is more delightful to do than to receive a kindness. . . .

"Plutarch was well-born, well-conditioned; eminently social, he was a king in his own house, surrounded himself with select friends, and knew the high value of good conversation. . . .

"He had that universal sympathy with genius which makes all its victories his own; though he never used verse, he had many qualities of the poet in the power of his imagination, the speed of his mental associations, and his sharp, objective eyes. But what specially marks him, he is a chief example of the illumination of the intellect by the force of morals."

How much of all this would have been recognized as just and true if it had been set down in an obituary notice of Emerson!

I have already made use of several of the other papers contained in this volume, and will merely enumerate all that follow the "Plutarch." Some of the titles will be sure to attract the reader. They are "Historic Notes of Life and Letters in New England;" "The Chardon Street Convention;" "Ezra Ripley, D. D.;" "Mary Moody Emerson;" "Samuel Hoar;" "Thoreau;" "Carlyle."

Mr. Cabot prefaces the eleventh and last volume of Emerson's writings with the following "Note:" —

"The first five pieces in this volume, and the Editorial Address from 'The Massachusetts Quarterly Review,' were published by Mr. Emerson long ago. The speeches at the John Brown, the Walter Scott, and the Free Religious Association meetings were published at the time, no doubt with his consent, but without any active co-operation on his part. 'The Fortune of the Republic' appeared separately in 1879; the rest have never been published. In none was any change from the original form made by me, except in 'The Fortune of the Republic,' which was made up from several lectures for the occasion upon which it was read."

The volume of "Miscellanies" contains no less than twenty-three pieces of very various lengths and relating to many different subjects. The five referred to as having been previously published are, "The Lord's Supper," the "Historical Discourse in Concord," the "Address at the Dedication of the Soldiers' Monument in Concord," the "Address on Emancipation in the British West Indies," and the lecture or essay on War, — all of which have been already spoken of.

Next in order comes a lecture on the Fugitive Slave Law. Emerson says, "I do not often speak on public questions. *. . .* My own habitual view is to the well-being of scholars." But he leaves his studies to attack the institution of slavery, from which he says he himself has never suffered any inconvenience, and the "Law," which the abolitionists would always call the "Fugitive Slave *Bill*." Emerson had a great admiration for Mr. Webster, but he did not spare him as he recalled his speech of the 7th of March, just four years before the delivery of this lecture. He warns against false leadership: —

"To make good the cause of Freedom, you must draw off from all foolish trust in others. He only who is able to stand alone is qualified for society. And that I understand to be the end for which a soul exists in this world, — to be himself the counter-balance of all falsehood and all wrong. The Anglo-Saxon race is proud and strong and selfish. England maintains trade, not liberty."

Cowper had said long before this : —

"Doing good,
Disinterested good, is not our trade."

And America found that England had not learned that trade when, fifteen years after this discourse was delivered, the conflict between the free and slave States threatened the ruin of the great Republic, and England forgot her anti-slavery in the prospect of the downfall of a "great empire which threatens to overshadow the whole earth."

It must be remembered that Emerson had never been identified with the abolitionists. But an individual act of wrong sometimes gives a sharp point to a blunt dagger which has been kept in its sheath too long : —

"The events of the last few years and months and days have taught us the lessons of centuries. I do not see how a barbarous community and a civilized community can constitute one State. I think we must get rid of slavery or we must get rid of freedom."

These were his words on the 26th of May, 1856, in his speech on "The Assault upon Mr. Sumner."

A few months later, in his "Speech on Affairs in Kansas," delivered almost five years before the first gun was fired at Fort Sumter, he spoke the following fatally prophetic and commanding words : —

"The hour is coming when the strongest will not be strong enough. A harder task will the new revolution of the nineteenth century be than was the revolution of the eighteenth century. I think the American Revolution bought its glory cheap. If the problem was new, it was simple. If there were few people, they were united, and the enemy three thousand miles off. But now, vast property, gigantic interests, family connections, webs of party, cover the land with a network that immensely multiplies the dangers of war.

"Fellow-citizens, in these times full of the fate of the Republic, I think the towns should hold town-meetings, and resolve themselves into Committees of Safety, go into permanent sessions, adjourning from week to week, from month to month. I wish we could send the sergeant-at-arms to stop every American who is about to leave the country. Send home every one who is abroad, lest they should find no country to return to. Come home and stay at home while there is a country to save. When it is lost it will be time enough then for any who are luckless enough to remain alive to gather up their clothes and depart to some land where freedom exists."

Two short speeches follow, one delivered at a meeting for the relief of the family of John Brown, on the 18th of November, 1859, the other after his execution: —

"Our blind statesmen," he says, "go up and down, with committees of vigilance and safety, hunting for the origin of this new heresy. They will need a very vigilant committee indeed to find its birthplace, and a very strong force to root it out. For the arch-Abolitionist, older than Brown, and older than the Shenandoah Mountains, is Love, whose other name is Justice, which was before Alfred, before Lycurgus, before Slavery, and will be after it."

From his discourse on Theodore Parker I take the following vigorous sentence: —

"His commanding merit as a reformer is this, that he insisted beyond all men in pulpits, — I cannot think of one rival, — that the essence of Christianity is its practical morals; it is there for use, or it is nothing; and if you combine it with sharp trading, or with ordinary city ambitions to gloze over municipal corruptions, or private intemperance, or successful fraud, or immoral politics, or unjust wars, or the cheating of Indians, or the robbery of frontier nations, or leaving your principles at home to follow on the high seas or in Europe a supple complaisance to tyrants, — it is hypocrisy, and the truth is not in you; and no love of religious music or of dreams of Swedenborg, or praise of John Wesley or of Jeremy Taylor, can save you from the Satan which you are."

The lecture on American Civilization, made up from two addresses, one of which was delivered at Washington on the 31st of January, 1862, is, as might be expected, full of anti-slavery. That on the Emancipation Proclamation, delivered in Boston in September, 1862, is as full of "silent joy" at the advent of "a day which most of us dared not hope to see, — an event worth the dreadful war, worth its costs and uncertainties."

From the "Remarks" at the funeral services for Abraham Lincoln, held in Concord on the 19th of April, 1865, I extract this admirably drawn character of the man: —

"He is the true history of the American people in his time. Step by step he walked before them; slow with their slowness, quickening his march by theirs, the true representative of this continent; an entirely public man; father of his country, the pulse of twenty millions throbbing in his heart, the thought of their minds articulated by his tongue."

The following are the titles of the remaining contents of this volume: "Harvard Commemoration Speech;" "Editors' Address: Massachusetts Quarterly Review;" "Woman;" "Address to Kossuth;" "Robert Burns;" "Walter Scott;" "Remarks at the Organization of the Free Religious Association;" "Speech at the Annual Meeting of the Free Religious Association;" "The Fortune of the Republic."

In treating of the "Woman Question," Emerson speaks temperately, delicately, with perfect fairness, but leaves it in the hands of the women themselves to determine whether they shall have an equal part in public affairs. "The new movement," he says, "is only a tide shared by the spirits of man and woman; and you may proceed in the faith that whatever the woman's heart is prompted to desire, the man's mind is simultaneously prompted to accomplish."

It is hard to turn a leaf in any book of Emerson's writing without finding some pithy remark or some striking image or witty comment which illuminates the page where we find it and tempts us to seize upon it for an extract. But I must content myself with these few sentences from "The Fortune of the Republic," the last address he ever delivered, in which his belief in America and her institutions, and his trust in the Providence which overrules all nations and all worlds, have found fitting utterance: —

"Let the passion for America cast out the passion for Europe. Here let there be what the earth waits for, — exalted manhood. What this country longs for is personalities, grand persons, to counteract its materialities. For it is the rule of the universe that corn shall serve man, and not man corn.

"They who find America insipid, — they for whom London and Paris have spoiled their own homes, can be spared to return to those cities. I not only see a career at home for more genius than we have, but for more than there is in the world. . . .

"Our helm is given up to a better guidance than our own; the course of events is quite too strong for any helmsman, and our little wherry is taken in tow by the ship of the great Admiral which knows the way, and has the force to draw men and states and planets to their good."

With this expression of love and respect for his country and trust in his country's God, we may take leave of Emerson's prose writings.

CHAPTER XIV.

EMERSON'S POEMS.

THE following "Prefatory Note" by Mr. Cabot introduces the ninth volume of the series of Emerson's collected works: —

"This volume contains nearly all the pieces included in the POEMS and MAY-DAY of former editions. In 1876 Mr. Emerson published a selection from his poems, adding six new ones, and omitting many. Of those omitted, several are now restored, in accordance with the expressed wishes of many readers and lovers of them. Also some pieces never before published are here given in an Appendix, on various grounds. Some of them appear to have had Mr. Emerson's approval, but to have been withheld because they were unfinished. These it seemed best not to suppress, now that they can never receive their completion. Others, mostly of an early date, remained unpublished doubtless because of their personal and private nature. Some of these seem to have an autobiographic interest sufficient to justify their publication. Others again, often mere fragments, have been admitted as characteristic, or as expressing in poetic form thoughts found in the essays.

"In coming to a decision in these cases, it seemed on the whole preferable to take the risk of including too much rather than the opposite, and to leave the task of further winnowing to the hands of time.

"As was stated in the Preface to the first volume of this edition of Mr. Emerson's writings, the readings adopted by him in the 'Selected Poems' have not always been followed here, but in some cases preference has been given to corrections made by him when he was in fuller strength than at the time of the last revision.

‧·A change in the arrangement of the stanzas of 'May-Day,' in the part representative of the march of Spring, received his sanction as bringing them more nearly in accordance with the events in Nature."

Emerson's verse has been a fertile source of discussion. Some have called him a poet and nothing but a poet, and some have made so much of the palpable defects of his verse that they have forgotten to recognize its true claims. His prose is often highly poetical, but his verse is something more than the most imaginative and rhetorical passages of his prose. An illustration presently to be given will make this point clear.

Poetry is to prose what the so-called full dress of the ball-room is to the plainer garments of the household and the street. Full dress, as we call it, is so full of beauty that it cannot hold it all, and the redundancy of nature overflows the narrowed margin of satin or velvet.

It reconciles us to its approach to nudity by the richness of its drapery and ornaments. A pearl or diamond necklace or a blushing bouquet excuses the liberal allowance of undisguised nature. We expect from the fine lady in her brocades and laces a generosity of display which we should reprimand with the virtuous severity of Tartuffe if ventured upon by the waiting-maid in her calicoes. So the poet reveals himself under the protection of his imaginative and melodious phrases, — the flowers and jewels of his vocabulary.

Here is a prose sentence from Emerson's "Works and Days:" —

"The days are ever divine as to the first Aryans.

They come and go like muffled and veiled figures, sent from a distant friendly party; but they say nothing, and if we do not use the gifts they bring, they carry them as silently away."

Now see this thought in full dress, and then ask what is the difference betweeen prose and poetry: —

DAYS.

Daughters of time, the hypocritic Days,
Muffled and dumb like barefoot dervishes,
And marching single in an endless file,
Bring diadems and fagots in their hands.
To each they offer gifts after his will,
Bread, kingdoms, stars, and sky that holds them all.
I, in my pleachéd garden, watched the pomp,
Forgot my morning wishes, hastily
Took a few herbs and apples, and the Day
Turned and departed silent. I too late
Under her solemn fillet saw the scorn.

Cinderella at the fireside, and Cinderella at the prince's ball! The full dress version of the thought is glittering with new images like bracelets and brooches and ear-rings, and fringed with fresh adjectives like edges of embroidery. That one word *pleachéd*, an heirloom from Queen Elizabeth's day, gives to the noble sonnet an antique dignity and charm like the effect of an ancestral jewel. But mark that now the poet reveals himself as he could not in the prosaic form of the first extract. It is his own neglect of his great opportunity of which he now speaks, and not merely the indolent indifference of others. It is himself who is the object of scorn. Self-revelation of beauty embellished by ornaments is the privilege of full dress; self-revelation in the florid costume of verse is the divine right of the poet. Passion that

must express itself longs always for the freedom of
rhythmic utterance.   And in spite of the exaggeration and extravagance which shield themselves under
the claim of poetic license, I venture to affirm that
"*In* vino *veritas*" is not truer than *In* carmine *veritas*.

As a further illustration of what has just been said
of the self-revelations to be looked for in verse, and
in Emerson's verse more especially, let the reader observe how freely he talks about his bodily presence
and infirmities in his poetry, — subjects he never
referred to in prose, except incidentally in private
letters.

Emerson is so essentially a poet that whole pages
of his are like so many litanies of alternating chants
and recitations.   His thoughts slip on and off their
light rhythmic robes just as the mood takes him, as
was shown in the passage I have quoted in prose and
in verse.   Many of the metrical preludes to his lectures are a versified and condensed abstract of the
leading doctrine of the discourse.   They are a curious
instance of survival; the lecturer, once a preacher,
still wants his text, and finds his scriptural motto in
his own rhythmic inspiration.

Shall we rank Emerson among the great poets or
not?

"The great poets are judged by the frame of mind
they induce; and to them, of all men, the severest criticism is due."

These are Emerson's words in the Preface to "Parnassus."

His own poems will stand this test as well as any

in the language. They lift the reader into a higher region of thought and feeling. This seems to me a better test to apply to them than the one which Mr. Arnold cited from Milton. The passage containing this must be taken, not alone, but with the context. Milton had been speaking of "Logic" and of "Rhetoric," and spoke of poetry "as being less subtile and fine, but more simple, sensuous, and passionate." This relative statement, it must not be forgotten, is conditioned by what went before. If the terms are used absolutely, and not comparatively, as Milton used them, they must be very elastic if they would stretch widely enough to include all the poems which the world recognizes as masterpieces, nay, to include some of the best of Milton's own.

In spite of what he said about himself in his letter to Carlyle, Emerson was not only a poet, but a very remarkable one. Whether a great poet or not will depend on the scale we use and the meaning we affix to the term. The heat at eighty degrees of Fahrenheit is one thing, and the heat at eighty degrees of Réaumur is a very different matter. The rank of poets is a point of very unstable equilibrium. From the days of Homer to our own, critics have been disputing about the place to be assigned to this or that member of the poetic hierarchy. It is not the most popular poet who is necessarily the greatest; Wordsworth never had half the popularity of Scott or Moore. It is not the multitude of remembered passages which settles the rank of a metrical composition as poetry. Gray's "Elegy," it is true, is full of lines we all remember, and is a great poem, if that term can be applied to any piece of verse of that length. But what shall we say to the "Ars Poetica" of Horace? It is crowded with lines worn smooth as old sesterces by constant quotation. And yet we should rather call it a versified criticism than a poem in the full sense of that word. And what shall we do with Pope's "Essay on Man," which has furnished more familiar lines than "Paradise Lost" and "Paradise Regained" both together? For all that, we know there is a school of writers who will not allow that Pope deserves the name of poet.

It takes a generation or two to find out what are the passages in a great writer which are to become commonplaces in literature and conversation. It is to be remembered that Emerson is one of those authors whose popularity must diffuse itself from above downwards. And after all, few will dare assert that "The Vanity of Human Wishes" is greater as a poem than Shelley's "Ode to the West Wind," or Keats's "Ode to a Nightingale," because no line in either of these poems is half so often quoted as

> "To point a moral or adorn a tale."

We cannot do better than begin our consideration of Emerson's poetry with Emerson's own self-estimate. He says in a fit of humility, writing to Carlyle: —

"I do not belong to the poets, but only to a low department of literature, the reporters, suburban men."

But Miss Peabody writes to Mr. Ireland: —

"He once said to me, 'I am not a great poet — but whatever is of me *is a poet*.'"

These opposite feelings were the offspring of different moods and different periods.

Here is a fragment, written at the age of twenty-eight, in which his self-distrust and his consciousness of the "vision," if not "the faculty, divine," are revealed with the brave nudity of the rhythmic confessional: —

> " A dull uncertain brain,
>   But gifted yet to know
>   That God has cherubim who go
>   Singing an immortal strain,
>   Immortal here below.
>   I know the mighty bards,
>   I listen when they sing,
>   And now I know
>   The secret store
>   Which these explore
>   When they with torch of genius pierce
>   The tenfold clouds that cover
>   The riches of the universe
>   From God's adoring lover.
>   And if to me it is not given
>   To fetch one ingot thence
>   Of that unfading gold of Heaven
>   His merchants may dispense,
>   Yet well I know the royal mine,
>   And know the sparkle of its ore,
>   Know Heaven's truth from lies that shine, —
>   Explored, they teach us to explore."

These lines are from "The Poet," a series of fragments given in the "Appendix," which, with his first volume, "Poems," his second, "May-Day and Other Pieces," form the complete ninth volume of the new series. These fragments contain some of the loftiest and noblest passages to be found in his poetical works, and if the reader should doubt which of Emerson's self-estimates in his two different moods spoken of above had most truth in it, he could question no longer after reading "The Poet."

Emerson has the most exalted ideas of the true

poetic function, as this passage from "Merlin" sufficiently shows: —

> " Thy trivial harp will never please
> Or fill my craving ear ;
> Its chords should ring as blows the breeze,
> Free, peremptory, clear.
> No jingling serenader's art
> Nor tinkling of piano-strings
> Can make the wild blood start
> In its mystic springs ;
> The kingly bard
> Must smite the chords rudely and hard,
> As with hammer or with mace ;
> That they may render back
> Artful thunder, which conveys
> Secrets of the solar track,
> Sparks of the supersolar blaze.
>
> .   .   .   .
>
> Great is the art,
> Great be the manners, of the bard.
> He shall not his brain encumber
> With the coil of rhythm and number ;
> But leaving rule and pale forethought
> He shall aye climb
> For his rhyme.
> ' Pass in, pass in,' the angels say,
> ' In to the upper doors,
> Nor count compartment of the floors,
> But mount to paradise
> By the stairway of surprise.' "

And here is another passage from "The Poet," mentioned in the quotation before the last, in which the
bard is spoken of as performing greater miracles than
those ascribed to Orpheus: —

> " A Brother of the world, his song
> Sounded like a tempest strong
> Which tore from oaks their branches broad,

And stars from the ecliptic road.
Time wore he as his clothing-weeds,
He sowed the sun and moon for seeds.
As melts the iceberg in the seas,
As clouds give rain to the eastern breeze,
As snow-banks thaw in April's beam,
The solid kingdoms like a dream
Resist in vain his motive strain,
They totter now and float amain.
For the Muse gave special charge
His learning should be deep and large,
And his training should not scant
The deepest lore of wealth or want:
His flesh should feel, his eyes should read
Every maxim of dreadful Need;
In its fulness he should taste
Life's honeycomb, but not too fast;
Full fed, but not intoxicated;
He should be loved; he should be hated;
A blooming child to children dear,
His heart should palpitate with fear."

We look naturally to see what poets were Emerson's chief favorites. In his poems "The Test" and "Solution," we find that the five whom he recognizes as defying the powers of destruction are Homer, Dante, Shakespeare, Swedenborg, Goethe.

Here are a few of his poetical characterizations from "The Harp:"—

" And this at least I dare affirm,
Since genius too has bound and term,
There is no bard in all the choir,
Not Homer's self the poet-sire,
Wise Milton's odes of pensive pleasure,
Or Shakespeare, whom no mind can measure,
Nor Collins' verse of tender pain,
Nor Byron's clarion of disdain,
Scott, the delight of generous boys,
Or Wordsworth, Pan's recording voice, —

Not one of all can put in verse,
Or to this presence could rehearse
The sights and voices ravishing
The boy knew on the hills in spring."

In the notice of "Parnassus" some of his prefer-
ences have been already mentioned.

Comparisons between men of genius for the sake of
aggrandizing the one at the expense of the other are
the staple of the meaner kinds of criticism. No lover
of art will clash a Venetian goblet against a Roman
amphora to see which is stronger; no lover of nature
undervalues a violet because it is not a rose. But
comparisons used in the way of description are not
odious.

The difference between Emerson's poetry and that
of the contemporaries with whom he would naturally
be compared is that of algebra and arithmetic. He
deals largely in general symbols, abstractions, and infinite series. He is always seeing the universal in the
particular. The great multitude of mankind care
more for two and two, something definite, a fixed
quantity, than for $a + b$'s and x^2's, — symbols used for
undetermined amounts and indefinite possibilities.
Emerson is a citizen of the universe who has taken up
his residence for a few days and nights in this travelling caravansary between the two inns that hang out
the signs of Venus and Mars. This little planet could
not provincialize such a man. The multiplication-
table is for the every-day use of every-day earth-people,
but the symbols he deals with are too vast, sometimes,
we must own, too vague, for the unilluminated terres-
trial and arithmetical intelligence. One cannot help
feeling that he might have dropped in upon us from

some remote centre of spiritual life, where, instead
of addition and subtraction, children were taught
quaternions, and where the fourth dimension of space
was as familiarly known to everybody as a foot-mea-
sure or a yard-stick is to us. Not that he himself
dealt in the higher or the lower mathematics, but he
saw the hidden spiritual meaning of things as Professor Cayley or Professor Sylvester see the meaning of
their mysterious formulæ. Without using the Ro-
setta-stone of Swedenborg, Emerson finds in every
phenomenon of nature a hieroglyphic. Others measure and describe the monuments, — he reads the
sacred inscriptions. How alive he makes Monadnoc !
Dinocrates undertook to "hew Mount Athos to the
shape of man " in the likeness of Alexander the Great.
Without the help of tools or workmen Emerson makes
"Cheshire's haughty hill" stand before us an imper-
sonation of kingly humanity, and talk with us as a
god from Olympus might have talked. This is the
fascination of Emerson's poetry; it moves in a world
of universal symbolism. The sense of the infinite
fills it with its majestic presence. It shows, also,
that he has a keen delight in the every-day aspects of
nature. But he looks always with the eye of a poet,
never with that of the man of science. The law of
association of ideas is wholly different in the two.
The scientific man connects objects in sequences and
series, and in so doing is guided by their collective resemblances. His aim is to classify and index all that
he sees and contemplates so as to show the relations
which unite, and learn the laws that govern, the subjects of his study. The poet links the most remote
objects together by the slender filament of wit, the
flowery chain of fancy, or the living, pulsating cord

of imagination, always guided by his instinct for the
beautiful.   The man of science clings to his object,
as the marsupial embryo to its teat, until he has filled
himself as full as he can hold; the poet takes a sip of
his dew-drop, throws his head up like a chick, rolls
his eyes around in contemplation of the heavens above
him and the universe in general, and never thinks of
asking a Linnæan question as to the flower that furnished him his dew-drop.   The poetical and scientific
natures rarely coexist; Haller and Goethe are examples which show that such a union may occur, but as
a rule the poet is contented with the colors of the
rainbow and leaves the study of Fraunhofer's lines
to the man of science.

Though far from being a man of science, Emerson
was a realist in the best sense of that word.   But his
realities reached to the highest heavens; like Milton,

> " He passed the flaming bounds of place and time ;
> The living throne, the sapphire blaze
> Where angels tremble while they gaze,
> HE SAW."

Everywhere his poetry abounds in celestial imagery.
If Galileo had been a poet as well as an astronomer,
he would hardly have sowed his verse thicker with
stars than we find them in the poems of Emerson.

Not less did Emerson clothe the common aspects
of life with the colors of his imagination.   He was
ready to see beauty everywhere: —

> " Thou canst not wave thy staff in air,
> Or dip thy paddle in the lake,
> But it carves the bow of beauty there,
> And the ripples in rhyme the oar forsake."

He called upon the poet to

> " Tell men what they knew before ;
> Paint the prospect from their door."

And his practice was like his counsel. He saw our plain New England life with as honest New England eyes as ever looked at a huckleberry-bush or into a milking-pail.

This noble quality of his had its dangerous side. In one of his exalted moods he would have us

> "Give to barrows, trays and pans
> Grace and glimmer of romance."

But in his lecture on Poetry and Imagination, he says: —

> "What we once admired as poetry has long since come to be a sound of tin pans; and many of our later books we have outgrown. Perhaps Homer and Milton will be tin pans yet."

The "grace and glimmer of romance" which were to invest the tin pan are forgotten, and he uses it as a belittling object for comparison. He himself was not often betrayed into the mistake of confounding the prosaic with the poetical, but his followers, so far as the "realists" have taken their hint from him, have done it most thoroughly. Mr. Whitman enumerates all the objects he happens to be looking at as if they were equally suggestive to the poetical mind, furnishing his reader a large assortment on which he may exercise the fullest freedom of selection. It is only giving him the same liberty that Lord Timothy Dexter allowed his readers in the matter of punctuation, by leaving all stops out of his sentences, and printing at the end of his book a page of commas, semicolons, colons, periods, notes of interrogation and exclamation, with which the reader was expected to "pepper" the pages as he might see fit.

French realism does not stop at the tin pan, but must

deal with the slop-pail and the wash-tub as if it were literally true that

> " In the mud and scum of things
> There alway, alway something sings."

Happy were it for the world if M. Zola and his tribe would stop even there; but when they cross the borders of science into its infected districts, leaving behind them the reserve and delicacy which the genuine scientific observer never forgets to carry with him, they disgust even those to whom the worst scenes they describe are too wretchedly familiar. The true realist is such a man as Parent du Chatelet; exploring all that most tries the senses and the sentiments, and reporting all truthfully, but soberly, chastely, without needless circumstance, or picturesque embellishment, for a useful end, and not for a mere sensational effect.

What a range of subjects from "The Problem" and "Uriel" and "Forerunners" to "The Humble-Bee" and "The Titmouse"! Nor let the reader who thinks the poet must go far to find a fitting theme fail to read the singularly impressive home-poem, "Hamatreya," beginning with the names of the successive owners of a piece of land in Concord, — probably the same he owned after the last of them, —

> " Bulkeley, Hunt, Willard, Hosmer, Meriam, Flint,"

and ending with the austere and solemn "Earth-Song."

Full of poetical feeling, and with a strong desire for poetical expression, Emerson experienced a difficulty in the mechanical part of metrical composition. His muse picked her way as his speech did in conversation and in lecturing. He made desperate work now and then with rhyme and rhythm, showing that though a born poet he was not a born singer. Think of making "feeble" rhyme with "people," "abroad" with "Lord," and contemplate the following couplet which one cannot make rhyme without actual verbicide:—

> "Where feeds the moose, and walks the surly bear,
> And up the tall mast runs the woodpeck"—are!

And how could prose go on all-fours more unmetrically than this?

> "In Adirondac lakes
> At morn or noon the guide rows bare-headed."

It was surely not difficult to say—

> "At morn or noon bare-headed rows the guide."

And yet while we note these blemishes, many of us will confess that we like his uncombed verse better, oftentimes, than if it were trimmed more neatly and disposed more nicely. When he is at his best, his lines flow with careless ease, as a mountain stream tumbles, sometimes rough and sometimes smooth, but all the more interesting for the rocks it runs against and the grating of the pebbles it rolls over.

There is one trick of verse which Emerson occasionally, not very often, indulges in. This is the crowding of a redundant syllable into a line. It is a liberty which is not to be abused by the poet. Shakespeare, the supreme artist, and Milton, the "mighty-mouth'd inventor of harmonies," knew how to use it effectively. Shelley employed it freely. Bryant indulged in it occasionally, and wrote an article in an early number of "The North American Review" in defence of its use. Willis was fond of it. As a relief to monotony it may be now and then allowed,—may even have an agreeable effect in breaking the monotony of too formal verse. But it may easily become a deformity and a cause of aversion. A humpback may add picturesqueness to a procession, but if there are too many humpbacks in line we turn away from the sight of them. Can any ear reconcile itself to the last of these three lines of Emerson's?

> "Oh, what is Heaven but the fellowship
> Of minds that each can stand against the world
> By its own meek and incorruptible will?"

These lines that lift their backs up in the middle — span-worm lines, we may call them — are not to be commended for common use because some great poets have now and then admitted them. They have invaded some of our recent poetry as the canker-worms gather on our elms in June. Emerson has one or two of them here and there, but they never swarm on his leaves so as to frighten us away from their neighborhood.

As for the violently artificial rhythms and rhymes which have reappeared of late in English and American literature, Emerson would as soon have tried to ride three horses at once in a circus as to shut himself up in triolets, or attempt any cat's-cradle tricks of rhyming sleight of hand.

If we allow that Emerson is not a born singer, that he is a careless versifier and rhymer, we must still recognize that there is something in his verse which belongs, indissolubly, sacredly, to his thought. Who would decant the wine of his poetry from its quaint and antique-looking *lagena?* Read his poem to the Æolian harp ("The Harp") and his model betrays itself: —

> "These syllables that Nature spoke,
> And the thoughts that in him woke,
> Can adequately utter none

Save to his ear the wind-harp lone.
Therein I hear the Parcæ reel
The threads of man at their humming wheel,
The threads of life and power and pain,
So sweet and mournful falls the strain.
And best can teach its Delphian chord
How Nature to the soul is moored,
If once again that silent string,
As erst it wont, would thrill and ring."

There is no need of quoting any of the poems which have become familiar to most true lovers of poetry. Emerson saw fit to imitate the Egyptians by placing "The Sphinx" at the entrance of his temple of song. This poem was not fitted to attract worshippers. It is not easy of comprehension, not pleasing in movement. As at first written it had one verse in it which sounded so much like a nursery rhyme that Emerson was prevailed upon to omit it in the later versions. There are noble passages in it, but they are for the adept and not for the beginner. A commonplace young person taking up the volume and puzzling his or her way along will come by and by to the verse: —

"Have I a lover
Who is noble and free ? —
I would he were nobler
Than to love me."

The commonplace young person will be apt to say or think *c'est magnifique, mais ce n'est pas — l'amour.*

The third poem in the volume, "The Problem," should have stood first in order. This ranks among the finest of Emerson's poems. All his earlier verse has a certain freshness which belongs to the first outburst of song in a poetic nature. "Each and All," "The Humble-Bee," "The Snow-Storm," should be read before "Uriel," "The World-Soul," or "Mithridates." "Monadnoc" will be a good test of the reader's taste for Emerson's poetry, and after this "Woodnotes."

In studying his poems we must not overlook the delicacy of many of their descriptive portions. If in the flights of his imagination he is like the strong-winged bird of passage, in his exquisite choice of descriptive epithets he reminds me of the *tenui-rostrals*. His subtle selective instinct penetrates the vocabulary for the one word he wants, as the long, slender bill of those birds dives deep into the flower for its drop of honey. Here is a passage showing admirably the two different conditions: wings closed and the selective instinct picking out its descriptive expressions; then suddenly wings flashing open and the imagination in the firmament, where it is always at home. Follow the pitiful inventory of insignificances of the forlorn being he describes with a pathetic humor more likely to bring a sigh than a smile, and then mark the grand hyperbole of the last two lines. The passage is from the poem called "Destiny:" —

> "Alas ! that one is born in blight,
> Victim of perpetual slight :
> When thou lookest on his face,
> Thy heart saith, 'Brother, go thy ways !
> None shall ask thee what thou doest,
> Or care a rush for what thou knowest,
> Or listen when thou repliest,
> Or remember where thou liest,
> Or how thy supper is sodden ;'
> And another is born
> To make the sun forgotten."

Of all Emerson's poems the "Concord Hymn" is the most nearly complete and faultless, — but it is not distinctively Emersonian. It is such a poem as Collins might have written, — it has the very movement and melody of the "Ode on the Death of Thomson," and of the "Dirge in Cymbeline," with the same sweetness and tenderness of feeling. Its one conspicuous line,

> "And fired the shot heard round the world,"

must not take to itself all the praise deserved by this perfect little poem, a model for all of its kind. Compact, expressive, serene, solemn, musical, in four brief stanzas it tells the story of the past, records the commemorative act of the passing day, and invokes the higher Power that governs the future to protect the memorial-stone sacred to Freedom and her martyrs.

These poems of Emerson's find the readers that must listen to them and delight in them, as the Ancient Mariner fastened upon the man who must hear him. If any doubter wishes to test his fitness for reading them, and if the poems already mentioned are not enough to settle the question, let him read the paragraph of "May-Day," beginning, —

> "I saw the bud-crowned Spring go forth,"

"Sea-Shore," the fine fragments in the "Appendix" to his published works, called, collectively, "The Poet," blocks bearing the mark of poetic genius, but left lying round for want of the structural instinct, and last of all, that which is, in many respects, first of all, the "Threnody," a lament over the death of his first-born son. This poem has the dignity of "Lycidas" without its refrigerating classicism, and with all the tenderness of Cowper's lines on the receipt of his mother's picture. It may well compare with others of the finest memorial poems in the language, — with Shelley's "Adonais," and Matthew Arnold's "Thyrsis," leaving out of view Tennyson's "In Memoriam" as of wider scope and larger pattern.

Many critics will concede that there is much truth in Mr. Arnold's remark on the want of "evolution" in Emerson's poems. One is struck with the fact that a great number of fragments lie about his poetical workshop: poems begun and never finished; scraps of poems, chips of poems, paving the floor with intentions never carried out. One cannot help remembering Coleridge with his incomplete "Christabel," and his "Abyssinian Maid" and her dulcimer which she never got a tune out of. We all know there was good reason why Coleridge should have been infirm of purpose. But when we look at that great unfinished picture over which Allston labored with the hopeless ineffectiveness of Sisyphus; when we go through a whole gallery of pictures by an American artist in which the backgrounds are slighted as if our midsummer heats had taken away half the artist's life and vigor; when we walk round whole rooms full of sketches, impressions, effects, symphonies, invisibilities, and other apologies for honest work, it would not be strange if it should suggest a painful course of reflections as to the possibility that there may be something in our climatic or other conditions which tends to scholastic and artistic anæmia and insufficiency, — the opposite of what we find showing itself in the full-blooded verse of poets like Browning and on the flaming canvas of painters like Henri Regnault. Life seemed lustier in Old England than in New England to Emerson, to Hawthorne, and to that admirable observer, Mr. John

Burroughs. Perhaps we require another century or two of acclimation.

Emerson never grappled with any considerable metrical difficulties. He wrote by preference in what I have ventured to call the normal respiratory measure, — octosyllabic verse, in which one common expiration is enough and not too much for the articulation of each line. The "fatal facility" for which this verse is noted belongs to it as recited and also as written, and it implies the need of only a minimum of skill and labor. I doubt if Emerson would have written a verse of poetry if he had been obliged to use the Spenserian stanza. In the simple measures he habitually employed he found least hindrance to his thought.

Every true poet has an atmosphere as much as every great painter. The golden sunshine of Claude and the pearly mist of Corot belonged to their way of looking at nature as much as the color of their eyes and hair belonged to their personalities. So with the poets; for Wordsworth the air is always serene and clear, for Byron the sky is uncertain between storm and sunshine. Emerson sees all nature in the same pearly mist that wraps the willows and the streams of Corot. Without its own characteristic atmosphere, illuminated by

> "The light that never was on sea or land,"

we may have good verse but no true poem. In his poetry there is not merely this atmosphere, but there is always a mirage in the horizon.

Emerson's poetry is eminently subjective, — if Mr. Ruskin, who hates the word, will pardon me for using it in connection with a reference to two of his own

chapters in his "Modern Painters." These are the
chapter on "The Pathetic Fallacy," and the one
which follows it "On Classical Landscape." In these
he treats of the transfer of a writer's mental or emotional conditions to the external nature which he contemplates. He asks his readers to follow him in a long
examination of what he calls by the singular name mentioned, "the pathetic fallacy," because, he says, "he
will find it eminently characteristic of the modern
mind; and in the landscape, whether of literature or
art, he will also find the modern painter endeavoring
to express something which he, as a living creature,
imagines in the lifeless object, while the classical and
mediæval painters were content with expressing the
unimaginary and actual qualities of the object itself."

Illustrations of Mr. Ruskin's "pathetic fallacy"
may be found almost anywhere in Emerson's poems.
Here is one which offers itself without search: —

> "Daily the bending skies solicit man,
>   The seasons chariot him from this exile,
>   The rainbow hours bedeck his glowing wheels,
>   The storm-winds urge the heavy weeks along,
>   Suns haste to set, that so remoter lights
>   Beckon the wanderer to his vaster home."

The expression employed by Ruskin gives the idea
that he is dealing with a defect. If he had called
the state of mind to which he refers the *sympathetic
illusion*, his readers might have looked upon it more
justly.

It would be a pleasant and not a difficult task to
trace the resemblances between Emerson's poetry and
that of other poets. Two or three such resemblances

have been incidentally referred to; a few others may
be mentioned.

In his contemplative study of Nature he reminds us
of Wordsworth, at least in certain brief passages, but
he has not the staying power of that long-breathed,
not to say long-winded, lover of landscapes. Both
are on the most intimate terms with Nature, but
Emerson contemplates himself as belonging to her,
while Wordsworth feels as if she belonged to him.

> "Good-bye, proud world,"

recalls Spenser and Raleigh. "The Humble-Bee" is
strongly marked by the manner and thought of Marvell. Marvell's

> "Annihilating all that's made
> To a green thought in a green shade"

may well have suggested Emerson's

> "The green silence dost displace
> With thy mellow, breezy bass."

"The Snow-Storm" naturally enough brings to
mind the descriptions of Thomson and of Cowper, and
fragment as it is, it will not suffer by comparison with
either.

"Woodnotes," one of his best poems, has passages
that might have been found in Milton's "Comus;"
this, for instance: —

> "All constellations of the sky
> Shed their virtue through his eye.
> Him Nature giveth for defence
> His formidable innocence."

Of course his Persian and Indian models betray
themselves in many of his poems, some of which,
called translations, sound as if they were original.

So we follow him from page to page and find him

passing through many moods, but with one pervading
spirit: —

> "Melting matter into dreams,
> Panoramas which I saw,
> And whatever glows or seems
> Into substance, into Law."

We think in reading his "Poems" of these words of
Sainte-Beuve: —

> "The greatest poet is not he who has done the best; it
> is he who suggests the most; he, not all of whose meaning
> is at first obvious, and who leaves you much to desire, to
> explain, to study; much to complete in your turn."

Just what he shows himself in his prose, Emerson
shows himself in his verse. Only when he gets into
rhythm and rhyme he lets us see more of his personality, he ventures upon more audacious imagery, his
flight is higher and swifter, his brief crystalline sentences have dissolved and pour in continuous streams.
Where they came from, or whither they flow to empty
themselves, we cannot always say, — it is enough to
enjoy them as they flow by us.

Incompleteness — want of beginning, middle, and
end — is their too common fault. His pages are too
much like those artists' studios all hung round with
sketches and "bits" of scenery. "The Snow-Storm"
and "Sea-Shore" are "bits" out of a landscape that
was never painted, admirable, so far as they go, but
forcing us to ask, "Where is the painting for which
these scraps are studies?" or "Out of what great picture have these pieces been cut?"

We do not want his fragments to be made wholes,
— if we did, what hand could be found equal to the
task? We do not want his rhythms and rhymes
smoothed and made more melodious. They are as

honest as Chaucer's, and we like them as they are, not modernized or manipulated by any versifying drill-sergeant, — if we wanted them reshaped whom could we trust to meddle with them?

His poetry is elemental; it has the rock beneath it in the eternal laws on which it rests; the roll of deep waters in its grander harmonies; its air is full of Æolian strains that waken and die away as the breeze wanders over them; and through it shines the white starlight, and from time to time flashes a meteor that startles us with its sudden brilliancy.

After all our criticisms, our selections, our analyses, our comparisons, we have to recognize that there is a charm in Emerson's poems which cannot be defined any more than the fragrance of a rose or a hyacinth, — any more than the tone of a voice which we should know from all others if all mankind were to pass before us, and each of its articulating representatives should call us by name.

All our crucibles and alembics leave unaccounted for the great mystery of *style*. "The style is of [a part of] the man himself," said Buffon, and this saying has passed into the stronger phrase, "The style is the man."

The "personal equation" which differentiates two observers is not confined to the tower of the astronomer. Every human being is individualized by a new arrangement of elements. His mind is a safe with a lock to which only certain letters are the key. His ideas follow in an order of their own. His words group themselves together in special sequences, in peculiar rhythms, in unlooked-for combinations, the total effect of which is to stamp all that he says or writes with his individuality. We may not be able to assign the reason of the fascination the poet we have been considering exercises over us. But this we can say, that he lives in the highest atmosphere of thought; that he is always in the presence of the infinite, and ennobles the accidents of human existence so that they partake of the absolute and eternal while he is looking at them; that he unites a royal dignity of manner with the simplicity of primitive nature; that his words and phrases arrange themselves, as if by an elective affinity of their own, with a *curiosa felicitas* which captivates and enthrals the reader who comes fully under its influence, and that through all he sings as in all he says for us we recognize the same serene, high, pure intelligence and moral nature, infinitely precious to us, not only in themselves, but as a promise of what the transplanted life, the air and soil and breeding of this western world may yet educe from their potential virtues, shaping themselves, at length, in a literature, as much its own as the Rocky Mountains and the Mississippi.

CHAPTER XV.

MR. CONWAY gives the following account of two visits to Emerson after the decline of his faculties had begun to make itself obvious: —

"In 1875, when I stayed at his house in Concord for a little time, it was sad enough to find him sitting as a listener before those who used to sit at his feet in silence. But when alone with him he conversed in the old way, and his faults of memory seemed at times to disappear. There was something striking in the kind of forgetfulness by which he suffered. He remembered the realities and uses of things when he could not recall their names. He would describe what he wanted or thought of; when he could not recall 'chair' he could speak of that which supports the human frame, and 'the implement that cultivates the soil' must do for plough."

"In 1880, when I was last in Concord, the trouble had made heavy strides. The intensity of his silent attention to every word that was said was painful, suggesting a concentration of his powers to break through the invisible walls closing around them. Yet his face was serene; he was even cheerful, and joined in our laughter at some letters his eldest daughter had preserved, from young girls, trying to coax autograph letters, and in one case asking for what price he would write a valedictory address she had to deliver at college. He was still able to joke about his 'naughty memory;' and no complaint came from him when he once rallied himself on living too long. Emerson appeared to me strangely beautiful at this time, and the sweetness of his voice, when he spoke of the love and providence at his side, is quite indescribable."

One of the later glimpses we have of Emerson is that preserved in the journal of Mr. Whitman, who visited Concord in the autumn of 1881. Mr. Ireland gives a long extract from this journal, from which I take the following: —

"On entering he had spoken very briefly, easily, and politely to several of the company, then settled himself in his chair, a trifle pushed back, and, though a listener and apparently an alert one, remained silent through the whole talk and discussion. And so, there Emerson sat, and I looking at him. A good color in his face, eyes clear, with the well-known expression of sweetness, and the old clear-peering aspect quite the same."

Mr. Whitman met him again the next day, Sunday, September 18, and records: —

"As just said, a healthy color in the cheeks, and good light in the eyes, cheery expression, and just the amount of talking that best suited, namely, a word or short phrase only where needed, and almost always with a smile."

Dr. Le Baron Russell writes to me of Emerson at a still later period: —

"One incident I will mention which occurred at my last visit to Emerson, only a few months before his death. I went by Mrs. Emerson's request to pass a Sunday at their house at Concord towards the end of June. His memory had been failing for some time, and his mind, as you know, was clouded, but the old charm of his voice and manner had never left him. On the morning after my arrival Mrs. Emerson took us into the garden to see the beautiful roses in which she took great delight. One red rose of most brilliant color she called our attention to especially; its 'hue' was so truly 'angry and brave' that I involuntarily repeated Herbert's line, —

> 'Bids the rash gazer wipe his eye,' —

from the verses which Emerson had first repeated to me so long ago.   Emerson looked at the rose admiringly, and then as if by a sudden impulse lifted his hat gently, and said with a low bow, 'I take off my hat to it.'"

Once a poet, always a poet.   It was the same reverence for the beautiful that he had shown in the same way in his younger days on entering the wood, as Governor Rice has told us the story, given in an earlier chapter.

I do not remember Emerson's last time of attendance at the Saturday Club, but I recollect that he came after the trouble in finding words had become well marked.   "My memory hides itself," he said. The last time I saw him, living, was at Longfellow's funeral.   I was sitting opposite to him when he rose, and going to the side of the coffin, looked intently upon the face of the dead poet.   A few minutes later he rose again and looked once more on the familiar features, not apparently remembering that he had just done so.   Mr. Conway reports that he said to a friend near him, "That gentleman was a sweet, beautiful soul, but I have entirely forgotten his name."

Dr. Edward Emerson has very kindly furnished me, in reply to my request, with information regarding his father's last years which will interest every one who has followed his life through its morning and midday to the hour of evening shadows.

"May-Day," which was published in 1867, was made up of the poems written since his first volume appeared.   After this he wrote no poems, but with some difficulty fitted the refrain to the poem "Boston," which had remained unfinished since the old anti-slavery days. "Greatness," and the Phi Beta Kappa Oration of 1867, were among his last pieces of work. His college lectures, "Natural History of Intellect," were merely notes recorded years before, and now gathered and welded together. In 1876 he revised his poems, and made the selections from them for the "Little Classic" edition of his works, then called "Selected Poems." In that year he gave his "Address to the Students of the University of Virginia." This was a paper written long before, and its revision, with the aid of his daughter Ellen, was accomplished with much difficulty.

The year 1867 was about the limit of his working life. During the last five years he hardly answered a letter. Before this time it had become increasingly hard for him to do so, and he always postponed and thought he should feel more able the next day, until his daughter Ellen was compelled to assume the correspondence. He did, however, write some letters in 1876, as, for instance, the answer to the invitation of the Virginia students.

Emerson left off going regularly to the Saturday Club probably in 1875. He used to depend on meeting Mr. Cabot there, but after Mr. Cabot began to come regularly to work on "Letters and Social Aims," Emerson, who relied on his friendly assistance, ceased attending the meetings. The trouble he had in finding the word he wanted was a reason for his staying away from all gatherings where he was called upon to take a part in conversation, though he the more willingly went to lectures and readings and to church. His hearing was very slightly impaired, and his sight

remained pretty good, though he sometimes said letters doubled, and that "M's" and "N's" troubled
him to read.   He recognized the members of his own
family and his *old* friends; but, as I infer from this
statement, he found a difficulty in remembering the
faces of new acquaintances, as is common with old
persons.

He continued the habit of reading, — read through
all his printed works with much interest and surprise,
went through all his manuscripts, and endeavored,
unsuccessfully, to index them.   In these Dr. Emerson found written "Examined 1877 or 1878," but he
found no later date.

In the last year or two he read anything which he
picked up on his table, but he read the same things
over, and whispered the words like a child.   He liked
to look over the "Advertiser," and was interested in
the "Nation."   He enjoyed pictures in books and
showed them with delight to guests.

All this with slight changes and omissions is from
the letter of Dr. Emerson in answer to my questions.
The twilight of a long, bright day of life may be sad-
dening, but when the shadow falls so gently and gradually, with so little that is painful and so much that is
soothing and comforting, we do not shrink from following the imprisoned spirit to the very verge of its
earthly existence.

But darker hours were in the order of nature very
near at hand.   From these he was saved by his not
untimely release from the imprisonment of the worn-
out bodily frame.

In April, 1882, Emerson took a severe cold, and
became so hoarse that he could hardly speak.   When
his son, Dr. Edward Emerson, called to see him, he

found him on the sofa, feverish, with more difficulty of expression than usual, dull, but not uncomfortable. As he lay on his couch he pointed out various objects, among others a portrait of Carlyle "the good man, — my friend." His son told him that he had seen Carlyle, which seemed to please him much. On the following day the unequivocal signs of pneumonia showed themselves, and he failed rapidly. He still recognized those around him, among the rest Judge Hoar, to whom he held out his arms for a last embrace. A sharp pain coming on, ether was administered with relief. And in a little time, surrounded by those who loved him and whom he loved, he passed quietly away. He lived very nearly to the completion of his seventy-ninth year, having been born May 25, 1803, and his death occurring on the 27th of April, 1882.

Mr. Ireland has given a full account of the funeral, from which are, for the most part, taken the following extracts: —

"The last rites over the remains of Ralph Waldo Emerson took place at Concord on the 30th of April. A special train from Boston carried a large number of people. Many persons were on the street, attracted by the services, but were unable to gain admission to the church where the public ceremonies were held. Almost every building in town bore over its entrance-door a large black and white rosette with other sombre draperies. The public buildings were heavily draped, and even the homes of the very poor bore outward marks of grief at the loss of their friend and fellow-townsman.

"The services at the house, which were strictly private, occurred at 2.30, and were conducted by Rev. W. H. Furness, of Philadelphia, a kindred spirit and an almost life-long friend. They were simple in character, and only

Dr. Furness took part in them. The body lay in the front northeast room, in which were gathered the family and close friends of the deceased. The only flowers were contained in three vases on the mantel, and were lilies of the valley, red and white roses, and arbutus. The adjoining room and hall were filled with friends and neighbors.

"At the church many hundreds of persons were awaiting the arrival of the procession, and all the space, except the reserved pews, was packed. In front of the pulpit were simple decorations, boughs of pine covered the desk, and in their centre was a harp of yellow jonquils, the gift of Miss Louisa M. Alcott. Among the floral tributes was one from the teachers and scholars in the Emerson school. By the sides of the pulpit were white and scarlet geraniums and pine boughs, and high upon the wall a laurel wreath.

"Before 3.30 the pall-bearers brought in the plain black walnut coffin, which was placed before the pulpit. The lid was turned back, and upon it was put a cluster of richly colored pansies and a small bouquet of roses. While the coffin was being carried in, 'Pleyel's Hymn' was rendered on the organ by request of the family of the deceased. Dr. James Freeman Clarke then entered the pulpit. Judge E. Rockwood Hoar remained by the coffin below, and when the congregation became quiet, made a brief and pathetic address, his voice many times trembling with emotion."

I subjoin this most impressive "Address" entire, from the manuscript with which Judge Hoar has kindly favored me: —

"The beauty of Israel is fallen in its high place! Mr. Emerson has died; and we, his friends and neighbors, with this sorrowing company, have turned aside the procession from his home to his grave, — to this temple of his fathers, that we may here unite in our parting tribute of memory and love.

"There is nothing to mourn for him. That brave and

manly life was rounded out to the full length of days. That dying pillow was softened by the sweetest domestic affection; and as he lay down to the sleep which the Lord giveth his beloved, his face was as the face of an angel, and his smile seemed to give a glimpse of the opening heavens.

"Wherever the English language is spoken throughout the world his fame is established and secure. Throughout this great land and from beyond the sea will come innumerable voices of sorrow for this great public loss. But we, his neighbors and townsmen, feel that he was *ours*. He was descended from the founders of the town. He chose our village as the place where his lifelong work was to be done. It was to our fields and orchards that his presence gave such value; it was our streets in which the children looked up to him with love, and the elders with reverence. He was our ornament and pride.

> " ' He is gone — is dust, —
> He the more fortunate ! Yea, he hath finished !
> For him there is no longer any future.
> His life is bright — bright without spot it was
> And cannot cease to be. No ominous hour
> Knocks at his door with tidings of mishap.
> Far off is he, above desire and fear ;
> No more submitted to the change and chance
> Of the uncertain planets. . . .

> " ' The bloom is vanished from my life,
> For, oh ! he stood beside me like my youth;
> Transformed for me the real to a dream,
> Clothing the palpable and the familiar
> With golden exhalations of the dawn.
> Whatever fortunes wait my future toils,
> The *beautiful* is vanished and returns not.'

"That lofty brow, the home of all wise thoughts and high aspirations, — those lips of eloquent music, — that great soul, which trusted in God and never let go its hope of immortality, — that large heart, to which everything that belonged to man was welcome, — that hospitable nature, loving and tender and generous, having no repulsion or scorn for anything but meanness and baseness, — oh, friend, brother, father, lover, teacher, inspirer, guide! is there no more that we can do now than to give thee this our hail and farewell! "

Judge Hoar's remarks were followed by the congregation singing the hymns, "Thy will be done," "I will not fear the fate provided by Thy love." The Rev. Dr. Furness then read selections from the Scriptures.

The Rev. James Freeman Clarke then delivered an "Address," from which I extract two eloquent and inspiring passages, regretting to omit any that fell from lips so used to noble utterances and warmed by their subject, — for there is hardly a living person more competent to speak or write of Emerson than this high-minded and brave-souled man, who did not wait until he was famous to be his admirer and champion.

"The saying of the Liturgy is true and wise, that 'in the midst of life we are in death.' But it is still more true that in the midst of death we are in life. Do we ever believe so much in immortality as when we look on such a dear and noble face, now so still, which a few hours ago was radiant with thought and love? ' He is not here: he is risen.' That power which we knew, — that soaring intelligence, that soul of fire, that ever-advancing spirit, — *that* cannot have been suddenly annihilated with the decay of these earthly organs. It has left its darkened dust behind. It has outsoared the shadow of our night. God does not trifle with his creatures by bringing to nothing the ripe fruit of the ages by the lesion of a cerebral cell, or some bodily tissue. Life does not die, but matter dies off from it. The highest energy we know, the soul of man, the unit in which meet intelligence, imagination, memory, hope, love, purpose, insight, — this agent of immense resource and boundless power, — this has not been

subdued by its instrument.   When we think of such an
one as he, we can only think of life, never of death.

"Such was his own faith, as expressed in his paper on
'Immortality.'   But he himself was the best argument for
immortality.   Like the greatest thinkers, he did not rely
on logical proof, but on the higher evidence of universal
instincts, — the vast streams of belief which flow through
human thought like currents in the ocean; those shoreless
rivers which forever roll along their paths in the Atlantic
and Pacific, not restrained by banks, but guided by the
revolutions of the globe and the attractions of the sun."

.   .   .   .

"Let us then ponder his words: —

> "'Wilt thou not ope thy heart to know
> What rainbows teach and sunsets show ?
> Voice of earth to earth returned,
> Prayers of saints that inly burned,
> Saying, *What is excellent,*
> *As God lives, is permanent ;*
> *Hearts are dust, hearts' loves remain ;*
> *Heart's love will meet thee again.*
>
> .   .   .   .   .   .
>
> House and tenant go to ground
> Lost in God, in Godhead found.'"

After the above address a feeling prayer was offered
by Rev. Howard N. Brown, of Brookline, and the
benediction closed the exercises in the church.   Immediately before the benediction, Mr. Alcott recited
the following sonnet, which he had written for the occasion: —

> "His harp is silent : shall successors rise,
> Touching with venturous hand the trembling string,
> Kindle glad raptures, visions of surprise,
> And wake to ecstasy each slumbering thing ?
> Shall life and thought flash new in wondering eyes,
> As when the seer transcendent, sweet, and wise,

World-wide his native melodies did sing,
Flushed with fair hopes and ancient memories ?
Ah, no ! That matchless lyre shall silent lie :
None hath the vanished minstrel's wondrous skill
To touch that instrument with art and will.
With him, winged poesy doth droop and die ;
While our dull age, left voiceless, must lament
The bard high heaven had for its service sent."

"Over an hour was occupied by the passing files of neighbors, friends, and visitors looking for the last time upon the face of the dead poet. The body was robed completely in white, and the face bore a natural and peaceful expression. From the church the procession took its way to the cemetery. The grave was made beneath a tall pine-tree upon the hill-top of Sleepy Hollow, where lie the bodies of his friends Thoreau and Hawthorne, the upturned sod being concealed by strewings of pine boughs. A border of hemlock spray surrounded the grave and completely lined its sides. The services here were very brief, and the casket was soon lowered to its final resting-place.

"The Rev. Dr. Haskins, a cousin of the family, an Episcopal clergyman, read the Episcopal Burial Service, and closed with the Lord's Prayer, ending at the words, 'and deliver us from evil.' In this all the people joined. Dr. Haskins then pronounced the benediction. After it was over, the grandchildren passed the open grave and threw flowers into it."

So vanished from human eyes the bodily presence of Ralph Waldo Emerson, and his finished record belongs henceforth to memory.

CHAPTER XVI.

EMERSON. — A RETROSPECT.

EMERSON'S earthly existence was in the estimate of
his own philosophy so slight an occurrence in his
career of being that his relations to the accidents of
time and space seem quite secondary matters to one
who has been long living in the companionship of his
thought. Still, he had to be born, to take in his
share of the atmosphere in which we are all immersed,
to have dealings with the world of phenomena, and at
length to let them all "soar and sing" as he left his
earthly half-way house. It is natural and pardonable
that we should like to know the details of the daily
life which the men whom we admire have shared with
common mortals, ourselves among the rest. But
Emerson has said truly, "Great geniuses have the
shortest biographies. Their cousins can tell you nothing about them. They lived in their writings, and
so their home and street life was trivial and commonplace."

The reader has had many extracts from Emerson's writings laid before him. It was no easy task to choose them, for his paragraphs are so condensed, so much in the nature of abstracts, that it is like distilling absolute alcohol to attempt separating the spirit of what he says from his undiluted thought. His books are all so full of his life to their last syllable that we might letter every volume *Emersoniana*, by Ralph Waldo Emerson.

From the numerous extracts I have given from Emerson's writings it may be hoped that the reader will have formed an idea for himself of the man and of the life which have been the subjects of these pages. But he may probably expect something like a portrait of the poet and moralist from the hand of his biographer, if the author of this Memoir may borrow the name which will belong to a future and better equipped laborer in the same field. He may not unreasonably look for some general estimate of the life-work of the scholar and thinker of whom he has been reading. He will not be disposed to find fault with the writer of the Memoir if he mentions many things which seem very trivial but for the interest they borrow from the individual to whom they relate.

Emerson's personal appearance was that of a scholar, the descendant of scholars. He was tall and slender, with the complexion which is bred in the alcove and not in the open air. He used to tell his son Edward that he measured six feet in his shoes, but his son thinks he could hardly have straightened himself to that height in his later years. He was very light for a man of his stature. He got on the scales at Cheyenne, on his trip to California, comparing his weight with that of a lady of the party. A little while afterwards he asked of his fellow-traveller, Professor Thayer, "How much did I weigh? A hundred and forty?" "A hundred and forty and a half," was the answer. "Yes, yes, a hundred and forty and a half! That *half* I prize; it is an index of better things!"

Emerson's head was not such as Schopenhauer insists upon for a philosopher. He wore a hat measuring six and seven eighths on the *cephalometer* used by hatters, which is equivalent to twenty-one inches and a quarter of circumference. The average size is from seven to seven and an eighth, so that his head was quite small in that dimension. It was long and narrow, but lofty, almost symmetrical, and of more nearly equal breadth in its anterior and posterior regions than many or most heads.

His shoulders sloped so much as to be commented upon for this peculiarity by Mr. Gilfillan, and like "Ammon's great son," he carried one shoulder a little higher than the other. His face was thin, his nose somewhat accipitrine, casting a broad shadow; his mouth rather wide, well formed and well closed, carrying a question and an assertion in its finely finished curves; the lower lip a little prominent, the chin shapely and firm, as becomes the corner - stone of the countenance. His expression was calm, sedate, kindly, with that look of refinement, centring about the lips, which is rarely found in the male New Englander, unless the family features have been for two or three cultivated generations the battle-field and the playground of varied thoughts and complex emotions as well as the sensuous and nutritive port of entry. His whole look was irradiated by an ever active inquiring intelligence. His manner was noble and gracious. Few of our fellow-countrymen have had larger opportunities of seeing distinguished personages than our present minister at the Court of St. James. In a recent letter to myself, which I trust Mr. Lowell will pardon my quoting, he says of Emerson: —

"There was a majesty about him beyond all other men I have known, and he habitually dwelt in that ampler and diviner air to which most of us, if ever, only rise in spurts."

From members of his own immediate family I have derived some particulars relating to his personality and habits which are deserving of record.

His hair was brown, quite fine, and, till he was fifty, very thick. His eyes were of the "strongest and brightest blue." The member of the family who tells me this says: —

"My sister and I have looked for many years to see whether any one else had such absolutely blue eyes, and have never found them except in sea-captains. I have seen three sea-captains who had them."

He was not insensible to music, but his gift in that direction was very limited, if we may judge from this family story. When he was in college, and the singing-master was gathering his pupils, Emerson presented himself, intending to learn to sing. The master received him, and when his turn came, said to him, "Chord!" "What?" said Emerson. "Chord! Chord! I tell you," repeated the master. "I don't know what you mean," said Emerson. "Why, sing! Sing a note." "So I made some kind of a noise, and the singing-master said, 'That will do, sir. You need not come again.'"

Emerson's mode of living was very simple: coffee in the morning, tea in the evening, animal food by choice only once a day, wine only when with others using it, but always *pie* at breakfast. "It stood before him and was the first thing eaten." Ten o'clock was his bed-time, six his hour of rising until the last ten years of his life, when he rose at seven. Work or company sometimes led him to sit up late, and this he could do night after night. He never was hungry, — could go any time from breakfast to tea without food and not know it, but was always ready for food when it was set before him.

He always walked from about four in the afternoon till tea-time, and often longer when the day was fine, or he felt that he should work the better.

It is plain from his writings that Emerson was possessed all his life long with the idea of his constitutional infirmity and insufficiency. He hated invalidism, and had little patience with complaints about ill-health, but in his poems, and once or twice in his letters to Carlyle, he expresses himself with freedom about his own bodily inheritance. In 1827, being then but twenty-four years old, he writes: —

> "I bear in youth the sad infirmities
> That use to undo the limb and sense of age."

Four years later: —

> "Has God on thee conferred
> A bodily presence mean as Paul's,
> Yet made thee bearer of a word
> Which sleepy nations as with trumpet calls?"

and again, in the same year: —

> "Leave me, Fear, thy throbs are base,
> Trembling for the body's sake."

Almost forty years from the first of these dates we

find him bewailing in "Terminus" his inherited weakness of organization.

And in writing to Carlyle, he says: —

"You are of the Anakim and know nothing of the debility and postponement of the blonde constitution."

Again, "I am the victim of miscellany — miscellany of designs, vast debility and procrastination."

He thought too much of his bodily insufficiencies, which, it will be observed, he refers to only in his private correspondence, and in that semi-nudity of self-revelation which is the privilege of poetry. His presence was fine and impressive, and his muscular strength was enough to make him a rapid and enduring walker.

Emerson's voice had a great charm in conversation, as in the lecture-room. It was never loud, never shrill, but singularly penetrating. He was apt to hesitate in the course of a sentence, so as to be sure of the exact word he wanted; picking his way through his vocabulary, to get at the best expression of his thought, as a well-dressed woman crosses the muddy pavement to reach the opposite sidewalk. It was this natural slight and not unpleasant semicolon pausing of the memory which grew upon him in his years of decline, until it rendered conversation laborious and painful to him.

He never laughed loudly. When he laughed it was under protest, as it were, with closed doors, his mouth shut, so that the explosion had to seek another respiratory channel, and found its way out quietly, while his eyebrows and nostrils and all his features betrayed the "ground swell," as Professor Thayer happily called it, of the half-suppressed convulsion. He was averse to loud laughter in others, and objected to Margaret Fuller that she made him laugh too much.

Emerson was not rich in some of those natural gifts which are considered the birthright of the New Englander. He had not the mechanical turn of the whittling Yankee. I once questioned him about his manual dexterity, and he told me he could split a shingle four ways with one nail, — which, as the intention is not to split it at all in fastening it to the roof of a house or elsewhere, I took to be a confession of inaptitude for mechanical works. He does not seem to have been very accomplished in the handling of agricultural implements either, for it is told in the family that his little son, Waldo, seeing him at work with a spade, cried out, "Take care, papa, — you will dig your leg."

He used to regret that he had no ear for music. I have said enough about his verse, which often jars on a sensitive ear, showing a want of the nicest perception of harmonies and discords in the arrangement of the words.

There are stories which show that Emerson had a retentive memory in the earlier part of his life. It is hard to say from his books whether he had or not, for he jotted down such a multitude of things in his diary that this was a kind of mechanical memory which supplied him with endless materials of thought and subjects for his pen.

Lover and admirer of Plato as Emerson was, the doors of the academy, over which was the inscription μηδείς ἀγεωμέτρητος ἔσειτω, — Let no one unacquainted with geometry enter here, — would have been closed to him. All the exact sciences found him an unwilling learner. He says of himself that he cannot multiply seven by twelve with impunity.

In an unpublished manuscript kindly submitted to me by Mr. Frothingham, Emerson is reported as saying, "God has given me the seeing eye, but not the working hand." His gift was insight; he saw the germ through its envelope; the particular in the light of the universal; the fact in connection with the principle; the phenomenon as related to the law; all this not by the slow and sure process of science, but by the sudden and searching flashes of imaginative double vision. He had neither the patience nor the method of the inductive reasoner; he passed from one thought to another not by logical steps but by airy flights, which left no footprints. This mode of intellectual action when found united with natural sagacity becomes poetry, philosophy, wisdom, or prophecy in its various forms of manifestation. Without that gift of natural sagacity (*odoratio quædam venatica*), — a good scent for truth and beauty, — it appears as extravagance, whimsicality, eccentricity, or insanity, according to its degree of aberration. Emerson was eminently sane for an idealist. He carried the same sagacity into the ideal world that Franklin showed in the affairs of common life.

He was constitutionally fastidious, and had to school himself to become able to put up with the terrible inflictions of uncongenial fellowships. We must go to his poems to get at his weaknesses. The clown of the first edition of "Monadnoc," "with heart of cat and eyes of bug," disappears in the after-thought of the later version of the poem, but the eye that recognized him and the nature that recoiled from him were there still. What must he not have endured from the persecutions of small-minded worshippers who fastened upon him for the interminable period between the in-

coming and the outgoing railroad train! He was a
model of patience and good temper. We might have
feared that he lacked the sensibility to make such intrusions and offences an annoyance. But when Mr.
Frothingham gratifies the public with those most interesting personal recollections which I have had the
privilege of looking over, it will be seen that his equanimity, admirable as it was, was not incapable of being disturbed, and that on rare occasions he could give
way to the feeling which showed itself of old in the
doom pronounced on the barren fig-tree.

Of Emerson's affections his home-life, and those
tender poems in memory of his brothers and his son,
give all the evidence that could be asked or wished
for. His friends were all who knew him, for none
could be his enemy; and his simple graciousness of
manner, with the sincerity apparent in every look and
tone, hardly admitted indifference on the part of any
who met him, were it but for a single hour. Even
the little children knew and loved him, and babes in
arms returned his angelic smile. Of the friends who
were longest and most intimately associated with him,
it is needless to say much in this place. Of those who
are living, it is hardly time to speak; of those who
are dead, much has already been written. Margaret
Fuller — I must call my early schoolmate as I best
remember her — leaves her life pictured in the mosaic
of five artists, Emerson himself among the number;
Thoreau is faithfully commemorated in the loving
memoir by Mr. Sanborn; Theodore Parker lives in
the story of his life told by the eloquent Mr. Weiss;
Hawthorne awaits his portrait from the master-hand
of Mr. Lowell.

How nearly any friend, other than his brothers

Edward and Charles, came to him, I cannot say, indeed I can hardly guess. That "majesty" Mr. Lowell speaks of always seemed to hedge him round like
the divinity that doth hedge a king. What man was
he who would lay his hand familiarly upon his shoulder and call him Waldo? No disciple of Father
Mathew would be likely to do such a thing. There
may have been such irreverent persons, but if any one
had so ventured at the Saturday Club, it would
have produced a sensation like Brummel's "George,
ring the bell," to the Prince Regent. His ideas of
friendship, as of love, seem almost too exalted for our
earthly conditions, and suggest the thought as do many
others of his characteristics, that the spirit which animated his mortal frame had missed its way on the
shining path to some brighter and better sphere of
being.

Not so did Emerson appear among the plain working farmers of the village in which he lived. He was
a good, unpretending fellow-citizen who put on no
airs, who attended town-meetings, took his part in
useful measures, was no great hand at farming, but
was esteemed and respected, and felt to be a principal
source of attraction to Concord, for strangers came
flocking to the place as if it held the tomb of Washington.

What was the errand on which he visited our
earth, — the message with which he came commis-
sioned from the Infinite source of all life?

Every human soul leaves its port with sealed orders.
These may be opened earlier or later on its voyage,
but until they are opened no one can tell what is to be
his course or to what harbor he is bound.

Emerson inherited the traditions of the Boston pulpit, such as they were, damaged, in the view of the prevailing sects of the country, perhaps by too long contact with the "Sons of Liberty," and their revolutionary notions. But the most "liberal" Boston pulpit still held to many doctrines, forms, and phrases open to the challenge of any independent thinker.

In the year 1832 this young priest, then a settled minister, "began," as was said of another, "to be about thirty years of age." He had opened his sealed orders and had read therein : —

Thou shalt not profess that which thou dost not believe.

Thou shalt not heed the voice of man when it agrees not with the voice of God in thine own soul.

Thou shalt study and obey the laws of the Universe and they will be thy fellow-servants.

Thou shalt speak the truth as thou seest it, without fear, in the spirit of kindness to all thy fellow-creatures, dealing with the manifold interests of life and the typical characters of history.

Nature shall be to thee as a symbol. The life of the soul, in conscious union with the Infinite, shall be for thee the only real existence.

This pleasing show of an external world through which thou art passing is given thee to interpret by the light which is in thee. Its least appearance is not unworthy of thy study. Let thy soul be open and thine eyes will reveal to thee beauty everywhere.

Go forth with thy message among thy fellow-creatures; teach them they must trust themselves as guided by that inner light which dwells with the pure in heart, to whom it was promised of old that they shall see God.

Teach them that each generation begins the world afresh, in perfect freedom; that the present is not the prisoner of the past, but that to-day holds captive all yesterdays, to compare, to judge, to accept, to reject their teachings, as these are shown by its own morning's sun.

To thy fellow-countrymen thou shalt preach the gospel of the New World, that here, here in our America, is the home of man; that here is the promise of a new and more excellent social state than history has recorded.

Thy life shall be as thy teachings, brave, pure, truthful, beneficent, hopeful, cheerful, hospitable to all honest belief, all sincere thinkers, and active according to thy gifts and opportunities.

He was true to the orders he had received. Through doubts, troubles, privations, opposition, he would not

> "bate a jot
> Of heart or hope, but still bear up and steer
> Right onward."

All through the writings of Emerson the spirit of these orders manifests itself. His range of subjects is very wide, ascending to the highest sphere of spiritual contemplation, bordering on that "intense inane" where thought loses itself in breathless ecstasy, and stooping to the homeliest maxims of prudence and the every-day lessons of good manners. And all his work was done, not so much

> "As ever in his great Taskmaster's eye,"

as in the ever-present sense of divine companionship.

He was called to sacrifice his living, his position, his intimacies, to a doubt, and he gave them all up

without a murmur.   He might have been an idol, and
he broke his own pedestal to attack the idolatry which
he saw all about him.   He gave up a comparatively
easy life for a toilsome and trying one; he accepted a
precarious employment, which hardly kept him above
poverty, rather than wear the golden padlock on his
lips which has held fast the conscience of so many
pulpit Chrysostoms.   Instead of a volume or two of
sermons, bridléd with a text and harnessed with a confession of faith, he bequeathed us a long series of discourses and essays in which we know we have his
honest thoughts, free from that professional bias which
tends to make the pulpit teaching of the fairest-minded
preacher follow a diagonal of two forces, — the promptings of his personal and his ecclesiastical opinions.

Without a church or a pulpit, he soon had a congregation.   It was largely made up of young persons
of both sexes, young by nature, if not in years, who,
tired of routine and formulæ, and full of vague aspirations, found in his utterances the oracles they sought.
To them, in the words of his friend and neighbor Mr.
Alcott, he

> " Sang his full song of hope and lofty cheer."

Nor was it only for a few seasons that he drew his audiences of devout listeners around him.   Another
poet, his Concord neighbor, Mr. Sanborn, who listened
to him many years after the first flush of novelty was
over, felt the same enchantment, and recognized the
same inspiring life in his words, which had thrilled
the souls of those earlier listeners.

> " His was the task and his the lordly gift
>   Our eyes, our hearts, bent earthward, to uplift."

This was his power, — to inspire others, to make life

purer, loftier, calmer, brighter. Optimism is what the young want, and he could no more help taking the hopeful view of the universe and its future than Claude could help flooding his landscapes with sunshine.

"Nature," published in 1836, "the first clear manifestation of his genius," as Mr. Norton calls it, revealed him as an idealist and a poet, with a tendency to mysticism. If he had been independent in circumstances, he would doubtless have developed more freely in these directions. But he had his living to get and a family to support, and he must look about him for some paying occupation. The lecture-room naturally presented itself to a scholar accustomed to speaking from the pulpit. This medium of communicating thought was not as yet very popular, and the rewards it offered were but moderate. Emerson was of a very hopeful nature, however, and believed in its possibilities.

"I am always haunted with brave dreams of what might be accomplished in the lecture-room, — so free and so unpretending a platform, — a Delos not yet made fast. I imagine an eloquence of infinite variety, rich as conversation can be, with anecdote, joke, tragedy, epics and pindarics, argument and confession."

So writes Emerson to Carlyle in 1841.

It would be as unfair to overlook the special form in which Emerson gave most of his thoughts to the world, as it would be to leave out of view the calling of Shakespeare in judging his literary character. Emerson was an essayist and a lecturer, as Shakespeare was a dramatist and a play-actor.

The exigencies of the theatre account for much that is, as it were, accidental in the writings of Shakespeare. The demands of the lecture-room account for many peculiarities which are characteristic of Emerson as an author. The play must be in five acts, each of a given length. The lecture must fill an hour and not overrun it. Both play and lecture must be vivid, varied, picturesque, stimulating, or the audience would tire before the allotted time was over.

Both writers had this in common: they were poets and moralists. They reproduced the conditions of life in the light of penetrative observation and ideal contemplation; they illustrated its duties in their breach and in their observance, by precepts and well-chosen portraits of character. The particular form in which they wrote makes little difference when we come upon the utterance of a noble truth or an elevated sentiment.

It was not a simple matter of choice with the dramatist or the lecturer in what direction they should turn their special gifts. The actor had learned his business on the stage; the lecturer had gone through his apprenticeship in the pulpit. Each had his bread to earn, and he must work, and work hard, in the way open before him. For twenty years the playwright wrote dramas, and retired before middle age with a good estate to his native town. For forty years Emerson lectured and published lectures, and established himself at length in competence in the village where his ancestors had lived and died before him. He never became rich, as Shakespeare did. He was never in easy circumstances until he was nearly seventy years old. Lecturing was hard work, but he was under the "base necessity," as he called it, of constant labor, writing in summer, speaking everywhere east and west in the trying and dangerous winter season.

He spoke in great cities to such cultivated audiences as no other man could gather about him, and in remote villages where he addressed plain people whose classics were the Bible and the "Farmer's Almanac." Wherever he appeared in the lecture-room, he fascinated his listeners by his voice and manner; the music of his speech pleased those who found his thought too subtle for their dull wits to follow.

When the lecture had served its purpose, it came before the public in the shape of an essay. But the essay never lost the character it borrowed from the conditions under which it was delivered; it was a lay sermon, — *concio ad populum*. We must always remember what we are dealing with. "Expect nothing more of my power of construction, — no ship-building, no clipper, smack, nor skiff even, only boards and logs tied together." "Here I sit and read and write, with very little system, and, as far as regards composition, with the most fragmentary result: paragraphs incompressible, each sentence an infinitely repellent particle." We have then a moralist and a poet appearing as a lecturer and an essayist, and now and then writing in verse. He liked the freedom of the platform. "I preach in the lecture-room," he says, "and there it tells, for there is no prescription. You may laugh, weep, reason, sing, sneer, or pray, according to your genius." In England, he says, "I find this lecturing a key which opens all doors." But he did not tend to overvalue the calling which from "base necessity" he followed so diligently. "Incorrigible spouting Yankee," he calls himself; and again, "I peddle out all the wit I can gather from Time or from Nature, and am pained at heart to see how thankfully that little is received."

Lecture-peddling was a hard business and a poorly paid one in the earlier part of the time when Emerson was carrying his precious wares about the country and offering them in competition with the cheapest itinerants, with shilling concerts and negro-minstrel entertainments. But one could get a kind of living out of it if he had invitations enough. I remember Emerson's coming to my house to know if I could fill his place at a certain lyceum so that he might accept a very advantageous invitation in another direction. I told him that I was unfortunately engaged for the evening mentioned. He smiled serenely, saying that then he supposed he must give up the new stove for that season.

No man would accuse Emerson of parsimony of ideas. He crams his pages with the very marrow of his thought. But in weighing out a lecture he was as punctilious as Portia about the pound of flesh. His utterance was deliberate and spaced with not infrequent slight delays. Exactly at the end of the hour the lecture stopped, — suddenly, abruptly, but quietly, without peroration of any sort, always with "a gentle shock of mild surprise" to the unprepared listener. He had weighed out the full measure to his audience with perfect fairness.

ὥστε τάλαντα γυνὴ χερνῆτις ἀληθὴς
῞Η τε σταθμὸν ἔχουσα καὶ εἴριον, ἀμφὶς ἀνέλκει
᾽Ισαζουσ, ἵνα παισὶν ἀεικέα μισθὸν ἄρηται,

or, in Bryant's version,

"as the scales
Are held by some just woman, who maintains
By spinning wool her household, — carefully
She poises both the wool and weights, to make
The balance even, that she may provide
A pittance for her babes."

As to the charm of his lectures all are agreed. It is needless to handle this subject, for Mr. Lowell has written upon it. Of their effect on his younger listeners he says,—

"To some of us that long past experience remains the most marvellous and fruitful we have ever had. Emerson awakened us, saved us from the body of this death. It is the sound of the trumpet that the young soul longs for, careless of what breath may fill it. Sidney heard it in the ballad of 'Chevy Chase,' and we in Emerson. Nor did it blow retreat, but called us with assurance of victory."

There was, besides these stirring notes, a sweet seriousness in Emerson's voice that was infinitely soothing. So might "Peace, be still," have sounded from the lips that silenced the storm. I remember that in the dreadful war-time, on one of the days of anguish and terror, I fell in with Governor Andrew, on his way to a lecture of Emerson's, where he was going, he said, to relieve the strain upon his mind. An hour passed in listening to that flow of thought, calm and clear as the diamond drops that distil from a mountain rock, was a true nepenthe for a care-worn soul.

An author whose writings are like mosaics must have borrowed from many quarries. Emerson had read more or less thoroughly through a very wide range of authors. I shall presently show how extensive was his reading. No doubt he had studied certain authors diligently, a few, it would seem, thoroughly. But let no one be frightened away from his pages by the terrible names of Plotinus and Proclus and Porphyry, of Behmen or Spinoza, or of those

modern German philosophers with whom it is not pretended that he had any intimate acquaintance. Mr.
George Ripley, a man of erudition, a keen critic, a
lover and admirer of Emerson, speaks very plainly of
his limitations as a scholar.

"As he confesses in the essay on Books, his learning is
second hand; but everything sticks which his mind can
appropriate. He defends the use of translations, and I
doubt whether he has ever read ten pages of his great
authorities, Plato, Plutarch, Montaigne, or Goethe, in the
original. He is certainly no friend of profound study
any more than of philosophical speculation. Give him a
few brilliant and suggestive glimpses and he is content."

One correction I must make to this statement.
Emerson says he has "contrived to read" almost
every volume of Goethe, and that he has fifty-five of
them, but that he has read nothing else in German,
and has not looked into him for a long time. This
was in 1840, in a letter to Carlyle. It was up-hill
work, it may be suspected, but he could not well be
ignorant of his friend's great idol, and his references
to Goethe are very frequent.

Emerson's quotations are like the miraculous
draught of fishes. I hardly know his rivals except
Burton and Cotton Mather. But no one would accuse him of pedantry. Burton quotes to amuse himself and his reader; Mather quotes to show his learning, of which he had a vast conceit; Emerson quotes
to illustrate some original thought of his own, or because another writer's way of thinking falls in with
his own, — never with a trivial purpose. Reading as
he did, he must have unconsciously appropriated a
great number of thoughts from others. But he was
profuse in his references to those from whom he bor-

rowed, — more profuse than many of his readers would believe without taking the pains to count his authorities. This I thought it worth while to have done, once for all, and I will briefly present the results of the examination. The named references, chiefly to authors, as given in the table before me, are three thousand three hundred and ninety-three, relating to eight hundred and sixty-eight different individuals. Of these, four hundred and eleven are mentioned more than once; one hundred and fifty-five, five times or more; sixty-nine, ten times or more; thirty-eight, fifteen times or more; and twenty-seven, twenty times or more. These twenty-seven names alone, the list of which is here given, furnish no less than one thousand and sixty-five references.

Authorities.	Number of times mentioned.	Authorities.	Number of times mentioned.
Shakespeare	112	Webster	27
Napoleon	84	Aristotle	25
Plato	81	Hafiz	25
Plutarch	70	Wordsworth	25
Goethe	62	Burke	24
Swift	49	Saint Paul	24
Bacon	47	Dante	22
Milton	46	Shattuck (Hist. of Concord)	21
Newton	43		
Homer	42	Chaucer	20
Socrates	42	Coleridge	20
Swedenborg	40	Michael Angelo	20
Montaigne	30	The name of Jesus occurs fifty-four times.	
Saadi	30		
Luther	30		

It is interesting to observe that Montaigne, Franklin, and Emerson all show the same fondness for Plutarch.

Montaigne says, "I never settled myself to the

reading of any book of solid learning but Plutarch and Seneca."

Franklin says, speaking of the books in his father's library, "There was among them Plutarch's Lives, which I read abundantly, and I still think that time spent to great advantage."

Emerson says, "I must think we are more deeply indebted to him than to all the ancient writers."

Studies of life and character were the delight of all these four moralists. As a judge of character, Dr. Hedge, who knew Emerson well, has spoken to me of his extraordinary gift, and no reader of "English Traits" can have failed to mark the formidable penetration of the intellect which looked through those calm cerulean eyes.

Noscitur a sociis is applicable to the books a man most affects as well as to the companions he chooses. It is with the kings of thought that Emerson most associates. As to borrowing from his royal acquaintances his ideas are very simple and expressed without reserve.

"All minds quote. Old and new make the warp and woof of every moment. There is no thread that is not a twist of these two strands. By necessity, by proclivity, and by delight, we all quote."

What Emerson says of Plutarch applies very nearly to himself.

"In his immense quotation and allusion we quickly cease to discriminate between what he quotes and what he invents. We sail on his memory into the ports of every nation, enter into every private property, and do not stop to discriminate owners, but give him the praise of all."

Mr. Ruskin and Lord Tennyson have thought it worth their while to defend themselves from the charge of plagiarism. Emerson would never have taken the trouble to do such a thing. His mind was overflowing with thought as a river in the season of flood, and was full of floating fragments from an endless variety of sources. He drew ashore whatever he wanted that would serve his purpose. He makes no secret of his mode of writing. "I dot evermore in my endless journal, a line on every knowable in nature; but the arrangement loiters long, and I get a brick-kiln instead of a house." His journal is "full of disjointed dreams and audacities." Writing by the aid of this, it is natural enough that he should speak of his "lapidary style" and say, "I build my house of boulders."

"It is to be remembered," says Mr. Ruskin, "that all men who have sense and feeling are continually helped; they are taught by every person they meet, and enriched by everything that falls in their way. The greatest is he who has been oftenest aided; and if the attainments of all human minds could be traced to their real sources, it would be found that the world had been laid most under contribution by the men of most original powers, and that every day of their existence deepened their debt to their race, while it enlarged their gifts to it."

The reader may like to see a few coincidences between Emerson's words and thoughts and those of others.

Some sayings seem to be a kind of family property. "Scorn trifles" comes from Aunt Mary Moody Emerson, and reappears in her nephew, Ralph Waldo. "What right have you, Sir, to your virtue? Is virtue piecemeal? This is a jewel among the rags of a beggar." So writes Ralph Waldo Emerson in his lecture, "New England Reformers." "Hiding the badges of royalty beneath the gown of the mendicant,

and ever on the watch lest their rank be betrayed by
the sparkle of a gem from under their rags." Thus
wrote Charles Chauncy Emerson in "The Harvard
Register" nearly twenty years before.

> "The hero is not fed on sweets,
> Daily his own heart he eats."

The image comes from Pythagoras *via* Plutarch.

Now and then, but not with any questionable fre-
quency, we find a sentence which recalls Carlyle.

> "The national temper, in the civil history, is not
> flashy or whiffling.   The slow, deep English mass
> smoulders with fire, which at lasts sets all its borders
> in flame.   The wrath of London is not French wrath,
> but has a long memory, and in hottest heat a register
> and rule."

Compare this passage from "English Traits" with
the following one from Carlyle's "French Revolution:" —

> "So long this Gallic fire, through its successive
> changes of color and character, will blaze over the face
> of Europe, and afflict and scorch all men; — till it pro-
> voke all men, till it kindle another kind of fire, the
> Teutonic kind, namely; and be swallowed up, so to
> speak, in a day!   For there is a fire comparable to the
> burning of dry jungle and grass; most sudden, high-
> blazing; and another fire which we liken to the burning
> of coal, or even of anthracite coal, but which no known
> thing will put out."

> "O what are heroes, prophets, men
>   But pipes through which the breath of man doth blow
>   A momentary music."

The reader will find a similar image in one of
Burns's letters, again in one of Coleridge's poetical

fragments, and long before any of them, in a letter of Leibnitz.

> "He builded better than he knew"

is the most frequently quoted line of Emerson. The thought is constantly recurring in our literature. It helps out the minister's sermon; and a Fourth of July Oration which does not borrow it is like the "Address without a Phœnix" among the Drury Lane mock poems. Can we find any trace of this idea elsewhere?

In a little poem of Coleridge's, "William Tell," are these two lines: —

> "On wave and wind the boy would toss,
> Was great, nor knew how great he was."

The thought is fully worked out in the celebrated essay of Carlyle called "Characteristics." It appears in Emerson's poem "Fate."

> "Unknown to Cromwell as to me
> Was Cromwell's measure or degree;
> Unknown to him as to his horse,
> If he than his groom be better or worse."

It is unnecessary to illustrate this point any further in this connection. In dealing with his poetry other resemblances will suggest themselves. All the best poetry the world has known is full of such resemblances. If we find Emerson's wonderful picture, "Initial Love," prefigured in the "Symposium" of Plato, we have only to look in the "Phædrus" and we shall find an earlier sketch of Shakespeare's famous group, —

> "The lunatic, the lover, and the poet."

Sometimes these resemblances are nothing more than accidental coincidences; sometimes the similar pas-

sages are unconsciously borrowed from another; sometimes they are paraphrases, variations, embellished
copies, *éditions de luxe* of sayings that all the world
knows are old, but which it seems to the writer worth
his while to say over again. The more improved versions of the world's great thoughts we have, the better, and we look to the great minds for them. The
larger the river, the more streams flow into it. The
wide flood of Emerson's discourse has a hundred rivers and thousands of streamlets for its tributaries.

It was not from books only that he gathered food
for thought and for his lectures and essays. He was
always on the lookout in conversation for things to be
remembered. He picked up facts one would not have
expected him to care for. He once corrected me in
giving Flora Temple's time at Kalamazoo. I made a
mistake of a quarter of a second, and he set me right.
He was not always so exact in his memory, as I have
already shown in several instances. Another example is where he speaks of Quintus Curtius, the historian, when he is thinking of Mettus Curtius, the self-
sacrificing equestrian. Little inaccuracies of this
kind did not concern him much; he was a wholesale
dealer in illustrations, and could not trouble himself
about a trifling defect in this or that particular article.

Emerson was a man who influenced others more
than others influenced him. Outside of his family
connections, the personalities which can be most
easily traced in his own are those of Carlyle, Mr. Alcott, and Thoreau. Carlyle's harsh virility could not
be without its effect on his valid, but sensitive nature.
Alcott's psychological and physiological speculations
interested him as an idealist. Thoreau lent him a new
set of organs of sense of wonderful delicacy. Emer-

son looked at nature as a poet, and his natural history, if left to himself, would have been as vague as that of Polonius. But Thoreau had a pair of eyes which, like those of the Indian deity, could see the smallest emmet on the blackest stone in the darkest night, — or come nearer to seeing it than those of most mortals. Emerson's long intimacy with him taught him to give an outline to many natural objects which would have been poetic nebulæ to him but for this companionship. A nicer analysis would detect many alien elements mixed with his individuality, but the family traits predominated over all the external influences, and the personality stood out distinct from the common family qualities. Mr. Whipple has well said: "Some traits of his mind and character may be traced back to his ancestors, but what doctrine of heredity can give us the genesis of his genius? Indeed, the safest course to pursue is to quote his own words, and despairingly confess that it is the nature of genius 'to spring, like the rainbow daughter of Wonder, from the invisible, to abolish the past and refuse all history.'"

Emerson's place as a thinker is somewhat difficult to fix. He cannot properly be called a psychologist. He made notes and even delivered lectures on the natural history of the intellect; but they seem to have been made up, according to his own statement, of hints and fragments rather than of the results of systematic study. He was a man of intuition, of insight, a seer, a poet, with a tendency to mysticism. This tendency renders him sometimes obscure, and once in a while almost, if not quite, unintelligible. We can, for this reason, understand why the great lawyer turned him over to his daughters, and Dr. Walter Channing complained that his lecture made his head ache.   But it is not always a writer's fault that he is not understood.   Many persons have poor heads for abstractions; and as for mystics, if they understand themselves it is quite as much as can be expected.   But that which is mysticism to a dull listener may be the highest and most inspiring imaginative clairvoyance to a brighter one.   It is to be hoped that no reader will take offence at the following anecdote, which may be found under the title "Diogenes," in the work of his namesake, Diogenes Laertius.   I translate from the Latin version.

"Plato was talking about ideas, and spoke of *mensality* and *cyathity* [*tableity* and *gobletity*].   'I can see a table and a goblet,' said the cynic, 'but I can see no such things as tableity and gobletity.'   'Quite so,' answered Plato, 'because you have the eyes to see a goblet and a table with, but you have not the brains to understand tableity and gobletity.'"

This anecdote may be profitably borne in mind in following Emerson into the spheres of intuition and mystical contemplation.

Emerson was an idealist in the Platonic sense of the word, a spiritualist as opposed to a materialist. He believes, he says, "as the wise Spenser teaches," that the soul makes its own body.   This, of course, involves the doctrine of preëxistence; a doctrine older than Spenser, older than Plato or Pythagoras, having its cradle in India, fighting its way down through Greek philosophers and Christian fathers and German professors, to our own time, when it has found Pierre Leroux, Edward Beecher, and Brigham Young among its numerous advocates.   Each has his fancies on the subject.   The geography of an undiscovered country and the soundings of an ocean that has never been sailed over may belong to romance and poetry, but they do not belong to the realm of knowledge.

That the organ of the mind brings with it inherited aptitudes is a simple matter of observation.   That it inherits truths is a different proposition.   The eye does not bring landscapes into the world on its retina, — why should the brain bring thoughts?   Poetry settles such questions very simply by saying it is so.

The poet in Emerson never accurately differentiated itself from the philosopher.   He speaks of Wordsworth's ode on the Intimations of Immortality as the high-water mark of the poetry of this century. It sometimes seems as if he had accepted the lofty rhapsodies of this noble ode as working truths.

> " Not in entire forgetfulness,
>   And not in utter nakedness,
>   But trailing clouds of glory do we come
>   From God, who is our home."

In accordance with this statement of a divine inheritance from a preëxisting state, the poet addresses the infant : —

> " Mighty prophet !   Seer blest !
>   On whom those truths do rest
> Which we are toiling all our lives to find."

These are beautiful fancies, but the philosopher will naturally ask the poet what are the truths which the child has lost between its cradle and the age of eight years, at which Wordsworth finds the little girl of whom he speaks in the lines, —

> " A simple child,
> That lightly draws its breath
> And feels its life in every limb, —
> What should it know of death ? "

What should it, sure enough, or of any other of those great truths which Time with its lessons, and the hardening of the pulpy brain, can alone render appreciable to the consciousness? Undoubtedly every brain has its own set of moulds ready to shape all material of thought into its own individual set of patterns. If the mind comes into consciousness with a good set of moulds derived by "traduction," as Dryden called it, from a good ancestry, it may be all very well to give the counsel to the youth to plant himself on his instincts. But the individual to whom this counsel is given probably has dangerous as well as wholesome instincts. He has also a great deal besides the instincts to be considered. His instincts are mixed up with innumerable acquired prejudices, erroneous conclusions, deceptive experiences, partial truths, one-sided tendencies. The clearest insight will often find it hard to decide what is the real instinct, and whether the instinct itself is, in theological language, from God or the devil. That which was a safe guide for Emerson might not work well with Lacenaire or Jesse Pomeroy. The cloud of glory which the babe brings with it into the world is a good set of instincts, which dispose it to accept moral and intellectual truths, — not the truths themselves. And too many children come into life trailing after them clouds which are anything but clouds of glory.

It may well be imagined that when Emerson proclaimed the new doctrine, — new to his young disciples, — of planting themselves on their instincts, consulting their own spiritual light for guidance, — trusting to intuition, without reference to any other authority, he opened the door to extravagances in any unbalanced minds, if such there were, which listened

to his teachings.   Too much was expected out of the
mouths of babes and sucklings.   The children shut up
by Psammetichus got as far as one word in their evolution of an original language, but *bekkos* was a very
small contribution towards a complete vocabulary.
"The Dial" was well charged with intuitions, but
there was too much vagueness, incoherence, aspiration
without energy, effort without inspiration, to satisfy
those who were looking for a new revelation.

The gospel of intuition proved to be practically nothing more or less than this: a new manifesto of intellectual and spiritual independence.   It was no great
discovery that we see many things as truths which
we cannot prove.   But it was a great impulse to
thought, a great advance in the attitude of our thinking community, when the profoundly devout religious
free-thinker took the ground of the undevout and ir-
religious free-thinker, and calmly asserted and peace-
ably established the right and the duty of the individual to weigh the universe, its laws and its legends, in
his own balance, without fear of authority, or names,
or institutions.

All this brought its dangers with it, like other
movements of emancipation.   For the Fay *ce que
voudras* of the revellers of Medmenham Abbey was
substituted the new motto, Pense *ce que voudras*.
There was an intoxication in this newly proclaimed
evangel which took hold of some susceptible natures
and betrayed itself in prose and rhyme, occasionally
of the Bedlam sort.   Emerson's disciples were never
accused of falling into the more perilous snares of antinomianism, but he himself distinctly recognizes the
danger of it, and the counterbalancing effect of household life, with its curtain lectures and other benign

influences. Extravagances of opinion cure themselves. Time wore off the effects of the harmless de-
bauch, and restored the giddy revellers to the regi-
men of sober thought, as reformed spiritual inebriates.

Such were some of the incidental effects of the Emersonian declaration of independence. It was followed
by a revolutionary war of opinion not yet ended or
at present like to be. A local outbreak, if you will,
but so was throwing the tea overboard. A provincial
affair, if the Bohemian press likes that term better,
but so was the skirmish where the gun was fired the
echo of which is heard in every battle for freedom all
over the world.

Too much has been made of Emerson's mysticism.
He was an intellectual rather than an emotional mystic, and withal a cautious one. He never let go the
string of his balloon. He never threw over all his
ballast of common sense so as to rise above an atmosphere in which a rational being could breathe. I
found in his library William Law's edition of Jacob
Behmen. There were all those wonderful diagrams
over which the reader may have grown dizzy, — just
such as one finds on the walls of lunatic asylums, —
evidences to all sane minds of cerebral strabismus in
the contrivers of them. Emerson liked to lose himself
for a little while in the vagaries of this class of minds,
the dangerous proximity of which to insanity he knew
and has spoken of. He played with the incommunicable, the inconceivable, the absolute, the antinomies,
as he would have played with a bundle of jackstraws.
"Brahma," the poem which so mystified the readers
of "The Atlantic Monthly," was one of his spiritual

divertisements. To the average Western mind it is
the nearest approach to a Torricellian vacuum of intel-
ligibility that language can pump out of itself. If
"Rejected Addresses" had not been written half a
century before Emerson's poem, one would think these
lines were certainly meant to ridicule and parody it :

> " The song of Braham is an Irish howl ;
> Thinking is but an idle waste of thought,
> And nought is everything and everything is nought."

Braham, Hazlitt might have said, is so obviously the
anagram of Brahma that dulness itself could not mistake the object intended.

Of course no one can hold Emerson responsible for
the "Yoga" doctrine of Brahmanism, which he has
amused himself with putting in verse. The oriental
side of Emerson's nature delighted itself in these nar-
cotic dreams, born in the land of the poppy and of
hashish. They lend a peculiar charm to his poems,
but it is not worth while to try to construct a philosophy out of them. The knowledge, if knowledge it
be, of the mystic is not transmissible. It is not cumu-
lative; it begins and ends with the solitary dreamer,
and the next who follows him has to build his own
cloud-castle as if it were the first aerial edifice that a
human soul had ever constructed.

Some passages of "Nature," "The Over-Soul,"
"The Sphinx," "Uriel," illustrate sufficiently this
mood of spiritual exaltation. Emerson's calm temperament never allowed it to reach the condition he
sometimes refers to, — that of ecstasy. The passage
in "Nature" where he says "I become a transparent
eyeball" is about as near it as he ever came. This
was almost too much for some of his admirers and

worshippers. One of his most ardent and faithful followers, whose gifts as an artist are well known, mounted the eyeball on legs, and with its cornea in front for a countenance and its optic nerve projecting behind as a queue, the spiritual cyclops was shown setting forth on his travels.

Emerson's reflections in the "transcendental" mood do beyond question sometimes irresistibly suggest the close neighborhood of the sublime to the ridiculous. But very near that precipitous border line there is a charmed region where, if the statelier growths of philosophy die out and disappear, the flowers of poetry next the very edge of the chasm have a peculiar and mysterious beauty. "Uriel" is a poem which finds itself perilously near to the gulf of unsounded obscurity, and has, I doubt not, provoked the mirth of profane readers; but read in a lucid moment, it is just obscure enough and just significant enough to give the voltaic thrill which comes from the sudden contacts of the highest imaginative conceptions.

Human personality presented itself to Emerson as a passing phase of universal being. Born of the Infinite, to the Infinite it was to return. Sometimes he treats his own personality as interchangeable with objects in nature, — he would put it off like a garment and clothe himself in the landscape. Here is a curious extract from "The Adirondacs," in which the reader need not stop to notice the parallelism with Byron's —

> "The sky is changed, — and such a change ! O night
> And storm and darkness, ye are wondrous strong."

Now Emerson : —

> "And presently the sky is changed ; O world !
> What pictures and what harmonies are thine !

The clouds are rich and dark, the air serene,
So like the soul of me, what if 't were me?"

We find this idea of confused personal identity also in a brief poem printed among the "Translations" in Emerson's "Poems." These are the last two lines of "The Flute, from Hilali:"—

"Saying, Sweetheart! the old mystery remains,
If I am I ; thou, thou ; or thou art I?"

The same transfer of personality is hinted in the line of Shelley's "Ode to the West Wind:"—

"Be thou, Spirit fierce,
My spirit! Be thou me, impetuous one!"

Once more, how fearfully near the abyss of the ridiculous! A few drops of alcohol bring about a confusion of mind not unlike this poetical metempsychosis.

The laird of Balnamoon had been at a dinner where they gave him cherry-brandy instead of port wine. In driving home over a wild tract of land called Munrimmon Moor his hat and wig blew off, and his servant got out of the gig and brought them to him. The hat he recognized, but not the wig. "It 's no my wig, Hairy [Harry], lad; it 's no my wig," and he would not touch it. At last Harry lost his patience: "Ye 'd better tak' it, sir, for there 's nae waile [choice] o' wigs on Munrimmon Moor." And in our earlier days we used to read of the bewildered market-woman, whose *Ego* was so obscured when she awoke from her slumbers that she had to leave the question of her personal identity to the instinct of her four-footed companion:—

"If it be I, he 'll wag his little tail ;
And if it be not I, he 'll loudly bark and wail."

I have not lost my reverence for Emerson in showing one of his fancies for a moment in the distorting mirror of the ridiculous. He would doubtless have smiled with me at the reflection, for he had a keen sense of humor. But I take the opportunity to disclaim a jesting remark about "a foresmell of the Infinite" which Mr. Conway has attributed to me, who am innocent of all connection with it.

The mystic appeals to those only who have an ear for the celestial concords, as the musician only appeals to those who have the special endowment which enables them to understand his compositions. It is not for organizations untuned to earthly music to criticise the great composers, or for those who are deaf to spiritual harmonies to criticise the higher natures which lose themselves in the strains of divine contemplation. The bewildered reader must not forget that passage of arms, previously mentioned, between Plato and Diogenes.

Emerson looked rather askance at Science in his early days. I remember that his brother Charles had something to say in "The Harvard Register" (1828) about its disenchantments. I suspect the prejudice may have come partly from Wordsworth. Compare this verse of his with the lines of Emerson's which follow it.

> " Physician art thou, one all eyes ;
> Philosopher, a fingering slave,
> One that would peep and botanize
> Upon his mother's grave ? "

Emerson's lines are to be found near the end of the Appendix in the new edition of his works.

> " Philosophers are lined with eyes within,
> And, being so, the sage unmakes the man.

> In love he cannot therefore cease his trade ;
> Scarce the first blush has overspread his cheek,
> He feels it, introverts his learned eye
> To catch the unconscious heart in the very act.
> His mother died, — the only friend he had, —
> Some tears escaped, but his philosophy,
> Couched like a cat, sat watching close behind
> And throttled all his passion.   Is 't not like
> That devil-spider that devours her mate
> Scarce freed from her embraces ? "

The same feeling comes out in the Poem "Blight," where he says the "young scholars who invade our hills "

> " Love not the flower they pluck, and know it not,
>   And all their botany is Latin names ; "

and in "The Walk," where the "learned men " with their glasses are contrasted with the sons of Nature, — the poets are no doubt meant, — much to the disadvantage of the microscopic observers.   Emerson's mind was very far from being of the scientific pattern. Science is quantitative, — loves the foot-rule and the balance, — methodical, exhaustive, indifferent to the beautiful as such.   The poet is curious, asks all manner of questions, and never thinks of waiting for the answer, still less of torturing Nature to get at it.   Emerson wonders, for instance, —

> " Why Nature loves the number five,"

but leaves his note of interrogation without troubling himself any farther.   He must have picked up some woodcraft and a little botany from Thoreau, and a few chemical notions from his brother-in-law, Dr. Jackson, whose name is associated with the discovery of artificial anæsthesia.   It seems probable that the genial companionship of Agassiz, who united with his

scientific genius, learning, and renown, most delightful social qualities, gave him a kinder feeling to men
of science and their pursuits than he had entertained
before that great master came among us. At any rate
he avails himself of the facts drawn from their spe-
cialties without scruple when they will serve his turn.
But he loves the poet always better than the scientific
student of nature. In his Preface to the Poems of
Mr. W. E. Channing, he says: —

"Here is a naturalist who sees the flower and the bud
with a poet's curiosity and awe, and does not count the
stamens in the aster, nor the feathers in the wood-thrush,
but rests in the surprise and affection they awake."

This was Emerson's own instinctive attitude to all
the phenomena of nature.

Emerson's style is epigrammatic, incisive, authoritative, sometimes quaint, never obscure, except when
he is handling nebulous subjects. His paragraphs are
full of brittle sentences that break apart and are independent units, like the fragments of a coral colony.
His imagery is frequently daring, leaping from the
concrete to the abstract, from the special to the general
and universal, and *vice versa*, with a bound that is like
a flight. Here are a few specimens of his pleasing
audacities: —

"There is plenty of wild azote and carbon unappro-
priated, but it is naught till we have made it up into
loaves and soup."

"He arrives at the sea-shore and a sumptuous ship
has floored and carpeted for him the stormy Atlantic."

"If we weave a yard of tape in all humility and as
well as we can, long hereafter we shall see it was no cotton tape at all, but some galaxy which we braided, and
that the threads were Time and Nature."

"Tapping the tempest for a little side wind."

"The locomotive and the steamboat, like enormous shuttles, shoot every day across the thousand various threads of national descent and employment and bind them fast in one web."

He is fond of certain archaisms and unusual phrases. He likes the expression "mother-wit," which he finds in Spenser, Marlowe, Shakespeare, and other old writers. He often uses the word "husband" in its earlier sense of economist. His use of the word "haughty" is so fitting, and it sounds so nobly from his lips, that we could wish its employment were forbidden henceforth to voices which vulgarize it. But his special, constitutional word is "fine," meaning something like dainty, as Shakespeare uses it, — "my dainty Ariel," — "fine Ariel." It belongs to his habit of mind and body as "faint" and "swoon" belong to Keats. This word is one of the ear-marks by which Emerson's imitators are easily recognized. "Melioration" is another favorite word of Emerson's. A clairvoyant could spell out some of his most characteristic traits by the aid of his use of these three words; his inborn fastidiousness, subdued and kept out of sight by his large charity and his good breeding, showed itself in his liking for the word "haughty;" his exquisite delicacy by his fondness for the word "fine," with a certain shade of meaning; his optimism in the frequent recurrence of the word "melioration."

We must not find fault with his semi-detached sentences until we quarrel with Solomon and criticise the Sermon on the Mount. The "point and surprise" which he speaks of as characterizing the style of Plutarch belong eminently to his own. His fertility of illustrative imagery is very great. His images are

noble, or, if borrowed from humble objects, ennobled
by his handling. He throws his royal robe over a
milking-stool and it becomes a throne. But chiefly
he chooses objects of comparison grand in themselves.
He deals with the elements at first hand. Such delicacy of treatment, with such breadth and force of
effect, is hard to match anywhere, and we know him
by his style at sight. It is as when the slight fingers
of a girl touch the keys of some mighty and many-
voiced organ, and send its thunders rolling along the
aisles and startling the stained windows of a great
cathedral. We have seen him as an unpretending
lecturer. We follow him round as he "peddles out
all the wit he can gather from Time or from Nature,"
and we find that "he has changed his market cart into
a chariot of the sun," and is carrying about the morning light as merchandise.

Emerson was as loyal an American, as thorough
a New Englander, as home-loving a citizen, as ever
lived. He arraigned his countrymen sharply for their
faults. Mr. Arnold made one string of his epithets
familiar to all of us, — "This great, intelligent, sensual, and avaricious America." This was from a private letter to Carlyle. In his essay, "Works and
Days," he is quite as outspoken: "This mendicant
America, this curious, peering, itinerant, imitative
America." "I see plainly," he says, "that our society is as bigoted to the respectabilities of religion
and education as yours." "The war," he says, "gave
back integrity to this erring and immoral nation."
All his life long he recognized the faults and errors
of the new civilization. All his life long he labored
diligently and lovingly to correct them. To the dark

prophecies of Carlyle, which came wailing to him
across the ocean, he answered with ever hopeful and
cheerful anticipations. "Here," he said, in words I
have already borrowed, "is the home of man — here
is the promise of a new and more excellent social state
than history has recorded."

Such a man as Emerson belongs to no one town or
province or continent; he is the common property of
mankind; and yet we love to think of him as breathing the same air and treading the same soil that we
and our fathers and our children have breathed and
trodden. So it pleases us to think how fondly he remembered his birthplace; and by the side of Franklin's bequest to his native city we treasure that golden
verse of Emerson's : —

> " A blessing through the ages thus
> Shield all thy roofs and towers !
> GOD WITH THE FATHERS, SO WITH US,
> Thou darling town of ours !"

Emerson sympathized with all generous public
movements, but he was not fond of working in associations, though he liked well enough to attend their
meetings as a listener and looker-on. His study was
his workshop, and he preferred to labor in solitude.
When he became famous he paid the penalty of celebrity in frequent interruptions by those "devastators
of the day" who sought him in his quiet retreat. His
courtesy and kindness to his visitors were uniform and
remarkable. Poets who come to recite their verses
and reformers who come to explain their projects are
among the most formidable of earthly visitations.
Emerson accepted his martyrdom with meek submission; it was a martyrdom in detail, but collectively
its petty tortures might have satisfied a reasonable

inquisitor as the punishment of a moderate heresy. Except in that one phrase above quoted, he never complained of his social oppressors, so far as I remember, in his writings. His perfect amiability was one of his most striking characteristics, and in a nature fastidious as was his in its whole organization, it implied a self-command worthy of admiration.

The natural purity and elevation of Emerson's character show themselves in all that he writes. His life corresponded to the ideal we form of him from his writings. This it was which made him invulnerable amidst all the fierce conflicts his gentle words excited. His white shield was so spotless that the least scrupulous combatants did not like to leave their defacing marks upon it. One would think he was protected by some superstition like that which Voltaire refers to as existing about Boileau, —

"Ne disons pas mal de Nicolas, — cela porte malheur."

(Don't let us abuse Nicolas, — it brings ill luck.) The cooped-up dogmatists whose very citadel of belief he was attacking, and who had their hot water and boiling pitch and flaming brimstone ready for the assailants of their outer defences, withheld their missiles from him, and even sometimes, in a movement of involuntary human sympathy, sprinkled him with rose-water. His position in our Puritan New England was in some respects like that of Burns in Presbyterian Scotland. The *dour* Scotch ministers and elders could not cage their minstrel, and they could not clip his wings; and so they let this morning lark rise above their theological mists, and sing to them at heaven's gate, until he had softened all their hearts and might nestle in their bosoms and find his perch on "the big ha' bible," if he would, — and as he did. So did the music of Emerson's words and life steal into the hearts of our stern New England theologians, and soften them to a temper which would have seemed treasonable weakness to their stiff-kneed forefathers. When a man lives a life commended by all the Christian virtues, enlightened persons are not so apt to cavil at his particular beliefs or unbeliefs as in former generations. We do, however, wish to know what are the convictions of any such persons in matters of highest interest about which there is so much honest difference of opinion in this age of deep and anxious and devout religious scepticism.

It was a very wise and a very prudent course which was taken by Simonides, when he was asked by his imperial master to give him his ideas about the Deity. He begged for a day to consider the question, but when the time came for his answer he wanted two days more, and at the end of these, four days. In short, the more he thought about it, the more he found himself perplexed.

The name most frequently applied to Emerson's form of belief is Pantheism. How many persons who shudder at the sound of this word can tell the difference between that doctrine and their own professed belief in the omnipresence of the Deity?

Theodore Parker explained Emerson's position, as he understood it, in an article in "The Massachusetts Quarterly Review." I borrow this quotation from Mr. Cooke: —

"He has an absolute confidence in God. He has been foolishly accused of Pantheism, which sinks God in nature, but no man is further from it. He never sinks

God in man; he does not stop with the law, in matter or morals, but goes to the Law-giver; yet probably it would not be so easy for him to give his definition of God, as it would be for most graduates at Andover or Cambridge."

We read in his essay, "Self-Reliance:"—

"This is the ultimate fact which we so quickly reach on this, as on every topic, the resolution of all into the ever-blessed ONE. Self-existence is the attribute of the Supreme Cause, and it constitutes the measure of good by the degree in which it enters into all lower forms."

The "ever-blessed ONE" of Emerson corresponds to the Father in the doctrine of the Trinity. The "Over-Soul" of Emerson is that aspect of Deity which is known to theology as the Holy Spirit. Jesus was for him a divine manifestation, but only as other great human souls have been in all ages and are to-day. He was willing to be called a Christian just as he was willing to be called a Platonist.

Explanations are apt not to explain much in dealing with subjects like this. "Canst thou by searching find out God? Canst thou find out the Almighty unto perfection?" But on certain great points nothing could be clearer than the teaching of Emerson. He believed in the doctrine of spiritual influx as sincerely as any Calvinist or Swedenborgian. His views as to fate, or the determining conditions of the character, brought him near enough to the doctrine of predestination to make him afraid of its consequences, and led him to enter a caveat against any denial of the self-governing power of the will.

His creed was a brief one, but he carried it everywhere with him. In all he did, in all he said, and, so far as all outward signs could show, in all his

thoughts, the indwelling Spirit was his light and
guide; through all nature he looked up to nature's
God; and if he did not worship the "man Christ
Jesus" as the churches of Christendom have done, he
followed his footsteps so nearly that our good Methodist, Father Taylor, spoke of him as more like Christ
than any man he had known.

Emerson was in friendly relations with many clergymen of the church from which he had parted.   Since
he left the pulpit, the lesson, not of tolerance, for that
word is an insult as applied by one set of well-behaved
people to another, not of charity, for that implies an
impertinent assumption, but of good feeling on the
part of divergent sects and their ministers, has been
taught and learned as never before.   Their official
Confessions of Faith make far less difference in their
human sentiments and relations than they did even
half a century ago.   These ancient creeds are handed
along down, to be kept in their phials with their
stoppers fast, as attar of rose is kept in its little bot-
tles; they are not to be opened and exposed to the
atmosphere so long as their perfume — the odor of
sanctity — is diffused from the carefully treasured
receptacles, — perhaps even longer than that.

Out of the endless opinions as to the significance
and final outcome of Emerson's religious teachings I
will select two as typical.

Dr. William Hague, long the honored minister
of a Baptist church in Boston, where I had the pleasure of friendly acquaintance with him, has written
a thoughtful, amiable paper on Emerson, which he
read before the New York Genealogical and Biographical Society.   This essay closes with the following
sentence: —

"Thus to-day, while musing, as at the beginning, over the works of Ralph Waldo Emerson, we recognize now as ever his imperial genius as one of the greatest of writers; at the same time, his life work, as a whole, tested by its supreme ideal, its method and its fruitage, shows also a great waste of power, verifying the saying of Jesus touching the harvest of human life: ' HE THAT GATHERETH NOT WITH ME SCATTERETH ABROAD.'"

"But when Dean Stanley returned from America, it was to report," says Mr. Conway ("Macmillan," June, 1879), "that religion had there passed through an evolution from Edwards to Emerson, and that ' the genial atmosphere which Emerson has done so much to promote is shared by all the churches equally.'"

What is this "genial atmosphere" but the very spirit of Christianity? The good Baptist minister's essay is full of it. He comes asking what has become of Emerson's "wasted power" and lamenting his lack of "fruitage," and lo! he himself has so ripened and mellowed in that same Emersonian air that the tree to which he belongs would hardly know him. The close-communion clergyman handles the arch-heretic as tenderly as if he were the nursing mother of a new infant Messiah. A few generations ago this preacher of a new gospel would have been burned; a little later he would have been tried and imprisoned; less than fifty years ago he was called infidel and atheist; names which are fast becoming relinquished to the intellectual half-breeds who sometimes find their way into pulpits and the so-called religious periodicals.

It is not within our best-fenced churches and creeds that the self-governing American is like to find the religious freedom which the Concord prophet asserted with the strength of Luther and the sweetness of Melancthon, and which the sovereign in his shirt-sleeves will surely claim. Milton was only the precursor of Emerson when he wrote: —

"Neither is God appointed and confined, where and out of what place these his chosen shall be first heard to speak; for he sees not as man sees, chooses not as man chooses, lest we should devote ourselves again to set places and assemblies, and outward callings of men, planting our faith one while in the old convocation house, and another while in the Chapel at Westminster, when all the faith and religion that shall be there canonized is not sufficient without plain convincement, and the charity of patient instruction, to supple the least bruise of conscience, to edify the meanest Christian who desires to walk in the spirit and not in the letter of human trust, for all the number of voices that can be there made; no, though Harry the Seventh himself there, with all his liege tombs about him, should lend their voices from the dead, to swell their number."

The best evidence of the effect produced by Emerson's writings and life is to be found in the attention he has received from biographers and critics. The ground upon which I have ventured was already occupied by three considerable Memoirs. Mr. George Willis Cooke's elaborate work is remarkable for its careful and thorough analysis of Emerson's teachings. Mr. Moncure Daniel Conway's "Emerson at Home and Abroad" is a lively picture of its subject by one long and well acquainted with him. Mr. Alexander Ireland's "Biographical Sketch" brings together, from a great variety of sources, as well as from his own recollections, the facts of Emerson's history and the comments of those whose opinions were best worth reproducing. I must refer to this volume for a bibliography of the various works and essays of which Emerson furnished the subject.

From the days when Mr. Whipple attracted the attention of our intelligent but unawakened reading community, by his discriminating and appreciative criticisms of Emerson's lectures, and Mr. Lowell drew the portrait of the New England "Plotinus-Montaigne" in his brilliant "Fable for Critics," to the recent essays of Mr. Matthew Arnold, Mr. John Morley, Mr. Henry Norman, and Mr. Edmund Clarence Stedman, Emerson's writings have furnished one of the most enduring *pièces de résistance* at the critical tables of the old and the new world.

He early won the admiration of distinguished European thinkers and writers: Carlyle accepted his friendship and his disinterested services; Miss Martineau fully recognized his genius and sounded his praises; Miss Bremer fixed her sharp eyes on him and pronounced him "a noble man;" Professor Tyndall found the inspiration of his life in Emerson's fresh thought; and Mr. Arnold, who clipped his medals reverently but unsparingly, confessed them to be of pure gold, even while he questioned whether they would pass current with posterity. He found discerning critics in France, Germany, and Holland. Better than all is the testimony of those who knew him best. They who repeat the saying that "a prophet is not without honor save in his own country" will find an exception to its truth in the case of Emerson. Read the impressive words spoken at his funeral by his fellow-townsman, Judge Hoar; read the glowing tributes of three of Concord's poets, — Mr. Alcott, Mr. Channing, and Mr. Sanborn, — and it will appear plainly enough that he, whose fame had gone out into all the earth, was most of all believed in, honored, beloved, lamented, in the little village circle that centred about his own fireside.

It is a not uninteresting question whether Emerson has bequeathed to the language any essay or poem which will resist the flow of time like "the adamant of Shakespeare," and remain a classic like the Essays of Addison or Gray's Elegy. It is a far more important question whether his thought entered into the spirit of his day and generation, so that it modified the higher intellectual, moral, and religious life of his time, and, as a necessary consequence, those of succeeding ages. *Corpora non agunt nisi soluta*, and ideas must be dissolved and taken up as well as material substances before they can act. "That which thou sowest is not quickened except it die," or rather lose the form with which it was sown. Eight stanzas of four lines each have made the author of "The Burial of Sir John Moore" an immortal, and endowed the language with a classic, perfect as the most finished cameo. But what is the gift of a mourning ring to the bequest of a perpetual annuity? How many lives have melted into the history of their time, as the gold was lost in Corinthian brass, leaving no separate monumental trace of their influence, but adding weight and color and worth to the age of which they formed a part and the generations that came after them! We can dare to predict of Emerson, in the words of his old friend and disciple, Mr. Cranch: —

> "The wise will know thee and the good will love,
> The age to come will feel thy impress given
> In all that lifts the race a step above
> Itself, and stamps it with the seal of heaven."

It seems to us, to-day, that Emerson's best literary work in prose and verse must live as long as the language lasts; but whether it live or fade from memory, the influence of his great and noble life, and the spoken and written words which were its exponents, blends, indestructible, with the enduring elements of civilization.

It is not irreverent, but eminently fitting, to compare any singularly pure and virtuous life with that of the great exemplar in whose footsteps Christendom professes to follow. The time was when the divine authority of his gospel rested chiefly upon the miracles he is reported to have wrought. As the faith in these exceptions to the general laws of the universe diminished, the teachings of the Master, of whom it was said that He spoke as never man spoke, were more largely relied upon as evidence of his divine mission. Now, when a comparison of these teachings with those of other religious leaders is thought by many to have somewhat lessened the force of this argument, the life of the sinless and self-devoted servant of God and friend of man is appealed to as the last and convincing proof that he was an immediate manifestation of the Divinity.

Judged by his life, Emerson comes very near our best ideal of humanity. He was born too late for the trial of the cross or the stake, or even the jail. But the penalty of having an opinion of his own and expressing it was a serious one, and he accepted it as cheerfully as any of Queen Mary's martyrs accepted his fiery baptism. His faith was too large and too deep for the formulæ he found built into the pulpit, and he was too honest to cover up his doubts under the flowing vestments of a sacred calling. His writings, whether in prose or verse, are worthy of admiration, but his manhood was the underlying quality which gave them their true value. It was in virtue of this that his rare genius acted on so many minds as a trumpet call, to awaken them to the meaning and the privileges of this earthly existence, with all its infinite promise. No matter of what he wrote or spoke, his words, his tones, his looks, carried the evidence of a sincerity which pervaded them all and was to his eloquence and poetry like the water of crystallization; without which they would effloresce into mere rhetoric. He shaped an ideal for the commonest life, he proposed an object to the humblest seeker after truth. Look for beauty in the world around you, he said, and you shall see it everywhere. Look within, with pure eyes and simple trust, and you shall find the Deity mirrored in your own soul. Trust yourself because you trust the voice of God in your inmost consciousness.

There are living organisms so transparent that we can see their hearts beating and their blood flowing through their glassy tissues. So transparent was the life of Emerson; so clearly did the true nature of the man show through it. What he taught others to be, he was himself. His deep and sweet humanity won him love and reverence everywhere among those whose natures were capable of responding to the highest manifestations of character. Here and there a narrow-eyed sectary may have avoided or spoken ill of him; but if He who knew what was in man had wandered from door to door in New England as of old in Palestine, we can well believe that one of the thresholds which "those blessed feet" would have crossed, to hallow and receive its welcome, would have been that of the lovely and quiet home of Emerson.

JOHN LOTHROP MOTLEY.

NOTE.

THE Memoir here given to the public is based on a biographical sketch prepared by the writer at the request of the Massachusetts Historical Society for its Proceedings. The questions involving controversies into which the Society could not feel called to enter are treated at considerable length in the following pages. Many details are also given which would have carried the paper written for the Society beyond the customary limits of such tributes to the memory of its deceased members. It is still but an outline which may serve a present need and perhaps be of some assistance to a future biographer.

John Lothrop Motley

JOHN LOTHROP MOTLEY.

I.

1814–1827. To Æt. 13.

Birth and Early Years.

JOHN MOTLEY, the great-grandfather of the subject of this Memoir, came in the earlier part of the last century from Belfast in Ireland to Falmouth, now Portland, in the District, now the State of Maine. He was twice married, and had ten children, four of the first marriage and six of the last. Thomas, the youngest son by his first wife, married Emma, a daughter of John Wait, the first Sheriff of Cumberland County under the government of the United States. Two of their seven sons, Thomas and Edward, removed from Portland to Boston in 1802 and established themselves as partners in commercial business, continuing united and prosperous for nearly half a century before the firm was dissolved.

The earlier records of New England have preserved the memory of an incident which deserves mention as showing how the historian's life was saved by a quick-witted handmaid, more than a hundred years before he was born. On the 29th of August, 1708, the French and Indians from Canada made an attack upon the town of Haverhill, in Massachusetts. Thirty or forty persons were slaughtered, and many others were carried captive into Canada.

The minister of the town, Rev. Benjamin Rolfe, was killed by a bullet through the door of his house. Two of his daughters, Mary, aged thirteen, and Elizabeth, aged nine, were sleeping in a room with the maid-servant, Hagar. When Hagar heard the whoop of the savages she seized the children, ran with them into the cellar, and, after concealing them under two large washtubs, hid herself. The Indians ransacked the cellar, but missed the prey. Elizabeth, the younger of the two girls, grew up and married the Rev. Samuel Checkley, first minister of the "New South" Church, Boston. Her son, Rev. Samuel Checkley, Junior, was minister of the Second Church, and his successor, Rev. John Lothrop, or Lathrop, as it was more commonly spelled, married his daughter. Dr. Lothrop was great-grandson of Rev. John Lothrop, of Scituate, who had been imprisoned in England for nonconformity. The Checkleys were from Preston Capes, in Northamptonshire. The name is probably identical with that of the Chicheles or Chichleys, a well-known Northamptonshire family.

Thomas Motley married Anna, daughter of the Rev. John Lothrop, granddaughter of the Rev. Samuel Checkley, Junior, the two ministers mentioned above, both honored in their day and generation. Eight children were born of this marriage, of whom four are still living.

JOHN LOTHROP MOTLEY, the second of these children, was born in Dorchester, now a part of Boston, Massachusetts, on the 15th of April, 1814. A member of his family gives a most pleasing and interesting picture, from his own recollections and from what his mother told him, of the childhood which was to develop into such rich maturity. The boy was rather delicate in organization, and not much given to out-door amusements, except skating and swimming, of which last exercise he was very fond in his young days, and in which he excelled. He was a great reader, never idle, but always had a book in his hand, — a volume of poetry or one of the novels of Scott or Cooper. His fondness for plays and declamation is illustrated by the story told by a younger brother, who remembers being wrapped up in a shawl and kept quiet by sweetmeats, while he figured as the dead Cæsar, and his brother, the future historian, delivered the speech of Antony over his prostrate body. He was of a most sensitive nature, easily excited, but not tenacious of any irritated feelings, with a quick sense of honor, and the most entirely truthful child, his mother used to say, that she had ever seen. Such are some of the recollections of those who knew him in his earliest years and in the most intimate relations.

His father's family was at this time living in the house No. 7 Walnut Street, looking down Chestnut Street over the water to the western hills. Near by, at the corner of Beacon Street, was the residence of the family of the first mayor of Boston, and at a little distance from the opposite corner was the house of one of the fathers of New England manufacturing enterprise, a man of superior intellect, who built up a great name and fortune in our city. The children from these three homes naturally became playmates. Mr. Motley's house was a very hospitable one, and Lothrop and two of his young companions were allowed to carry out their schemes of amusement in

the garden and the garret. If one with a prescient
glance could have looked into that garret on some
Saturday afternoon while our century was not far advanced in its second score of years, he might have
found three boys in cloaks and doublets and plumed
hats, heroes and bandits, enacting more or less im-
promptu melodramas. In one of the boys he would
have seen the embryo dramatist of a nation's life history, John Lothrop Motley; in the second, a famous
talker and wit who has spilled more good things on
the wasteful air in conversation than would carry a
"diner-out" through half a dozen London seasons,
and waked up somewhat after the usual flowering-time
of authorship to find himself a very agreeable and
cordially welcomed writer, — Thomas Gold Appleton.
In the third he would have recognized a champion of
liberty known wherever that word is spoken, an orator whom to hear is to revive all the traditions of the
grace, the address, the commanding sway of the silver-
tongued eloquence of the most renowned speakers, —
Wendell Phillips.

Both of young Motley's playmates have furnished
me with recollections of him and of those around him
at this period of his life, and I cannot do better than
borrow freely from their communications. His father
was a man of decided character, social, vivacious,
witty, a lover of books, and himself not unknown as a
writer, being the author of one or more of the well-
remembered "Jack Downing" letters. He was fond
of having the boys read to him from such authors as
Channing and Irving, and criticised their way of reading with discriminating judgment and taste.   Mrs.
Motley was a woman who could not be looked upon
without admiration. I remember well the sweet dig-

nity of her aspect, her "regal beauty," as Mr. Phillips truly styles it, and the charm of her serene and
noble presence, which made her the type of a perfect
motherhood. Her character corresponded to the promise of her gracious aspect. She was one of the fond-
est of mothers, but not thoughtlessly indulgent to the
boy from whom she hoped and expected more than she
thought it wise to let him know. The story used to
be current that in their younger days this father and
mother were the handsomest pair the town of Boston
could show. This son of theirs was "rather tall,"
says Mr. Phillips, "lithe, very graceful in movement
and gesture, and there was something marked and
admirable in the set of his head on his shoulders," —
a peculiar elegance which was most noticeable in those
later days when I knew him. Lady Byron long afterwards spoke of him as more like her husband in appearance than any other person she had met; but
Mr. Phillips, who remembers the first bloom of his
boyhood and youth, thinks he was handsomer than
any portrait of Byron represents the poet. "He could
not have been eleven years old," says the same correspondent, "when he began writing a novel. It opened,
I remember, not with one solitary horseman, but with
two, riding up to an inn in the valley of the Housatonic. Neither of us had ever seen the Housatonic,
but it sounded grand and romantic. Two chapters
were finished."

There is not much remembered of the single summer he passed at Mr. Green's school at Jamaica Plain.
From that school he went to Round Hill, Northampton, then under the care of Mr. Cogswell and Mr.
Bancroft. The historian of the United States could

hardly have dreamed that the handsome boy of ten years was to take his place at the side of his teacher in the first rank of writers in his own department. Motley came to Round Hill, as one of his school-mates tells me, with a great reputation, especially as a declaimer. He had a remarkable facility for acquiring languages, excelled as a reader and as a writer, and was the object of general admiration for his many gifts. There is some reason to think that the flattery he received was for a time a hindrance to his progress and the development of his character. He obtained praise too easily, and learned to trust too much to his genius. He had everything to spoil him, — beauty, precocious intelligence, and a personal charm which might have made him a universal favor-ite. Yet he does not seem to have been generally popular at this period of his life. He was wilful, im-petuous, sometimes supercilious, always fastidious. He would study as he liked, and not by rule. His school and college mates believed in his great possi-bilities through all his forming period, but it may be doubted if those who counted most confidently on his future could have supposed that he would develop the heroic power of concentration, the long-breathed tenacity of purpose, which in after years gave effect to his brilliant mental endowments. "I did wonder," says Mr. Wendell Phillips, "at the diligence and painstaking, the drudgery shown in his historical works. In early life he had no industry, not needing it. All he cared for in a book he caught quickly, — the spirit of it, and all his mind needed or would use. This quickness of apprehension was marvellous." I do not find from the recollections of his schoolmates at Northampton that he was reproached for any grave offences, though he may have wandered beyond the prescribed boundaries now and then, and studied according to his inclinations rather than by rule. While at that school he made one acquisition much less common then than now, — a knowledge of the German language and some degree of acquaintance with its literature, under the guidance of one of the few thorough German scholars this country then possessed, Mr. George Bancroft.

College Life.

SUCH then was the boy who at the immature, we might almost say the tender, age of thirteen entered Harvard College. Though two years after me in college standing, I remember the boyish reputation which he brought with him, especially that of a wonderful linguist, and the impression which his striking personal beauty produced upon us as he took his seat in the college chapel. But it was not until long after this period that I became intimately acquainted with him, and I must again have recourse to the classmates and friends who have favored me with their reminiscences of this period of his life. Mr. Phillips says:

"During our first year in college, though the youngest in the class, he stood third, I think, or second in college rank, and ours was an especially able class. Yet to maintain this rank he neither cared nor needed to make any effort. Too young to feel any responsibilities, and not yet awake to any ambition, he became so negligent that he was 'rusticated' [that is, sent away from college for a time]. He came back sobered, and worked rather more, but with no effort for college rank thenceforward."

I must finish the portrait of the collegian with all its lights and shadows by the help of the same friends from whom I have borrowed the preceding outlines.

He did not care to make acquaintances, was haughty in manner and cynical in mood, at least as he appeared to those in whom he felt no special interest. It is no wonder, therefore, that he was not a popular favorite, although recognized as having very brilliant qualities. During all this period his mind was doubtless fermenting with projects which kept him in a fevered and irritable condition. "He had a small writing-table," Mr. Phillips says, "with a shallow drawer; I have often seen it half full of sketches, unfinished poems, soliloquies, a scene or two of a play, prose portraits of some pet character, etc. These he would read to me, though he never volunteered to do so, and every now and then he burnt the whole and began to fill the drawer again."

My friend, Mr. John Osborne Sargent, who was a year before him in college, says, in a very interesting letter with which he has favored me: —

"My first acquaintance with him [Motley] was at Cambridge, when he came from Mr. Cogswell's school at Round Hill. He then had a good deal of the shyness that was just pronounced enough to make him interesting, and which did not entirely wear off till he left college. . . . I soon became acquainted with him, and we used to take long walks together, sometimes taxing each other's memory for poems or passages from poems that had struck our fancy. Shelley was then a great favorite of his, and I remember that Praed's verses then appearing in the 'New Monthly' he thought very clever and brilliant, and was fond of repeating them. You have forgotten, or perhaps never knew, that Motley's first appearance in print was in the 'Collegian.' He brought me one day, in a very modest mood, a translation from Goethe, which I was most happy to oblige him by inserting. It was very prettily done, and will now be a curiosity. . . . How it happened that Motley wrote only one piece I do not remember. I had the pleasure about that time of initiating him as a member of the Knights of the Square Table, — always my favorite college club, for the reason, perhaps, that I was a sometime Grand Master. He was always a genial and jovial companion at our supper-parties at Fresh Pond and Gallagher's."

We who live in the days of photographs know how many faces belong to every individual. We know too under what different aspects the same character appears to those who study it from different points of view and with different prepossessions. I do not hesitate, therefore, to place side by side the impressions of two of his classmates as to one of his personal traits as they observed him at this period of his youth.

"He was a manly boy, with no love for or leaning to girls' company; no care for dress; not a trace of personal vanity. . . . He was, or at least seemed, wholly unconscious of his rare beauty and of the fascination of his manner; not a trace of pretence, the simplest and most natural creature in the world."

Look on that picture and on this: —

"He seemed to have a passion for dress. But as in everything else, so in this, his fancy was a fitful one. At one time he would excite our admiration by the splendor of his outfit, and perhaps the next week he would seem to take equal pleasure in his slovenly or careless appearance."

It is not very difficult to reconcile these two portraitures. I recollect it was said by a witty lady of a handsome clergyman well remembered among us, that he had *dressy eyes*. Motley so well became everything he wore, that if he had sprung from his bed and slipped his clothes on at an alarm of fire, his costume would have looked like a prince's undress. His natural presentment, like that of Count D'Orsay, was of the kind which suggests the intentional effects of an elaborate toilet, no matter how little thought or care may have been given to make it effective. I think the "passion for dress" was really only a seeming, and that he often excited admiration when he had not taken half the pains to adorn himself that many a youth less favored by nature has wasted upon his unblest exterior only to be laughed at.

I gather some other interesting facts from a letter which I have received from his early playmate and school and college classmate, Mr. T. G. Appleton.

"In his Sophomore year he kept abreast of the prescribed studies, but his heart was out of bounds, as it often had been at Round Hill when chasing squirrels or rabbits through forbidden forests. Already his historical interest was shaping his life. A tutor coming — by chance, let us hope — to his room remonstrated with him upon the heaps of novels upon his table.

"'Yes,' said Motley, 'I am reading historically, and have come to the novels of the nineteenth century. Taken in the lump, they are very hard reading.'"

All Old Cambridge people know the Brattle House, with its gambrel roof, its tall trees, its perennial spring, its legendary fame of good fare and hospitable board in the days of the kindly old *bon vivant*, Major Brattle. In this house the two young students, Appleton and Motley, lived during a part of their college course.

"Motley's room was on the ground floor, the room to the left of the entrance. He led a very pleasant life there, tempering his college duties with the literature he loved, and receiving his friends amidst elegant surroundings, which added to the charm of his society. Occasionally we amused ourselves by writing for the magazines and papers of the day. Mr. Willis had just started a slim monthly, written chiefly by himself, but with the true magazine flavor. We wrote for that, and sometimes verses in the corner of a paper called 'The Anti-Masonic Mirror,' and in which corner was a woodcut of Apollo, and inviting to destruction ambitious youths by the legend underneath, —

'Much yet remains unsung.'

These pieces were usually dictated to each other, the poet recumbent upon the bed and a classmate ready to carry off the manuscript for the paper of the following day. 'Blackwood's' was then in its glory, its pages redolent of 'mountain dew' in every sense; the humor of the Shepherd, the elegantly brutal onslaughts upon Whigs and Cockney poets by Christopher North, intoxicated us youths.

"It was young writing, and made for the young. The opinions were charmingly wrong, and its enthusiasm was half Glenlivet. But this delighted the boys. There were no reprints then, and to pass the paper-cutter up the fresh inviting pages was like swinging over the heather arm in arm with Christopher himself. It is a little singular that though we had a college magazine of our own, Motley rarely if ever wrote for it. I remember a translation from Goethe, 'The Ghost-Seer,' which he may have written for it, and a poem upon the White Mountains. Motley spoke at one of the college exhibitions an essay on Goethe so excellent that Mr. Joseph Cogswell sent it to Madam Goethe, who, after reading it, said, 'I wish to see the first book that young man will write.'"

Although Motley did not aim at or attain a high college rank, the rules of the Phi Beta Kappa Society, which confine the number of members to the first sixteen of each class, were stretched so as to include him, — a tribute to his recognized ability, and an evidence that a distinguished future was anticipated for him.

III.

1832–1833. ÆT. 18–19.

Study and Travel in Europe.

Of the two years divided between the Universities of Berlin and Göttingen I have little to record. That he studied hard I cannot doubt; that he found himself in pleasant social relations with some of his fellow-students seems probable from the portraits he has drawn in his first story, "Morton's Hope," and is rendered certain so far as one of his companions is concerned. Among the records of the past to which he referred during his last visit to this country was a letter which he took from a collection of papers and handed me to read one day when I was visiting him. The letter was written in a very lively and exceedingly familiar vein. It implied such intimacy, and called up in such a lively way the gay times Motley and himself had had together in their youthful days, that I was puzzled to guess who could have addressed him from Germany in that easy and off-hand fashion. I knew most of his old friends who would be likely to call him by his baptismal name in its most colloquial form, and exhausted my stock of guesses unsuccessfully before looking at the signature. I confess that I was surprised, after laughing at the hearty and almost boyish tone of the letter, to read at the bottom of the page the signature of Bismarck. I will not say that I suspect Motley of having drawn the portrait of his friend in one of the characters of "Morton's Hope," but it is not hard to point out traits in one of them which we can believe may have belonged to the great Chancellor at an earlier period of life than that at which the world contemplates his overshadowing proportions.

Hoping to learn something of Motley during the two years while we had lost sight of him, I addressed a letter to His Highness Prince Bismarck, to which I received the following reply: —

FOREIGN OFFICE, BERLIN, *March* 11, 1878.

SIR, — I am directed by Prince Bismarck to acknowledge the receipt of your letter of the 1st of January, relating to the biography of the late Mr. Motley. His Highness deeply regrets that the state of his health and pressure of business do not allow him to contribute personally, and as largely as he would be delighted to do, to your depicting of a friend whose memory will be ever dear to him. Since I had the pleasure of making the acquaintance of Mr. Motley at Varzin, I have been intrusted with communicating to you a few details I have gathered from the mouth of the Prince. I enclose them as they are jotted down, without any attempt of digestion.

I have the honor to be
Your obedient servant,
LOTHAIR BUCHER.

"Prince Bismarck said: —

"'I met Motley at Göttingen in 1832, I am not sure if at the beginning of Easter Term or Michaelmas Term. He kept company with German students, though more addicted to study than we members of the fighting clubs (: corps :). Although not having mastered yet the German language, he exercised a marked attraction by a conversation sparkling with wit, humor, and originality. In autumn of 1833, having both of us migrated from Göttingen to Berlin for the prosecution of our studies, we became fellow-lodgers in the house No. 161 Friedrich Strasse. There we lived in the closest intimacy, sharing meals and outdoor exercise. Motley by that time had arrived at talking German fluently; he occupied himself not only in translating Goethe's poem "Faust," but tried his hand even in composing German verses. Enthusiastic admirer of Shakespeare, Byron, Goethe, he used to spice his conversation abundantly with quotations from these his favorite authors. A pertinacious arguer, so much so that sometimes he watched my awakening in order to continue a discussion on some topic of science, poetry, or practical life, cut short by the chime of the small hours, he never lost his mild and amiable temper. Our faithful companion was Count Alexander Keyserling, a native of Courland, who has since achieved distinction as a botanist.

"'Motley having entered the diplomatic service of his country, we had frequently the opportunity of renewing our friendly intercourse; at Frankfort he used to stay with me, the welcome guest of my wife; we also met at Vienna, and, later, here. The last time I saw him was in 1872 at Varzin, at the celebration of my "silver wedding," namely, the twenty-fifth anniversary.

"'The most striking feature of his handsome and delicate appearance was uncommonly large and beautiful eyes. He never entered a drawing-room without exciting the curiosity and sympathy of the ladies.'"

It is but a glimpse of their young life which the great statesman gives us, but a bright and pleasing one. Here were three students, one of whom was to range in the flowery fields of the loveliest of the sciences, another to make the dead past live over again in his burning pages, and a third to extend an empire as the botanist spread out a plant and the historian laid open a manuscript.

1834–1839.   ÆT. 20–25.

Return to America. — Study of Law. — Marriage. — His first
Novel, " Morton's Hope."

OF the years passed in the study of law after his
return from Germany I have very little recollection,
and nothing of importance to record.   He never became seriously engaged in the practice of the profession he had chosen.   I had known him pleasantly
rather than intimately, and our different callings
tended to separate us.   I met him, however, not very
rarely, at one house where we were both received with
the greatest cordiality, and where the attractions
brought together many both young and old to enjoy
the society of its charming and brilliant inmates.   This
was at No. 14 Temple Place, where Mr. Park Benjamin was then living with his two sisters, both in the
bloom of young womanhood.   Here Motley found the
wife to whom his life owed so much of its success and
its happiness.   Those who remember Mary Benjamin
find it hard to speak of her in the common terms of
praise which they award to the good and the lovely.
She was not only handsome and amiable and agreeable, but there was a cordial frankness, an open-
hearted sincerity about her which made her seem like
a sister to those who could help becoming her lovers.
She stands quite apart in the memory of the friends

who knew her best, even from the circle of young persons whose recollections they most cherish. Yet hardly could one of them have foreseen all that she was to be to him whose life she was to share. They were married on the 2d of March, 1837. His intimate friend, Mr. Joseph Lewis Stackpole, was married at about the same time to her sister, thus joining still more closely in friendship the two young men who were already like brothers in their mutual affection.

Two years after his marriage, in 1839, appeared his first work, a novel in two volumes, called "Morton's Hope." He had little reason to be gratified with its reception. The general verdict was not favorable to it, and the leading critical journal of America, not usually harsh or cynical in its treatment of native authorship, did not even give it a place among its "Critical Notices," but dropped a small-print extinguisher upon it in one of the pages of its "List of New Publications." Nothing could be more utterly disheartening than the unqualified condemnation passed upon the story. At the same time the critic says that "no one can read 'Morton's Hope' without perceiving it to have been written by a person of uncommon resources of mind and scholarship."

It must be confessed that, as a story, "Morton's Hope" cannot endure a searching or even a moderately careful criticism. It is wanting in cohesion, in character, even in a proper regard to circumstances of time and place; it is a map of dissected incidents which has been flung out of its box and has arranged itself without the least regard to chronology or geography. It is not difficult to trace in it many of the influences which had helped in forming or deforming the mind of the young man of twenty-five, not yet come into possession of his full inheritance of the slowly ripening qualities which were yet to assert their robust independence. How could he help admiring Byron and falling into more or less unconscious imitation of his moods if not of his special affectations? Passion showing itself off against a dark foil of cynicism; sentiment, ashamed of its own self-betrayal, and sneering at itself from time to time for fear of the laugh of the world at its sincerity, — how many young men were spoiled and how many more injured by becoming bad copies of a bad ideal! The blood of Don Juan ran in the veins of Vivian Grey and of Pelham. But if we read the fantastic dreams of Disraeli, the intellectual dandyisms of Bulwer, remembering the after careers of which these were the preludes, we can understand how there might well be something in those earlier efforts which would betray itself in the way of thought and in the style of the young men who read them during the plastic period of their minds and characters. Allow for all these influences, allow for whatever impressions his German residence and his familiarity with German literature had produced; accept the fact that the story is to the last degree disjointed, improbable, impossible; lay it aside as a complete failure in what it attempted to be, and read it, as "Vivian Grey" is now read, in the light of the career which it heralded.

"Morton's Hope" is not to be read as a novel: it is to be studied as an autobiography, a prophecy, a record of aspirations, disguised under a series of incidents which are flung together with no more regard to the unities than a pack of shuffled playing-cards. I can do nothing better than let him picture himself, for it is impossible not to recognize the portrait. It

is of little consequence whether every trait is an exact
copy from his own features, but it is so obvious that
many of the lines are direct transcripts from nature
that we may believe the same thing of many others.
Let us compare his fictitious hero's story with what
we have read of his own life.

In early boyhood Morton amused himself and astonished those about him by enacting plays for a pup-
pet theatre. This was at six years old, and at twelve
we find him acting in a play with other boys, just as
Motley's playmates have already described him. The
hero may now speak for himself, but we shall all perceive that we are listening to the writer's own story.

"I was always a huge reader; my mind was essentially craving and insatiable. Its appetite was enormous,
and it devoured too greedily for health. I rejected all
guidance in my studies. I already fancied myself a mis-
anthrope. I had taken a step very common for boys of
my age, and strove with all my might to be a cynic."

He goes on to describe, under the perfectly transparent mask of his hero, the course of his studies.
"To poetry, like most infants, I devoted most of my
time." From modern poetry he went back to the earlier sources, first with the idea of systematic reading
and at last through Chaucer and Gower and early
ballads, until he lost himself "in a dismal swamp of
barbarous romances and lying Latin chronicles. I
got hold of the Bibliotheca Monastica, containing a
copious account of Anglo-Norman authors, with notices of their works, and set seriously to reading every
one of them." One profit of his antiquarianism, however, was, as he says, his attention to foreign languages, — French, Spanish, German, especially in
their earliest and rudest forms of literature. From

these he ascended to the ancient poets, and from Latin to Greek. He would have taken up the study of the Oriental languages, but for the advice of a relative, who begged him seriously to turn his attention to history. The paragraph which follows must speak for itself as a true record under a feigned heading.

"The groundwork of my early character was plasticity and fickleness. I was mortified by this exposure of my ignorance, and disgusted with my former course of reading. I now set myself violently to the study of history. With my turn of mind, and with the preposterous habits which I had been daily acquiring, I could not fail to make as gross mistakes in the pursuit of this as of other branches of knowledge. I imagined, on setting out, a system of strict and impartial investigation of the sources of history. I was inspired with the absurd ambition, not uncommon to youthful students, of knowing as much as their masters. I imagined it necessary for me, stripling as I was, to study the authorities; and, imbued with the strict necessity of judging for myself, I turned from the limpid pages of the modern historians to the notes and authorities at the bottom of the page. These, of course, sent me back to my monastic acquaintances, and I again found myself in such congenial company to a youthful and ardent mind as Florence of Worcester and Simeon of Durham, the Venerable Bede and Matthew Paris; and so on to Gregory and Fredegarius, down to the more modern and elegant pages of Froissart, Hollinshed, Hooker, and Stowe. Infant as I was, I presumed to grapple with masses of learning almost beyond the strength of the giants of history. A spendthrift of my time and labor, I went out of my way to collect materials, and to build for myself, when I should have known that older and abler architects had already appropriated all that was worth preserving; that the edifice was built, the quarry exhausted, and that I was, consequently, only delving amidst rubbish.

"This course of study was not absolutely without its advantages. The mind gained a certain proportion of vigor even by this exercise of its faculties, just as my bodily health would have been improved by transporting the refuse ore of a mine from one pit to another, instead of coining the ingots which lay heaped before my eyes. Still, however, my time was squandered. There was a constant want of fitness and concentration of my energies. My dreams of education were boundless, brilliant, indefinite; but alas! they were only dreams. There was nothing accurate and defined in my future course of life. I was ambitious and conceited, but my aspirations were vague and shapeless. I had crowded together the most gorgeous and even some of the most useful and durable materials for my woof, but I had no pattern, and consequently never began to weave.

"I had not made the discovery that an individual cannot learn, nor be, everything; that the world is a factory in which each individual must perform his portion of work: — happy enough if he can choose it according to his taste and talent, but must renounce the desire of observing or superintending the whole operation. . . .

"From studying and investigating the sources of history with my own eyes, I went a step further; I refused the guidance of modern writers; and proceeding from one point of presumption to another, I came to the magnanimous conviction that I could not know history as I ought to know it unless I *wrote* it for myself. . . .

"It would be tedious and useless to enlarge upon my various attempts and various failures. I forbear to comment upon mistakes which I was in time wise enough to retrieve. Pushing out as I did, without compass and without experience, on the boundless ocean of learning, what could I expect but an utter and a hopeless shipwreck?

"Thus I went on, becoming more learned, and therefore more ignorant, more confused in my brain, and more awkward in my habits, from day to day. I was ever at my studies, and could hardly be prevailed upon to allot a moment to exercise or recreation. I breakfasted with a pen behind my ear, and dined in company with a folio bigger than the table. I became solitary and morose, the necessary consequence of reckless study; talked impatiently of the value of my time, and the immensity of my labors; spoke contemptuously of the learning and acquirements of the whole world, and threw out mysterious hints of the magnitude and importance of my own project.

"In the midst of all this study and this infant authorship the perusal of such masses of poetry could not fail to produce their effect. Of a youth whose mind, like mine at that period, possessed some general capability, without perhaps a single prominent and marked talent, a proneness to imitation is sure to be the besetting sin. I consequently, for a large portion of my earlier life, never read a work which struck my fancy, without planning a better one upon its model; for my ambition, like my vanity, knew no bounds. It was a matter of course that I should be attacked by the poetic mania. I took the infection at the usual time, went through its various stages, and recovered as soon as could be expected. I discovered soon enough that emulation is not capability, and he is fortunate to whom is soonest revealed the relative extent of his ambition and his powers.

"My ambition was boundless; my dreams of glory were not confined to authorship and literature alone; but every sphere in which the intellect of man exerts itself revolved in a blaze of light before me. And there I sat in my solitude and dreamed such wondrous dreams! Events were thickening around me which were soon to change the world, — but they were unmarked by me. The country was changing to a mighty theatre, on whose stage those who were as great as I fancied myself to be were to enact a stupendous drama in which I had no part. I saw it not; I knew it not; and yet how infinitely beautiful were the imaginations of my solitude! Fancy shook her kaleidoscope each moment as chance directed, and lo! what new, fantastic, brilliant, but what unmeaning visions. My ambitious anticipations were as boundless as they were various and conflicting. There was not a path which leads to glory in which I was not destined to gather laurels. As a warrior I would conquer and overrun the world. As a statesman I would reorganize and govern it. As a historian I would consign it all to immortality; and in my leisure moments I would be a great poet and a man of the world.

"In short, I was already enrolled in that large category of what are called young men of genius, — men who are the pride of their sisters and the glory of their grandmothers, — men of whom unheard-of things are expected, till after long preparation comes a portentous failure, and then they are forgotten; subsiding into indifferent apprentices and attorneys' clerks.

"Alas for the golden imaginations of our youth! They are bright and beautiful, but they fade. They glitter brightly enough to deceive the wisest and most cautious, and we garner them up in the most secret caskets of our hearts; but are they not like the coins which the Dervise gave the merchant in the story? When we look for them the next morning, do we not find them withered leaves? "

The ideal picture just drawn is only a fuller portraiture of the youth whose outlines have been already sketched by the companions of his earlier years. If his hero says, "I breakfasted with a pen behind my ear and dined in company with a folio bigger than the table," one of his family says of the boy Motley that "if there were five minutes before dinner, when he came into the parlor he always took up some book near at hand and began to read until dinner was announced." The same unbounded thirst for knowledge, the same history of various attempts and various failures, the same ambition, not yet fixed in its aim, but showing itself in restless effort, belong to the hero of the story and its narrator.

Let no man despise the first efforts of immature

genius. Nothing can be more crude as a novel, nothing more disappointing, than "Morton's Hope."
But in no other of Motley's writings do we get such
an inside view of his character with its varied impulses, its capricious appetites, its unregulated forces,
its impatient grasp for all kinds of knowledge. With
all his university experiences at home and abroad,
it might be said with a large measure of truth that
he was a self-educated man, as he had been a self-
taught boy. His instincts were too powerful to let
him work quietly in the common round of school and
college training. Looking at him as his companions
describe him, as he delineates himself *mutato nomine*,
the chances of success would have seemed to all but
truly prophetic eyes very doubtful, if not decidedly
against him. Too many brilliant young novel-readers
and lovers of poetry, excused by their admirers for
their shortcomings on the strength of their supposed
birthright of "genius," have ended where they began;
flattered into the vain belief that they were men at
eighteen or twenty, and finding out at fifty that they
were and always had been nothing more than boys.
It was but a tangled skein of life that Motley's book
showed us at twenty-five, and older men might well
have doubted whether it would ever be wound off in
any continuous thread. To repeat his own words, he
had crowded together the materials for his work, but
he had no pattern, and consequently never began to
weave.

The more this first work of Motley's is examined,
the more are its faults as a story and its interest as
a self-revelation made manifest to the reader. The
future historian, who spared no pains to be accurate,
falls into the most extraordinary anachronisms in al-

most every chapter. Brutus in a bob-wig, Othello in a
swallow-tail coat, could hardly be more incongruously
equipped than some of his characters in the manner
of thought, the phrases, the way of bearing themselves
which belong to them in the tale, but never could
have belonged to characters of our Revolutionary
period. He goes so far in his carelessness as to mix
up dates in such a way as almost to convince us that
he never looked over his own manuscript or proofs.
His hero is in Prague in June, 1777, reading a letter
received from America in less than a fortnight from
the date of its being written; in August of the same
year he is in the American camp, where he is found
in the company of a certain Colonel Waldron, an
officer of some standing in the Revolutionary Army,
with whom he is said to have been constantly associated for some three months, having arrived in America, as he says, on the 15th of May, that is to say,
six weeks or more before he sailed, according to his
previous account. Bohemia seems to have bewitched
his chronology as it did Shakespeare's geography.
To have made his story a consistent series of contra-
dictions, Morton should have sailed from that Bohemian seashore which may be found in "A Winter's
Tale," but not in the map of Europe.

And yet in the midst of all these marks of haste
and negligence, here and there the philosophical student of history betrays himself, the ideal of noble
achievement glows in an eloquent paragraph, or is
embodied in a loving portrait like that of the professor and historian Harlem. The novel, taken in
connection with the subsequent developments of the
writer's mind, is a study of singular interest. It is a
chaos before the creative epoch; the light has not been

divided from the darkness; the firmament has not yet divided the waters from the waters. The forces at work in a human intelligence to bring harmony out of its discordant movements are as mysterious, as miraculous, we might truly say, as those which give shape and order to the confused materials out of which habitable worlds are evolved. It is too late now to be sensitive over this unsuccessful attempt as a story and unconscious success as a self-portraiture. The first sketches of Paul Veronese, the first patterns of the Gobelin tapestry, are not to be criticised for the sake of pointing out their inevitable and too manifest imperfections. They are to be carefully studied as the earliest efforts of the hand which painted the Marriage at Cana, of the art which taught the rude fabrics made to be trodden under foot to rival the glowing canvas of the great painters. None of Motley's subsequent writings give such an insight into his character and mental history. It took many years to train the as yet undisciplined powers into orderly obedience, and to bring the unarranged materials into the organic connection which was needed in the construction of a work that should endure. There was a long interval between his early manhood and the middle term of life, during which the slow process of evolution was going on. There are plants which open their flowers with the first rays of the sun; there are others that wait until evening to spread their petals. It was already the high noon of life with him before his genius had truly shown itself; if he had not lived beyond this period, he would have left nothing to give him a lasting name.

V.

1841–1842. Æt. 27–28.

First Diplomatic Appointment, Secretary of Legation to the Russian Mission. — Brief Residence at St. Petersburg. — Letter to his Mother. — Return.

In the autumn of 1841, Mr. Motley received the appointment of Secretary of Legation to the Russian Mission, Mr. Todd being then the Minister. Arriving at St. Petersburg just at the beginning of winter, he found the climate acting very unfavorably upon his spirits if not upon his health, and was unwilling that his wife and his two young children should be exposed to its rigors. The expense of living, also, was out of proportion to his income, and his letters show that he had hardly established himself in St. Petersburg before he had made up his mind to leave a place where he found he had nothing to do and little to enjoy. He was homesick, too, as a young husband and father with an affectionate nature like his ought to have been under these circumstances. He did not regret having made the experiment, for he knew that he should not have been satisfied with himself if he had not made it. It was his first trial of a career in which he contemplated embarking, and in which afterwards he had an eventful experience. In his private letters to his family, many of which I have had the privilege of looking over, he mentions in detail all the reasons which influenced him in forming his own opinion about the expediency of a continued residence at St. Petersburg, and leaves the decision to her in whose judgment he always had the greatest confidence. No unpleasant circumstance attended his resignation of his secretaryship, and though it must have been a disappointment to find that the place did not suit him, as he and his family were then situated, it was only at the worst an experiment fairly tried and not proving satisfactory. He left St. Petersburg after a few months' residence, and returned to America. On reaching New York he was met by the sad tidings of the death of his first-born child, a boy of great promise, who had called out all the affections of his ardent nature. It was long before he recovered from the shock of this great affliction. The boy had shown a very quick and bright intelligence, and his father often betrayed a pride in his gifts and graces which he never for a moment made apparent in regard to his own.

Among the letters which he wrote from St. Petersburg are two miniature ones directed to this little boy. His affectionate disposition shows itself very sweetly in these touching mementos of a love of which his first great sorrow was so soon to be born. Not less charming are his letters to his mother, showing the tenderness with which he always regarded her, and full of all the details which he thought would entertain one to whom all that related to her children was always interesting. Of the letters to his wife it is needless to say more than that they always show the depth of the love he bore her and the absolute trust he placed in her, consulting her at all times as his nearest and wisest friend and adviser, — one in all respects fitted

"To warn, to comfort, and command."

I extract a passage from one of his letters to his mother, as much for the sake of lending a character of reality to his brief residence at St. Petersburg as for that of the pleasant picture it gives us of an interior in that Northern capital.

"We entered through a small vestibule, with the usual arrangement of treble doors, padded with leather to exclude the cold and guarded by two 'proud young porters' in severe cocked hats and formidable batons, into a broad hall, — threw off our furred boots and cloaks, ascended a carpeted marble staircase, in every angle of which stood a statuesque footman in gaudy coat and unblemished unmentionables, and reached a broad landing upon the top thronged as usual with servants. Thence we passed through an antechamber into a long, high, brilliantly lighted, saffron-papered room, in which a dozen card-tables were arranged, and thence into the receiving-room. This was a large room, with a splendidly inlaid and polished floor, the walls covered with crimson satin, the cornices heavily incrusted with gold, and the ceiling beautifully painted in arabesque. The massive fauteuils and sofas, as also the drapery, were of crimson satin with a profusion of gilding. The ubiquitous portrait of the Emperor was the only picture, and was the same you see everywhere. This crimson room had two doors upon the side facing the three windows. The innermost opened into a large supper-room, in which a table was spread covered with the usual refreshments of European parties, — tea, ices, lemonade, and et ceteras, — and the other opened into a ball-room which is a sort of miniature of the 'salle blanche' of the Winter Palace, being white and gold, and very brilliantly lighted with 'ormolu' chandeliers filled with myriads of candles. This room (at least forty feet long by perhaps twenty-five) opened into a carpeted conservatory of about the same size, filled with orange-trees and japonica plants covered with fruit and flowers, arranged very gracefully into arbors, with luxurious seats under the pendent boughs, and with here and there a pretty marble statue gleaming through the green and glossy leaves. One might almost have imagined one's self in the 'land of the cypress and myrtle' instead of our actual whereabout upon the polar banks of the Neva. Wandering through these mimic groves, or reposing from the fatigues of the dance, was many a fair and graceful form, while the brilliantly lighted ball-room, filled with hundreds of exquisitely dressed women (for the Russian ladies, if not very pretty, are graceful, and make admirable toilettes), formed a dazzling contrast with the tempered light of the 'Winter Garden.' The conservatory opened into a library, and from the library you reach the antechamber, thus completing the 'giro' of one of the prettiest houses in St. Petersburg. I waltzed one waltz and quadrilled one quadrille, but it was hard work; and as the sole occupation of these parties is dancing and card-playing — conversation apparently not being customary — they are to me not very attractive."

He could not be happy alone, and there were good reasons against his being joined by his wife and children.

"With my reserved habits," he says, "it would take a great deal longer to become intimate here than to thaw the Baltic. I have only to 'knock that it shall be opened to me,' but that is just what I hate to do. . . . 'Man delights not me, no, nor woman neither.' "

Disappointed in his expectations, but happy in the thought of meeting his wife and children, he came back to his household to find it clad in mourning for the loss of its first-born.

VI

1844. Æt. 30.

Letter to Park Benjamin. — Political Views and Feelings.

A LETTER to Mr. Park Benjamin, dated December 17, 1844, which has been kindly lent me by Mrs. Mary Lanman Douw of Poughkeepsie, gives a very complete and spirited account of himself at this period. He begins with a quiet, but tender reference to the death of his younger brother, Preble, one of the most beautiful youths seen or remembered among us, "a great favorite," as he says, "in the family and indeed with every one who knew him." He mentions the fact that his friends and near connections, the Stackpoles, are in Washington, which place he considers as exceptionally odious at the time when he is writing. The election of Mr. Polk as the opponent of Henry Clay gives him a discouraged feeling about our institutions. The question, he thinks, is now settled that a *statesman* can never again be called to administer the government of the country. He is almost if not quite in despair "because it is now proved that a man, take him for all in all, better qualified by intellectual power, energy and purity of character, knowledge of men, a great combination of personal qualities, a frank, high-spirited, manly bearing, keen sense of honor, the power of attracting and winning men, united with a vast experience in affairs, such as no man (but John Quincy Adams) now living has had and no man in this country can ever have again, — I say it is proved that a man better qualified by an extraordinary combination of advantages to administer the government than any man now living, or any man we can ever produce again, can be beaten by anybody. . . . It has taken forty years of public life to prepare such a man for the Presidency, and the result is that he can be beaten by anybody, — Mr. Polk is anybody, — he is Mr. Quelconque."

I do not venture to quote the most burning sentences of this impassioned letter. It shows that Motley had not only become interested most profoundly in the general movements of parties, but that he had followed the course of political events which resulted in the election of Mr. Polk with careful study, and that he was already looking forward to the revolt of the slave States which occurred sixteen years later. The letter is full of fiery eloquence, now and then extravagant and even violent in expression, but throbbing with a generous heat which shows the excitable spirit of a man who wishes to be proud of his country and does not wish to keep his temper when its acts make him ashamed of it. He is disgusted and indignant to the last degree at seeing "Mr. Quelconque" chosen over the illustrious statesman who was his favorite candidate. But all his indignation cannot repress a sense of humor which was one of his marked characteristics. After fatiguing his vocabulary with hard usage, after his unsparing denunciation of "the very dirty politics" which he finds mixed up with our popular institutions, he says, — it must be remembered that this was an offhand letter to one nearly connected with him, —

"All these things must in short, to use the energetic

language of the Balm of Columbia advertisement, 'bring every generous thinking youth to that heavy sinking gloom which not even the loss of property can produce, but only the loss of hair, which brings on premature decay, causing many to shrink from being uncovered, and even to shun society, to avoid the jests and sneers of their acquaintances. The remainder of their lives is consequently spent in retirement.' "

He continues: —

"Before dropping the subject, and to show the perfect purity of my motives, I will add that I am not at all anxious about the legislation of the new government. I desired the election of Clay as a moral triumph, and because the *administration* of the country, at this moment of ten thousand times more importance than its legislation, would have been placed in pure, strong, and determined hands."

Then comes a dash of that satirical and somewhat cynical way of feeling which he had not as yet outgrown. He had been speaking about the general want of attachment to the Union and the absence of the sentiment of loyalty as bearing on the probable dissolution of the Union.

"I don't mean to express any opinions on these matters, — I have n't got any. It seems to me that the best way is to look at the hodge-podge, be good-natured if possible, and laugh,

> ' As from the height of contemplation
> We view the feeble joints men totter on.'

I began a tremendous political career during the election, having made two stump speeches of an hour and a half each, — after you went away, — one in Dedham town-hall and one in Jamaica Plain, with such eminent success that many invitations came to me from the surrounding villages, and if I had continued in active political life I might have risen to be vote-distributor, or fence-viewer, or selectman, or hog-reeve, or something of the kind."

The letter from which the above passages are quoted gives the same portrait of the writer, only seen in profile, as it were, which we have already seen drawn in full face in the story of "Morton's Hope." It is charged with that *sæva indignatio* which at times verges on misanthropic contempt for its objects, not unnatural to a high-spirited young man who sees his lofty ideals confronted with the ignoble facts which strew the highways of political life. But we can recognize real conviction and the deepest feeling beneath his scornful rhetoric and his bitter laugh. He was no more a mere *dilettante* than Swift himself, but now and then in the midst of his most serious thought some absurd or grotesque image will obtrude itself, and one is reminded of the lines on the monument of Gay rather than of the fierce epitaph of the Dean of Saint Patrick's.

VII.

1845–1847.   Æt. 31–33.

First Historical and Critical Essays. — Peter the Great. —
Novels of Balzac. — Polity of the Puritans.

MR. MOTLEY'S first serious effort in historical
composition was an article of fifty pages in "The
North American Review" for October, 1845.   This
was nominally a notice of two works, one on Russia,
the other "A Memoir of the Life of Peter the Great."
It is, however, a narrative rather than a criticism, a
rapid, continuous, brilliant, almost dramatic narrative.
If there had been any question as to whether the young
novelist who had missed his first mark had in him the
elements which might give him success as an author,
this essay would have settled the question.   It shows
throughout that the writer has made a thorough study
of his subject, but it is written with an easy and
abundant, yet scholarly freedom, not as if he were
surrounded by his authorities and picking out his
material piece by piece, but rather as if it were
the overflow of long-pursued and well-remembered
studies recalled without effort and poured forth almost
as a recreation.

As he betrayed or revealed his personality in his
first novel, so in this first effort in another department
of literature he showed in epitome his qualities as a
historian and a biographer.   The hero of his narra-

tive makes his entrance at once in his character as the
shipwright of Saardam, on the occasion of a visit of
the great Duke of Marlborough. The portrait instantly arrests attention. His ideal personages had
been drawn in such a sketchy way, they presented
so many imperfectly harmonized features, that they
never became real, with the exception, of course, of
the story-teller himself. But the vigor with which the
presentment of the imperial ship-carpenter, the sturdy,
savage, eager, fiery Peter, was given in the few opening sentences, showed the movement of the hand, the
glow of the color, that were in due time to display on
a broader canvas the full-length portraits of William
the Silent and of John of Barneveld. The style of
the whole article is rich, fluent, picturesque, with
light touches of humor here and there, and perhaps a
trace or two of youthful jauntiness, not quite as yet
outgrown. His illustrative poetical quotations are
mostly from Shakespeare, — from Milton and Byron
also in a passage or two, — and now and then one is
reminded that he is not unfamiliar with Carlyle's
"Sartor Resartus" and the "French Revolution" of
the same unmistakable writer, more perhaps by the
way in which phrases borrowed from other authorities
are set in the text than by any more important evidence of unconscious imitation.

The readers who had shaken their heads over the
unsuccessful story of "Morton's Hope" were startled
by the appearance of this manly and scholarly essay.
This young man, it seemed, had been studying, —
studying with careful accuracy, with broad purpose.
He could paint a character with the ruddy life-blood
coloring it as warmly as it glows in the cheeks of one

of Van der Helst's burgomasters. He could sweep the horizon in a wide general outlook, and manage his perspective and his lights and shadows so as to place and accent his special subject with its due relief and just relations. It was a sketch, or rather a study for a larger picture, but it betrayed the hand of a master. The feeling of many was that expressed in the words of Mr. Longfellow in his review of the "Twice-Told Tales" of the unknown young writer, Nathaniel Hawthorne: "When a new star rises in the heavens, people gaze after it for a season with the naked eye, and with such telescopes as they may find. . . . This star is but newly risen; and erelong the observation of numerous star-gazers, perched up on arm-chairs and editor's tables, will inform the world of its magnitude and its place in the heaven of " — not poetry in this instance, but that serene and unclouded region of the firmament where shine unchanging the names of Herodotus and Thucydides. Those who had always believed in their brilliant schoolmate and friend at last felt themselves justified in their faith. The artist that sent this unframed picture to be hung in a corner of the literary gallery was equal to larger tasks. There was but one voice in the circle that surrounded the young essayist. He must redeem his pledge, he can and will redeem it, if he will only follow the bent of his genius and grapple with the heroic labor of writing a great history.

And this was the achievement he was already meditating.

In the mean time he was studying history for its facts and principles, and fiction for its scenery and portraits. In "The North American Review" for July, 1847, is a long and characteristic article on

Balzac, of whom he was an admirer, but with no blind worship. The readers of this great story-teller, who was so long in obtaining recognition, who "made twenty assaults upon fame and had forty books killed under him" before he achieved success, will find his genius fully appreciated and fairly weighed in this discriminating essay. A few brief extracts will show its quality.

"Balzac is an artist, and only an artist. In his tranquil, unimpassioned, remorseless diagnosis of morbid phenomena, in his cool method of treating the morbid anatomy of the heart, in his curiously accurate dissection of the passions, in the patient and painful attention with which, stethoscope in hand, finger on pulse, eye everywhere, you see him watching every symptom, alive to every sound and every breath, and in the scientific accuracy with which he portrays the phenomena which have been the subject of his investigation, — in all this calm and conscientious study of nature he often reminds us of Goethe. Balzac, however, is only an artist. . . . He is neither moral nor immoral, but a calm and profound observer of human society and human passions, and a minute, patient, and powerful delineator of scenes and characters in the world before his eyes. His readers must moralize for themselves. . . . It is, perhaps, his defective style more than anything else which will prevent his becoming a classic, for style above all other qualities seems to embalm for posterity. As for his philosophy, his principles, moral, political, or social, we repeat that he seems to have none whatever. He looks for the picturesque and the striking. He studies sentiments and sensations from an artistic point of view. He is a physiognomist, a physiologist, a bit of an anatomist, a bit of a mesmerist, a bit of a geologist, a Flemish painter, an upholsterer, a micrological, misanthropical, sceptical philosopher; but he is no moralist, and certainly no reformer."

Another article contributed by Mr. Motley to "The

North American Review" is to be found in the number for October, 1849. It is nominally a review of Talvi's (Mrs. Robinson's) "Geschichte der Colonisation von New England," but in reality an essay on the Polity of the Puritans, — an historical disquisition on the principles of self-government evolved in New England, broad in its views, eloquent in its language. Its spirit is thoroughly American, and its estimate of the Puritan character is not narrowed by the near-sighted liberalism which sees the past in the pitiless light of the present, — which looks around at high noon and finds fault with early dawn for its long and dark shadows. Here is a sentence or two from the article : —

"With all the faults of the system devised by the Puritans, it was a practical system. With all their foibles, with all their teasing, tyrannical, and arbitrary notions, the Pilgrims were lovers of liberty as well as sticklers for authority. . . . Nowhere can a better description of liberty be found than that given by Winthrop, in his defence of himself before the General Court on a charge of arbitrary conduct. 'Nor would I have you mistake your own liberty,' he says. 'There is a freedom of doing what we list, without regard to law or justice; this liberty is indeed inconsistent with authority; but civil, moral, and federal liberty consists in every man's enjoying his property and having the benefit of the laws of his country; which is very consistent with a due subjection to the civil magistrate.' . . .

"We enjoy an inestimable advantage in America. One can be a republican, a democrat, without being a radical. A *radical*, one who would *uproot*, is a man whose trade is dangerous to society. Here is but little to uproot. The trade cannot flourish. All classes are conservative by necessity, for none can wish to change the structure of our polity. . . .

"The country without a past cannot be intoxicated by visions of the past of other lands. Upon this absence of the past it seems to us that much of the security of our institutions depends. Nothing interferes with the development of what is now felt to be the true principle of government, the will of the people legitimately expressed. To establish that great truth, nothing was to be torn down, nothing to be uprooted. It grew up in New England out of the seed unconsciously planted by the first Pilgrims, was not crushed out by the weight of a thousand years of error spread over the whole continent, and the Revolution was proclaimed and recognized."

VIII.

1847–1849. ÆT. 33–35.

Joseph Lewis Stackpole, the Friend of Motley. His Sudden
Death. — Motley in the Massachusetts House of Representa-
tives. — Second Novel, "Merry-Mount, A Romance of the
Massachusetts Colony."

THE intimate friendships of early manhood are
not very often kept up among our people. The eager
pursuit of fortune, position, office, separates young
friends, and the indoor home life imprisons them in
the domestic circle so generally that it is quite exceptional to find two grown men who are like brothers,
— or rather unlike most brothers, in being constantly
found together. An exceptional instance of such a
more than fraternal relation was seen in the friendship
of Mr. Motley and Mr. Joseph Lewis Stackpole.
Mr. William Amory, who knew them both well, has
kindly furnished me with some recollections, which I
cannot improve by changing his own language.

"Their intimacy began in Europe, and they returned to
this country in 1835. In 1837 they married sisters, and
this cemented their intimacy, which continued to Stackpole's death in 1847. The contrast in the temperament
of the two friends — the one sensitive and irritable, and
the other always cool and good-natured — only increased
their mutual attachment to each other, and Motley's dependence upon Stackpole. Never were two friends more
constantly together or more affectionately fond of each

other. As Stackpole was about eight years older than Motley, and much less impulsive and more discreet, his death was to his friend irreparable, and at the time an overwhelming blow."

Mr. Stackpole was a man of great intelligence, of remarkable personal attractions, and amiable character. His death was a loss to Motley even greater than he knew, for he needed just such a friend, older, calmer, more experienced in the ways of the world, and above all capable of thoroughly understanding him and exercising a wholesome influence over his excitable nature without the seeming of a Mentor preaching to a Telemachus. Mr. Stackpole was killed by a railroad accident on the 20th of July, 1847.

In the same letter Mr. Amory refers to a very different experience in Mr. Motley's life, — his one year of service as a member of the Massachusetts House of Representatives, 1849.

"In respect to the one term during which he was a member of the Massachusetts House of Representatives, I can recall only one thing, to which he often and laughingly alluded. Motley, as the Chairman of the Committee on Education, made, as he thought, a most masterly report. It was very elaborate, and, as he supposed, unanswerable; but Boutwell, then a young man from some country town [Groton, Mass.], rose, and as Motley always said, demolished the report, so that he was unable to defend it against the attack. You can imagine his disgust, after the pains he had taken to render it unassailable, to find himself, as he expressed it, 'on his own dunghill,' ignominiously beaten. While the result exalted his opinion of the speech-making faculty of a Representative of a common school education, it at the same time cured him of any ambition for political promotion in Massachusetts."

To my letter of inquiry about this matter, Hon. George S. Boutwell courteously returned the following answer: —

BOSTON, *October* 14, 1878.

MY DEAR SIR, — As my memory serves me, Mr. Motley was a member of the Massachusetts House of Representatives in the year 1847 [1849]. It may be well to consult the manual for that year. I recollect the controversy over the report from the Committee on Education.

His failure was not due to his want of faculty or to the vigor of his opponents.

In truth he espoused the weak side of the question and the unpopular one also. His proposition was to endow the colleges at the expense of the fund for the support of the common schools. Failure was inevitable. Neither Webster nor Choate could have carried the bill.

Very truly,

GEO. S. BOUTWELL.

No one could be more ready and willing to recognize his own failures than Motley. He was as honest and manly, perhaps I may say as sympathetic with the feeling of those about him, on this occasion, as was Charles Lamb, who, sitting with his sister in the front of the pit, on the night when his farce was damned at its first representation, gave way to the common feeling, and hissed and hooted lustily with the others around him. It was what might be expected from his honest and truthful nature, sometimes too severe in judging itself.

The commendation bestowed upon Motley's historical essays in "The North American Review" must have gone far towards compensating him for the ill success of his earlier venture. It pointed clearly towards the field in which he was to gather his laurels. And

it was in the year following the publication of the first
essay, or about that time (1846), that he began collecting materials for a history of Holland.   Whether
to tell the story of men that have lived and of events
that have happened, or to create the characters and
invent the incidents of an imaginary tale be the higher
task, we need not stop to discuss.   But the young
author was just now like the great actor in Sir Joshua's
picture, between the allurements of Thalia and Mel-
pomene, still doubtful whether he was to be a romancer or a historian.

The tale of which the title is given at the beginning
of this section had been written several years before
the date of its publication.   It is a great advance in
certain respects over the first novel, but wants the
peculiar interest which belonged to that as a partially
autobiographical memoir.   The story is no longer disjointed and impossible.   It is carefully studied in
regard to its main facts.   It has less to remind us of
"Vivian Grey" and "Pelham," and more that recalls
"Woodstock" and "Kenilworth."   The personages
were many of them historical, though idealized; the
occurrences were many of them such as the record
authenticated; the localities were drawn largely from
nature.   The story betrays marks of haste or carelessness in some portions, though others are elabo-
rately studied.   His preface shows that the reception
of his first book had made him timid and sensitive
about the fate of the second, and explains and excuses
what might be found fault with, to disarm the criticism he had some reason to fear.

That old watch-dog of our American literature,
"The North American Review," always ready with
lambent phrases in stately "Articles" for native talent

of a certain pretension, and wagging its appendix of "Critical Notices" kindly at the advent of humbler merit, treated "Merry-Mount" with the distinction implied in a review of nearly twenty pages. This was a great contrast to the brief and slighting notice of "Morton's Hope." The reviewer thinks the author's descriptive power wholly exceeds his conception of character and invention of circumstances.

"He dwells, perhaps, too long and fondly upon his imagination of the landscape as it was before the stillness of the forest had been broken by the axe of the settler; but the picture is so finely drawn, with so much beauty of language and purity of sentiment, that we cannot blame him for lingering upon the scene. . . . The story is not managed with much skill, but it has variety enough of incident and character, and is told with so much liveliness that few will be inclined to lay it down before reaching the conclusion. . . . The writer certainly needs practice in elaborating the details of a consistent and interesting novel; but in many respects he is well qualified for the task, and we shall be glad to meet him again on the half-historical ground he has chosen. His present work, certainly, is not a fair specimen of what he is able to accomplish, and its failure, or partial success, ought only to inspirit him for further effort."

The "half-historical ground" he had chosen had already led him to the entrance into the broader domain of history. The "further effort" for which he was to be inspirited had already begun. He had been for some time, as was before mentioned, collecting materials for the work which was to cast all his former attempts into the kindly shadow of oblivion, save when from time to time the light of his brilliant after success is thrown upon them to illustrate the path by which it was at length attained.

IX.

Plan of a History. — Letters.

THE reputation of Mr. Prescott was now co-extensive with the realm of scholarship. The histories of the reign of Ferdinand and Isabella and of the conquest of Mexico had met with a reception which might well tempt the ambition of a young writer to emulate it, but which was not likely to be awarded to any second candidate who should enter the field in rivalry with the great and universally popular historian. But this was the field on which Mr. Motley was to venture.

After he had chosen the subject of the history he contemplated, he found that Mr. Prescott was occupied with a kindred one, so that there might be too near a coincidence between them. I must borrow from Mr. Ticknor's beautiful life of Prescott the words which introduce a letter of Motley's to Mr. William Amory, who has kindly allowed me also to make use of it.

"The moment, therefore, that he [Mr. Motley] was aware of this condition of things, and the consequent possibility that there might be an untoward interference in their plans, he took the same frank and honorable course with Mr. Prescott that Mr. Prescott had taken in relation to Mr. Irving, when he found that they had both been contemplating a 'History of the Conquest of Mexico.' The result was the same. Mr. Prescott, instead of treating the matter as an interference, earnestly encouraged Mr. Motley to go on, and placed at his disposition such of the books in his library as could be most useful to him. How amply and promptly he did it, Mr. Motley's own account will best show. It is in a letter dated at Rome, 26th February, 1859, the day he heard of Mr. Prescott's death, and was addressed to his intimate friend, Mr. William Amory, of Boston, Mr. Prescott's much-loved brother-in-law."

"It seems to me but as yesterday," Mr. Motley writes, "though it must be now twelve years ago, that I was talking with our ever-lamented friend Stackpole about my intention of writing a history upon a subject to which I have since that time been devoting myself. I had then made already some general studies in reference to it, without being in the least aware that Prescott had the intention of writing the 'History of Philip the Second.' Stackpole had heard the fact, and that large preparations had already been made for the work, although 'Peru' had not yet been published. I felt naturally much disappointed. I was conscious of the immense disadvantage to myself of making my appearance, probably at the same time, before the public, with a work not at all similar in plan to 'Philip the Second,' but which must of necessity traverse a portion of the same ground.

"My first thought was inevitably, as it were, only of myself. It seemed to me that I had nothing to do but to abandon at once a cherished dream, and probably to renounce authorship. For I had not first made up my mind to write a history, and then cast about to take up a subject. My subject had taken me up, drawn me on, and absorbed me into itself. It was necessary for me, it seemed, to write the book I had been thinking much of, even if it were destined to fall dead from the press, and I had no inclination or interest to write any other. When I had made up my mind accordingly, it then occurred to me that Prescott might not be pleased that I should come

forward upon his ground.   It is true that no announcement of his intentions had been made, and that he had
not, I believe, even commenced his preliminary studies
for Philip.   At the same time I thought it would be dis-
loyal on my part not to go to him at once, confer with
him on the subject, and if I should find a shadow of dis-
satisfaction on his mind at my proposition, to abandon my
plan altogether.

"I had only the slightest acquaintance with him at that
time.   I was comparatively a young man, and certainly
not entitled on any ground to more than the common courtesy which Prescott never could refuse to any one.   But
he received me with such a frank and ready and liberal
sympathy, and such an open-hearted, guileless expansive-
ness, that I felt a personal affection for him from that
hour.   I remember the interview as if it had taken place
yesterday.   It was in his father's house, in his own library,
looking on the garden - house and garden, — honored
father and illustrious son, — alas ! all numbered with the
things that were !   He assured me that he had not the
slightest objection whatever to my plan, that he wished
me every success, and that, if there were any books in his
library bearing on my subject that I liked to use, they
were entirely at my service.   After I had expressed my
gratitude for his kindness and cordiality, by which I had
been in a very few moments set completely at ease, — so
far as my fears of his disapprobation went, — I also very
naturally stated my opinion that the danger was entirely
mine, and that it was rather wilful of me thus to risk
such a collision at my first venture, the probable consequence of which was utter shipwreck.   I recollect how
kindly and warmly he combated this opinion, assuring me
that no two books, as he said, ever injured each other, and
encouraging me in the warmest and most earnest manner to proceed on the course I had marked out for myself.

"Had the result of that interview been different, —
had he distinctly stated, or even vaguely hinted, that it
would be as well if I should select some other topic, or

had he only sprinkled me with the cold water of conventional and commonplace encouragement, — I should have gone from him with a chill upon my mind, and, no doubt, have laid down the pen at once; for, as I have already said, it was not that I cared about writing a history, but that I felt an inevitable impulse to write *one particular history*.

"You know how kindly he always spoke of and to me; and the generous manner in which, without the slightest hint from me, and entirely unexpected by me, he attracted the eyes of his hosts of readers to my forthcoming work, by so handsomely alluding to it in the Preface to his own, must be almost as fresh in your memory as it is in mine.

"And although it seems easy enough for a man of world-wide reputation thus to extend the right hand of fellowship to an unknown and struggling aspirant, yet I fear that the history of literature will show that such instances of disinterested kindness are as rare as they are noble."

It was not from any feeling that Mr. Motley was a young writer from whose rivalry he had nothing to apprehend. Mr. Amory says that Prescott expressed himself very decidedly to the effect that an author who had written such descriptive passages as were to be found in Mr. Motley's published writings was not to be undervalued as a competitor by any one. The reader who will turn to the description of Charles River in the eighth chapter of the second volume of "Merry-Mount," or of the autumnal woods in the sixteenth chapter of the same volume, will see good reason for Mr. Prescott's appreciation of the force of the rival whose advent he so heartily and generously welcomed.

1851–1856.   Æt. 37–42.

Historical Studies in Europe. — Letter from Brussels.

AFTER working for several years on his projected "History of the Dutch Republic," he found that, in order to do justice to his subject, he must have recourse to the authorities to be found only in the libraries and state archives of Europe.   In the year 1851 he left America with his family, to begin his task over again, throwing aside all that he had already done, and following up his new course of investigations at Berlin, Dresden, the Hague, and Brussels during several succeeding years.   I do not know that I can give a better idea of his mode of life during this busy period, his occupations, his state of mind, his objects of interest outside of his special work, than by making the following extracts from a long letter to myself, dated Brussels, 20th November, 1853.

After some personal matters he continued: —

"I don't really know what to say to you.   I am in a town which, for aught I know, may be very gay.   I don't know a living soul in it.   We have not a single acquaintance in the place, and we glory in the fact.   There is something rather sublime in thus floating on a single spar in the wide sea of a populous, busy, fuming, fussy world like this.   At any rate it is consonant to both our tastes.   You may suppose, however, that I find it rather difficult to amuse my friends out of the incidents of so isolated an

existence.   Our daily career is very regular and monoto-
nous.   Our life is as stagnant as a Dutch canal.   Not
that I complain of it, — on the contrary, the canal may
be richly freighted with merchandise and be a short cut
to the ocean of abundant and perpetual knowledge; but,
at the same time, few points rise above the level of so
regular a life, to be worthy of your notice.   You must,
therefore, allow me to meander along the meadows of commonplace.   Don't expect anything of the impetuous and
boiling style.   We go it weak here.   I don't know whether
you were ever in Brussels.   It is a striking, picturesque
town, built up a steep promontory, the old part at the
bottom, very dingy and mouldy, the new part at the top,
very showy and elegant.   Nothing can be more exquisite
in its way than the *grande place* in the very heart of the
city, surrounded with those toppling, zigzag, ten-storied
buildings bedizened all over with ornaments and emblems
so peculiar to the Netherlands, with the brocaded Hotel de
Ville on one side, with its impossible spire rising some
three hundred and seventy feet into the air and embroi-
dered to the top with the delicacy of needle-work, sugar-
work, spider-work, or what you will.   I haunt this place
because it is my scene, — my theatre.   Here were en-
acted so many deep tragedies, so many stately dramas,
and even so many farces, which have been familiar to me
so long that I have got to imagine myself invested with a
kind of property in the place, and look at it as if it were
merely the theatre with the coulisses, machinery, drapery,
etc., for representing scenes which have long since vanished, and which no more enter the minds of the men and
women who are actually moving across its pavements than
if they had occurred in the moon.   When I say that I
knew no soul in Brussels I am perhaps wrong.   With the
present generation I am not familiar.   *En revanche*, the
dead men of the place are my intimate friends.   I am at
home in any cemetery.   With the fellows of the sixteenth
century I am on the most familiar terms.   Any ghost that
ever flits by night across the moonlight square is at once
hailed by me as a man and a brother.   I call him by his

Christian name at once. When you come out of this place, however, which, as I said, is in the heart of the town, — the antique gem in the modern setting, — you may go either up or down. If you go down, you will find yourself in the very nastiest complications of lanes and culs-de-sac possible, a dark entanglement of gin-shops, beer-houses, and hovels, through which charming valley dribbles the Senne (whence, I suppose, is derived Senna), the most nauseous little river in the world, which receives all the outpourings of all the drains and houses, and is then converted into beer for the inhabitants, all the many breweries being directly upon its edge. If you go up the hill instead of down, you come to an arrangement of squares, palaces, and gardens as trim and fashionable as you will find in Europe. Thus you see that our Cybele sits with her head crowned with very stately towers and her feet in a tub of very dirty water.

"My habits here for the present year are very regular. I came here, having, as I thought, finished my work, or rather the first Part (something like three or four volumes, 8vo), but I find so much original matter here, and so many emendations to make, that I am ready to despair. However, there is nothing for it but to penelopize, pull to pieces, and stitch away again. Whatever may be the result of my labor, nobody can say that I have not worked like a brute beast, — but I don't care for the result. The labor is in itself its own reward and all I want. I go day after day to the archives here (as I went all summer at the Hague), studying the old letters and documents of the fifteenth century. Here I remain among my fellow-worms, feeding on these musty mulberry-leaves, out of which we are afterwards to spin our silk. How can you expect anything interesting from such a human cocoon? It is, however, not without its amusement in a mouldy sort of way, this reading of dead letters. It is something to read the real, bona fide signs-manual of such fellows as William of Orange, Count Egmont, Alexander Farnese, Philip II., Cardinal Granvelle, and the rest of them. It gives a 'realizing sense,' as the Americans have it. . . . There are not many public resources of amusement in this place, — if we wanted them, — which we don't. I miss the Dresden Gallery very much, and it makes me sad to think that I shall never look at the face of the Sistine Madonna again, — that picture beyond all pictures in the world, in which the artist certainly did get to heaven and painted a face which was never seen on earth — so pathetic, so gentle, so passionless, so prophetic. . . . There are a few good Rubenses here, — but the great wealth of that master is in Antwerp. The great picture of the Descent from the Cross is free again, after having been ten years in the repairing room. It has come out in very good condition. What a picture! It seems to me as if I had really stood at the cross and seen Mary weeping on John's shoulder, and Magdalen receiving the dead body of the Saviour in her arms. Never was the grand tragedy represented in so profound and dramatic a manner. For it is not only in his *color* in which this man so easily surpasses all the world, but in his life-like, flesh-and-blood action, — the tragic power of his composition. And is it not appalling to think of the 'large constitution of this man,' when you reflect on the acres of canvas which he has covered? How inspiriting to see with what muscular, masculine vigor this splendid Fleming rushed in and plucked up drowning Art by the locks when it was sinking in the trashy sea of such creatures as the Luca Giordanos and Pietro Cortonas and the like. Well might Guido exclaim, 'The fellow mixes blood with his colors !'. . . How providentially did the man come in and invoke living, breathing, moving men and women out of his canvas! Sometimes he is ranting and exaggerated, as are all men of great genius who wrestle with Nature so boldly. No doubt his heroines are more expansively endowed than would be thought genteel in our country, where cryptogams are so much in fashion, nevertheless there is always something very tremendous about him, and very often much that is sublime, pathetic, and moving. I defy any one of the average amount of imagination and sentiment to stand long before the Descent from the Cross without being moved more nearly to tears than he would care to acknowledge. As for color, his effects are as sure as those of the sun rising in a tropical landscape. There is something quite genial in the cheerful sense of his own omnipotence which always inspired him. There are a few fine pictures of his here, and I go in sometimes of a raw, foggy morning merely to warm myself in the blaze of their beauty."

I have been more willing to give room to this description of Rubens's pictures and the effect they produced upon Motley, because there is a certain affinity between those sumptuous and glowing works of art and the prose pictures of the historian who so admired them. He was himself a colorist in language, and called up the image of a great personage or a splendid pageant of the past with the same affluence, the same rich vitality, that floods and warms the vast areas of canvas over which the full-fed genius of Rubens disported itself in the luxury of imaginative creation.

XI.

1856–1857.   Æt. 42–43.

Publication of his first Historical Work, "Rise of the Dutch
Republic." — Its Reception. — Critical Notices.

THE labor of ten years was at last finished.   Carrying his formidable manuscript with him, — and how
formidable the manuscript which melts down into
three solid octavo volumes is, only writers and publishers know, — he knocked at the gate of that terrible fortress from which Lintot and Curll and Tonson
looked down on the authors of an older generation.
So large a work as the "History of the Rise of the
Dutch Republic," offered for the press by an author
as yet unknown to the British public, could hardly expect a warm welcome from the great dealers in literature as merchandise.   Mr. Murray civilly declined the
manuscript which was offered to him, and it was published at its author's expense by Mr. John Chapman.
The time came when the positions of the first-named
celebrated publisher and the unknown writer were
reversed.   Mr. Murray wrote to Mr. Motley asking
to be allowed to publish his second great work, the
"History of the United Netherlands," expressing at
the same time his regret at what he candidly called his
mistake in the first instance, and thus they were at
length brought into business connection as well as the
most agreeable and friendly relations.   An American

edition was published by the Harpers at the same time
as the London one.

If the new work of the unknown author found it
difficult to obtain a publisher, it was no sooner given
to the public than it found an approving, an admiring,
an enthusiastic world of readers, and a noble welcome
at the colder hands of the critics.

"The Westminster Review" for April, 1856, had
for its leading article a paper by Mr. Froude, in which
the critic awarded the highest praise to the work of
the new historian. As one of the earliest as well as
one of the most important recognitions of the work, I
quote some of its judgments.

"A history as complete as industry and genius can make
it now lies before us of the first twenty years of the Revolt
of the United Provinces; of the period in which those
provinces finally conquered their independence and established the Republic of Holland. It has been the result
of many years of silent, thoughtful, unobtrusive labor, and
unless we are strangely mistaken, unless we are ourselves
altogether unfit for this office of criticising which we have
here undertaken, the book is one which will take its place
among the finest histories in this or in any language. . . .
All the essentials of a great writer Mr. Motley eminently
possesses. His mind is broad, his industry unwearied.
In power of dramatic description no modern historian, except perhaps Mr. Carlyle, surpasses him, and in analysis
of character he is elaborate and distinct. His principles
are those of honest love for all which is good and admirable in human character wherever he finds it, while
he unaffectedly hates oppression, and despises selfishness
with all his heart."

After giving a slight analytical sketch of the series
of events related in the history, Mr. Froude objects
to only one of the historian's estimates, that, namely,
of the course of Queen Elizabeth.

"It is ungracious, however," he says, "even to find so slight a fault with these admirable volumes. Mr. Motley has written without haste, with the leisurely composure of a master. . . . We now take our leave of Mr. Motley, desiring him only to accept our hearty thanks for these volumes, which we trust will soon take their place in every English library. Our quotations will have sufficed to show the ability of the writer. Of the scope and general character of his work we have given but a languid conception. The true merit of a great book must be learned from the book itself. Our part has been rather to select varied specimens of style and power. Of Mr. Motley's antecedents we know nothing. If he has previously appeared before the public, his reputation has not crossed the Atlantic. It will not be so now. We believe that we may promise him as warm a welcome among ourselves as he will receive even in America; that his place will be at once conceded to him among the first historians in our common language."

The faithful and unwearied Mr. Allibone has swept the whole field of contemporary criticism, and shown how wide and universal was the welcome accorded to the hitherto unknown author. An article headed "Prescott and Motley," attributed to M. Guizot, which must have been translated, I suppose, from his own language, judging by its freedom from French idioms, is to be found in "The Edinburgh Review" for January, 1857. The praise, not unmingled with criticisms, which that great historian bestowed upon Motley is less significant than the fact that he superintended a translation of the "Rise of the Dutch Republic," and himself wrote the Introduction to it.

A general chorus of approbation followed or accompanied these leading voices. The reception of the work in Great Britain was a triumph. On the Continent, in addition to the tribute paid to it by M.

Guizot, it was translated into Dutch, into German, and into Russian. At home his reception was not less hearty. "The North American Review," which had set its foot on the semi-autobiographical medley which he called "Morton's Hope," which had granted a decent space and a tepid recognition to his "semi-historical" romance, in which he had already given the reading public a taste of his quality as a narrator of real events and a delineator of real personages, — this old and awe-inspiring New England and more than New England representative of the Fates, found room for a long and most laudatory article, in which the son of one of our most distinguished historians did the honors of the venerable literary periodical to the new-comer, for whom the folding-doors of all the critical headquarters were flying open as if of themselves. Mr. Allibone has recorded the opinions of some of our best scholars as expressed to him.

Dr. Lieber wrote a letter to Mr. Allibone in the strongest terms of praise. I quote one passage which in the light of after events borrows a cruel significance: —

"Congress and Parliament decree thanks for military exploits, — rarely for diplomatic achievements. If they ever voted their thanks for books, — and what deeds have influenced the course of human events more than some books? — Motley ought to have the thanks of our Congress; but I doubt not that he has already the thanks of every American who has read the work. It will leave its distinct mark upon the American mind."

Mr. Everett writes: —

"Mr. Motley's 'History of the Dutch Republic' is in my judgment a work of the highest merit. Unwearying research for years in the libraries of Europe, patience and

Wm H. Prescott

judgment in arranging and digesting his materials, a fine
historical tact, much skill in characterization, the perspective of narration, as it may be called, and a vigorous style unite to make it a very capital work, and place
the name of Motley by the side of those of our great historical trio, — Bancroft, Irving, and Prescott."

Mr. Irving, Mr. Bancroft, Mr. Sumner, Mr. Hillard, united their voices in the same strain of commendation. Mr. Prescott, whose estimate of the new
history is of peculiar value for obvious reasons, writes
to Mr. Allibone thus : —

"The opinion of any individual seems superfluous in respect to a work on the merits of which the public both at
home and abroad have pronounced so unanimous a verdict.
As Motley's path crosses my own historic field, I may be
thought to possess some advantage over most critics in my
familiarity with the ground.

"However this may be, I can honestly bear my testimony to the extent of his researches and to the accuracy
with which he has given the results of them to the public.
Far from making his book a mere register of events, he
has penetrated deep below the surface and explored the
cause of these events. He has carefully studied the phys-
iognomy of the times and given finished portraits of the
great men who conducted the march of the revolution.
Every page is instinct with the love of freedom and with
that personal knowledge of the working of free institutions
which could alone enable him to do justice to his subject.
We may congratulate ourselves that it was reserved for
one of our countrymen to tell the story — better than it
had yet been told — of this memorable revolution, which
in so many of its features bears a striking resemblance to
our own."

The public welcomed the work as cordially as the
critics. Fifteen thousand copies had already been
sold in London in 1857. In America it was equally

popular. Its author saw his name enrolled by common consent among those of the great writers of his time. Europe accepted him, his country was proud to claim him, scholarship set its jealously guarded seal upon the result of his labors, the reading world, which had not cared greatly for his stories, hung in delight over a narrative more exciting than romances; and the lonely student, who had almost forgotten the look of living men in the solitude of archives haunted by dead memories, found himself suddenly in the full blaze of a great reputation.

XII.

1856–1857. ÆT. 42–43.

Visit to America. — Residence in Boylston Place.

HE visited this country in 1856, and spent the winter of 1856–57 in Boston, living with his family in a house in Boylston Place.   At this time I had the pleasure of meeting him often, and of seeing the changes which maturity, success, the opening of a great literary and social career, had wrought in his character and bearing.   He was in every way greatly improved; the interesting, impulsive youth had ripened into a noble manhood.   Dealing with great themes, his own mind had gained their dignity.   Accustomed to the company of dead statesmen and heroes, his own ideas had risen to a higher standard. The flattery of society had added a new grace to his natural modesty.   He was now a citizen of the world by his reputation; the past was his province, in which he was recognized as a master; the idol's pedestal was ready for him, but he betrayed no desire to show himself upon it.

Return to England. — Social Relations. — Lady Harcourt's
Letter.

DURING the years spent in Europe in writing his
first history, from 1851 to 1856, Mr. Motley had lived
a life of great retirement and simplicity, devoting
himself to his work and to the education of his children, to which last object he was always ready to
give the most careful supervision. He was as yet unknown beyond the circle of his friends, and he did
not seek society. In this quiet way he had passed the
two years of residence in Dresden, the year divided
between Brussels and the Hague, and a very tranquil
year spent at Vevay on the Lake of Geneva. His
health at this time was tolerably good, except for nervous headaches, which frequently recurred and were
of great severity. His visit to England with his
manuscript in search of a publisher has already been
mentioned.

In 1858 he revisited England. His fame as a successful author was there before him, and he naturally
became the object of many attentions. He now made
many acquaintances who afterwards became his kind
and valued friends. Among those mentioned by his
daughter, Lady Harcourt, are Lord Lyndhurst, Lord
Carlisle, Lady William Russell, Lord and Lady
Palmerston, Dean Milman, with many others. The

following winter was passed in Rome, among many
English and American friends.

"In the course of the next summer," his daughter
writes to me, "we all went to England, and for the next
two years, marked chiefly by the success of the 'United
Netherlands,' our social life was most agreeable and most
interesting. He was in the fulness of his health and
powers; his works had made him known in intellectual
society, and I think his presence, on the other hand, increased their effects. As no one knows better than you
do, his belief in his own country and in its institutions at
their best was so passionate and intense that it was a part
of his nature, yet his refined and fastidious tastes were
deeply gratified by the influences of his life in England,
and the spontaneous kindness which he received added
much to his happiness. At that time Lord Palmerston
was Prime Minister; the weekly receptions at Cambridge
House were the centre of all that was brilliant in the political and social world, while Lansdowne House, Holland House, and others were open to the *sommités* in all
branches of literature, science, rank, and politics. . . .
It was the last year of Lord Macaulay's life, and as a few
out of many names which I recall come Dean Milman,
Mr. Froude (whose review of the 'Dutch Republic' in the
'Westminster' was one of the first warm recognitions it
ever received), the Duke and Duchess of Argyll, Sir
William Stirling Maxwell, then Mr. Stirling of Keir, the
Sheridan family in its different brilliant members, Lord
Wensleydale, and many more."

There was no society to which Motley would not
have added grace and attraction by his presence, and
to say that he was a welcome guest in the best houses
of England is only saying that these houses are always
open to those whose abilities, characters, achievements, are commended to the circles that have the
best choice by the personal gifts which are nature's
passport everywhere.

XIV.

1859. Æt. 45.

Letter to Mr. Francis H. Underwood. — Plan of Mr. Motley's Historical Works. — Second Great Work, "History of the United Netherlands."

I AM enabled by the kindness of Mr. Francis H. Underwood to avail myself of a letter addressed to him by Mr. Motley in the year before the publication of this second work, which gives us an insight into his mode of working and the plan he proposed to follow. It begins with an allusion which recalls a literary event interesting to many of his American friends.

ROME, *March* 4, 1859.

F. H. UNDERWOOD, ESQ.

My dear Sir, — . . . I am delighted to hear of the great success of "The Atlantic Monthly." In this remote region I have not the chance of reading it as often as I should like, but from the specimens which I have seen I am quite sure it deserves its wide circulation. A serial publication, the contents of which are purely original and of such remarkable merit, is a novelty in our country, and I am delighted to find that it has already taken so prominent a position before the reading world. . . .

The whole work [his history], of which the three volumes already published form a part, will be called "The Eighty Years' War for Liberty."

Epoch I. is the Rise of the Dutch Republic.
Epoch II. Independence Achieved. From the Death of

William the Silent till the Twelve Years' Truce.
1584–1609.

Epoch III. Independence Recognized. From the Twelve
Years' Truce to the Peace of Westphalia. 1609–
1648.

My subject is a very vast one, for the struggle of the
United Provinces with Spain was one in which all the
leading states of Europe were more or less involved.
After the death of William the Silent, the history assumes
world-wide proportions. Thus the volume which I am
just about terminating . . . is almost as much English
history as Dutch. The Earl of Leicester, very soon after
the death of Orange, was appointed governor of the provinces, and the alliance between the two countries almost
amounted to a political union. I shall try to get the
whole of the Leicester administration, terminating with the
grand drama of the Invincible Armada, into one volume;
but I doubt, my materials are so enormous. I have been
personally very hard at work, nearly two years, ransacking
the British State Paper Office, the British Museum, and
the Holland archives, and I have had two copyists constantly engaged in London, and two others at the Hague.
Besides this, I passed the whole of last winter at Brussels,
where, by special favor of the Belgian Government, I was
allowed to read what no one else has ever been permitted
to see, — the great mass of copies taken by that government from the Simancas archives, a translated epitome of
which has been published by Gachard. This correspondence reaches to the death of Philip II., and is of immense
extent and importance. Had I not obtained leave to read
the invaluable and, for my purpose, indispensable documents at Brussels, I should have gone to Spain, for they
will not be published these twenty years, and then only in
a translated and excessively abbreviated and unsatisfactory
form. I have read the whole of this correspondence, and
made very copious notes of it. In truth, I devoted three
months of last winter to that purpose alone.

The materials I have collected from the English archives

are also extremely important and curious. I have hundreds of interesting letters never published or to be published, by Queen Elizabeth, Burghley, Walsingham, Sidney, Drake, Willoughby, Leicester, and others. For the whole of that portion of my subject in which Holland and England were combined into one whole, to resist Spain in its attempt to obtain the universal empire, I have very abundant collections. For the history of the United Provinces is not at all a provincial history. It is the history of European liberty. Without the struggle of Holland and England against Spain, all Europe might have been Catholic and Spanish. It was Holland that saved England in the sixteenth century, and, by so doing, secured the triumph of the Reformation, and placed the independence of the various states of Europe upon a sure foundation. Of course, the materials collected by me at the Hague are of great importance. As a single specimen, I will state that I found in the archives there an immense and confused mass of papers, which turned out to be the autograph letters of Olden Barneveld during the last few years of his life; during, in short, the whole of that most important period which preceded his execution. These letters are in such an intolerable handwriting that no one has ever attempted to read them. I could read them only imperfectly myself, and it would have taken me a very long time to have acquired the power to do so; but my copyist and reader there is the most patient and indefatigable person alive, and he has quite mastered the handwriting, and he writes me that they are a mine of historical wealth for me. I shall have complete copies before I get to that period, one of signal interest, and which has never been described. I mention these matters that you may see that my work, whatever its other value may be, is built upon the only foundation fit for history, — original contemporary documents. These are all unpublished. Of course, I use the contemporary historians and pamphleteers, — Dutch, Spanish, French, Italian, German, and English, — but the most valuable of my sources are manuscript ones. I have said the little which I have said in order to vindicate the largeness of the subject. The kingdom of Holland is a small power now, but the Eighty Years' War, which secured the civil and religious independence of the Dutch Commonwealth and of Europe, was the great event of that whole age.

The whole work will therefore cover a most remarkable epoch in human history, from the abdication of Charles Fifth to the Peace of Westphalia, at which last point the political and geographical arrangements of Europe were established on a permanent basis, — in the main undisturbed until the French Revolution. . . .

I will mention that I received yesterday a letter from the distinguished M. Guizot, informing me that the first volume of the French translation, edited by him, with an introduction, has just been published. The publication was hastened in consequence of the appearance of a rival translation at Brussels. The German translation is very elegantly and expensively printed in handsome octavos; and the Dutch translation, under the editorship of the archivist general of Holland, Bakhuyzen v. d. Brink, is enriched with copious notes and comments by that distinguished scholar.

There are also three different piratical reprints of the original work at Amsterdam, Leipzig, and London. I must add that I had nothing to do with the translation in any case. In fact, with the exception of M. Guizot, no one ever obtained permission of me to publish translations, and I never knew of the existence of them until I read of it in the journals. . . . I forgot to say that among the collections already thoroughly examined by me is that portion of the Simancas archives still retained in the Imperial archives of France. I spent a considerable time in Paris for the purpose of reading these documents. There are many letters of Philip II. there, with *apostilles* by his own hand. . . . I would add that I am going to pass this summer at Venice for the purpose of reading and procuring copies from the very rich archives of that Republic, of the correspondence of their envoys in Madrid, London, and Brussels during the epoch of which I am treating.

I am also not without hope of gaining access to the archives of the Vatican here, although there are some difficulties in the way.

     With kind regards . . .

       I remain very truly yours,

          J. L. MOTLEY.

XV.

1860.   ÆT. 46.

Publication of the First Two Volumes of the "History of the United Netherlands." — Their Reception.

WE know something of the manner in which Mr. Motley collected his materials.   We know the labors, the difficulties, the cost of his toils among the dusty records of the past.   What he gained by the years he spent in his researches is so well stated by himself that I shall borrow his own words: —

"Thanks to the liberality of many modern governments of Europe, the archives where the state secrets of the buried centuries have so long mouldered are now open to the student of history.   To him who has patience and industry, many mysteries are thus revealed which no political sagacity or critical acumen could have divined.   He leans over the shoulder of Philip the Second at his writing-table, as the King spells patiently out, with cipher-key in hand, the most concealed hieroglyphics of Parma, or Guise, or Mendoza.   He reads the secret thoughts of 'Fabius' [Philip II.] as that cunctative Roman scrawls his marginal *apostilles* on each dispatch; he pries into all the stratagems of Camillus, Hortensius, Mucius, Julius, Tullius, and the rest of those ancient heroes who lent their names to the diplomatic masqueraders of the sixteenth century; he enters the cabinet of the deeply pondering Burghley, and takes from the most private drawer the memoranda which record that minister's unutterable doubtings; he pulls from the dressing-gown folds of the stealthy, soft-gliding Walsingham the last secret which he has picked from the Emperor's pigeon-holes or the Pope's pocket, and which not Hatton, nor Buckhurst, nor Leicester, nor the Lord Treasurer is to see, — nobody but Elizabeth herself; he sits invisible at the most secret councils of the Nassaus and Barneveld and Buys, or pores with Farnese over coming victories and vast schemes of universal conquest; he reads the latest bit of scandal, the minutest characteristic of king or minister, chronicled by the gossiping Venetians for the edification of the Forty; and after all this prying and eavesdropping, having seen the cross-purposes, the bribings, the windings in the dark, he is not surprised if those who were systematically deceived did not always arrive at correct conclusions." [1]

The fascination of such a quest is readily conceivable. A drama with real characters, and the spectator at liberty to go behind the scenes and look upon and talk with the kings and queens between the acts; to examine the scenery, to handle the properties, to study the "make up" of the imposing personages of full-dress histories; to deal with them all as Thackeray has done with the Grand Monarque in one of his caustic sketches, — this would be as exciting, one might suppose, as to sit through a play one knows by heart at Drury Lane or the Théâtre Français, and might furnish occupation enough to the curious idler who was only in search of entertainment. The mechanical obstacles of half-illegible manuscript, of antiquated forms of speech, to say nothing of the intentional obscurities of diplomatic correspondence, stand, however, in the way of all but the resolute and unwearied scholar. These difficulties, in all their complex obstinacy, had been met and overcome by the heroic efforts, the concentrated devotion, of the new laborer in the unbroken fields of secret history.

[1] *History of the United Netherlands,* i. p. 54.

Without stopping to take breath, as it were, — for his was a task *de longue haleine*, — he proceeded to his second great undertaking.

The first portion — consisting of two volumes — of the "History of the United Netherlands" was published in the year 1860. It maintained and increased the reputation he had already gained by his first history.

"The London Quarterly Review" devoted a long article to it, beginning with this handsome tribute to his earlier and later volumes: —

"Mr. Motley's 'History of the Rise of the Dutch Republic' is already known and valued for the grasp of mind which it displays, for the earnest and manly spirit in which he has communicated the results of deep research and careful reflection. Again he appears before us, rich with the spoils of time, to tell the story of the United Netherlands from the time of William the Silent to the end of the eventful year of the Spanish Armada, and we still find him in every way worthy of this 'great argument.' Indeed, it seems to us that he proceeds with an increased facility of style, and with a more complete and easy command over his materials. These materials are indeed splendid, and of them most excellent use has been made. The English State Paper Office, the Spanish archives from Simancas, and the Dutch and Belgian repositories, have all yielded up their secrets; and Mr. Motley has enjoyed the advantage of dealing with a vast mass of unpublished documents, of which he has not failed to avail himself to an extent which places his work in the foremost rank as an authority for the period to which it relates. By means of his labor and his art we can sit at the council board of Philip and Elizabeth, we can read their most private dispatches. Guided by his demonstration, we are enabled to dissect out to their ultimate issues the minutest ramifications of intrigue. We join in the amusement of the popular lampoon; we visit the prison-house; we stand by the scaffold; we are present at the battle and the siege. We can scan the inmost characters of men and can view them in their habits as they lived."

After a few criticisms upon lesser points of form and style, the writer says: —

"But the work itself must be read to appreciate the vast and conscientious industry bestowed upon it. His delineations are true and life-like, because they are not mere compositions written to please the ear, but are really taken from the facts and traits preserved in those authentic records to which he has devoted the labor of many years. Diligent and painstaking as the humblest chronicler, he has availed himself of many sources of information which have not been made use of by any previous historical writer. At the same time he is not oppressed by his materials, but has sagacity to estimate their real value, and he has combined with scholarly power the facts which they contain. He has rescued the story of the Netherlands from the domain of vague and general narrative, and has labored, with much judgment and ability, to unfold the *Belli causas, et vitia, et modos*, and to assign to every man and every event their own share in the contest, and their own influence upon its fortunes. We do not wonder that his earlier publication has been received as a valuable addition, not only to English, but to European literature."

One or two other contemporary criticisms may help us with their side lights. A critic in "The Edinburgh Review" for January, 1861, thinks that "Mr. Motley has not always been successful in keeping the graphic variety of his details subordinate to the main theme of his work." Still, he excuses the fault, as he accounts it, in consideration of the new light thrown on various obscure points of history, and

"it is atoned for by striking merits, by many narratives of great events faithfully, powerfully, and vividly executed, by the clearest and most life-like conceptions of character, and by a style which, if it sacrifices the severer principles of composition to a desire to be striking and picturesque, is always vigorous, full of animation, and glowing with the genuine enthusiasm of the writer.   Mr. Motley combines as an historian two qualifications seldom found united, — to great capacity for historical research he adds much power of pictorial representation.   In his pages we find characters and scenes minutely set forth in elaborate and characteristic detail, which is relieved and heightened in effect by the artistic breadth of light and shade thrown across the broader prospects of history.   In an American author, too, we must commend the hearty English spirit in which the book is written; and fertile as the present age has been in historical works of the highest merit, none of them can be ranked above these volumes in the grand qualities of interest, accuracy, and truth."

A writer in "Blackwood" (May, 1861) contrasts Motley with Froude somewhat in the way in which another critic had contrasted him with Prescott.   Froude, he says, remembers that there are some golden threads in the black robe of the Dominican.   Motley "finds it black and thrusts it farther into the darkness."

Every writer carries more or less of his own character into his book, of course.   A great professor has told me that there is a personal flavor in the mathematical work of a man of genius like Poisson.   Those who have known Motley and Prescott would feel sure beforehand that the impulsive nature of the one and the judicial serenity of the other would as surely betray themselves in their writings as in their conversation and in their every movement.   Another point which the critic of "Blackwood's Magazine" has noticed has not been so generally observed: it is what he calls "a dashing, offhand, rattling " style, — "fast" writing.   It cannot be denied that here and there may be detected slight vestiges of the way of writing of an earlier period of Motley's literary life, with which I have no reason to think the writer just mentioned was acquainted.   Now and then I can trace in the turn of a phrase, in the twinkle of an epithet, a faint reminiscence of a certain satirical levity, airiness, jauntiness, if I may hint such a word, which is just enough to remind me of those perilous shallows of his early time through which his richly freighted argosy had passed with such wonderful escape from their dangers and such very slight marks of injury.   That which is pleasant gayety in conversation may be quite out of place in formal composition, and Motley's wit must have had a hard time of it struggling to show its spangles in the processions while his gorgeous tragedies went sweeping by.

Residence in England. — Outbreak of the Civil War. — Letters
to the London "Times." — Visit to America. — Appointed
Minister to Austria. — Lady Harcourt's Letter. — Miss Motley's Memorandum.

THE winter of 1859–60 was passed chiefly at Oat-
lands Hotel, Walton-on-Thames. In 1860 Mr. Motley hired the house No. 31 Hertford Street, May Fair,
London. He had just published the first two volumes
of his "History of the Netherlands," and was ready
for the further labors of its continuation, when the
threats, followed by the outbreak, of the great civil
contention in his native land brought him back from
the struggles of the sixteenth and seventeenth centuries to the conflict of the nineteenth.

His love of country, which had grown upon him so
remarkably of late years, would not suffer him to be
silent at such a moment. All around him he found
ignorance and prejudice. The quarrel was like to be
prejudged in default of a champion of the cause which
to him was that of Liberty and Justice. He wrote
two long letters to the London "Times," in which he
attempted to make clear to Englishmen and to Europe
the nature and conditions of our complex system of
government, the real cause of the strife, and the
mighty issues at stake. Nothing could have been
more timely, nothing more needed. Mr. William

Everett, who was then in England, bears strong testimony to the effect these letters produced. Had Mr. Motley done no other service to his country, this alone would entitle him to honorable remembrance as among the first defenders of the flag, which at that moment had more to fear from what was going on in the cabinet councils of Europe than from all the armed hosts that were gathering against it.

He returned to America in 1861, and soon afterwards was appointed by Mr. Lincoln Minister to Austria. Mr. Burlingame had been previously appointed to the office, but having been objected to by the Austrian Government for political reasons, the place unexpectedly left vacant was conferred upon Motley, who had no expectation of any diplomatic appointment when he left Europe. For some interesting particulars relating to his residence in Vienna I must refer to the communications addressed to me by his daughter, Lady Harcourt, and her youngest sister, and the letters I received from him while at the Austrian capital. Lady Harcourt writes: —

"He held the post for six years, seeing the civil war fought out and brought to a triumphant conclusion, and enjoying, as I have every reason to believe, the full confidence and esteem of Mr. Lincoln to the last hour of the President's life. In the first dark years the painful interest of the great national drama was so all-absorbing that literary work was entirely put aside, and with his countrymen at home he lived only in the varying fortunes of the day, his profound faith and enthusiasm sustaining him and lifting him above the natural influence of a by no means sanguine temperament. Later, when the tide was turning and success was nearing, he was more able to work. His social relations during the whole period of his mission were of the most agreeable character. The society of Vienna was at that time, and I believe is still, the absolute reverse of that of England, where all claims to distinction are recognized and welcomed. There the old feudal traditions were still in full force, and diplomatic representatives admitted to the court society by right of official position found it to consist exclusively of an aristocracy of birth, sixteen quarterings of nobility being necessary to a right of presentation to the Emperor and Empress. The society thus constituted was distinguished by great charm and grace of manner, the exclusion of all outer elements not only limiting the numbers, but giving the ease of a family party within the charmed circle. On the other hand, larger interests suffered under the rigid exclusion of all occupations except the army, diplomacy, and court place. The intimacy among the different members of the society was so close that, beyond a courtesy of manner that never failed, the tendency was to resist the approach of any stranger as a *gêne*. A single new face was instantly remarked and commented on in a Vienna saloon to an extent unknown in any other large capital. This peculiarity, however, worked in favor of the old resident. Kindliness of feeling increased with familiarity and grew into something better than acquaintance, and the parting with most sincere and affectionately disposed friends in the end was deeply felt on both sides. Those years were passed in a pleasant house in the Weiden Faubourg, with a large garden at the back, and I do not think that during this time there was one disagreeable incident in his relations to his colleagues, while in several cases the relations, agreeable with all, became those of close friendship. We lived constantly, of course, in diplomatic and Austrian society, and during the latter part of the time particularly his house was as much frequented and the centre of as many dancing and other receptions as any in the place. His official relations with the Foreign Office were courteous and agreeable, the successive Foreign Ministers during his stay being Count Richberg, Count Mensdorff, and Baron Beust. Austria was so far removed from any real contact with our own country that, though the interest in our war may have been languid, they did not pretend to a knowledge which might have inclined them to controversy, while an instinct that we were acting as a constituted government against rebellion rather inclined them to sympathy. I think I may say that as he became known among them his keen patriotism and high sense of honor and truth were fully understood and appreciated, and that what he said always commanded a sympathetic hearing among men with totally different political ideas, but with chivalrous and loyal instincts to comprehend his own. I shall never forget his account of the terrible day when the news of Mr. Lincoln's death came. By some accident a rumor of it reached him first through a colleague. He went straight to the Foreign Office for news, hoping against hope, was received by Count Mensdorff, who merely came forward and laid his arm about his shoulder with an intense sympathy beyond words."

Miss Motley, the historian's youngest daughter, has added a note to her sister's communication: —

"During his residence in Vienna the most important negotiations which he had to carry on with the Austrian Government were those connected with the Mexican affair. Maximilian at one time applied to his brother the Emperor for assistance, and he promised to accede to his demand. Accordingly a large number of volunteers were equipped and had actually embarked at Trieste, when a dispatch from Seward arrived, instructing the American Minister to give notice to the Austrian Government that if the troops sailed for Mexico he was to leave Vienna at once. My father had to go at once to Count Mensdorff with these instructions, and in spite of the Foreign Minister being annoyed that the United States Government had not sooner intimated that this extreme course would be taken, the interview was quite amicable and the troops were not allowed to sail. We were in Vienna during the war in which Denmark fought alone against Austria and Prussia, and when it was over Bismarck came to Vienna to settle the terms of peace with the Emperor. He dined with us

twice during his short stay, and was most delightful and
agreeable.   When he and my father were together they
seemed to live over the youthful days they had spent together as students, and many were the anecdotes of their
boyish frolics which Bismarck related."

XVII.

1861–1863.   Æt. 47–49.

Letters from Vienna.

Soon after Mr. Motley's arrival in Vienna I received a long letter from him, most of which relates to personal matters, but which contains a few sentences of interest to the general reader as showing his zealous labors, wherever he found himself, in behalf of the great cause then in bloody debate in his own country: —

November 14, 1861.

. . . What can I say to you of cis-Atlantic things? I am almost ashamed to be away from home. You know that I had decided to remain, and had sent for my family to come to America, when my present appointment altered my plans. I do what good I can. I think I made some impression on Lord John Russell, with whom I spent two days soon after my arrival in England, and I talked very frankly and as strongly as I could to Palmerston, and I have had long conversations and correspondences with other leading men in England. I have also had an hour's [conversation] with Thouvenel in Paris. I hammered the Northern view into him as soundly as I could. For this year there will be no foreign interference with us. I don't anticipate it at any time, unless we bring it on ourselves by bad management, which I don't expect. Our fate is in our own hands, and Europe is looking on to see which side is strongest, — when it has made the discovery it will back it as also the best and the most moral. Yesterday I had my audience with the Emperor. He re-

ceived me with much cordiality, and seemed interested in
a long account which I gave him of our affairs. You may
suppose I inculcated the Northern views. We spoke in
his vernacular, and he asked me afterwards if I was a
German. I mention this not from vanity, but because
he asked it with earnestness, and as if it had a political
significance. Of course I undeceived him. His appearance interested me, and his manner is very pleasing.

I continued to receive long and interesting letters
from him at intervals during his residence as Minister at Vienna. Relating as they often did to public
matters, about which he had private sources of information, his anxiety that they should not get into print
was perfectly natural. As, however, I was at liberty
to read his letters to others at my discretion, and as
many parts of these letters have an interest as showing how American affairs looked to one who was behind the scenes in Europe, I may venture to give some
extracts without fear of violating the spirit of his injunctions, or of giving offence to individuals. The
time may come when his extended correspondence can
be printed in full with propriety, but it must be in a
future year and after it has passed into the hands of
a younger generation. Meanwhile these few glimpses
at his life and records of his feelings and opinions will
help to make the portrait of the man we are studying
present itself somewhat more clearly.

LEGATION OF THE U. S. A., VIENNA, *January* 14, 1862.

MY DEAR HOLMES, — I have two letters of yours,
November 29 and December 17, to express my thanks for.
It is quite true that it is difficult for me to write with the
same feeling that inspires you, — that everything around
the inkstand within a radius of a thousand miles is full
of deepest interest to writer and reader. I don't even

intend to try to amuse you with Vienna matters. What is it to you that we had a very pleasant dinner-party last week at Prince Esterhazy's, and another this week at Prince Liechtenstein's, and that to-morrow I am to put on my cocked hat and laced coat to make a visit to her Imperial Majesty, the Empress Mother, and that to-night there is to be the first of the assembly balls, the Vienna Almack's, at which — I shall be allowed to absent myself altogether?

It strikes me that there is likely to be left a fair field for us a few months longer, say till midsummer. The Trent affair I shall not say much about, except to state that I have always been for giving up the prisoners. I was awfully afraid, knowing that the demand had gone forth, —

> "Send us your prisoners or you'll hear of it,"

that the answer would have come back in the Hotspur vein —

> "And if the Devil come and roar for them,
> We will not send them."

The result would have been most disastrous, for in order to secure a most trifling advantage, — that of keeping Mason and Slidell at Fort Warren a little longer, — we should have turned our backs on all the principles maintained by us when neutral, and should have been obliged to accept a war at an enormous disadvantage. . . .

But I hardly dared to hope that we should have obtained such a victory as we have done. To have disavowed the illegal transaction at once, — before any demand came from England, — to have placed that disavowal on the broad ground of principle which we have always cherished, and thus with a clear conscience, and to our entire honor, to have kept ourselves clear from a war which must have given the Confederacy the invincible alliance of England, — was exactly what our enemies in Europe did not suppose us capable of doing. But we have done it in the handsomest manner, and there is not one liberal heart in this hemisphere that is not rejoiced, nor one hater of us and of our institutions that is not gnashing his teeth with rage.

The letter of ten close pages from which I have quoted these passages is full of confidential information, and contains extracts from letters of leading statesmen. If its date had been 1762, I might feel authorized in disobeying its injunctions of privacy. I must quote one other sentence, as it shows his animus at that time towards a distinguished statesman of whom he was afterwards accused of speaking in very hard terms by an obscure writer whose intent was to harm him. In speaking of the Trent affair, Mr. Motley says: "The English premier has been foiled by our much maligned Secretary of State, of whom, on this occasion at least, one has the right to say, with Sir Henry Wotton, —

> ' His armor was his honest thought,
> And simple truth his utmost skill.' "

He says at the close of this long letter: —

"I wish I could bore you about something else but American politics. But there is nothing else *worth* thinking of in the world. All else is leather and prunella. We are living over again the days of the Dutchmen or the seventeenth-century Englishmen."

My next letter, of fourteen closely written pages, was of similar character to the last. Motley could think of nothing but the great conflict. He was alive to every report from America, listening too with passionate fears or hopes, as the case might be, to the whispers not yet audible to the world which passed from lip to lip of the statesmen who were watching the course of events from the other side of the Atlantic

with the sweet complacency of the looker-on of Lucre-
tius; too often rejoicing in the storm that threatened
wreck to institutions and an organization which they
felt to be a standing menace to the established order
of things in their older communities.

A few extracts from this very long letter will be
found to have a special interest from the time at which
they were written.

LEGATION OF U. S. A., VIENNA, February 26, 1862.

MY DEAR HOLMES, — . . . I take great pleasure in
reading your prophecies, and intend to be just as free in
hazarding my own, for, as you say, our mortal life is but
a string of guesses at the future, and no one but an idiot
would be discouraged at finding himself sometimes far out
in his calculations. If I find you *signally right* in any
of your predictions, be sure that I will congratulate and
applaud. If you make mistakes, you shall never hear of
them again, and I promise to forget them. Let me ask
the same indulgence from you in return. This is what
makes letter-writing a comfort and journalizing dangerous.
. . . The ides of March will be upon us before this letter reaches you. We have got to squash the rebellion
soon, or be squashed forever as a nation. I don't pretend
to judge military plans or the capacities of generals.
But, as you suggest, perhaps I can take a more just view
of the whole picture of the eventful struggle at this great
distance than do those absolutely acting and suffering on
the scene. Nor can I resist the desire to prophesy any
more than you can do, knowing that I may prove utterly
mistaken. I say, then, that one great danger comes
from the chance of foreign interference. What will prevent that?

Our utterly defeating the Confederates in some *great*
and *conclusive* battle; or,

Our possession of the cotton ports and opening them
to European trade; or,

A *most unequivocal policy* of slave emancipation.

Any one of these three conditions would stave off recognition by foreign powers, until we had ourselves abandoned the attempt to reduce the South to obedience.

The last measure is to my mind the most important. The South has, by going to war with the United States government, *thrust into our hands against our will* the invincible weapon which constitutional reasons had hitherto forbidden us to employ. At the same time it has given us the power to remedy a great wrong to four millions of the human race, in which we had hitherto been obliged to acquiesce. We are threatened with national annihilation, and defied to use the only means of national preservation.

The question is distinctly proposed to us, Shall Slavery die, or the great Republic? It is most astounding to me that there can be two opinions in the free States as to the answer.

If we do fall, we deserve our fate. At the beginning of the contest, constitutional scruples might be respectable. But now we are fighting to subjugate the South; that is, Slavery. We are fighting for nothing else that I know of. We are fighting for the Union. Who wishes to destroy the Union? The slaveholder, nobody else. Are we to spend twelve hundred millions, and raise six hundred thousand soldiers, in order to *protect* slavery? It really does seem to me too simple for argument. I am anxiously waiting for the coming Columbus who will set this egg of ours on end by smashing in the slavery end. We shall be rolling about in every direction until that is done. I don't know that it is to be done by proclamation. Rather perhaps by facts. . . . Well, I console myself with thinking that the people — the American people, at least — is about as wise collectively as less numerous collections of individuals, and that the people has really declared emancipation, and is only puzzling how to carry it into effect. After all, it seems to be a law of Providence, that progress should be by a spiral movement; so that when it seems most tortuous, we may perhaps be going ahead. I am firm in the faith that slavery is now wriggling itself to death. With slavery in its pristine vigor,

I should think the restored Union neither possible nor desirable. Don't understand me as not taking into account all the strategical considerations against premature governmental utterances on this great subject. But are there any trustworthy friends to the Union among the slaveholders? Should we lose many Kentuckians and Virginians who are now with us, if we boldly confiscated the slaves of all rebels? — and a confiscation of property which has legs and so confiscates itself, at command, is not only a legal, but would prove a very practical measure in time of war. In brief, the time is fast approaching, I think, when 'Thorough' should be written on all our banners. Slavery will never accept a subordinate position. The great Republic and Slavery cannot both survive. We have been defied to mortal combat, and yet we hesitate to strike. These are my poor thoughts on this great subject. Perhaps you will think them crude. I was much struck with what you quote from Mr. Conway, that if emancipation was proclaimed on the Upper Mississippi it would be known to the negroes of Louisiana in advance of the telegraph. And if once the blacks had leave to run, how many whites would have to stay at home to guard their dissolving property?

You have had enough of my maunderings. But before I conclude them, may I ask you to give all our kindest regards to Lowell, and to express our admiration for the Yankee Idyl. I am afraid of using too extravagant language if I say all I think about it. Was there ever anything more stinging, more concentrated, more vigorous, more just? He has condensed into those few pages the essence of a hundred diplomatic papers and historical disquisitions and Fourth of July orations. I was dining a day or two since with his friend Lytton (Bulwer's son, *attaché* here) and Julian Fane (secretary of the embassy), both great admirers of him, — and especially of the "Biglow Papers;" they begged me to send them the Mason and Slidell Idyl, but I would n't, — I don't think it is in English nature (although theirs is very cosmopolitan and liberal) to take such punishment and come up smiling. I would rather they got it in some other way, and then told me what they thought voluntarily.

I have very pleasant relations with all the J. B.'s here. They are all friendly and well disposed to the North, — I speak of the embassy, which, with the ambassador and ——dress, numbers eight or ten souls, some of them very intellectual ones. There are no other J. B.'s here. I have no fear at present of foreign interference. We have got three or four months to do our work in, — a fair field and no favor. There is no question whatever that the Southern commissioners have been thoroughly snubbed in London and Paris. There is to be a blockade debate in Parliament next week, but no bad consequences are to be apprehended. The Duke de Gramont (French ambassador, and an intimate friend of the Emperor) told my wife last night that it was entirely false that the Emperor had ever urged the English government to break the blockade. "Don't believe it, — don't believe a word of it," he said. He has *always* held that language to me. He added that Prince Napoleon had just come out with a strong speech about us, — you will see it, doubtless, before you get this letter, — but it has not yet reached us.

Shall I say anything of Austria, — what can I say that would interest you? That's the reason why I hate to write. All my thoughts are in America. Do you care to know about the Archduke Ferdinand Maximilian, that shall be King hereafter of Mexico (if L. N. has his way)? He is next brother to the Emperor, but although I have had the honor of private audiences of many archdukes here, this one is a resident of Trieste.

He is about thirty, — has an adventurous disposition, — some imagination, — a turn for poetry, — has voyaged a good deal about the world in the Austrian ship-of-war, — for in one respect he much resembles that unfortunate but anonymous ancestor of his, the King of Bohemia with the seven castles, who, according to Corporal Trim, had such a passion for navigation and sea-affairs, "with never a seaport in all his dominions." But now the present

King of Bohemia has got the sway of Trieste, and is Lord
High Admiral and Chief of the Marine Department.   He
has been much in Spain, also in South America; I have
read some travels, "Reise Skizzen," of his — printed, not
published.   They are not without talent, and he ever and
anon relieves his prose jog-trot by breaking into a canter
of poetry.   He adores bull-fights, and rather regrets the
Inquisition, and considers the Duke of Alva everything
noble and chivalrous, and the most abused of men.   It
would do your heart good to hear his invocations to that
deeply injured shade, and his denunciations of the ignorant and vulgar protestants who have defamed him.   (N.
B.   Let me observe that the R. of the D. R. was not published until long after the "Reise Skizzen" were written.)
Du armer Alva! weil du dem Willen deines Herrn uner-
schütterlich treu wast, weil die festbestimmten grundsätze
der Regierung, etc., etc., etc.   You can imagine the rest.

Dear me! I wish I could get back to the sixteenth
and seventeenth century. . . . But alas! the events of
the nineteenth are too engrossing.

If Lowell cares to read this letter, will you allow me
to "make it over to him jointly," as Captain Cuttle says.
I wished to write to him, but I am afraid only you would
tolerate my writing so much when I have nothing to say.
If he would ever send me a line I should be infinitely
obliged, and would quickly respond.   We read the "Wash-
ers of the Shroud" with fervid admiration.

Always remember me most sincerely to the Club, one
and all.   It touches me nearly when you assure me that I
am not forgotten by them.   To-morrow is *Saturday* and
the last of the month.[1]   We are going to dine with our
Spanish colleague.   But the first bumper of the Don's
champagne I shall drain to the health of my Parker House
friends.

From another long letter dated August 31, 1862, I
extract the following passages: —

"I quite agree in all that you said in your last letter.

[1] See Appendix A.

'The imp of secession can't reënter its mother's womb.'
It is merely childish to talk of the Union 'as it was.'
You might as well bring back the Saxon Heptarchy.   But
the great Republic is destined to live and flourish, I can't
doubt. . . . Do you remember that wonderful scene in
Faust in which Mephistopheles draws wine for the rabble
with a gimlet out of the wooden table; and how it changes
to fire as they drink it, and how they all go mad, draw
their knives, grasp each other by the nose, and think they
are cutting off bunches of grapes at every blow, and how
foolish they all look when they awake from the spell and
see how the Devil has been mocking them?   It always
seems to me a parable of the great Secession.

"I repeat, I can't doubt as to the ultimate result.
But I dare say we have all been much mistaken in our
calculations as to time.   Days, months, years, are nothing
in history.   *Men* die, *man* is immortal, practically, even
on this earth.   We are so impatient, — and we are always
watching for the last scene of the tragedy.   Now I hum-
bly opine that the drop is only about falling on the first
act, or perhaps only the prologue.   This act or prologue
will be called, in after days, War for the *status quo*.

"Such enthusiasm, heroism, and manslaughter as *status
quo* could inspire, has, I trust, been not entirely in vain,
but it has been proved insufficient.

"I firmly believe that when the slaveholders declared
war on the United States government they began a series
of events that, in the logical chain of history, cannot come
to a conclusion until the last vestige of slavery is gone.
Looking at the whole field for a moment dispassionately,
objectively, as the dear Teutonic philosophers say, and
merely as an exhibition of phenomena, I cannot imagine
any other issue.   Everything else *may* happen.   This
alone *must* happen.

"But after all this is n't a war.   It is a revolution.
It is n't strategists that are wanted so much as *believers*.
In revolutions the men who win are those who are in earnest.   Jeff and Stonewall and the other Devil-worshippers
are in earnest, but it was not written in the book of fate

that the slaveholders' rebellion should be vanquished by a pro-slavery general. History is never so illogical. No, the coming 'man on horseback' on our side must be a great strategist, with the soul of that insane lion, mad old John Brown, in his belly. That is your only Promethean recipe: —

> ' et insani leonis
> Vim stomacho apposuisse nostro.'

"I don't know why Horace runs so in my head this morning. . . .

"There will be work enough for all; but I feel awfully fidgety just now about Port Royal and Hilton Head, and about affairs generally for the next three months. After that iron-clads and the new levies must make us invincible."

In another letter, dated November 2, 1862, he expresses himself very warmly about his disappointment in the attitude of many of his old English friends with reference to our civil conflict. He had recently heard the details of the death of "the noble Wilder Dwight."

"It is unnecessary," he says, "to say how deeply we were moved. I had the pleasure of knowing him well, and I always appreciated his energy, his manliness, and his intelligent cheerful heroism. I look back upon him now as a kind of heroic type of what a young New Englander ought to be and was. I tell you that one of these days — after a generation of mankind has passed away — these youths will take their places in our history, and be regarded by the young men and women now unborn with the admiration which the Philip Sidneys and the Max Piccolominis now inspire. After all, what was your Chevy Chace to stir blood with like a trumpet? What noble principle, what deathless interest, was there at stake? Nothing but a bloody fight between a lot of noble game-keepers on one side and of noble poachers on the other.

And because they fought well and hacked each other to pieces like devils, they have been heroes for centuries."

The letter was written in a very excited state of feeling, and runs over with passionate love of country and indignation at the want of sympathy with the cause of freedom which he had found in quarters where he had not expected such coldness or hostile tendencies.

From a letter dated Vienna, September 22, 1863.

. . . "When you wrote me last you said on general matters this: 'In a few days we shall get the news of the success or failure of the attacks on Port Hudson and Vicksburg. If both are successful, many will say that the whole matter is about settled.' You may suppose that when I got the great news I shook hands warmly with you in the spirit across the Atlantic. Day by day for so long we had been hoping to hear the fall of Vicksburg. At last when that little concentrated telegram came, announcing Vicksburg and Gettysburg on the same day and in two lines, I found myself almost alone. . . . There was nobody in the house to join in my huzzahs but my youngest infant. And my conduct very much resembled that of the excellent Philip II. when he heard the fall of Antwerp, — for I went to her door, screeching through the key-hole 'Vicksburg is ours!' just as that other *père de famille*, more potent, but I trust not more respectable than I, conveyed the news to his Infanta. (*Vide*, for the incident, an American work on the Netherlands, i. p. 263, and the authorities there cited.) It is contemptible on my part to speak thus frivolously of events which will stand out in such golden letters so long as America has a history, but I wanted to illustrate the yearning for sympathy which I felt. You who were among people grim and self-contained usually, who, I *trust*, were falling on each other's necks in the public streets, shouting, with tears in their eyes and triumph in their hearts, can picture my isolation.

"I have never faltered in my faith, and in the darkest hours, when misfortunes seemed thronging most thickly upon us, I have never felt the want of anything to lean against; but I own I did feel like shaking hands with a few hundred people when I heard of our Fourth of July, 1863, work, and should like to have heard and joined in an American cheer or two. . . .

"I have not much to say of matters here to interest you. We have had an intensely hot, historically hot, and very long and very dry summer. I never knew before what a drought meant. In Hungary the suffering is great, and the people are killing the sheep to feed the pigs with the mutton. Here about Vienna the trees have been almost stripped of foliage ever since the end of August. There is no glory in the grass nor verdure in anything.

"In fact, we have nothing green here but the Archduke Max, who firmly believes that he is going forth to Mexico to establish an American empire, and that it is his divine mission to destroy the dragon of democracy and reëstablish the true Church, the Right Divine, and all sorts of games. Poor young man! . . .

"Our information from home is to the 12th. Charleston seems to be in *articulo mortis*, but how forts nowadays seem to fly in the face of Scripture. Those founded on a rock, and built of it, fall easily enough under the rain of Parrotts and Dahlgrens, while the house built of sand seems to bid defiance to the storm."

In quoting from these confidential letters I have been restrained from doing full justice to their writer by the fact that he spoke with such entire freedom of persons as well as events. But if they could be read from beginning to end, no one could help feeling that his love for his own country, and passionate absorption of every thought in the strife upon which its existence as a nation depended, were his very life during all this agonizing period. He can think and talk of nothing else, or, if he turns for a moment to other subjects, he reverts to the one great central interest of "American politics," of which he says in one of the letters from which I have quoted, "There is nothing else *worth* thinking of in the world."

But in spite of his public record as the historian of the struggle for liberty and the champion of its defenders, and while every letter he wrote betrayed in every word the intensity of his patriotic feeling, he was not safe against the attacks of malevolence. A train laid by unseen hands was waiting for the spark to kindle it, and this came at last in the shape of a letter from an unknown individual, — a letter the existence of which ought never to have been a matter of official recognition.

XVIII.

1866–1867. Æt. 52–53.

Resignation of his Office. — Causes of his Resignation.

IT is a relief to me that just here, where I come to
the first of two painful episodes in this brilliant and
fortunate career, I can preface my statement with the
generous words of one who speaks with authority of
his predecessor in office.

The Hon. John Jay, Ex-Minister to Austria, in
the tribute to the memory of Motley read at a meeting of the New York Historical Society, wrote as
follows: —

"In singular contrast to Mr. Motley's brilliant career
as an historian stands the fact recorded in our diplomatic
annals that he was twice forced from the service as one
who had forfeited the confidence of the American government. This society, while he was living, recognized his
fame as a statesman, diplomatist, and patriot, as belonging to America, and now that death has closed the career
of Seward, Sumner, and Motley, it will be remembered
that the great historian, twice humiliated, by orders from
Washington, before the diplomacy and culture of Europe,
appealed from the passions of the hour to the verdict of
history.

"Having succeeded Mr. Motley at Vienna some two
years after his departure, I had occasion to read most of
his dispatches, which exhibited a mastery of the subjects
of which they treated, with much of the clear perception,
the scholarly and philosophic tone and decided judgment,

which, supplemented by his picturesque description, full of life and color, have given character to his histories. They are features which might well have served to extend the remark of Madame de Staël that a great historian is almost a statesman. I can speak also from my own observation of the reputation which Motley left in the Austrian capital. Notwithstanding the decision with which, under the direction of Mr. Seward, he had addressed the minister of foreign affairs, Count Mensdorff, afterwards the Prince Diedrickstein, protesting against the departure of an Austrian force of one thousand volunteers, who were about to embark for Mexico in aid of the ill-fated Maximilian, — a protest which at the last moment arrested the project, — Mr. Motley and his amiable family were always spoken of in terms of cordial regard and respect by members of the imperial family and those eminent statesmen, Count de Beust and Count Andrassy. His death, I am sure, is mourned to-day by the representatives of the historic names of Austria and Hungary, and by the surviving diplomats then residing near the Court of Vienna, wherever they may still be found, headed by their venerable Doyen, the Baron de Heckéren."

The story of Mr. Motley's resignation of his office and its acceptance by the government is this.

The President of the United States, Andrew Johnson, received a letter professing to be written from the Hotel Meurice, Paris, dated October 23, 1866, and signed "George W. M'Crackin, of New York." This letter was filled with accusations directed against various public agents, ministers, and consuls, representing the United States in different countries. Its language was coarse, its assertions were improbable, its spirit that of the lowest of party scribblers. It was bitter against New England, especially so against Massachusetts, and it singled out Motley for the most particular abuse. I think it is still questioned whether

there was any such person as the one named, — at any
rate, it bore the characteristic marks of those vulgar
anonymous communications which rarely receive any
attention unless they are important enough to have
the police set on the track of the writer to find his rat-
hole, if possible. A paragraph in the "Daily Advertiser" of June 7, 1869, quotes from a Western paper
a story to the effect that one *William R.* M'Cracken,
who had recently died at ——, confessed to having
written the M'Crackin letter. Motley, he said, had
snubbed him and refused to lend him money. "He
appears to have been a Bohemian of the lowest order."
Between such authorship and the anonymous there
does not seem to be much to choose. But the dying
confession sounds in my ears as decidedly apocryphal.
As for the letter, I had rather characterize it than
reproduce it. It is an offence to decency and a disgrace to the national record on which it is found.

This letter of "George W. M'Crackin" passed into
the hands of Mr. Seward, the Secretary of State.
Most gentlemen, I think, would have destroyed it
on the spot, as it was not fit for the waste-basket.
Some, more cautious, might have smothered it among
the piles of their private communications. If any notice was taken of it, one would say that a private note
to each of the gentlemen attacked might have warned
him that there were malicious eavesdroppers about,
ready to catch up any careless expression he might let
fall and make a scandalous report of it to his detri-
ment.

The secretary, acquiescing without resistance in a
suggestion of the President, saw fit to address a formal note to several of the gentlemen mentioned in
the M'Crackin letter, repeating some of its offensive

expressions, and requesting those officials to deny or confirm the report that they had uttered them.

A gentleman who is asked whether he has spoken in a "malignant" or "offensive" manner, whether he has "railed violently and shamefully" against the President of the United States, or against anybody else, might well wonder who would address such a question to the humblest citizen not supposed to be wanting in a common measure of self-respect. A gentleman holding an important official station in a foreign country, receiving a letter containing such questions, signed by the prime minister of his government, if he did not think himself imposed upon by a forgery, might well consider himself outraged. It was a letter of this kind which was sent by the Secretary of State to the Minister Plenipotentiary to the Empire of Austria. Not quite all the vulgar insolence of the M'Crackin letter was repeated. Mr. Seward did not ask Mr. Motley to deny or confirm the assertion of the letter that he was a "thorough flunky" and "un-American functionary." But he did insult him with various questions suggested by the anonymous letter, — questions that must have been felt as an indignity by the most thick-skinned of battered politicians.

Mr. Motley was very sensitive, very high-spirited, very impulsive, very patriotic, and singularly truthful. The letter of Mr. Seward to such a man was like a buffet on the cheek of an unarmed officer. It stung like the thrust of a stiletto. It roused a resentment that could not find any words to give it expression. He could not wait to turn the insult over in his mind, to weigh the exact amount of affront in each question, to take counsel, to sleep over it, and reply to it with diplomatic measure and suavity. One hour had scarcely elapsed before his answer was written. As to his feelings as an American, he appeals to his record. This might have shown that if he erred it was on the side of enthusiasm and extravagant expressions of reverence for the American people during the heroic years just passed. He denounces the accusations as pitiful fabrications and vile calumny. He blushes that such charges could have been uttered; he is deeply wounded that Mr. Seward could have listened to such falsehood. He does not hesitate to say what his opinions are with reference to home questions, and especially to that of reconstruction.

"These opinions," he says, "in the privacy of my own household, and to occasional American visitors, I have not concealed. The great question now presenting itself for solution demands the conscientious scrutiny of every American who loves his country and believes in the human progress of which that country is one of the foremost representatives. I have never thought, during my residence at Vienna, that because I have the honor of being a public servant of the American people I am deprived of the right of discussing within my own walls the gravest subjects that can interest freemen. A minister of the United States does not cease to be a citizen of the United States, as deeply interested as others in all that relates to the welfare of his country."

Among the "occasional American visitors" spoken of above must have been some of those self-appointed or hired agents called "interviewers," who do for the American public what the Venetian spies did for the Council of Ten, what the familiars of the Inquisition did for the priesthood, who invade every public man's privacy, who listen at every key-hole, who tamper with every guardian of secrets; purveyors to the insatiable appetite of a public which must have a slain reputation to devour with its breakfast, as the monster of antiquity called regularly for his tribute of a spotless virgin.

The "interviewer" has his use, undoubtedly, and often instructs and amuses his public with gossip they could not otherwise listen to. He serves the politician by repeating the artless and unstudied remarks which fall from his lips in a conversation which the reporter has been invited to take notes of. He tickles the author's vanity by showing him off as he sits in his library unconsciously uttering the engaging items of self-portraiture which, as he well knows, are to be given to the public in next week's illustrated paper. The feathered end of his shaft titillates harmlessly enough, but too often the arrowhead is crusted with a poison worse than the Indian gets by mingling the wolf's gall with the rattlesnake's venom. No man is safe whose unguarded threshold the mischief-making questioner has crossed. The more unsuspecting, the more frank, the more courageous, the more social is the subject of his vivisection, the more easily does he get at his vital secrets, if he has any to be extracted. No man is safe if the hearsay reports of his conversation are to be given to the public without his own careful revision. When we remember that a proof-text bearing on the mighty question of the future life, words of supreme significance, uttered as they were in the last hour, and by the lips to which we listen as to none other, — that this text depends for its interpretation on the position of a single comma, we can readily see what wrong may be done by the unintentional blunder of the most conscientious reporter. But too frequently it happens that the careless talk of an honest and high-minded man only reaches the public after filtering through the drain of some reckless hireling's memory, — one who has played so long with other men's characters and good name that he forgets they have any value except to fill out his morning paragraphs.

Whether the author of the scandalous letter which it was disgraceful to the government to recognize was a professional interviewer or only a malicious amateur, or whether he was a paid "spotter," sent by some jealous official to report on the foreign ministers as is sometimes done in the case of conductors of city horse-cars, or whether the dying miscreant before mentioned told the truth, cannot be certainly known. But those who remember Mr. Hawthorne's account of his consular experiences at Liverpool are fully aware to what intrusions and impertinences and impositions our national representatives in other countries are subjected. Those fellow-citizens who "often came to the consulate in parties of half a dozen or more, on no business whatever, but merely to subject their public servant to a rigid examination, and see how he was getting on with his duties," may very possibly have included among them some such mischief-maker as the author of the odious letter which received official recognition. Mr. Motley had spoken in one of his histories of "a set of venomous familiars who glided through every chamber and coiled themselves at every fireside." He little thought that under his own roof he himself was to be the victim of an equally base espionage.

It was an insult on the part of the government to have sent Mr. Motley such a letter with such questions as were annexed to it. No very exact rule can be laid down as to the manner in which an insult shall be dealt with. Something depends on temperament, and his was of the warmer complexion. His first impulse, he says, was to content himself with a flat denial of the truth of the accusations. But his scrupulous honesty compelled him to make a plain statement of his opinions, and to avow the fact that he had made no secret of them in conversation under conditions where he had a right to speak freely of matters quite apart from his official duties. His answer to the accusation was denial of its charges; his reply to the insult was his resignation.

It may be questioned whether this was the wisest course, but wisdom is often disconcerted by an indignity, and even a meek Christian may forget to turn the other cheek after receiving the first blow until the natural man has asserted himself by a retort in kind. But the wrong was committed; his resignation was accepted; the vulgar letter, not fit to be spread out on these pages, is enrolled in the records of the nation, and the first deep wound was inflicted on the proud spirit of one whose renown had shed lustre on the whole country.

That the burden of this wrong may rest where it belongs, I quote the following statement from Mr. Jay's paper, already referred to.

"It is due to the memory of Mr. Seward to say, and there would seem now no further motive for concealing the truth, that I was told in Europe, on what I regarded as reliable authority, that there was reason to believe that on the receipt of Mr. Motley's resignation Mr. Seward had written to him declining to accept it, and that this letter, by a telegraphic order of President Johnson, had been arrested in the hands of a dispatch agent before its delivery to Mr. Motley, and that the curt letter of the 18th of April had been substituted in its stead."

The Hon. John Bigelow, late Minister to France, has published an article in "The International Review" for July–August, 1878, in which he defends his late friend Mr. Seward's action in this matter at the expense of the President, Mr. Andrew Johnson, and not without inferences unfavorable to the discretion of Mr. Motley. Many readers will think that the simple record of Mr. Seward's unresisting acquiescence in the action of the President is far from being to his advantage. I quote from his own conversation as carefully reported by his friend Mr. Bigelow. "Mr. Johnson was in a state of intense irritation, and more or less suspicious of everybody about him." "Instead of throwing the letter into the fire," the President handed it to him, the secretary, and suggested answering it, and without a word, so far as appears, he simply answered, "Certainly, sir." Again, the secretary having already written to Mr. Motley that "his answer was satisfactory," the President, on reaching the last paragraph of Mr. Motley's letter, in which he begged respectfully to resign his post, "without waiting to learn what Mr. Seward had done or proposed to do, exclaimed, with a not unnatural asperity, 'Well, let him go,' and 'on hearing this,' said Mr. Seward, laughing, 'I did not read my dispatch.'" Many persons will think that the counsel for the defence has stated the plaintiff's case so strongly that there is nothing left for him but to show his ingenuity and his friendship for the late secretary in a hopeless argument. At any rate, Mr. Seward appears not to have made the slightest effort to protect Mr. Motley against his coarse and jealous chief at two critical moments, and though his own continuance in office may have been more important to the State than

that of the Vicar of Bray was to the Church, he ought
to have risked something, as it seems to me, to shield
such a patriot, such a gentleman, such a scholar, from
ignoble treatment; he ought to have been as ready to
guard Mr. Motley from wrong as Mr. Bigelow has
shown himself to shield Mr. Seward from reproach,
and his task, if more delicate, was not more difficult.
I am willing to accept Mr. Bigelow's loyal and honorable defence of his friend's memory as the best that
could be said for Mr. Seward, but the best defence in
this case is little better than an impeachment. As for
Mr. Johnson, he had held the weapon of the most
relentless of the Parcæ so long that his suddenly clip-
ping the thread of a foreign minister's tenure of office
in a fit of jealous anger is not at all surprising.

Thus finished Mr. Motley's long and successful
diplomatic service at the Court of Austria. He may
have been judged hasty in resigning his place; he may
have committed himself in expressing his opinions too
strongly before strangers, whose true character as
spies and eavesdroppers he was too high-minded to
suspect. But no caution could have protected him
against a slanderer who hated the place he came from,
the company he kept, the name he had made famous,
to whom his very look and bearing — such as belong
to a gentleman of natural refinement and good breeding — must have been a personal grievance and an
unpardonable offence.

I will add, in illustration of what has been said, and
as showing his feeling with reference to the matter,
an extract from a letter to me from Vienna, dated the
12th of March, 1867.

. . . "As so many friends and so many strangers
have said so much that is gratifying to me in public and

private on this very painful subject, it would be like affectation, in writing to so old a friend as you, not to touch upon it. I shall confine myself, however, to one fact, which, so far as I know, may be new to you.

"Geo. W. M'Cracken is a man and a name utterly unknown to me.

"With the necessary qualification which every man who values truth must make when asserting such a negation, — viz., to the very best of my memory and belief, — I never set eyes on him nor heard of him until now, in the whole course of my life. Not a member of my family or of the legation has the faintest recollection of any such person. I am quite convinced that he never saw me nor heard the sound of my voice. That his letter was a tissue of vile calumnies, shameless fabrications, and unblushing and contemptible falsehoods, — by whomsoever uttered, — I have stated in a reply to what ought never to have been an official letter. No man can regret more than I do that such a correspondence is enrolled in the capital among American state papers. I shall not trust myself to speak of the matter. It has been a sufficiently public scandal."

XIX.

1867–1868.   Æt. 53–54.

Last Two Volumes of the "History of the United Netherlands."
— General Criticisms of Dutch Scholars on Motley's Historical Works.

In his letter to me of March 12, 1867, just cited,
Mr. Motley writes : —

"My two concluding volumes of the United Netherlands
are passing rapidly through the press.   Indeed, Volume
III. is entirely printed and a third of Volume IV.

"If I live ten years longer I shall have probably written the natural sequel to the first two works, — viz., the
Thirty Years' War.   After that I shall cease to scourge
the public.

"I don't know whether my last two volumes are good
or bad; I only know that they are true — but that need n't
make them amusing.

"Alas! one never knows when one becomes a bore."

In 1868 the two concluding volumes of the "History
of the Netherlands" were published at the same time
in London and in New York.   The events described
and the characters delineated in these two volumes
had, perhaps, less peculiar interest for English and
American readers than some of those which had lent
attraction to the preceding ones.   There was no scene
like the siege of Antwerp, no story like that of the
Spanish Armada.   There were no names that sounded
to our ears like those of Sir Philip Sidney and Lei-

cester and Amy Robsart. But the main course of his narrative flowed on with the same breadth and depth of learning and the same brilliancy of expression. The monumental work continued as nobly as it had begun. The facts had been slowly, quietly gathered, one by one, like pebbles from the empty channel of a brook. The style was fluent, impetuous, abundant, impatient, as it were, at times, and leaping the sober boundaries prescribed to it, like the torrent which rushes through the same channel when the rains have filled it. Thus there was matter for criticism in his use of language. He was not always careful in the construction of his sentences. He introduced expressions now and then into his vocabulary which reminded one of his earlier literary efforts. He used stronger language at times than was necessary, coloring too highly, shading too deeply in his pictorial delineations. To come to the matter of his narrative, it must be granted that not every reader will care to follow him through all the details of diplomatic intrigues which he has with such industry and sagacity extricated from the old manuscripts in which they had long lain hidden. But we turn a few pages and we come to one of those descriptions which arrest us at once and show him in his power and brilliancy as a literary artist. His characters move before us with the features of life; we can see Elizabeth, or Philip, or Maurice, not as a name connected with events, but as a breathing and acting human being, to be loved or hated, admired or despised, as if he or she were our contemporary. That all his judgments would not be accepted as final we might easily anticipate; he could not help writing more or less as a partisan, but he was a partisan on the side of freedom in politics and religion, of human nature as against every form of tyranny, secular or priestly, of noble manhood wherever he saw it as against meanness and violence and imposture, whether clad in the soldier's mail or the emperor's purple. His sternest critics, and even these admiring ones, were yet to be found among those who with fundamental beliefs at variance with his own followed him in his long researches among the dusty annals of the past.

The work of the learned M. Groen van Prinsterer,[1] devoted expressly to the revision and correction of what the author considers the erroneous views of Mr. Motley on certain important points, bears, notwithstanding, such sincere and hearty tribute to his industry, his acquisitions, his brilliant qualities as a historian, that some extracts from it will be read, I think, with interest.

"My first interview, more than twenty years ago, with Mr. Lothrop Motley, has left an indelible impression on my memory.

"It was the 8th of August, 1853. A note is handed me from our eminent archivist Bakhuyzen van den Brink. It informs me that I am to receive a visit from an American, who, having been struck by the analogies between the United Provinces and the United States, between Washington and the founder of our independence, has interrupted his diplomatic career to write the life of William the First; that he has already given proof of ardor and perseverance, having worked in libraries and among collections of manuscripts, and that he is coming to pursue his studies at the Hague.

"While I am surprised and delighted with this intelligence, I am informed that Mr. Motley himself is waiting for my answer. My eagerness to make the acquaintance of such an associate in my sympathies and my labors may

[1] *Maurice et Barnevelt, Étude Historique.* Utrecht, 1875.

be well imagined.   But how shall I picture my surprise,
in presently discovering that this unknown and indefatigable fellow-worker has really read, I say read and reread,
our Quartos, our Folios, the enormous volumes of Bor, of
van Meteren, besides a multitude of books, of pamphlets,
and even of unedited documents.   Already he is familiar
with the events, the changes of condition, the characteristic details of the life of his and my hero.   Not only is he
acquainted with my Archives, but it seems as if there
was nothing in this voluminous collection of which he was
ignorant. . . .

   "In sending me the last volume of his 'History of the
Foundation of the Republic of the Netherlands,' Mr. Motley wrote to me: 'Without the help of the Archives I could
never have undertaken the difficult task I had set myself,
and you will have seen at least from my numerous cita-
tions that I have made a sincere and conscientious study
of them.'   Certainly in reading such a testimonial I con-
gratulated myself on the excellent fruit of my labors, but
the gratitude expressed to me by Mr. Motley was sincerely
reciprocated.   The Archives are a scientific collection,
and my 'Manual of National History,' written in Dutch,
hardly gets beyond the limits of my own country.   And
here is a stranger, become our compatriot in virtue of the
warmth of his sympathies, who has accomplished what was
not in my power.   By the detail and the charm of his
narrative, by the matter and form of a work which the universality of the English language and numerous translations were to render cosmopolitan, Mr. Motley, like that
other illustrious historian, Prescott, lost to science by too
early death, has popularized in both hemispheres the sublime devotion of the Prince of Orange, the exceptional
and providential destinies of my country, and the bene-
dictions of the Eternal for all those who trust in Him and
tremble only at his Word."

   The old Dutch scholar differs in many important
points from Mr. Motley, as might be expected from
his creed and his life-long pursuits.   This I shall

refer to in connection with Motley's last work, "John of Barneveld." An historian among archivists and annalists reminds one of Sir John Lubbock in the midst of his ant-hills. Undoubtedly he disturbs the ants in their praiseworthy industry, much as his attentions may flatter them. Unquestionably the ants (if their means of expressing themselves were equal to their apparent intellectual ability) could teach him many things that he has overlooked and correct him in many mistakes. But the ants will labor ingloriously without an observer to chronicle their doings, and the archivists and annalists will pile up facts forever like so many articulates or mollusks or radiates, until the vertebrate historian comes with his generalizing ideas, his beliefs, his prejudices, his idiosyncrasies of all kinds, and brings the facts into a more or less imperfect, but still organic series of relations. The history which is not open to adverse criticism is worth little, except as material, for it is written without taking cognizance of those higher facts about which men must differ; of which Guizot writes as follows, as quoted in the work of M. Groen van Prinsterer himself.

"It is with *facts* that our minds are exercised, it has nothing but facts as its materials, and when it discovers general laws these laws are themselves facts which it determines. . . . In the study of *facts* the intelligence may allow itself to be crushed; it may lower, narrow, materialize itself; it may come to believe that there are no facts except those which strike us at the first glance, which come close to us, which fall, as we say, under our senses; a great and gross error; there are *remote facts*, immense, obscure, sublime, very difficult to reach, to observe, to describe, and which are not any less *facts* for these reasons, and which man is not less obliged to study and to know; and if he fails to recognize them or forgets them, his thought will be prodigiously abashed, and all his ideas carry the stamp of this deterioration."

In that higher region of facts which belongs to the historian, whose task it is to interpret as well as to transcribe, Mr. Motley showed, of course, the political and religious school in which he had been brought up. Every man has a right to his "personal equation" of prejudice, and Mr. Motley, whose ardent temperament gave life to his writings, betrayed his sympathies in the disputes of which he told the story, in a way to insure sharp criticism from those of a different way of thinking. Thus it is that in the work of M. Groen van Prinsterer, from which I have quoted, he is considered as having been betrayed into error, while his critic recognizes "his manifest desire to be scrupulously impartial and truth-telling." And M. Fruin, another of his Dutch critics, says, "His sincerity, his perspicacity, the accuracy of his laborious researches, are incontestable."

Some of the criticisms of Dutch scholars will be considered in the pages which deal with his last work, "The Life of John of Barneveld."

XX

1868–1869. Æt. 54–55.

Visit to America. — Residence at No. 2 Park Street, Boston. —
Address on the coming Presidential Election. — Address on
Historic Progress and American Democracy. — Appointed
Minister to England.

In June, 1868, Mr. Motley returned with his family to Boston, and established himself in the house
No. 2 Park Street.   During his residence here he entered a good deal into society, and entertained many
visitors in a most hospitable and agreeable way.

On the 20th of October, 1868, he delivered an
address before the Parker Fraternity, in the Music
Hall, by special invitation.   Its title was "Four Questions for the People, at the Presidential Election."
This was of course what is commonly called an elec-
tioneering speech, but a speech full of noble sentiments and eloquent expression.   Here are two of its
paragraphs : —

"Certainly there have been bitterly contested elections
in this country before.   Party spirit is always rife, and
in such vivid, excitable, disputatious communities as ours
are, and I trust always will be, it is the very soul of freedom.   To those who reflect upon the means and end of
popular government, nothing seems more stupid than in
grand generalities to deprecate party spirit.   Why, government by parties and through party machinery is the
only possible method by which a free government can accomplish the purpose of its existence.   The old republics

of the past may be said to have fallen, not because of
party spirit, but because there was no adequate machinery
by which party spirit could develop itself with facility and
regularity. . . .

"And if our Republic be true to herself, the future
of the human race is assured by our example.   No sweep
of overwhelming armies, no ponderous treatises on the
rights of man, no hymns to liberty, though set to martial
music and resounding with the full diapason of a million human throats, can exert so persuasive an influence
as does the spectacle of a great republic, occupying a quarter of the civilized globe, and governed quietly and sagely
by the people itself."

A large portion of this address is devoted to the
proposition that it is just and reasonable to pay our
debts rather than to repudiate them, and that the
nation is as much bound to be honest as is the individual. "It is an awful thing," he says, "that this
should be a question at all," but it was one of the
points on which the election turned, for all that.

In his advocacy of the candidate with whom, and
the government of which he became the head, his relations became afterwards so full of personal antagonism, he spoke as a man of his ardent nature might
be expected to speak on such an occasion. No one
doubts that his admiration of General Grant's career
was perfectly sincere, and no one at the present day
can deny that the great captain stood before the historian with such a record as one familiar with the
deeds of heroes and patriots might well consider as
entitling him to the honors too often grudged to the
living to be wasted on the dead. The speaker only
gave voice to the widely prevailing feelings which had
led to his receiving the invitation to speak. The time
was one which called for outspoken utterance, and

there was not a listener whose heart did not warm as he heard the glowing words in which the speaker recorded the noble achievements of the soldier who must in so many ways have reminded him of his favorite character, William the Silent.

On the 16th of December of this same year, 1868, Mr. Motley delivered an address before the New York Historical Society, on the occasion of the sixty-fourth anniversary of its foundation. The president of the society, Mr. Hamilton Fish, introduced the speaker as one "whose name belongs to no single country, and to no single age. As a statesman and diplomatist and patriot, he belongs to America; as a scholar, to the world of letters; as a historian, all ages will claim him in the future."

His subject was "Historic Progress and American Democracy." The discourse is, to use his own words, "a rapid sweep through the eons and the centuries," illustrating the great truth of the development of the race from its origin to the time in which we are living. It is a long distance from the planetary fact of the obliquity of the equator, which gave the earth its alternation of seasons, and rendered the history, if not the existence of man and of civilization a possibility, to the surrender of General Lee under the apple-tree at Appomattox Court-House. No one but a scholar familiar with the course of history could have marshalled such a procession of events into a connected and intelligible sequence. It is indeed a flight rather than a march; the reader is borne along as on the wings of a soaring poem, and sees the rising and decaying empires of history beneath him as a bird of passage marks the succession of cities and wilds and deserts as he keeps pace with the sun in his journey.

Its eloquence, its patriotism, its crowded illustrations, drawn from vast resources of knowledge, its epigrammatic axioms, its occasional pleasantries, are all characteristic of the writer.

Mr. Gulian C. Verplanck, the venerable senior member of the society, proposed the vote of thanks to Mr. Motley with words of warm commendation.

Mr. William Cullen Bryant rose and said: —

"I take great pleasure in seconding the resolution which has just been read. The eminent historian of the Dutch Republic, who has made the story of its earlier days as interesting as that of Athens and Sparta, and who has infused into the narrative the generous glow of his own genius, has the highest of titles to be heard with respectful attention by the citizens of a community which, in its origin, was an offshoot of that renowned republic. And cheerfully has that title been recognized, as the vast audience assembled here to-night, in spite of the storm, fully testifies; and well has our illustrious friend spoken of the growth of civilization and of the improvement in the condition of mankind, both in the Old World — the institutions of which he has so lately observed — and in the country which is proud to claim him as one of her children."

Soon after the election of General Grant, Mr. Motley received the appointment of Minister to England. That the position was one which was in many respects most agreeable to him cannot be doubted. Yet it was not with unmingled feelings of satisfaction, not without misgivings which warned him but too truly of the dangers about to encompass him, that he accepted the place. He writes to me on April 16, 1869: —

"I feel anything but exultation at present, — rather the opposite sensation. I feel that I am placed higher than I deserve, and at the same time that I am taking

greater responsibilities than ever were assumed by me
before. *You* will be indulgent to my mistakes and
shortcomings, — and who can expect to avoid them? But
the world will be cruel, and the times are threatening.
I shall do my best, — but the best may be poor enough, —
and keep 'a heart for any fate.' "

XXI

Recall from the English Mission. — Its Alleged and its Probable Reasons.

THE misgivings thus expressed to me in confidence, natural enough in one who had already known what it is to fall on evil days and evil tongues, were but too well justified by after events.   I could have wished to leave untold the story of the English mission, an episode in Motley's life full of heart-burnings, and long to be regretted as a passage of American history. But his living appeal to my indulgence comes to me from his grave as a call for his defence, however little needed, at least as a part of my tribute to his memory.   It is little needed, because the case is clear enough to all intelligent readers of our diplomatic history, and because his cause has been amply sustained by others in many ways better qualified than myself to do it justice.   The task is painful, for if a wrong was done him it must be laid at the doors of those whom the nation has delighted to honor, and whose services no error of judgment or feeling or conduct can ever induce us to forget.   If he confessed himself liable, like the rest of us, to mistakes and short-comings, we must remember that the great officers of the government who decreed his downfall were not less the subjects of human infirmity.

The outline to be filled up is this: A new administration had just been elected. The "Alabama Treaty," negotiated by Motley's predecessor, Mr. Reverdy Johnson, had been rejected by the Senate. The minister was recalled, and Motley, nominated without opposition and unanimously confirmed by the Senate, was sent to England in his place. He was welcomed most cordially on his arrival at Liverpool, and replied in a similar strain of good feeling, expressing the same kindly sentiments which may be found in his instructions. Soon after arriving in London he had a conversation with Lord Clarendon, the British Foreign Secretary, of which he sent a full report to his own government. While the reported conversation was generally approved of in the government's dispatch acknowledging it, it was hinted that some of its expressions were stronger than were required by the instructions, and that one of its points was not conveyed in precise conformity with the President's view. The criticism was very gently worded, and the dispatch closed with a somewhat guarded paragraph repeating the government's approbation.

This was the first offence alleged against Mr. Motley. The second ground of complaint was that he had shown written minutes of this conversation to Lord Clarendon to obtain his confirmation of its exactness, and that he had — as he said, inadvertently, — omitted to make mention to the government of this circumstance until some weeks after the time of the interview.

He was requested to explain to Lord Clarendon that a portion of his presentation and treatment of the subject discussed at the interview immediately after his arrival was disapproved by the Secretary of State, and he did so in a written communication, in which he used the very words employed by Mr. Fish in his criticism of the conversation with Lord Clarendon.

An alleged mistake; a temperate criticism, coupled with a general approval; a rectification of the mistake criticised. All this within the first two months of Mr. Motley's official residence in London.

No further fault was found with him, so far as appears, in the discharge of his duties, to which he must have devoted himself faithfully, for he writes to me, under the date of December 27, 1870: "I have worked harder in the discharge of this mission than I ever did in my life." This from a man whose working powers astonished the old Dutch archivist, Groen van Prinsterer, means a good deal.

More than a year had elapsed since the interview with Lord Clarendon, which had been the subject of criticism. In the mean time a paper of instructions was sent to Motley, dated September 25, 1869, in which the points in the report of his interview which had been found fault with are so nearly covered by similar expressions, that there seemed no real ground left for difference between the government and the minister. Whatever over-statement there had been, these new instructions would imply that the government was now ready to go quite as far as the minister had gone, and in some points to put the case still more strongly. Everything was going on quietly. Important business had been transacted, with no sign of distrust or discontent on the part of the government as regarded Motley. Whatever mistake he was thought to have committed was condoned by amicable treatment, neutralized by the virtual indorsement of the government in the instructions of the 25th of September, and obsolete as a ground of quarrel by lapse of time. The question about which the misunderstanding, if such it deserves to be called, had taken place, was no longer a possible source of disagreement, as it had long been settled that the Alabama case should only be opened again at the suggestion of the British government, and that it should be transferred to Washington whenever that suggestion should again bring it up for consideration.

Such was the aspect of affairs at the American Legation in London. No foreign minister felt more secure in his place than Mr. Motley. "I thought myself," he says in the letter of December 27, "entirely in the confidence of my own government, and I know that I had the thorough confidence and the friendship of the leading personages in England." All at once, on the first of July, 1870, a letter was written by the Secretary of State, requesting him to resign. This gentle form of violence is well understood in the diplomatic service. Horace Walpole says, speaking of Lady Archibald Hamilton: "They have civilly asked her and grossly forced her to ask civilly to go away, which she has done, with a pension of twelve hundred a year." Such a request is like the embrace of the "virgin" in old torture-chambers. She is robed in soft raiment, but beneath it are the knife-blades which are ready to lacerate and kill the victim, if he awaits the pressure of the machinery already in motion.

Mr. Motley knew well what was the logical order in an official execution, and saw fit to let the government work its will upon him as its servant. In November he was recalled.

The recall of a minister under such circumstances is an unusual if not an unprecedented occurrence. The government which appoints a citizen to represent

the country at a foreign court assumes a very serious
obligation to him. The next administration may turn
him out and nothing will be thought of it. He may
be obliged to ask for his passports and leave all at
once if war is threatened between his own country and
that which he represents. He may, of course, be recalled for gross misconduct. But his dismissal is a
very serious matter to him personally, and not to be
thought of on the ground of passion or caprice. Marriage is a simple business, but divorce is a very different thing. The world wants to know the reason of it;
the law demands its justification. It was a great blow
to Mr. Motley, a cause of indignation to those who
were interested in him, a surprise and a mystery to
the world in general.

When he, his friends, and the public, all startled
by this unexpected treatment, looked to find an explanation of it, one was found which seemed to many
quite sufficient. Mr. Sumner had been prominent
among those who had favored his appointment. A
very serious breach had taken place between the President and Mr. Sumner on the important San Domingo
question. It was a quarrel, in short, neither more
nor less, at least so far as the President was concerned.
The proposed San Domingo treaty had just been
rejected by the Senate, on the thirtieth day of June,
and immediately thereupon, — the very next day, —
the letter requesting Mr. Motley's resignation was
issued by the executive. This fact was interpreted
as implying something more than a mere coincidence.
It was thought that Sumner's friend, who had been
supported by him as a candidate for high office, who
shared many of his political ideas and feelings, who
was his intimate associate, his fellow-townsman, his

companion in scholarship and cultivation, his sympathetic co-laborer in many ways, had been accounted
and dealt with as the ally of an enemy, and that the
shaft which struck to the heart of the sensitive envoy
had glanced from the *œs triplex* of the obdurate Senator.

Mr. Motley wrote a letter to the Secretary of State
immediately after his recall, in which he reviewed his
relations with the government from the time of his
taking office, and showed that no sufficient reason
could be assigned for the treatment to which he had
been subjected. He referred finally to the public
rumor which assigned the President's hostility to his
friend Sumner, growing out of the San Domingo
treaty question, as the cause of his own removal, and
to the coincidence between the dates of the rejection
of the treaty and his dismissal, with an evident belief
that these two occurrences were connected by something more than accident.

To this, a reply was received from the Secretary of
State's office, signed by Mr. Fish, but so objectionable in its tone and expressions that it has been generally doubted whether the paper could claim anything
more of the secretary's hand than his signature. It
travelled back to the old record of the conversation
with Lord Clarendon, more than a year and a half before, took up the old exceptions, warmed them over
into grievances, and joined with them whatever the
captatores verborum, not extinct since Daniel Webster's time, could add to their number. This was the
letter which was rendered so peculiarly offensive by
a most undignified comparison which startled every
well-bred reader. No answer was possible to such a
letter, and the matter rested until the death of Mr.

Motley caused it to be brought up once more for judgment.

The Honorable John Jay, in his tribute to the memory of Mr. Motley, read at a meeting of the New York Historical Society, vindicated his character against the attacks of the late executive in such a way as to leave an unfavorable impression as to the course of the government. Objection was made on this account to placing the tribute upon the minutes of the society. This led to a publication by Mr. Jay, entitled "Motley's Appeal to History," in which the propriety of the society's action is questioned, and the wrong done to him insisted upon and further illustrated.

The defence could not have fallen into better hands. Bearing a name which is, in itself, a title to the confidence of the American people, a diplomatist familiar with the rights, the customs, the traditions, the courtesies, which belong to the diplomatic service, the successor of Mr. Motley at Vienna, and therefore familiar with his official record, not self-made, which too commonly means half-made, but with careful training added to the instincts to which he had a right by inheritance, he could not allow the memory of such a scholar, of such a high-minded lover of his country, of so true a gentleman as Mr. Motley, to remain without challenge under the stigma of official condemnation. I must refer to Mr. Jay's memorial tribute as printed in the newspapers of the day, and to his "Appeal" published in "The International Review," for his convincing presentation of the case, and content myself with a condensed statement of the general and special causes of complaint against Mr. Motley, and the explanations which suggest themselves, as abundantly competent to show the insufficiency of the reasons alleged by the government as an excuse for the manner in which he was treated.

The grounds of complaint against Mr. Motley are to be looked for: —

1. In the letter of Mr. Fish to Mr. Moran, of December 30, 1870.

2. In Mr. Bancroft Davis's letter to the New York "Herald" of January 4, 1878, entitled, "Mr. Sumner, the Alabama Claims and their Settlement."

3. The reported conversations of General Grant.

4. The reported conversations of Mr. Fish.

In considering Mr. Fish's letter, we must first notice its animus. The manner in which Dickens's two old women are brought in is not only indecorous, but it shows a state of feeling from which nothing but harsh interpretation of every questionable expression of Mr. Motley's was to be expected.

There is not the least need of maintaining the perfect fitness and rhetorical felicity of every phrase and every word used by him in his interview with Lord Clarendon. It is not to be expected that a minister, when about to hold a conversation with a representative of the government to which he is accredited, will commit his instructions to memory and recite them, like a school-boy "speaking his piece." He will give them more or less in his own language, amplifying, it may be, explaining, illustrating, at any rate paraphrasing in some degree, but endeavoring to convey an idea of their essential meaning. In fact, as any one can see, a *conversation* between two persons must necessarily imply a certain amount of extemporization on the part of both. I do not believe any long and important conference was ever had between two able men without each of them feeling that he had not spoken exactly in all respects as he would if he could say all over again.

Doubtless, therefore, Mr. Motley's report of his conversation shows that some of his expressions might have been improved, and others might as well have been omitted. A man does not change his temperament on taking office. General Jackson still swore "by the Eternal," and his illustrious military successor of a more recent period seems, by his own showing, to have been liable to sudden impulses of excitement. It might be said of Motley, as it was said of Shakespeare by Ben Jonson, "aliquando sufflaminandus erat." Yet not too much must be made of this concession. Only a determination to make out a case could, as it seems to me, have framed such an indictment as that which the secretary constructed by stringing together a slender list of pretended peccadillos. One instance will show the extreme slightness which characterizes many of the grounds of inculpation: —

The instructions say, "The government, in rejecting the recent convention, abandons neither its own claims nor those of its citizens," etc.

Mr. Motley said, in the course of his conversation, "At present, the United States government, while withdrawing neither its national claims nor the claims of its individual citizens against the British government," etc.

Mr. Fish says, "The determination of this government not to abandon its claims nor those of its citizens was stated parenthetically, and in such a subordinate way as not necessarily to attract the attention of Lord Clarendon."

What reported conversation can stand a captious

criticism like this? Are there not two versions of the
ten commandments which were given out in the thun-
der and smoke of Sinai, and would the secretary hold
that this would have been a sufficient reason to recall
Moses from his "Divine Legation" at the court of the
Almighty?

There are certain expressions which, as Mr. Fish
shows them *apart from their connection*, do very certainly seem in bad taste, if not actually indiscreet and
unjustifiable. Let me give an example: —

"Instead of expressing the hope entertained by this
government that there would be an early, satisfactory,
and friendly settlement of the questions at issue, he volunteered the unnecessary, and from the manner in which
it was thrust in, the highly objectionable statement that
'the United States government had no insidious purposes,'" etc.

This sounds very badly as Mr. Fish puts it; let us
see how it stands in its proper connection: —

"He [Lord Clarendon] added with some feeling, that
in his opinion it would be highly objectionable that the
question should be hung up on a peg, to be taken down
at some convenient moment for us, when it might be difficult for the British government to enter upon its solution, and when they might go into the debate at a disadvantage. These were, as nearly as I can remember, his
words, and I replied very earnestly that I had already
answered that question when I said that my instructions
were to propose as brief a delay as would probably be
requisite for the cooling of passions and for producing the
calm necessary for discussing the defects of the old treaty
and a basis for a new one. The United States government had no insidious purposes," etc.

Is it not evident that Lord Clarendon suggested the
idea which Mr Motley repelled as implying an insid-

ious mode of action? Is it not just as clear that Mr.
Fish's way of reproducing the expression without the
insinuation which called it forth is a practical mis-
statement which does Mr. Motley great wrong?

One more example of the method of wringing a dry
cloth for drops of evidence ought to be enough to show
the whole spirit of the paper.

Mr. Fish, in his instructions: —

"It might, indeed, well have occurred in the event of
the selection by lot of the arbitrator or umpire in different cases, involving however precisely the same principles,
that different awards, resting upon antagonistic principles, might have been made."

Mr. Motley, in the conversation with Lord Clarendon: —

"I called his lordship's attention to your very judicious
suggestion that the throwing of the dice for umpires might
bring about opposite decisions in cases arising out of identical principles. He agreed entirely that no principle
was established by the treaty, but that the throwing of
dice or drawing of lots was not a new invention on that
occasion, but a not uncommon method in arbitrations. I
only expressed the opinion that such an aleatory process
seemed an unworthy method in arbitrations," etc.

Mr. Fish, in his letter to Mr. Moran: —

"That he had in his mind at that interview something
else than his letter of instructions from this department
would appear to be evident, when he says that ' he called
his lordship's attention to your [my] very judicious suggestion that the throwing of dice for umpire might bring
about opposite decisions.' The instructions which Mr.
Motley received from me contained no suggestion about
' throwing of dice.' That idea is embraced in the suggestive words 'aleatory process' (adopted by Mr. Motley),

but previously applied in a speech made in the Senate on
the question of ratifying the treaty."

Charles Sumner's Speech on the Johnson-Claren-
don Treaty, April 13, 1869 : —

"In the event of failure to agree, the arbitrator is determined 'by lot' out of two persons named by each side.
Even if this aleatory proceeding were a proper device in
the umpirage of private claims, it is strongly inconsistent with the solemnity which belongs to the present
question."

It is "suggestive" that the critical secretary, so
keen in detecting conversational inaccuracies, having
but two words to quote from a printed document, got
one of them wrong. But this trivial comment must
not lead the careful reader to neglect to note how
much is made of what is really nothing at all. The
word *aleatory*, whether used in its original and limited sense, or in its derived extension as a technical
term of the civil law, was appropriate and convenient; one especially likely to be remembered by any
person who had read Mr. Sumner's speech, — and
everybody *had* read it; the secretary himself doubtless got the suggestion of determining the question
"by lot" from it. What more natural than that it
should be used again when the subject of appealing
to chance came up in conversation? It "was an excellent good word before it was ill-sorted," and we
were fortunate in having a minister who was scholar
enough to know what it meant. The language used
by Mr. Motley conveyed the idea of his instructions
plainly enough, and threw in a compliment to their
author which should have saved this passage at least
from the wringing process. The example just given
is, like the concession of belligerency to the insur-

gents by Great Britain, chiefly important as "showing animus."

It is hardly necessary to bring forward other instances of virtual misrepresentation. If Mr. Motley could have talked his conversation over again, he would very probably have changed some expressions. But he felt bound to repeat the interview exactly as it occurred, with all the errors to which its extemporaneous character exposed it. When a case was to be made out against him, the secretary wrote, December 30, 1870 : —

"Well might he say, as he did in a subsequent dispatch on the 15th of July, 1869, that he had gone beyond the strict letter of his instructions. He might have added, in direct opposition to their temper and spirit."

Of the same report the secretary had said, June 28, 1869: "Your general presentation and treatment of the several subjects discussed in that interview meet the approval of this department." This general approval is qualified by mild criticism of a single statement as not having been conveyed in "precise conformity" to the President's view. The minister was told he might be well content to rest the question on the very forcible presentation he had made of the American side of the question, and that if there were expressions used stronger than were required by his instructions, they were in the right direction. The mere fact that a minute of this conversation was confidentially submitted to Lord Clarendon in order that our own government might have his authority for the accuracy of the record, which was intended exclusively for its own use, and that this circumstance was overlooked and not reported to the government until some weeks afterward, are the additional charges against Mr. Motley. The submission of the dispatch containing an account of the interview, the secretary says, is not inconsistent with diplomatic usage, but it is inconsistent with the duty of a minister not to inform his government of that submission. "Mr. Motley submitted the draft of his No. 8 to Lord Clarendon, and failed to communicate that fact to his government." He did inform Mr. Fish, at any rate, on the 30th of July, and alleged "inadvertence" as the reason for his omission to do it before.

Inasmuch as submitting the dispatch was not inconsistent with diplomatic usage, nothing seems left to find fault with but the not very long delay in mentioning the fact, or in his making the note "private and confidential," as is so frequently done in diplomatic correspondence.

Such were the grounds of complaint. On the strength of the conversation which had met with the general approval of the government, tempered by certain qualifications, and of the omission to report *immediately* to the government the fact of its verification by Lord Clarendon, the secretary rests the case against Mr. Motley. On these grounds it was that, according to him, the President withdrew all right to discuss the Alabama question from the minister whose dismissal was now only a question of time. But other evidence comes in here.

Mr. Motley says: —

"It was, as I supposed, understood before my departure for England, although not publicly announced, that the so-called Alabama negotiations, whenever renewed, should be conducted at Washington, in case of the consent of the British government."

Mr. Sumner says, in his "Explanation in Reply to an Assault:"—

"The secretary in a letter to me at Boston, dated at Washington, October 9, 1869, informs me that the discussion of the question was withdrawn from London '*because* (the italics are the secretary's) we think that when renewed it can be carried on here with a better prospect of settlement, than where the late attempt at a convention which resulted so disastrously and was conducted so strangely was had;' and what the secretary thus wrote he repeated in conversation when we met, carefully making the transfer to Washington depend upon our advantage here, from the presence of the Senate, — thus showing that the pretext put forth to wound Mr. Motley was an afterthought."

Again we may fairly ask how the government came to send a dispatch like that of September 25, 1869, in which the views and expressions for which Mr. Motley's conversation had been criticised were so nearly reproduced, and with such emphasis that Mr. Motley says, in a letter to me, dated April 8, 1871, "It not only covers all the ground which I ever took, but goes far beyond it. No one has ever used stronger language to the British government than is contained in that dispatch. . . . It is very able and well worth your reading. Lord Clarendon called it to me 'Sumner's speech over again.' It was thought by the English cabinet to have 'out-Sumnered Sumner,' and now our government, thinking that every one in the United States had forgotten the dispatch, makes believe that I was removed because my sayings and doings in England were too much influenced by Sumner!" Mr. Motley goes on to speak of the report that an offer of his place in England was made to Sumner "to get him out of the way of San Domingo." The facts concerning this offer are now sufficiently known to the public.

Here I must dismiss Mr. Fish's letter to Mr. Moran, having, as I trust, sufficiently shown the spirit in which it was written and the strained interpretations and manifest overstatements by which it attempts to make out its case against Mr. Motley. I will not parade the two old women, whose untimely and unseemly introduction into the dress-circle of diplomacy was hardly to have been expected of the high official whose name is at the bottom of this paper. They prove nothing, they disprove nothing, they illustrate nothing — except that a statesman may forget himself. Neither will I do more than barely allude to the unfortunate reference to the death of Lord Clarendon as connected with Mr. Motley's removal, so placidly disposed of by a sentence or two in the London "Times" of January 24, 1871. I think we may consider ourselves ready for the next witness.

Mr. J. C. Bancroft Davis, Assistant Secretary of State under President Grant and Secretary Fish, wrote a letter to the New York "Herald," under the date of January 4, 1878, since reprinted as a pamphlet and entitled "Mr. Sumner, the Alabama Claims and their Settlement." Mr. Sumner was never successfully attacked when living, — except with a bludgeon, — and his friends have more than sufficiently vindicated him since his death. But Mr. Motley comes in for his share of animadversion in Mr. Davis's letter. He has nothing of importance to add to Mr. Fish's criticisms on the interview with Lord Clarendon. Only he brings out the head and front of Mr. Motley's offending by italicizing three very brief passages from his conversation at this interview; not discreetly, as it seems to me, for they will not bear the strain that is put upon them. These are the passages: —

1. "*but that such measures must always be taken with a full view of the grave responsibilities assumed.*"

2. "*and as being the fountain head of the disasters which had been caused to the American people.*"

3. "*as the fruits of the proclamation.*"

1. It is true that nothing was said of *responsibility* in Mr. Motley's instructions. But the idea was necessarily involved in their statements. For if, as Mr. Motley's instructions say, the right of a power "to define its own relations," etc., when a civil conflict has arisen in another state depends on its (the conflict's) having "attained a sufficient complexity, magnitude, and completeness," inasmuch as that Power has to judge whether it has or has not fulfilled these conditions, and is of course liable to judge wrong, every such act of judgment must be attended with grave responsibilities. The instructions say that "the necessity and propriety of the original concession of belligerency by Great Britain at the time it was made have been contested and are not admitted." It follows beyond dispute that Great Britain may in this particular case have incurred grave responsibilities; in fact, the whole negotiations implied as much. Perhaps Mr. Motley need not have used the word "responsibilities." But considering that the government itself said in dispatch No. 70, September 25, 1869, "The President does not deny, on the contrary he maintains, that every sovereign power decides for itself on its *responsibility* whether or not it will, at a

given time, accord the status of belligerency," etc., it was hardly worth while to use italics about Mr. Motley's employment of the same language as constituting a grave cause of offence.

2. Mr. Motley's expression, "as being the fountain head of the disasters," is a conversational paraphrase of the words of his instructions, "as it shows the beginning and the animus of that course of conduct which resulted so disastrously," which is not "in precise conformity" with his instructions, but is just such a variation as is to be expected when one is talking with another and using the words that suggest themselves at the moment, just as the familiar expression, "hung up on a peg," probably suggested itself to Lord Clarendon.

3. "The fruits of the proclamation" is so inconsiderable a variation on the text of the instructions, "supplemented by acts causing direct damage," that the secretary's hint about want of precise conformity seems hardly to have been called for.

It is important to notice this point in the instructions: With other powers Mr. Motley was to take the position that the "recognition of the insurgents' state of war" was made "*no* ground of complaint;" with Great Britain that the cause of grievance was "*not so much*" placed upon the issuance of this recognition as upon her conduct under, and subsequent to, such recognition.

There is no need of maintaining the exact fitness of every expression used by Mr. Motley. But any candid person who will carefully read the government's dispatch No. 70, dated September 25, 1869, will see that a government holding such language could find nothing in Mr. Motley's expressions in a conversation held at his first official interview to visit with official capital punishment more than a year afterwards. If Mr. Motley had, as it was pretended, followed Sumner, Mr. Fish had "out-Sumnered" the Senator himself.

Mr. Davis's pamphlet would hardly be complete without a mysterious letter from an unnamed writer, whether a faithless friend, a disguised enemy, a secret emissary, or an injudicious alarmist, we have no means of judging for ourselves. The minister appears to have been watched by somebody in London, as he was in Vienna. This somebody wrote a private letter in which he expressed "fear and regret that Mr. Motley's bearing in his social intercourse was throwing obstacles in the way of a future settlement." The charge as mentioned in Mr. Davis's letter is hardly entitled to our attention. Mr. Sumner considered it the work of an enemy, and the recollection of the M'Crackin letter might well have made the government cautious of listening to complaints of such a character. This Somebody may have been one whom we should call Nobody. We cannot help remembering how well *Outis* served *Odusseus* of old, when he was puzzled to extricate himself from an embarrassing position. *Stat nominis umbra* is a poor showing for authority to support an attack on a public servant exposed to every form of open and insidious abuse from those who are prejudiced against his person or his birthplace, who are jealous of his success, envious of his position, hostile to his politics, dwarfed by his reputation, or hate him by the divine right of idiosyncrasy, always liable, too, to questioning comment from well-meaning friends who happen to be suspicious or sensitive in their political or social relations.

The reported sayings of General Grant and of Mr.
Fish to the correspondents who talked with them may
be taken for what they are worth.   They sound naturally enough to have come from the speakers who are
said to have uttered them.   I quote the most important part of the Edinburgh letter, September 11, 1877,
to the New York "Herald."   These are the words
attributed to General Grant: —

"Mr. Motley was certainly a very able, very honest
gentleman, fit to hold any official position.   But he knew
long before he went out that he would have to go.   When
I was making these appointments, Mr. Sumner came to
me and asked me to appoint Mr. Motley as minister to
the court of St. James.   I told him I would, and did.
Soon after Mr. Sumner made that violent speech about
the Alabama claims, and the British government was
greatly offended.   Mr. Sumner was at the time chairman
of the committee on foreign affairs.   Mr. Motley had
to be instructed.   The instructions were prepared very
carefully, and after Governor Fish and I had gone over
them for the last time I wrote an addendum charging him
that above all things he should handle the subject of the
Alabama claims with the greatest delicacy.   Mr. Motley,
instead of obeying his explicit instructions, deliberately
fell in line with Sumner, and thus added insult to the previous injury.   As soon as I heard of it I went over to
the State Department and told Governor Fish to dismiss
Motley at once.   I was very angry indeed, and I have
been sorry many a time since that I did not stick to my
first determination.   Mr. Fish advised delay because of
Sumner's position in the Senate and attitude on the treaty
question.   We did not want to stir him up just then.
We dispatched a note of severe censure to Motley at once,
and ordered him to abstain from any further connection
with that question.   We thereupon commenced negotiations with the British minister at Washington, and the
result was the joint high commission and the Geneva

award.   I supposed Mr. Motley would be manly enough to resign after that snub, but he kept on till he was removed.   Mr. Sumner promised me that he would vote for the treaty.   But when it was before the Senate he did all he could to beat it."

General Grant talked again at Cairo, in Egypt.

"Grant then referred to the statement published at an interview with him in Scotland, and said the publication had some omissions and errors.   He had no ill-will towards Mr. Motley, who, like other estimable men, made mistakes, and Motley made a mistake which made him an improper person to hold office under me."

"It is proper to say of me that I killed Motley, or that I made war upon Sumner for not supporting the annexation of San Domingo.   But if I dare to answer that I removed Motley from the highest considerations of duty as an executive; if I presume to say that he made a mistake in his office which made him no longer useful to the country; if Fish has the temerity to hint that Sumner's temper was so unfortunate that business relations with him became impossible, we are slandering the dead."

"Nothing but Mortimer."   Those who knew both men — the Ex-President and the late Senator — would agree, I do not doubt, that they would not be the most promising pair of human beings to make harmonious members of a political happy family. " Cedant arma togæ," the life-long sentiment of Sumner, in conflict with "Stand fast and stand sure," the well-known device of the clan of Grant, reminds one of the problem of an irresistible force in collision with an insuperable resistance.   But the President says, — or is reported as saying, — "I may be blamed for my opposition to Mr. Sumner's tactics, but I was not guided so much by reason of his personal hatred of myself, as I was by a desire to protect our national interests in diplomatic affairs."

"It would be useless," says Mr. Davis in his letter to the "Herald," "to enter into a controversy whether the President may or may not have been influenced in the final determination of the moment for requesting Motley's resignation by the feeling caused by Sumner's personal hostility and abuse of himself." Unfortunately, this controversy *had been* entered into, and the idleness of suggesting any relation of cause and effect between Mr. Motley's dismissal and the irritation produced in the President's mind by the rejection of the San Domingo treaty — which rejection was mainly due to Motley's friend Sumner's opposition — strongly insisted upon in a letter signed by the Secretary of State. *Too* strongly, for here it was that he failed to remember what was due to his office, to himself, and to the gentleman of whom he was writing; if indeed it was the secretary's own hand which held the pen, and not another's.

We might as well leave out the wrath of Achilles from the Iliad, as the anger of the President with Sumner from the story of Motley's dismissal. The sad recital must always begin with Μῆνιν ἄειδε. He was, he is reported as saying, "very angry indeed" with Motley because he had *fallen in line* with Sumner. He couples them together in his conversation as closely as Chang and Eng were coupled. The death of Lord Clarendon would have covered up the coincidence between the rejection of the San Domingo treaty and Mr. Motley's dismissal very neatly, but for the inexorable facts about its date, as revealed by the London "Times." It betrays itself as an afterthought, and its failure as a defence reminds us too nearly of the trial in which Mr. Webster said suicide is confession.

It is not strange that the spurs of the man who had so lately got out of the saddle should catch in the scholastic robe of the man on the floor of the Senate. But we should not have looked for any such antagonism between the Secretary of State and the envoy to Great Britain. On the contrary, they must have had many sympathies, and it must have cost the secretary pain, as he said it did, to be forced to communicate with Mr. Moran instead of with Mr. Motley.

He, too, was inquired of by one of the emissaries of the American Unholy Inquisition. His evidence is thus reported: —

"The reason for Mr. Motley's removal was found in considerations of state. He misrepresented the government on the Alabama question, especially in the two speeches made by him before his arrival at his post."

These must be the two speeches made to the American and the Liverpool chambers of commerce. If there is anything in these short addresses beyond those civil generalities which the occasion called out, I have failed to find it. If it was in these that the reason of Mr. Motley's removal was to be looked for, it is singular that they are not mentioned in the secretary's letter to Mr. Moran, or by Mr. Davis in his letter to the New York "Herald." They must have been as unsuccessful as myself in the search after anything in these speeches which could be construed into misinterpretation of the government on the Alabama question.

We may much more readily accept "considerations of state" as a reason for Mr. Motley's removal. Considerations of state have never yet failed the axe or the bowstring when a reason for the use of those

convenient implements was wanted, and they are quite
equal to every emergency which can arise in a republican autocracy. But for the very reason that a
minister is absolutely in the power of his government,
the manner in which that power is used is always
open to the scrutiny, and, if it has been misused, to
the condemnation, of a tribunal higher than itself; a
court that never goes out of office, and which no personal feelings, no lapse of time, can silence.

The ostensible grounds on which Mr. Motley was
recalled are plainly insufficient to account for the action of the government. If it was in great measure
a manifestation of personal feeling on the part of the
high officials by whom and through whom the act was
accomplished, it was a wrong which can never be re-
paired and never sufficiently regretted.

Stung by the slanderous report of an anonymous
eavesdropper to whom the government of the day was
not ashamed to listen, he had quitted Vienna, too
hastily, it may be, but wounded, indignant, feeling
that he had been unworthily treated. The sudden
recall from London, on no pretext whatever but an
obsolete and overstated incident which had ceased to
have any importance, was under these circumstances
a deadly blow. It fell upon "the new-healed wound
of malice," and though he would not own it, and bore
up against it, it was a shock from which he never fully
recovered.

"I hope I am one of those," he writes to me from
the Hague, in 1872, "who 'fortune's buffets and rewards can take with equal thanks.' I am quite aware
that I have had far more than I deserve of political
honors, and they might have had my post as a voluntary gift on my part had they remembered that I was

an honorable man, and not treated me as a detected
criminal deserves to be dealt with."

Mr. Sumner naturally felt very deeply what he
considered the great wrong done to his friend. He
says: —

"How little Mr. Motley merited anything but respect
and courtesy from the secretary is attested by all who
know his eminent position in London, and the service he
rendered to his country. Already the London press, usually slow to praise Americans when strenuous for their
country, has furnished its voluntary testimony. The
'Daily News' of August 16, 1870, spoke of the insulted
minister in these terms: —

"'We are violating no confidence in saying that all the
hopes of Mr. Motley's official residence in England have
been amply fulfilled, and that the announcement of his unexpected and unexplained recall was received with extreme
astonishment and unfeigned regret. The vacancy he
leaves cannot possibly be filled by a minister more sensitive to the honor of his government, more attentive to the
interests of his country, and more capable of uniting the
most vigorous performance of his public duties with the
high-bred courtesy and conciliatory tact and temper that
make those duties easy and successful. Mr. Motley's successor will find his mission wonderfully facilitated by the
firmness and discretion that have presided over the conduct of American affairs in this country during too brief
a term, too suddenly and unaccountably concluded.' "

No man can escape being found fault with when it
is necessary to make out a case against him. A diplomatist is watched by the sharpest eyes and commented on by the most merciless tongues. The best
and wisest has his defects, and sometimes they would
seem to be very grave ones if brought up against him
in the form of accusation. Take these two portraits,
for instance, as drawn by John Quincy Adams. The

first is that of Stratford Canning, afterwards Lord
Stratford de Redcliffe : —

"He is to depart to-morrow. I shall probably see him
no more. He is a proud, high-tempered Englishman, of
good but not extraordinary parts; stubborn and punctilious, with a disposition to be overbearing, which I have
often been compelled to check in its own way. He is, of
all the foreign ministers with whom I have had occasion
to treat, the man who has most severely tried my temper. Yet he has been long in the diplomatic career, and
treated with governments of the most opposite characters.
He has, however, a great respect for his word, and there
is nothing false about him. This is an excellent quality
for a negotiator. Mr. Canning is a man of forms, studi-
ous of courtesy, and tenacious of private morals. As a
diplomatic man, his great want is suppleness, and his great
virtue is sincerity."

The second portrait is that of the French minister,
Hyde de Neuville : —

"No foreign minister who ever resided here has been
so universally esteemed and beloved, nor have I ever
been in political relations with any foreign statesman of
whose moral qualities I have formed so good an opinion,
with the exception of Count Romanzoff. He has not sufficient command of his temper, is quick, irritable, sometimes punctilious, occasionally indiscreet in his discourse,
and tainted with Royalist and Bourbon prejudices. But
he has strong sentiments of honor, justice, truth, and
even liberty. His flurries of temper pass off as quickly
as they rise. He is neither profound nor sublime nor
brilliant; but a man of strong and good feelings, with the
experience of many vicissitudes of fortune, a good but common understanding, and good intentions biassed by party
feelings, occasional interests, and personal affections."

It means very little to say that a man has some
human imperfections, or that a public servant might

have done some things better.   But when a questionable cause is to be justified, the victim's excellences
are looked at with the eyes of Liliput and his failings
with those of Brobdingnag.

The recall of a foreign minister for alleged misconduct in office is a kind of capital punishment.   It is
the nearest approach to the Sultan's bowstring which
is permitted to the chief magistrate of our Republic.
A general can do nothing under martial law more peremptory than a President can do with regard to the
public functionary whom he has appointed with the
advice and consent of the Senate, but whom he can
officially degrade and disgrace at his own pleasure for
insufficient cause or for none at all.   Like the cen-
turion of Scripture, he says Go, and he goeth.   The
nation's representative is less secure in his tenure of
office than his own servant, to whom he must give
warning of his impending dismissal.

> " A breath *unmakes him* as a breath has made."

The chief magistrate's responsibility to duty, to the
fellow-citizen at his mercy, to his countrymen, to mankind, is in proportion to his power.   His prime minister, the agent of his edicts, should feel bound to
withstand him if he seeks to gratify a personal feeling
under the plea of public policy, unless the minister,
like the slaves of the harem, is to find his qualification
for office in leaving his manhood behind him.

The two successive administrations, which treated
Mr. Motley in a manner unworthy of their position
and cruel, if not fatal to him, have been heard, directly or through their advocates.   I have attempted
to show that the defence set up for their action is any-

thing but satisfactory. A later generation will sit in judgment upon the evidence more calmly than our own. It is not for a friend, like the writer, to anticipate its decision, but unless the reasons alleged to justify his treatment, and which have so much the air of afterthoughts, shall seem stronger to that future tribunal than they do to him, the verdict will be that Mr. Motley was twice sacrificed to personal feelings which should never have been cherished by the heads of the government, and should never have been countenanced by their chief advisers.

XXII

"Life of John of Barneveld." — Criticisms. — Groen van Prinsterer.

THE full title of Mr. Motley's next and last work
is "The Life and Death of John of Barneveld, Advocate of Holland; with a View of the Primary
Causes and Movements of the Thirty Years' War."

In point of fact this work is a history rather than a
biography. It is an interlude, a pause between the
acts which were to fill out the complete plan of the
"Eighty Years' Tragedy," and of which the last act,
the Thirty Years' War, remains unwritten. The "Life
of Barneveld" was received as a fitting and worthy
continuation of the series of intellectual labor in which
he was engaged.   I will quote but two general expressions of approval from the two best known British
critical reviews.   In connection with his previous
works, it forms, says "The London Quarterly," "a
fine and continuous story, of which the writer and
the nation celebrated by him have equal reason to be
proud; a narrative which will remain a prominent ornament of American genius, while it has permanently
enriched English literature on this as well as on the
other side of the Atlantic."

"The Edinburgh Review" speaks no less warmly:
"We can hardly give too much appreciation to that
subtile alchemy of the brain which has enabled him

to produce out of dull, crabbed, and often illegible state papers, the vivid, graphic, and sparkling narrative which he has given to the world."

In a literary point of view, M. Groen van Prinsterer, whose elaborate work has been already referred to, speaks of it as perhaps the most classical of Motley's productions, but it is upon this work that the force of his own and other Dutch criticisms has been chiefly expended.

The key to this biographical history or historical biography may be found in a few sentences from its opening chapter.

"There have been few men at any period whose lives have been more closely identical than his [Barneveld's] with a national history. There have been few great men in any history whose names have become less familiar to the world, and lived less in the mouths of posterity. Yet there can be no doubt that if William the Silent was the founder of the independence of the United Provinces, Barneveld was the founder of the Commonwealth itself. . . .

"Had that country of which he was so long the first citizen maintained until our own day the same proportional position among the empires of Christendom as it held in the seventeenth century, the name of John of Barneveld would have perhaps been as familiar to all men as it is at this moment to nearly every inhabitant of the Netherlands. Even now political passion is almost as ready to flame forth, either in ardent affection or enthusiastic hatred, as if two centuries and a half had not elapsed since his death. His name is so typical of a party, a polity, and a faith, so indelibly associated with a great historical cataclysm, as to render it difficult even for the grave, the conscientious, the learned, the patriotic, of his own compatriots to speak of him with absolute impartiality.

"A foreigner who loves and admires all that is great and noble in the history of that famous republic, and can have no hereditary bias as to its ecclesiastical or political theories, may at least attempt the task with comparative coldness, although conscious of inability to do thorough justice to a most complex subject."

With all Mr. Motley's efforts to be impartial, to which even his sternest critics bear witness, he could not help becoming a partisan of the cause which for him was that of religious liberty and progress, as against the accepted formula of an old ecclesiastical organization. For the quarrel which came near being a civil war, which convulsed the state, and cost Barneveld his head, had its origin in a difference on certain points, and more especially on a single point, of religious doctrine.

As a great river may be traced back until its fountain-head is found in a thread of water streaming from a cleft in the rocks, so a great national movement may sometimes be followed until its starting-point is found in the cell of a monk or the studies of a pair of wrangling professors.

The religious quarrel of the Dutchmen in the seventeenth century reminds us in some points of the strife between two parties in our own New England, sometimes arraying the "church" on one side against the "parish," or the general body of worshippers, on the other. The portraits of Gomarus, the great orthodox champion, and Arminius, the head and front of the "liberal theology" of his day, as given in the little old quarto of Meursius, recall two ministerial types of countenance familiar to those who remember the earlier years of our century.

Under the name of "Remonstrants" and "Contra-

Remonstrants,"—Arminians and old-fashioned Calvinists, as we should say,—the adherents of the two Leyden professors disputed the right to the possession of the churches, and the claim to be considered as representing the national religion. Of the seven United Provinces, two, Holland and Utrecht, were prevailingly Arminian, and the other five Calvinistic. Barneveld, who, under the title of Advocate, represented the province of Holland, the most important of them all, claimed for each province a right to determine its own state religion. Maurice the Stadholder, son of William the Silent, the military chief of the republic, claimed the right for the States-General. *Cujus regio ejus religio* was then the accepted public doctrine of Protestant nations. Thus the provincial and the general governments were brought into conflict by their creeds, and the question whether the republic was a confederation or a nation, the same question which has been practically raised, and for the time at least settled, in our own republic, was in some way to be decided. After various disturbances and acts of violence by both parties, Maurice, representing the States-General, pronounced for the Calvinists or Contra-Remonstrants, and took possession of one of the great churches, as an assertion of his authority. Barneveld, representing the Arminian or Remonstrant provinces, levied a body of mercenary soldiers in several of the cities. These were disbanded by Maurice, and afterwards by an act of the States-General. Barneveld was apprehended, imprisoned, and executed, after an examination which was in no proper sense a trial. Grotius, who was on the Arminian side and involved in the inculpated proceedings, was also arrested and imprisoned. His escape, by a stratagem successfully repeated by a slave in our own times, may challenge comparison for its romantic interest with any chapter of fiction. How his wife packed him into the chest supposed to contain the folios of the great oriental scholar Erpenius, how the soldiers wondered at its weight and questioned whether it did not hold an Arminian, how the servant-maid, Elsje van Houwening, quick-witted as Morgiana of the "Forty Thieves," parried their questions and convoyed her master safely to the friendly place of refuge, — all this must be read in the vivid narrative of the author.

The questions involved were political, local, personal, and above all religious. Here is the picture which Motley draws of the religious quarrel as it divided the people: —

"In burghers' mansions, peasants' cottages, mechanics' back-parlors; on board herring-smacks, canal-boats, and East Indiamen; in shops, counting-rooms, farm-yards, guard-rooms, alehouses; on the exchange, in the tennis-court, on the mall; at banquets, at burials, christenings, or bridals; wherever and whenever human creatures met each other, there was ever to be found the fierce wrangle of Remonstrant and Contra-Remonstrant, the hissing of red-hot theological rhetoric, the pelting of hostile texts. The blacksmith's iron cooled on the anvil, the tinker dropped a kettle half mended, the broker left a bargain unclinched, the Scheveningen fisherman in his wooden shoes forgot the cracks in his pinkie, while each paused to hold high converse with friend or foe on fate, free-will, or absolute foreknowledge; losing himself in wandering mazes whence there was no issue. Province against province, city against city, family against family; it was one vast scene of bickering, denunciation, heart-burnings, mutual excommunication and hatred."

The religious grounds of the quarrel which set these

seventeenth-century Dutchmen to cutting each other's throats were to be looked for in the "Five Points" of the Arminians as arrayed against the "Seven Points" of the Gomarites, or Contra-Remonstrants. The most important of the differences which were to be settled by fratricide seem to have been these: —

According to the Five Points, "God has from eternity resolved to choose to eternal life those who through his grace believe in Jesus Christ," etc. According to the Seven Points, "God in his election has not looked at the belief and the repentance of the elect," etc. According to the Five Points, all good deeds must be ascribed to God's grace in Christ, but it does not work irresistibly. The language of the Seven Points implies that the elect cannot resist God's eternal and unchangeable design to give them faith and steadfastness, and that they can never wholly and for always lose the true faith. The language of the Five Points is unsettled as to the last proposition, but it was afterwards maintained by the Remonstrant party that a true believer could, through his own fault, fall away from God and lose faith.

It must be remembered that these religious questions had an immediate connection with politics. Independently of the conflict of jurisdiction, in which they involved the parties to the two different creeds, it was believed or pretended that the new doctrines of the Remonstrants led towards Romanism, and were allied with designs which threatened the independence of the country. "There are two factions in the land," said Maurice, "that of Orange and that of Spain, and the two chiefs of the Spanish faction are those political and priestly Arminians, Uytenbogaert and Olden-barneveld."

The heads of the two religious and political parties were in such hereditary, long-continued, and intimate relations up to the time when one signed the other's death-warrant, that it was impossible to write the life of one without also writing that of the other. For his biographer John of Barneveld is the true patriot, the martyr, whose cause was that of religious and political freedom. For him Maurice is the ambitious soldier who hated his political rival, and never rested until this rival was brought to the scaffold.

The questions which agitated men's minds two centuries and a half ago are not dead yet in the country where they produced such estrangement, violence, and wrong. No stranger could take them up without encountering hostile criticism from one party or the other. It may be and has been conceded that Mr. Motley writes as a partisan, — a partisan of freedom in politics and religion, as he understands freedom. This secures him the antagonism of one class of critics. But these critics are themselves partisans, and themselves open to the cross-fire of their antagonists. M. Groen van Prinsterer, "the learned and distinguished" editor of the "Archives et Correspondance" of the Orange and Nassau family, published a considerable volume, before referred to, in which many of Motley's views are strongly controverted. But he himself is far from being in accord with "that eminent scholar," M. Bakhuyzen van den Brink, whose name, he says, is celebrated enough to need no comment, or with M. Fruin, of whose impartiality and erudition he himself speaks in the strongest terms. The ground upon which he is attacked is thus stated in his own words: —

"People have often pretended to find in my writings the deplorable influence of an extreme Calvinism.

The Puritans of the seventeenth century are my fellow - religionists. I am a *sectarian* and not an *historian.*"

It is plain enough to any impartial reader that there are at least plausible grounds for this accusation against Mr. Motley's critic. And on a careful examination of the formidable volume, it becomes obvious that Mr. Motley has presented a view of the events and the personages of the stormy epoch with which he is dealing, which leaves a battle-ground yet to be fought over by those who come after him. The dispute is not and cannot be settled.

The end of all religious discussion has come when one of the parties claims that it is thinking or acting under immediate Divine guidance. "It is God's affair, and his honor is touched," says William Lewis to Prince Maurice. Mr. Motley's critic is not less confident in claiming the Almighty as on the side of his own views. Let him state his own ground of departure : —

"To show the difference, let me rather say the contrast, between the point of view of Mr. Motley and my own, between the *Unitarian* and the *Evangelical* belief. I am *issue of* CALVIN, child of the *Awakening (reveil).* Faithful to the device of the Reformers : *Justification* by *faith alone, and the Word of God endures eternally.* I consider history from the point of view of *Merle d'Aubigné,* Chalmers, Guizot. I desire to be *disciple* and *witness* of our Lord and Saviour, Jesus Christ."

He is therefore of necessity antagonistic to a writer whom he describes in such words as these : —

"Mr. Motley is *liberal* and *rationalist.*

"He becomes, in attacking the principle of the Reformation, the passionate opponent of the Puritans and of

Maurice, the ardent apologist of Barnevelt and the *Arminians*.

"It is understood, and he makes no mystery of it, that he inclines towards the vague and undecided doctrine of the Unitarians."

What M. Groen's idea of Unitarians is may be gathered from the statement about them which he gets from a letter of De Tocqueville.

"They are pure deists; they talk about the Bible, because they do not wish to shock too severely public opinion, which is prevailingly *Christian*. They have a service on Sundays; I have been there. At it they read verses from Dryden or other English poets on the existence of God and the immortality of the soul. They deliver a discourse on some point of morality, and all is said."

In point of fact the wave of protest which stormed the dikes of Dutch orthodoxy in the seventeenth century stole gently through the bars of New England Puritanism in the eighteenth.

"Though the large number," says Mr. Bancroft, "still acknowledged the fixedness of the divine decrees, and the resistless certainty from all eternity of election and of reprobation, there were not wanting, even among the clergy, some who had modified the sternness of the ancient doctrine by making the self-direction of the active powers of man with freedom of inquiry and private judgment the central idea of a protest against Calvinism."

Protestantism, cut loose from an infallible church, and drifting with currents it cannot resist, wakes up once or oftener in every century, to find itself in a new locality. Then it rubs its eyes and wonders whether it has found its harbor or only lost its anchor. There is no end to its disputes, for it has nothing but a fallible vote as authority for its oracles, and these appeal only to fallible interpreters.

It is as hard to contend in argument against "the oligarchy of heaven," as Motley calls the Calvinistic party, as it was formerly to strive with them in arms.

To this "aristocracy of God's elect" belonged the party which framed the declaration of the Synod of Dort; the party which under the forms of justice shed the blood of the great statesman who had served his country so long and so well. To this chosen body belonged the late venerable and truly excellent as well as learned M. Groen van Prinsterer, and he exercised the usual right of examining in the light of his privileged position the views of a "liberal" and "rationalist" writer who goes to meeting on Sunday to hear verses from Dryden. This does not diminish his claim for a fair reading of the "intimate correspondence," which he considers Mr. Motley has not duly taken into account, and of the other letters to be found printed in his somewhat disjointed and fragmentary volume.

This "intimate correspondence" shows Maurice the Stadholder indifferent and lax in internal administration and as being constantly advised and urged by his relative Count William of Nassau. This need of constant urging extends to religious as well as other matters, and is inconsistent with M. Groen van Prinsterer's assertion that the question was for Maurice above all religious, and for Barneveld above all political. Whether its negative evidence can be considered as neutralizing that which is adduced by Mr. Motley to show the Stadholder's hatred of the Advocate may be left to the reader who has just risen from the account of the mock trial and the swift execution of the

great and venerable statesman. The formal entry on
the record upon the day of his "judicial murder" is
singularly solemn and impressive: —

"Monday, 13th May, 1619. To-day was executed
with the sword here in the Hague, on a scaffold thereto
erected in the Binnenhof before the steps of the great
hall, Mr. John of Barneveld, in his life Knight, Lord of
Berkel, Rodenrys, etc., Advocate of Holland and West
Friesland, for reasons expressed in the sentence and otherwise, with confiscation of his property, after he had
served the state thirty-three years two months and five
days, since 8th March, 1586; a man of great activity,
business, memory, and wisdom, — yea, extraordinary in
every respect. He that stands let him see that he does
not fall."

Maurice gave an account of the execution of Barneveld to Count William Lewis on the same day in a
note "painfully brief and dry."

Most authors write their own biography consciously
or unconsciously. We have seen Mr. Motley por-
traying much of himself, his course of life and his future, as he would have had it, in his first story. In
this, his last work, it is impossible not to read much
of his own external and internal personal history told
under other names and with different accessories. The
parallelism often accidentally or intentionally passes
into divergence. He would not have had it too close if
he could, but there are various passages in which it is
plain enough that he is telling his own story.

Mr. Motley was a diplomatist, and he writes of
other diplomatists, and one in particular, with most
significant detail. It need not be supposed that he
intends the "arch intriguer" Aerssens to stand for
himself, or that he would have endured being thought

to identify himself with the man of whose "almost devilish acts" he speaks so freely. But the sagacious reader — and he need not be very sharp-sighted — will very certainly see something more than a mere historical significance in some of the passages which I shall cite for him to reflect upon. Mr. Motley's standard of an ambassador's accomplishments may be judged from the following passage : —

"That those ministers [those of the Republic] were second to the representatives of no other European state in capacity and accomplishment was a fact well known to all who had dealings with them, for the states required in their diplomatic representatives knowledge of history and international law, modern languages, and the classics, as well as familiarity with political customs and social courtesies; the breeding of gentlemen, in short, and the accomplishments of scholars."

The story of the troubles of Aerssens, the ambassador of the United Provinces at Paris, must be given at some length, and will repay careful reading.

"Francis Aerssens . . . continued to be the Dutch ambassador after the murder of Henry IV. . . . He was beyond doubt one of the ablest diplomatists in Europe. Versed in many languages, a classical student, familiar with history and international law, a man of the world and familiar with its usages, accustomed to associate with dignity and tact on friendliest terms with sovereigns, eminent statesmen, and men of letters; endowed with a facile tongue, a fluent pen, and an eye and ear of singular acuteness and delicacy; distinguished for unflagging industry and singular aptitude for secret and intricate affairs; — he had by the exercise of these various qualities during a period of nearly twenty years at the court of Henry the Great been able to render inestimable services to the Republic which he represented.

"He had enjoyed the intimacy and even the confidence

of Henry IV., so far as any man could be said to possess
that monarch's confidence, and his friendly relations and
familiar access to the king gave him political advantages
superior to those of any of his colleagues at the same
court.

"Acting entirely and faithfully according to the instructions of the Advocate of Holland, he always grate-
fully and copiously acknowledged the privilege of being
guided and sustained in the difficult paths he had to traverse by so powerful and active an intellect. I have seldom alluded in terms to the instructions and dispatches
of the chief, but every position, negotiation, and opinion
of the envoy — and the reader has seen many of them —
is pervaded by their spirit. . . .

"It had become a question whether he was to remain
at his post or return. It was doubtful whether he wished
to be relieved of his embassy or not. The States of
Holland voted 'to leave it to his candid opinion if in his
free conscience he thinks he can serve the public any
longer. If yes, he may keep his office one year more. If
no, he may take leave and come home.'

"Surely the States, under the guidance of the Advocate,
had thus acted with consummate courtesy towards a diplomatist whose position, from no apparent fault of his own,
but by the force of circumstances, — and rather to his
credit than otherwise, — was gravely compromised."

The Queen, Mary de' Medici, had a talk with him,
got angry, "became very red in the face," and wanted
to be rid of him.

"Nor was the envoy at first desirous of remaining. . . .
Nevertheless, he yielded reluctantly to Barneveld's request that he should, for the time at least, remain at his
post. Later on, as the intrigues against him began to
unfold themselves, and his faithful services were made
use of at home to blacken his character and procure his
removal, he refused to resign, as to do so would be to play
into the hands of his enemies, and, by inference at least,
to accuse himself of infidelity to his trust. . . .

"It is no wonder that the ambassador was galled to the quick by the outrage which those concerned in the government were seeking to put upon him. How could an honest man fail to be overwhelmed with rage and anguish at being dishonored before the world by his masters for scrupulously doing his duty, and for maintaining the rights and dignity of his own country? He knew that the charges were but pretexts, that the motives of his enemies were as base as the intrigues themselves, but he also knew that the world usually sides with the government against the individual, and that a man's reputation is rarely strong enough to maintain itself unsullied in a foreign land when his own government stretches forth its hand, not to shield, but to stab him. . . .

"'I know,' he said, 'that this plot has been woven partly in Holland and partly here by good correspondence, in order to drive me from my post with disreputation. . . .

"'But as I have discovered this accurately, I have resolved to offer to my masters the continuance of my very humble service for such time and under such conditions as they may think good to prescribe. I prefer forcing my natural and private inclinations to giving an opportunity for the ministers of this kingdom to discredit us, and to my enemies to succeed in injuring me, and by fraud and malice to force me from my post. . . . I am truly sorry, being ready to retire, wishing to have an honorable testimony in recompense of my labors, that one is in such hurry to take advantage of my fall. . . . What envoy will ever dare to speak with vigor if he is not sustained by the government at home? . . . My enemies have misrepresented my actions, and my language as passionate, exaggerated, mischievous, but I have no passion except for the service of my superiors.' . . .

"Barneveld, from well-considered motives of public policy, was favoring his honorable recall. But he allowed a decorous interval of more than three years to elapse in which to terminate his affairs, and to take a deliberate departure from that French embassy to which the Advo-

cate had originally promoted him, and in which there had
been so many years of mutual benefit and confidence between the two statesmen. He used no underhand means.
He did not abuse the power of the States-General which
he wielded to cast him suddenly and brutally from the
distinguished post which he occupied, and so to attempt
to dishonor him before the world. Nothing could be
more respectful and conciliatory than the attitude of the
government from first to last towards this distinguished
functionary. The Republic respected itself too much to
deal with honorable agents whose services it felt obliged to
dispense with as with vulgar malefactors who had been
detected in crime. . . .

"This work aims at being a political study. I would
attempt to exemplify the influence of individual humors
and passions — some of them among the highest, and others certainly the basest that agitate humanity — upon the
march of great events, upon general historical results at
certain epochs, and upon the destiny of eminent personages."

Here are two suggestive portraits: —

"The Advocate, while acting only in the name of a
slender confederacy, was in truth, so long as he held his
place, the prime minister of European Protestantism.
There was none other to rival him, few to comprehend
him, fewer still to sustain him. As Prince Maurice was
at that time the great soldier of Protestantism, without
clearly scanning the grandeur of the field in which he was
a chief actor, or foreseeing the vastness of its future, so
the Advocate was its statesman and its prophet. Could
the two have worked together as harmoniously as they had
done at an earlier day, it would have been a blessing for
the common weal of Europe. But, alas! the evil genius
of jealousy, which so often forbids cordial relations between soldier and statesman, already stood shrouded in
the distance, darkly menacing the strenuous patriot, who
was wearing his life out in exertions for what he deemed
the true cause of progress and humanity. . . .

"All history shows that the brilliant soldier of a republic is apt to have the advantage, in a struggle for popular affection and popular applause, over the statesman, however consummate. . . . The great battles and sieges of the prince had been on a world's theatre, had enchained the attention of Christendom, and on their issue had frequently depended, or seemed to depend, the very existence of the nation. The labors of the statesman, on the contrary, had been comparatively secret. His noble orations and arguments had been spoken with closed doors to assemblies of colleagues, rather envoys than senators, . . . while his vast labors in directing both the internal administration and especially the foreign affairs of the commonwealth had been by their very nature as secret as they were perpetual and enormous."

The reader of the "Life of Barneveld" must judge for himself whether in these and similar passages the historian was thinking solely of Maurice, the great military leader, of Barneveld, the great statesman, and of Aerssens, the recalled ambassador. He will certainly find that there were "burning questions" for ministers to handle then as now, and recognize in "that visible atmosphere of power the poison of which it is so difficult to resist" a respiratory medium as well known to the nineteenth as to the seventeenth century.

XXIII.

1874–1877.   Æt. 60–63.

**Death of Mrs. Motley. — Last Visit to America. — Illness and
Death. — Lady Harcourt's Communication.**

On the last day of 1874, the beloved wife, whose
health had for some years been failing, was taken from
him by death.   She had been the pride of his happier
years, the stay and solace of those which had so tried
his sensitive spirit.   The blow found him already
weakened by mental suffering and bodily infirmity,
and he never recovered from it.   Mr. Motley's last
visit to America was in the summer and autumn of
1875.   During several weeks which he passed at Nahant, a seaside resort near Boston, I saw him almost
daily.   He walked feebly and with some little difficulty, and complained of a feeling of great weight in
the right arm, which made writing laborious.   His
handwriting had not betrayed any very obvious change,
so far as I had noticed in his letters.   His features
and speech were without any paralytic character.   His
mind was clear except when, as on one or two occasions, he complained of some confused feeling, and
walked a few minutes in the open air to compose himself.   His thoughts were always tending to revert to
the almost worshipped companion from whom death
had parted him a few months before.   Yet he could
often be led away to other topics, and in talking of
them could be betrayed into momentary cheerfulness of

manner. His long-enduring and all-pervading grief
was not more a tribute to the virtues and graces of her
whom he mourned than an evidence of the deeply affectionate nature which in other relations endeared
him to so many whose friendship was a title to love
and honor.

I have now the privilege of once more recurring to
the narrative of Mr. Motley's daughter, Lady Harcourt.

"The harassing work and mental distress of this time
[after the recall from England], acting on an acutely nervous organization, began the process of undermining his
constitution, of which we were so soon to see the results.
It was not the least courageous act of his life, that, smart-
ing under a fresh wound, tired and unhappy, he set his
face immediately towards the accomplishment of fresh
literary labor. After my sister's marriage in January he
went to the Hague to begin his researches in the archives
for John of Barneveld. The Queen of the Netherlands
had made ready a house for us, and personally superintended every preparation for his reception. We remained
there until the spring, and then removed to a house more
immediately in the town, a charming old-fashioned mansion, once lived in by John de Witt, where he had a large
library and every domestic comfort during the year of his
sojourn. The incessant literary labor in an enervating
climate with enfeebled health may have prepared the way
for the first break in his constitution, which was to show
itself soon after. There were many compensations in the
life about him. He enjoyed the privilege of constant
companionship with one of the warmest hearts and finest
intellects which I have ever known in a woman, — the *âme
d'élite* which has passed beyond this earth. The gracious
sentiment with which the Queen sought to express her
sense of what Holland owed him would have been deeply
felt even had her personal friendship been less dear to us

all.   From the King, the society of the Hague, and the
diplomatic circle we had many marks of kindness.   Once
or twice I made short journeys with him for change of air
to Amsterdam, to look for the portraits of John of Barneveld and his wife; to Bohemia, where, with the lingering hope of occupying himself with the Thirty Years'
War, he looked carefully at the scene of Wallenstein's
death near Prague, and later to Varzin in Pomerania for
a week with Prince Bismarck, after the great events of
the Franco-German war.   In the autumn of 1872 we moved
to England, partly because it was evident that his health
and my mother's required a change; partly for private
reasons to be near my sister and her children.   The day
after our arrival at Bournemouth occurred the rupture of
a vessel on the lungs, without any apparently sufficient
cause.   He recovered enough to revise and complete his
manuscript, and we thought him better, when at the end
of July, in London, he was struck down by the first attack of the head, which robbed him of all after power of
work, although the intellect remained untouched.   Sir
William Gull sent him to Cannes for the winter, where he
was seized with a violent internal inflammation, in which
I suppose there was again the indication of the lesion of
blood-vessels.   I am nearing the shadow now, — the time
of which I can hardly bear to write.   You know the terrible sorrow which crushed him on the last day of 1874,
— the grief which broke his heart and from which he never
rallied.   From that day it seems to me that his life may
be summed up in the two words, — patient waiting.
Never for one hour did her spirit leave him, and he strove
to follow its leading for the short and evil days left and
the hope of the life beyond.   I think I have never watched
quietly and reverently the traces of one personal character
remaining so strongly impressed on another nature.   With
her self-depreciation and unselfishness she would have been
the last to believe how much of him was in her very existence; nor could we have realized it until the parting came.
Henceforward, with the mind still there, but with the
machinery necessary to set it in motion disturbed and

shattered, he could but try to create small occupations with which to fill the hours of a life which was only valued for his children's sake. Kind and loving friends in England and America soothed the passage, and our gratitude for so many gracious acts is deep and true. His love for children, always a strong feeling, was gratified by the constant presence of my sister's babies, the eldest, a little girl who bore my mother's name, and had been her idol, being the companion of many hours and his best comforter. At the end the blow came swiftly and suddenly, as he would have wished it. It was a terrible shock to us who had vainly hoped to keep him a few years longer, but at least he was spared what he had dreaded with a great dread, a gradual failure of mental or bodily power. The mind was never clouded, the affections never weakened, and after a few hours of unconscious physical struggle he lay at rest, his face beautiful and calm, without a trace of suffering or illness. Once or twice he said, 'It has come, it has come,' and there were a few broken words before consciousness fled, but there was little time for messages or leave-taking. By a strange coincidence his life ended near the town of Dorchester, in the mother country, as if the last hour brought with it a reminiscence of his birthplace, and of his own dearly loved mother. By his own wish only the dates of his birth and death appear upon his gravestone, with the text chosen by himself, 'In God is light, and in him is no darkness at all.' "

XXIV.

Conclusion. — His Character. — His Labors. — His Reward.

In closing this restricted and imperfect record of a life which merits, and in due time will, I trust, receive an ampler tribute, I cannot refrain from adding a few thoughts which naturally suggest themselves, and some of which may seem quite unnecessary to the reader who has followed the story of the historian and diplomatist's brilliant and eventful career.

Mr. Motley came of a parentage which promised the gifts of mind and body very generally to be accounted for, in a measure at least, wherever we find them, by the blood of one or both of the parents. They gave him special attractions and laid him open to not a few temptations. Too many young men born to shine in social life, to sparkle, it may be, in conversation, perhaps in the lighter walks of literature, become agreeable idlers, self-indulgent, frivolous, incapable of large designs or sustained effort, lose every aspiration and forget every ideal. Our gilded youth want such examples as this of Motley, not a solitary, but a conspicuous one, to teach them how much better is the restlessness of a noble ambition than the narcotized stupor of club-life or the vapid amusement of a dressed-up intercourse which too often requires a questionable flavor of forbidden license to render it endurable to persons of vivacious character and temperament.

It would seem difficult for a man so flattered from his earliest days to be modest in his self-estimate; but Motley was never satisfied with himself. He was impulsive, and was occasionally, I have heard it said, over excited, when his prejudices were roughly handled. In all that related to the questions involved in our civil war, he was, no doubt, very sensitive. He had heard so much that exasperated him in the foreign society which he had expected to be in full sympathy with the cause of liberty as against slavery, that he might be excused if he showed impatience when he met with similar sentiments among his own countrymen. He felt that he had been cruelly treated by his own government, and no one who conceives himself to have been wronged and insulted must be expected to reason in naked syllogisms on the propriety of the liberties which have been taken with his name and standing. But with all his quickness of feeling, his manners were easy and courteous, simply because his nature was warm and kindly, and with all his natural fastidiousness there was nothing of the coxcomb about him.

He must have had enemies, as all men of striking individuality are sure to have; his presence cast more uncouth patriots into the shade; his learning was a reproach to the ignorant, his fame was too bright a distinction; his high-bred air and refinement, which he could not help, would hardly commend him to the average citizen in an order of things in which mediocrity is at a premium, and the natural nobility of presence, which rarely comes without family antecedents to account for it, is not always agreeable to the many whose two ideals are the man on horseback and the man in his shirt-sleeves. It may well be questioned whether Washington, with his grand manner, would be nearly as popular with what are called "the masses" as Lincoln, with his homely ways and broad stories. The experiment of universal suffrage must render the waters of political and social life more or less turbid even if they remain innoxious. The Cloaca Maxima can hardly mingle its contents with the stream of the Aqua Claudia, without taking something from its crystal clearness. We need not go so far as one of our well-known politicians has recently gone in saying that no great man can reach the highest position in our government, but we can safely say that, apart from military fame, the loftiest and purest and finest personal qualities are not those which can be most depended upon at the ballot-box. Strange stories are told of avowed opposition to Mr. Motley on the ground of the most trivial differences in point of taste in personal matters, — so told that it is hard to disbelieve them, and they show that the caprices which we might have thought belonged exclusively to absolute rulers among their mistresses or their minions may be felt in the councils of a great people which calls itself self-governing. It is perfectly true that Mr. Motley did not illustrate the popular type of politician. He was too high-minded, too scholarly, too generously industrious, too polished, too much at home in the highest European circles, too much courted for his personal fascinations, too remote from the trading world of caucus managers. To degrade him, so far as official capital punishment could do it, was not merely to wrong one whom the nation should have delighted to honor as showing it to the world in the fairest flower of its young civilization, but it was an indignity to a representative of the highest scholarship of native growth, which every student in the land felt as a discouragement to all sound learning and noble ambition.

If he was disappointed in his diplomatic career, he had enough, and more than enough, to console him in his brilliant literary triumphs. He had earned them all by the most faithful and patient labor. If he had not the "frame of adamant" of the Swedish hero, he had his "soul of fire." No labors could tire him, no difficulties affright him. What most surprised those who knew him as a young man was, not his ambition, not his brilliancy, but his dogged, continuous capacity for work. We have seen with what astonishment the old Dutch scholar, Groen van Prinsterer, looked upon a man who had wrestled with authors like Bor and Van Meteren, who had grappled with the mightiest folios and toiled undiscouraged among half-illegible manuscript records. Having spared no pains in collecting his materials, he told his story, as we all know, with flowing ease and stirring vitality. His views may have been more or less partial; Philip the Second may have deserved the pitying benevolence of poor Maximilian; Maurice may have wept as sincerely over the errors of Arminius as any one of "the crocodile crew that believe in election;" Barneveld and Grotius may have been on the road to Rome; none of these things seem probable, but if they were all proved true in opposition to his views, we should still have the long roll of glowing tapestry he has woven for us, with all its life-like portraits, its almost moving pageants, its sieges where we can see the artillery flashing, its battle-fields with their smoke and fire, — pictures which cannot fade, and which will preserve his name interwoven with their own enduring colors.

Republics are said to be ungrateful; it might be truer to say that they are forgetful. They forgive those who have wronged them as easily as they forget those who have done them good service. But History never forgets and never forgives. To her decision we may trust the question, whether the warm-hearted patriot who had stood up for his country nobly and manfully in the hour of trial, the great scholar and writer who had reflected honor upon her throughout the world of letters, the high-minded public servant, whose shortcomings it taxed the ingenuity of experts to make conspicuous enough to be presentable, was treated as such a citizen should have been dealt with. His record is safe in her hands, and his memory will be precious always in the hearts of all who enjoyed his friendship.

APPENDIX.

A.

THE SATURDAY CLUB.

THIS club, of which we were both members, and which is still flourishing, came into existence in a very quiet sort of way at about the same time as "The Atlantic Monthly," and, although entirely unconnected with that magazine, included as members some of its chief contributors. Of those who might have been met at some of the monthly gatherings in its earlier days I may mention Emerson, Hawthorne, Longfellow, Lowell, Motley, Whipple, Whittier; Professors Agassiz and Peirce; John S. Dwight; Governor Andrew, Richard H. Dana, Junior, Charles Sumner. It offered a wide gamut of intelligences, and the meetings were noteworthy occasions. If there was not a certain amount of "mutual admiration" among some of those I have mentioned it was a great pity, and implied a defect in the nature of men who were otherwise largely endowed. The vitality of this club has depended in a great measure on its utter poverty in statutes and by-laws, its entire absence of formality, and its blessed freedom from speech-making.

That holy man, Richard Baxter, says in his Preface to Alleine's "Alarm:" —

"I have done, when I have sought to remove a little scandal, which I foresaw, that I should myself write the Preface to his Life where himself and two of his friends make such a mention of my name, which I cannot own; which will seem a praising him for praising me. I confess it looketh ill-favoredly in me.

But I had not the power of other men's writings, and durst not forbear that which was his due."

I do not know that I have any occasion for a similar apology in printing the following lines read at a meeting of members of the Saturday Club and other friends who came together to bid farewell to Motley before his return to Europe in 1857.

A PARTING HEALTH.

Yes, we knew we must lose him, — though friendship may
    claim
To blend her green leaves with the laurels of fame,
Though fondly, at parting, we call him our own,
'T is the whisper of love when the bugle has blown.

As the rider that rests with the spur on his heel,
As the guardsman that sleeps in his corselet of steel,
As the archer that stands with his shaft on the string,
He stoops from his toil to the garland we bring.

What pictures yet slumber unborn in his loom
Till their warriors shall breathe and their beauties shall bloom,
While the tapestry lengthens the life-glowing dyes
That caught from our sunsets the stain of their skies !

In the alcoves of death, in the charnels of time,
Where flit the dark spectres of passion and crime,
There are triumphs untold, there are martyrs unsung,
There are heroes yet silent to speak with his tongue !

Let us hear the proud story that time has bequeathed
From lips that are warm with the freedom they breathed !
Let him summon its tyrants, and tell us their doom,
Though he sweep the black past like Van Tromp with his
    broom !

. . . .

The dream flashes by, for the west-winds awake
On pampas, on prairie, o'er mountain and lake,

To bathe the swift bark, like a sea-girdled shrine
With incense they stole from the rose and the pine.

So fill a bright cup with the sunlight that gushed
When the dead summer's jewels were trampled and crushed ;
THE TRUE KNIGHT OF LEARNING, — the world holds him
      dear, —
Love bless him, joy crown him, God speed his career !

B.

HABITS AND METHODS OF STUDY.

MR. MOTLEY'S daughter, Lady Harcourt, has favored
me with many interesting particulars which I could not
have learned except from a member of his own family.
Her description of his way of living and of working will
be best given in her own words : —

"He generally rose early, the hour varying somewhat at different parts of his life, according to his work and health. Sometimes when much absorbed by literary labor he would rise before
seven, often lighting his own fire, and with a cup of tea or coffee
writing until the family breakfast hour, after which his work
was immediately resumed, and he usually sat over his writing-
table until late in the afternoon, when he would take a short
walk. His dinner hour was late, and he rarely worked at night.
During the early years of his literary studies he led a life of
great retirement. Later, after the publication of the 'Dutch Republic' and during the years of official place, he was much in
society in England, Austria, and Holland. He enjoyed social
life, and particularly dining out, keenly, but was very moderate and simple in all his personal habits, and for many years
before his death had entirely given up smoking. His work,
when not in his own library, was in the Archives of the Netherlands, Brussels, Paris, the English State Paper Office, and the
British Museum, where he made his own researches, patiently
and laboriously consulting original manuscripts and reading
masses of correspondence, from which he afterwards sometimes
caused copies to be made, and where he worked for many con-
secutive hours a day. After his material had been thus painfully

and toilfully amassed, the writing of his own story was always done at home, and his mind, having digested the necessary matter, always poured itself forth in writing so copiously that his revision was chiefly devoted to reducing the over-abundance. He never shrank from any of the drudgery of preparation, but I think his own part of the work was sheer pleasure to him."

I should have mentioned that his residence in London while minister was at the house No. 17 Arlington Street, belonging to Lord Yarborough.

C.

SIR WILLIAM GULL'S ACCOUNT OF HIS ILLNESS.

I HAVE availed myself of the permission implied in the subjoined letter of Sir William Gull to make large extracts from his account of Mr. Motley's condition while under his medical care. In his earlier years he had often complained to me of those "nervous feelings connected with the respiration" referred to by this very distinguished physician. I do not remember any other habitual trouble to which he was subject.

74 BROOK STREET, GROSVENOR SQUARE, W.
February 13, 1878.

MY DEAR SIR, — I send the notes of Mr. Motley's last illness, as I promised. They are too technical for general readers, but you will make such exception as you require. The medical details may interest your professional friends. Mr. Motley's case was a striking illustration that the renal disease of so-called Bright's disease may supervene as part and parcel of a larger and antecedent change in the blood-vessels in other parts than the kidney. . . . I am, my dear sir,

Yours very truly,
WILLIAM W. GULL.

To OLIVER WENDELL HOLMES, ESQ.

I first saw Mr. Motley, I believe, about the year 1870, on account of some nervous feelings connected with the respiration. At that time his general health was good, and all he complained of was occasionally a feeling of oppression about the chest. There were no physical signs of anything abnormal, and the symptoms quite passed away in the course of time, and with the use of simple antispasmodic remedies, such as camphor and the like. This was my first interview with Mr. Motley, and I was naturally glad to have the opportunity of making his acquaintance. I remember that in our conversation I jokingly said that my wife could hardly forgive him for not making her hero, Henri IV., a perfect character, and the earnestness with which he replied *au sérieux*, " I assure you I have fairly recorded the facts." After this date I did not see Mr. Motley for some time. He had three slight attacks of hæmoptysis in the autumn of 1872, but no physical signs of change in the lung tissue resulted. So early as this I noticed that there were signs of commencing thickening in the heart, as shown by the degree and extent of its impulse. The condition of his health, though at that time not very obviously failing, a good deal arrested my attention, as I thought I could perceive in the occurrence of the hæmoptysis, and in the cardiac hypertrophy, the early beginnings of vascular degeneration.

In August, 1873, occurred the remarkable seizure, from the effects of which Mr. Motley never recovered. I did not see him in the attack, but was informed, as far as I can remember, that he was on a casual visit at a friend's house at luncheon (or it might have been dinner), when he suddenly became strangely excited, but not quite unconscious. . . . I believed at the time, and do so still, that there was some capillary apoplexy of the convolutions. The attack was attended with some hemiplegic weakness on the right side, and altered sensation, and ever after there was a want of freedom and ease both in the gait and in the use of the arm of that side. To my inquiries from time to time how the arm was, the patient would always flex and extend it freely, but nearly always used the expression, " There is a bedevilment in it ; " though the handwriting was not much, if at all, altered.

In December, 1873, Mr. Motley went by my advice to Cannes. I wrote the following letter [1] at the time to my friend Dr. Frank, who was practising there : —

---

[1] This letter, every word of which was of value to the practitioner who was to have charge of the patient, relates many of the facts given above, and I shall therefore only give extracts from it.

December 29, 1873.

MY DEAR DR. FRANK, — My friend Mr. Motley, the historian and late American Minister, whose name and fame no doubt you know very well, has by my advice come to Cannes for the winter and spring, and I have promised him to give you some account of his case. To me it is one of special interest, and personally, as respects the subject of it, of painful interest. I have known Mr. Motley for some time, but he consulted me for the present condition about midsummer.

. . . If I have formed a correct opinion of the pathology of the case, I believe the smaller vessels are degenerating in several parts of the *vascular area*, lung, brain, and kidneys. With this view I have suggested a change of climate, a nourishing diet, etc. ; and it is to be hoped, and I trust expected, that by great attention to the conditions of hygiene, internal and external, the progress of degeneration may be retarded. I have no doubt you will find, as time goes on, increasing evidence of renal change, but this is rather a coincidence and consequence than a cause, though no doubt when the renal change has reached a certain point, it becomes in its own way a factor of other lesions. I have troubled you at this length because my mind is much occupied with the pathology of these cases, and because no case can, on personal grounds, more strongly challenge our attention.

Yours very truly,
WILLIAM W. GULL.

During the spring of 1874, whilst at Cannes, Mr. Motley had a sharp attack of nephritis, attended with fever ; but on returning to England in July there was no important change in the health. The weakness of the side continued, and the inability to undertake any mental work. The signs of cardiac hypertrophy were more distinct. In the beginning of the year 1875 I wrote as follows : —

February 20, 1875.

MY DEAR MR. MOTLEY, — . . . The examination I have just made appears to indicate that the main conditions of your health are more stable than they were some months ago, and would therefore be so far in favor of your going to America in the summer, as we talked of. The ground of my doubt has lain in the possibility of such a trip further disordering the circulation. Of this, I hope, there is now less risk.

On the 4th of June, 1875, I received the following letter: —

CALVERLY PARK HOTEL, TUNBRIDGE WELLS,
June 4, 1875.

MY DEAR SIR WILLIAM, — I have been absent from town for a long time, but am to be there on the 9th and 10th. Could I make an appointment with you for either of those days? I am anxious to have a full consultation with you before leaving for America. Our departure is fixed for the 19th of this month. I have not been worse than usual of late. I think myself, on the contrary, rather stronger, and it is almost impossible for me not to make my visit to America this summer, unless you should absolutely prohibit it. If neither of those days should suit you, could you kindly suggest another day? I hope, however, you can spare me half an hour on one of those days, as I like to get as much of this bracing air as I can. Will you kindly name the hour when I may call on you, and address me at this hotel. Excuse this slovenly note in pencil, but it fatigues my head and arm much more to sit at a writing-table with pen and ink.

Always most sincerely yours,
My dear Sir William,
J. L. MOTLEY.

On Mr. Motley's return from America I saw him, and found him, I thought, rather better in general health than when he left England.

In December, 1875, Mr. Motley consulted me for trouble of vision in reading or walking, from sensations like those produced by flakes of falling snow coming between him and the objects he was looking at. Mr. Bowman, one of our most excellent oculists, was then consulted. Mr. Bowman wrote to me as follows: "Such symptoms as exist point rather to disturbed retinal function than to any brain-mischief. It is, however, quite likely that what you fear for the brain may have had its counterpart in the nerve-structures of the eye, and as he is short-sighted, this tendency may be further intensified."

Mr. Bowman suggested no more than such an arrangement of glasses as might put the eyes, when in use, under better optic conditions.

The year 1876 was passed over without any special change worth notice. The walking powers were much impeded by the want of control over the right leg. The mind was entirely clear, though Mr. Motley did not feel equal, and indeed had been advised not to apply himself, to any literary work. Occasional conversations, when I had interviews with him on the subject of his health, proved that the attack which had weakened the movements of the right side had not impaired the mental power. The most noticeable change which had come over Mr. Motley since I first knew him was due to the death of Mrs. Motley in December, 1874. It had in fact not only profoundly depressed him, but, if I may so express it, had removed the centre of his thought to a new world. In long conversations with me of a speculative kind, after that painful event, it was plain how much his point of view of the whole course and relation of things had changed. His mind was the last to dogmatize on any subject. There was a candid and childlike desire to know, with an equal confession of the incapacity of the human intellect. I wish I could recall the actual expressions he used, but the sense was that which has been so well stated by Hooker in concluding an exhortation against the pride of the human intellect, where he remarks : —

" Dangerous it were for the feeble brain of man to wade far into the doings of the Most High ; whom although to know be life, and joy to make mention of His Name, yet our soundest knowledge is to know that we know Him, not indeed as He is, neither can know Him ; and our safest eloquence concerning Him is our silence, when we confess without confession that His glory is inexplicable, His greatness above our capacity and reach. He is above and we upon earth ; therefore it behoveth our words to be wary and few."

Mrs. Motley's illness was not a long one, and the nature of it was such that its course could with certainty be predicted. Mr. Motley and her children passed the remaining days of her life, extending over about a month, with her, in the mutual understanding that she was soon to part from them. The character of the illness, and the natural exhaustion of her strength by suffering, lessened the shock of her death, though not the loss, to those who survived her.

The last time I saw Mr. Motley was, I believe, about two

months before his death, March 28, 1877. There was no great change in his health, but he complained of indescribable sensations in his nervous system, and felt as if losing the whole power of walking, but this was not obvious in his gait, although he walked shorter distances than before. I heard no more of him until I was suddenly summoned on the 29th of May into Devonshire to see him. The telegram I received was so urgent, that I suspected some rupture of a blood-vessel in the brain, and that I should hardly reach him alive ; and this was the case. About two o'clock in the day he complained of a feeling of faintness, said he felt ill and should not recover ; and in a few minutes was insensible with symptoms of ingravescent apoplexy. There was extensive hæmorrhage into the brain, as shown by post-mortem examination, the cerebral vessels being atheromatous. The fatal hæmorrhage had occurred into the lateral ventricles, from rupture of one of the middle cerebral arteries.

I am, my dear Sir,

Yours very truly,

WILLIAM W. GULL.

D.

PLACE OF BURIAL. — FUNERAL SERVICE. — EPITAPHS. — DEAN STANLEY'S FUNERAL SERMON.

MR. MOTLEY was buried by the side of his wife in Kensal Green Cemetery, just outside of London. Services were held in the chapel at the cemetery.

The following account of the funeral is extracted from a letter of Mr. Smalley to the "New York Tribune: " —

"Mr. Motley was buried on Monday in Kensal Green Cemetery, Dean Stanley performing the service. The funeral was neither quite public nor quite private. It had been Dean Stanley's wish that it should take place in Westminster Abbey. He had proposed that the body, when brought from Dorsetshire, should lie over night in the Abbey ; that a ceremony should be held there in the morning, and that the friends of the deceased should assemble at the Abbey and accompany the body thence to the cemetery. But some difficulties — I could not make out what — stood in the way of this arrangement. It is cause for regret that the kind purposes of the Dean could not be carried out. Mr. Motley's friends — and all Americans, because he was an American — would have liked that some of the last words said over him should have been said in the great church which has so peculiar an interest for Americans, — which Americans in general venerate as they venerate no cathedral and no other church. As it was not to be, we can only express our gratitude to Dean Stanley for his readiness to bring it about.

" The service at the Kensal Green Chapel was of course the burial service of the Church of England, of which Mr. Motley was a member. His three daughters, Lady Harcourt, Mrs. Sheridan, and Miss Motley, were present, and with Sir William Harcourt, Mr. Russell Sturgis, and Mr. Sheridan, followed the coffin from the chapel to the grave. Among others present were Mr. Bright, the Duke of Argyll, Mr. Froude, Lord Houghton, Mr. Thomas Hughes, the Minister of the Netherlands, the Minister of Belgium, the Hon. Lyulph Stanley, Mr. Lecky, Mr. Hoppin, Mr. Murray, Mr. Edward Dicey, and Mr. Conway."

The inscriptions on the gravestones are these: —

JOHN LOTHROP MOTLEY.

BORN AT DORCHESTER, MASS., APRIL 15, 1814:
DIED NEAR DORCHESTER, DORSET, MAY 29, 1877.
In God is light, and in him is no darkness at all.

MARY ELIZABETH, WIFE OF JOHN LOTHROP MOTLEY.

BORN APRIL 7, 1813.
DIED DECEMBER 31, 1874.
Truth shall make you free.

On the 3d of June Dean Stanley preached a sermon in Westminster Abbey, in which he referred with much feeling to the death of Mr. Motley. I give a few extracts from the manuscript notes sent me by Miss Motley.

. . . " But there is a yet deeper key of harmony that has just been struck within the last week. The hand of death has removed from his dwelling-place amongst us one of the brightest lights of the Western hemisphere, — the high-spirited patriot, the faithful friend of England's best and purest spirits, the brilliant, the indefatigable historian who told, as none before him had told, the history of the rise and struggle of the Dutch Republic, almost a part of his own.

"We sometimes ask what room or place is left in the crowded temple of Europe's fame for one of the Western world to occupy. But a sufficient answer is given in the work which was reserved to be accomplished by him who has just departed. So long as the tale of the greatness of the house of Orange, of the siege of Leyden, of the tragedy of Barneveld, interests mankind, so long will Holland be indissolubly connected with the name of Motley in that union of the ancient culture of Europe with the aspirations of America which was so remarkable in the ardent, laborious, soaring soul that has passed away. He loved that land of his with a passionate zeal, he loved the land of his adoption with a surpassing love. . . . He loved the fatherland, the mother tongue of the literature which he had made his own. He loved the land which was the happy home of his children, and which contained the dearly cherished grave of her beside whom he will be laid to-morrow. Whenever any gifted spirit passes from our world to the other it brings both within our nearer view, — the world of this mortal life with its contentions and strifes, its joys and griefs, now to him closed forever, but amidst which he won his fame, and in which his name shall long endure, and the other world of our ideal vision, of our inexhaustible longings, of our blank misgivings, of our inextinguishable hopes, of our everlasting reunions, the eternal love in which live the spirits of the just made perfect, the heavenly Jerusalem, which being above is free, the city of which God himself is the light, and in whose light we shall see light."

E.

FROM THE PROCEEDINGS OF THE MASSACHUSETTS HISTORICAL SOCIETY.

AT a meeting of the Massachusetts Historical Society, held on Thursday, the 14th of June, 1877, after the reading of the records of the preceding meeting, the president, the Hon. Robert C. Winthrop, spoke as follows: —

" Our first thoughts to-day, gentlemen, are of those whom we may not again welcome to these halls. We shall be in no mood, certainly, for entering on other subjects this morning until we have given some expression to our deep sense of the loss — the double loss — which our Society has sustained since our last monthly meeting." [1] . . .

After a most interesting and cordial tribute to his friend, Mr. Quincy, Mr. Winthrop continued : —

" The death of our distinguished associate, Motley, can hardly have taken many of us by surprise. Sudden at the moment of its occurrence, we had long been more or less prepared for it by his failing health. It must, indeed, have been quite too evident to those who had seen him, during the last two or three years, that his life-work was finished. I think he so regarded it himself.

" Hopes may have been occasionally revived in the hearts of his friends, and even in his own heart, that his long-cherished purpose of completing a History of the Thirty Years' War, as the grand consummation of his historical labors, — for which all his other volumes seemed to him to have been but the preludes and overtures, — might still be accomplished. But such hopes, faint and flickering from his first attack, had wellnigh died away. They were like Prescott's hopes of completing his ' Philip the Second,' or like Macaulay's hopes of finishing his brilliant ' History of England.'

" But great as may be the loss to literature of such a crowning work from Motley's pen, it was by no means necessary to the completeness of his own fame. His ' Rise of the Dutch Republic,' his ' History of the United Netherlands,' and his ' Life of John of Barneveld,' had abundantly established his reputation, and given him a fixed place among the most eminent historians of our country and of our age.

" No American writer, certainly, has secured a wider recognition or a higher appreciation from the scholars of the Old World. The universities of England and the learned societies of Europe have bestowed upon him their largest honors. It happened to me to be in Paris when he was first chosen a corre-

[1] Edmund Quincy died May 17. John Lothrop Motley died May 29.

sponding member of the Institute, and when his claims were canvassed with the freedom and earnestness which peculiarly characterize such a candidacy in France. There was no mistaking the profound impression which his first work had made on the minds of such men as Guizot and Mignet. Within a year or two past, a still higher honor has been awarded him from the same source. The journals not long ago announced his election as one of the six foreign associates of the French Academy of Moral and Political Sciences, — a distinction which Prescott would probably have attained had he lived a few years longer, until there was a vacancy, but which, as a matter of fact, I believe, Motley was the only American writer, except the late Edward Livingston, of Louisiana, who has actually enjoyed.

" Residing much abroad, for the purpose of pursuing his historical researches, he had become the associate and friend of the most eminent literary men in almost all parts of the world, and the singular charms of his conversation and manners had made him a favorite guest in the most refined and exalted circles.

" Of his relations to political and public life, this is hardly the occasion or the moment for speaking in detail. Misconstructions and injustices are the proverbial lot of those who occupy eminent position. It was a duke of Vienna, if I remember rightly, whom Shakespeare, in his ' Measure for Measure,' introduces as exclaiming, —

> ' O place and greatness, millions of false eyes
> Are stuck upon thee! Volumes of report
> Run with these false and most contrarious quests
> Upon thy doings! Thousand 'scapes of wit
> Make thee the father of their idle dream,
> And rack thee in their fancies! '

" I forbear from all application of the lines. It is enough for me, certainly, to say here, to-day, that our country was proud to be represented at the courts of Vienna and London successively by a gentleman of so much culture and accomplishment as Mr. Motley, and that the circumstances of his recall were deeply regretted by us all.

" His fame, however, was quite beyond the reach of any such accidents, and could neither be enhanced nor impaired by appointments or removals. As a powerful and brilliant historian we pay him our unanimous tribute of admiration and regret, and give him a place in our memories by the side of Prescott and Irving. I do not forget how many of us lament him, also, as a cherished friend.

"He died on the 29th ultimo, at the house of his daughter, Mrs. Sheridan, in Dorsetshire, England, and an impressive tribute to his memory was paid, in Westminster Abbey, on the following Sunday, by our Honorary Member, Dean Stanley. Such a tribute, from such lips, and with such surroundings, leaves nothing to be desired in the way of eulogy. He was buried in Kensal Green Cemetery, by the side of his beloved wife.

"One might well say of Motley precisely what he said of Prescott, in a letter from Rome to our associate, Mr. William Amory, immediately on hearing of Prescott's death : 'I feel inexpressibly disappointed — speaking now for an instant purely from a literary point of view — that the noble and crowning monument of his life, for which he had laid such massive foundations, and the structure of which had been carried forward in such a grand and masterly manner, must remain uncompleted, like the unfinished peristyle of some stately and beautiful temple on which the night of time has suddenly descended. But, still, the works which his great and untiring hand had already thoroughly finished will remain to attest his learning and genius, — a precious and perpetual possession for his country.'

"I am authorized by the Council to offer the following resolutions : —

. . . .

"'*Resolved*, That by the death of the Hon. John Lothrop Motley this Society has lost one of its most distinguished members, and American literature one of its brightest ornaments ; a son of Massachusetts, who, in illustrating so powerfully the annals of another land, has reflected the highest honor on his own, and whose fame as an historian will ever be cherished among the treasures of his native State.

"'*Resolved*, That the President be requested to nominate one of our associates to prepare a Memoir of Mr. Motley.'"

William Amory, Esq., spoke as follows: —

"I thank you cordially, Mr. President, for affording to me at this time the opportunity of paying the tribute of a few remarks to the memory of one whom I had so long known, loved, and honored as Mr. Motley ; and, though I may fail to do it in words suitable to the occasion, or satisfactory to myself, I am compelled by the promptings of my heart, not alone in silence to mingle my tears with those of the family and friends who mourn the loss of a father, brother, and friend, but to join also my voice with the voices of those who are gathered here to-day to deplore the loss and honor the memory of him who, as our associate, by his writings and character has contributed so largely to elevate the reputation of this Society, to embellish the name of this community, and to reflect throughout the civilized world the lustre of his own name on the literature of his native country. Till about 1840 I personally knew little of Mr. Motley ; but since then our intimacy has been unbroken and our intercourse uninterrupted, except by his absence in Europe. The lapse of almost forty years since I first saw him has scarcely effaced from the freshness of my memory my first impression of the transparent nature and striking idiosyncrasies of his remarkable character, which made it easy to imagine the past, and not difficult to divine the future of his brilliant career. The expressive beauty of his face, the manly elegance of his person, his winning ways, his sparkling wit, and the irresistible charm of his conversation, all gave even then assurance of distinction and promise of fame in his riper years. A few years later, at about thirty, not inclined to the practice of the law, which he had studied partly as an accomplishment, partly as a possible means of support, and partly as a preparation for any other pursuit he might embrace as more congenial to his temperament or taste, he determined upon a literary career, and, as his genius, attainments, studies, and tastes inclined him thereto, he, fortunately for himself and the world, adopted history as a specialty, and selected ' The Rise of the Dutch Republic ' as the subject of his first historical work.

"His brilliant success a few years later, on the publication of that book, showed how wisely he had chosen for his own reputation, for the honor of the republic whose history he faithfully, picturesquely, and elegantly depicted, and for that of the republic at home, upon which he at once shed such glory as a writer. By this, his first history, published in London in 1856, he was raised by common consent at one bound to the front rank of illustrious historians in the English language, and by his subsequent works, though perhaps less attractive to the general reader, he has sustained the reputation he at that time acquired.

"With a few of his friends in this country, I was favored with the privilege of a perusal of those volumes before they were published in England ; and, though already entertaining a high appreciation of his genius and powers, I was inexpressibly surprised at the eloquence of the style, the interest of the narrative, the variety, aptitude, and brilliancy of the illustrations, and the life-like fidelity of the portraits of the chief actors in that wonderful historical drama, but above all by the untiring industry and diligent research displayed throughout in procuring, preparing, and using so ably such copious materials from such various sources. Three years after its publication, in 1859, Mr. Motley, on hearing of the death of W. H. Prescott, his friend and brother historian, wrote from Rome a long letter, containing a very interesting account of an interview he had sought with Mr. Prescott about twelve years before, in relation to the subject of the Rise of the Dutch Republic. That letter was read by Mr. Sears at a meeting of this Society, holden in April, 1859, and recorded in full on page 266 of the published 'Proceedings' of 1858–60. Though too long to be read here, it is so touching and beautiful a letter, and so creditable and honorable to both Mr. Motley and Mr. Prescott, that I have ventured to allude to it for the benefit of such members of this Society as have either forgotten or never seen it, and to whom at this moment it may have a peculiar interest, if they possess the volume of the 'Proceedings' referred to. The subject of the letter may be briefly stated thus : About 1846, Mr. Motley had collected materials and made preparations to write 'The Rise of the Dutch Republic,' ignorant of the fact that Mr. Prescott had still earlier also made still larger preparations to write the History of Philip II. As, in writing upon subjects so closely identified in time and events, it was obvious that Mr. Motley must often traverse the same ground occupied by Mr. Prescott, he determined, when informed by a friend of Mr. Prescott's intention, to go to him and confer with him on the subject ; and, if he should find that Mr. Prescott had a shadow of objection to his proceeding with his history, to abandon it at once, though already so enamored of the subject he had selected that it was to him, as he said, like surrendering his historical career. He did so, was most kindly received, and cordially encouraged to proceed with the work at once by Mr. Prescott, who, at the same time, generously volunteered to offer any aid in his power and the free use of his library.

"Such is the summary of the purpose and result of that interview ; but to realize the sacrifice which the young aspirant to authorship was ready to make to a nice sense of honor and courtesy to the perhaps doubtful priority of the conventional claim of one with whom at that time he was only slightly acquainted, or to appreciate the genuine gratitude and pleasure inspired by the cordial aid and generous encouragement offered him by Mr. Prescott, it is necessary to read the letter itself.

"I have, Mr. President, perhaps dwelt too long on this subject ; but the temptation to present in one picture, and to illustrate by one anecdote, the different, but equally beautiful, traits of character exhibited in the same story by the two most illustrious historians of this country must be my excuse.

"You may well be proud, sir, that during your presidency of the Massachusetts Historical Society the names of Prescott and Motley, both your associates, have been enrolled by universal consent in the same rank with those of Hume, Gibbon, and Robertson, of the eighteenth century, and Hallam and Macaulay, of the nineteenth ; and it is worth recording on the same page that these friends and brother historians of the same subject were natives of the same State, citizens of the same city, graduates of the same college, equally remarkable for their personal beauty and the charms of their manners, published their first histories at the same time of life, and died in precisely the same manner, at about the same age. With more time, it would be gratifying to compare and contrast those elements of moral, intellectual, and social character, which, though so different in each of these distinguished men, contributed so equally to the charms and celebrity of both in the world of letters and in the society of the world ; but it is too late, and I am conscious that already I have encroached upon the ground of his literary friends, instead of confining myself to those social and domestic beauties of his character, so much richer in interest and materials, and upon which I am so much better authority. One of these attributes, and, as I think, the most prominent and characteristic of all, was the tender affectionateness of his nature, which, within the small circle of his home and friends, was irresistibly winning, and which, though less known to the outside world, pervaded his whole being, and was often the hidden source of that magnetism and fascination which captivated all, and won for him hosts of friends and admirers wherever he was known.

"His ready and deep sympathy in the hour of sorrow or affliction, as indicated by the tones of his voice, the expression of his face, or the simple eloquence of his words, will be long remembered by many. Passing by that greatest and last domestic affliction, which made his home so desolate and his life so sad for the last two years, as too recent and sacred to be more than glanced at, I recall that agony of grief occasioned many years before by the sudden and shocking death of his nearest and dearest friend, Mr. Stackpole. Mr. Motley, for a while at that time a near neighbor of mine, spent every afternoon with me on my piazza at Longwood; and I shall never forget the touching words and manner in which he bewailed his loss in all the variety of thought and language which death and friendship could suggest, and with all the eloquence of an 'In Memoriam.' He could think and talk of nothing else. Subdued and softened by his sorrow, he seemed an altered man, and in the tenderness of his grief he was more like a mother weeping for an only child than a strong man mourning the loss even of his dearest friend. How easy it would be, Mr. President, to select from a character so rich in its endless variety many other equally interesting peculiarities, and to illustrate them by similiar reminiscences, no one can imagine without a familiar acquaintance with the incidents of his life, and a nice appreciation of those fine impulses of his nature which have shaped his career; and this can be fitly done only by the eloquent pen of a biographer who has known him from his youth.

"I have made no allusion to Mr. Motley's diplomatic career, which, but for circumstances beyond his control and not attributable to any fault of his, might have been as distinguished as his career as a writer, because I am sure that, to all who knew him, or the history of the termination of his missions to Vienna and London, any defence of *him certainly*, on either side of the water, would be entirely superfluous."

The President now called on Dr. Oliver Wendell Holmes, who said: —

" The thoughts which suggest themselves upon this occasion are such as belong to the personal memories of the dear friends whom we have lost, rather than to their literary labors, the just tribute to which must wait for a calmer hour than the present, following so closely as it does on our bereavement.

"To those of us who remember Mr. Motley during his last visit to this country, his death, though it was a blow to many lingering hopes, was hardly a surprise. But if we go back a few more years, and recall him as he appeared at our meeting of November, 1868, he comes before us with the promise of a long afternoon and evening to a life which was still in the brightness of its intellectual meridian. It fell to him on that occasion to speak before us of his friend, the late Dean Milman, and I am sure that not one of those who listened to him can forget the effect his words and his presence produced upon all who were gathered around him.

"He stood before us, a scholar speaking of a man of letters, and his words had the fitness, the balance, the flow, which belong to an imperial master of language. He was speaking of one who was, as he said, 'his life long a conspicuous ornament of the most cultivated society of London and of England;' and here was in his own person and address that harmonious union of rare qualities which all the world over is the master-key that opens every door, the countersign that passes every sentinel, the unsealed letter of introduction to all the highest circles of the highest civilization. Scholars are frequently forgetful of the outward graces which commend the man of the world to social favor. Here was a scholar who, to say the least, had rivalled the most robust and patient of our workers in drudgery, who had ploughed through manuscripts without number, whose crabbed characters and uncouth phrases might well have tried Champollion's temper; yet here was a man of such natural graces and such distinguished bearing, that he seemed to belong rather to the gilded saloon than to the dusty library.

"Let me touch briefly upon a few periods in his life. I remember him as a handsome, spirited-looking boy at Harvard College, where, at the early age of thirteen, he joined the class two years after my own, graduating in 1831. He was probably the youngest student in college, said to be as bright as he looked, and with the reputation of a remarkable talent for learning languages. Two years make a wide gulf in college life, and my intercourse with him was less frequent than at a later period. I recollect him in those earlier days as vivacious, attractive, brilliant, with such a lustre of promise about him as belonged to hardly any other of my own date, and after it, in my four years' college experience, if I perhaps except William Sturgis, whom a swift summons called from our side in all the beauty of his early youth. Motley was more nearly the ideal of a young poet than any boy — for he was only a boy as yet — who sat on the benches of the college chapel. In after years, one who knew Lord Byron most nearly noted his resemblance to that great poet, and spoke of it to one of my friends ; but in our young days many pretty youths affected that resemblance, and were laughed at for their pains, so that if Motley recalled Byron's portrait, it was only because he could not help it. His finely shaped and expressive features ; his large, luminous eyes ; his dark, waving hair ; the singularly spirited set of his head, which was most worthy of note for its shapely form and poise ; his well-outlined figure, — all gave promise of his manly beauty, and commended him to those even who could not fully appreciate the richer endowments of which they were only the outward signature. How often such gifts and promises disappoint those who count upon their future we who have seen the November of so many Aprils know too well. But with every temptation to a life of pleasant self-indulgence, flattery and the love of luxury could not spoil him. None knew better what they meant. 'Give me the luxuries, and I will dispense with the necessaries, of life,' was a playful saying of his, which is one of the three wittiest things that have been said in Boston in our time, and which, I think, has not been fairly claimed for any other wit of any period.

" Soon after graduation, Motley left this country for Germany, where he studied two years longer in the universities of Berlin and Göttingen. I myself was absent from the country when he returned, and only renewed an acquaintance, which then grew to intimacy with him, after my own return from a residence in Europe, at the end of the year 1835. He was at that time just entering upon the practice of law, the profession which he had studied, but in the labors of which he never became very seriously engaged.

" His first literary venture of any note was the story called 'Morton's Hope ; or, The Memoirs of a Provincial.' This first effort failed to satisfy the critics, the public, or himself. His personality pervaded the characters and times which he portrayed, so that there was a discord between the actor and his costume. Brilliant passages could not save it; and it was plain enough that he must ripen into something better before the world would give him the reception which surely awaited him if he should find his true destination.

"The early failures of a great writer are like the first sketches of a great artist, and well reward patient study. More than this, the first efforts of poets and story-tellers are very commonly palimpsests: beneath the rhymes or the fiction one can almost always spell out the characters which betray the writer's self. Take these passages from the story just referred to:—

"'Ah! flattery is a sweet and intoxicating potion, whether we drink it from an earthen ewer or a golden chalice. . . . Flattery from man to woman is expected: it is a part of the courtesy of society; but when the divinity descends from the altar to burn incense to the priest, what wonder if the idolater should feel himself transformed into a god!'

"He had run the risk of being spoiled, but he had a safeguard in his aspirations.

"'My ambitious anticipations,' says Morton, in the story, 'were as boundless as they were various and conflicting. There was not a path which leads to glory in which I was not destined to gather laurels. As a warrior, I would conquer and overrun the world; as a statesman, I would reorganize and govern it; as a historian, I would consign it all to immortality; and, in my leisure moments, I would be a great poet and a man of the world.'

"Who can doubt that in this passage of his story he is picturing his own visions, one of the fairest of which was destined to become reality?

"But there was another element in his character, which those who knew him best recognized as one with which he had to struggle hard,—that is, a modesty which sometimes tended to collapse into self-distrust. This, too, betrays itself in the sentences which follow those just quoted:—

"'In short,' says Morton, 'I was already enrolled in that large category of what are called young men of genius, . . . men of whom unheard-of things are expected; till after long

preparation comes a portentous failure, and then they are forgotten. . . . Alas ! for the golden imaginations of our youth.
. . . They are all disappointments. They are bright and beautiful, but they fade.'

"Mr. Motley's diplomatic experience began with his appointment as Secretary of Legation to the American Embassy to
Russia, in 1840, — a position which he held for a few months
only, and then returned to this country.

"In 1845 he wrote an article on Peter the Great for 'The North
American Review,' which suggested to many of his friends that,
though he had not taken the place as a novelist he might have
hoped for, there was in him the stronger fibre of an historian.
He did not, however, give up the idea of succeeding in his earlier
field of effort ; and in 1849 he published his second story, —
'Merry-Mount, a Romance of the Massachusetts Colony ;' which
again, with all its merits of style and its brilliancy of description,
was found wanting in some of the qualities demanded by an historical novel, and settled the question for him that his genius
was not in every way adapted to that kind of composition. The
truth was, he could not divest himself of his personality and
lose his individual character in that of his own creations. It
will be noticed, that, while his first story turned on the adven-
tures of an individual, his second story came much nearer to the
complexion of a true history. It was at about this uncertain
period of his career that a friend of his found him at work one
day with a Dutch folio and a dictionary of that language. On
being asked what he was doing with those uninviting books, he
spoke of his turning his studies in the direction of history. 'I
must break myself on something,' he said.

"What came of the studies which began with that Dutch dictionary you all know, the whole literary world knows, and I
need not recite the story. Neither will I take up your time
with criticisms upon those noble works, which have passed their
ordeal, and stand among the foremost contributions of the New
World to the literature of the Old. The personal enthusiasm
which gives a glow to every page, the inborn love of freedom, the
generous sympathy with all that is lofty, and the passionate scorn
of all that is petty and base, the richness of his descriptions, the
vigor of his portraits, — to speak of these is to repeat the commonplaces of all our literary tribunals. I cannot refrain from
adding a single thought which I do not remember having met
with.

"The sturdy little State of Holland — a nation with a population comparable for numbers with that of the city of London — offers itself to too many English and American minds with the unheroic aspect in which the Dutchman has been presented in the satirical verse of Marvell and the ludicrous travesty of Irving. We cannot keep the pictures and figures of Diedrich Knickerbocker out of our fancies when we think of a Hollander. Mr. Graham, the English historian of the United States, complains that Mr. Irving 'has by anticipation ridiculed my topic and parodied my narrative.' We can still smile, or laugh, as Sir Walter Scott did, over the extravagances of our great American humorist ; but it remained for an American historian to assert the true dignity of the valiant people who conquered an empire from the waves, and rescued it from the tyranny of still more lawless masters. The world can forgive all the playful mischief of the satirist so long as it contemplates the majestic figure of William the Silent, and reads the story of the defence of Leyden, the record of John of Barneveld, and the romantic episode of Hugo Grotius in the pages of Motley.

"I shall not do more than allude to the further diplomatic career of our honored associate. I know that it ended in disappointment, and a feeling that a great wrong had been done him. But I know, also, that his highest office was undertaken with a profound sense of responsibility ; that its duties were discharged as faithfully as he knew how to perform them ; and that, whatever sting was left by the manner in which he had been dealt with, there was no poison of self-reproach to rankle in the wound. Those who will search curiously enough in the 'Life of John of Barneveld' will discover at least one passage in which the writer's own violated sensibilities find an expression in the record of another's grievance, — the natural device by which men and women of all ages have sought relief : —

'Πάτροκλον πρόφασιν, σφῶν δ' αὐτῶν κήδε' ἑκάστη.'

I do not believe that the violence which reached the nervous centres of Sumner's life told on him with more fatal effect than the rude shock of Mr. Motley's sudden recall from England upon his proud and excitable spirit, and through his sensibilities on the organ of thought, from the internal laceration of which he died.

"A slight attack — hardly serious enough in its effects to be called paralytic — interrupted the literary labors which he had resumed after the close of his diplomatic career. His speech never seems to have been affected, and his handwriting showed no remarkable change, though he complained of weight and weakness of the right side, and found it a considerable effort to write. He was slowly regaining something of his usual health and spirits, when the death, in December, 1874, of the lovely and noble woman who had made the happiness of his life, cast the deep shadow over him which was never lifted. He passed the summer which followed his bereavement in this country, where for some weeks I saw him daily, and under those conditions which revealed his inmost nature more completely than I had ever known it in my long intimacy with him. He appeared to have forgotten all lesser trials in the one great sorrow which had left his life so nearly desolate. One thought, one feeling, seemed ever present ; an undercurrent which betrayed itself not by unmanly signs of weakness, but by the tenderness and the reverence to which the memory of her from whom he had been parted saddened and subdued every accent. The language in which he spoke of his wife was the highest tribute to womanhood that ever found words on living lips in my hearing. And not to womanhood, not to that noble woman alone, for they revealed the passionate intensity of his own loving nature, and showed us better than we ever understood before what was his peculiar underlying charm, and why we who loved him had loved him with such strong affection.

"But time has anodynes for griefs it cannot cure, and his letters showed that he was doing his best to bear his burden of sorrow, and that the affection of those who were left him was not without its healing influences. He had even hoped to be able to do something more in the way of literary labor, when suddenly, on the 29th of May, without any immediate warning, the thread by which his fate hung over him parted. The summons, though at an unexpected moment, might have been looked for at any time. The stroke fell like a blow on the already suffering organ through which his untiring intellect had wrought its vast and exhausting labors. 'It has come !' he said, and, after a few hours of unconscious life in death, he passed quietly away.

"He leaves all his uncounted honors, which I need not try to enumerate ; he leaves the unblazoned record of a social career hardly rivalled for the brilliancy of its success ; his works, sacred to heroism, the spirit of freedom and humanity, are his monument ; and, amidst the sorrowing tears of those who dearly loved him, in many lands and in every station of life, from the lowliest to the loftiest, he is laid by the side of her from whom he would not have been parted in death, to sleep in the mausoleum of a nation surrounded by the sepulchres of those who have made her history."

The Rev. R. C. Waterston then said : —

"It is a pleasant thought, Mr. President, to remember that the two members whom we to-day commemorate were personal friends. I have here a brief letter from Mr. Motley to Mr. Quincy, — the last letter which Mr. Quincy ever received from him, — written in pencil, from Nahant, during his last visit to this country. It may have some interest at this moment.

"'MY DEAR QUINCY, — Many thanks for your kind words of remembrance, and for your Memoir of Charles Sprague. I perfectly remember our visit to the venerable poet, and am highly gratified that he should have been pleased by it. I have read your Memoir with much interest and sympathy, and should think it a very just, and not in the least an over-appreciative, tribute to his delicate genius and genuine and honorable character.

"'There are a good many lines of his poetry which I can repeat now, and could do ever since I was a Sophomore. I hope to see you in Boston before I leave, which will be in October, as people seem to decide that the winter here will be too severe for me.

"'Pray excuse my illegible pencilling, but it is very hard work for me to write.

"'I am your sincere friend,
"'J. L. MOTLEY.'"

Mr. Waterston continued : —

"Mr. Motley, after the publication of his 'Merry-Mount,' expressed his regret to Mr. Quincy that it had met with so little success. Mr. Quincy replied : 'Motley, turn your attention to history. Your style is admirably adapted to that, and every power of your mind would there find ample scope, and the result, I am sure, would meet with success.' 'Do you think so ?'

he said. 'I feel certain of your perfect triumph in that field,' continued Mr. Quincy. It is pleasant to think that these life-long friends went so nearly together. United in their lives, in their death they were not divided."

Professor William Everett then spoke as follows: —

"There is one incident, sir, in Mr. Motley's career that has not been mentioned to-day, which is, perhaps, most vividly re-membered by those of us who were in Europe at the outbreak of our civil war in 1861. At that time, the ignorance of English-men, friendly or otherwise, about America, was infinite : they knew very little of us, and that little wrong. Americans were overwhelmed with questions, taunts, threats, misrepresentations, the outgrowth of ignorance, and ignoring worse than ignorance, from every class of Englishmen. Never was an authoritative exposition of our hopes and policy worse needed ; and there was no one to do it. The outgoing diplomatic agents represented a bygone order of things ; the representatives of Mr. Lincoln's administration had not come. At that time of anxiety, Mr. Motley, living in England as a private person, came forward with two letters in the 'Times,' which set forth the cause of the United States once and for all. No unofficial, and few official, men could have spoken with such authority, and been so certain of obtaining a hearing from Englishmen. Thereafter, amid all the clouds of falsehood and ridicule which we had to encounter, there was one lighthouse fixed on a rock to which we could go for foothold, from which we could not be driven, and against which all assaults were impotent.

"There can be no question that the effect produced by these letters helped, if help had been needed, to point out Mr. Motley as a candidate for high diplomatic place who could not be over-looked. Their value was recognized alike by his fellow-citizens in America and his admirers in England ; but none valued them more than the little band of exiles, who were struggling against terrible odds, and who rejoiced with a great joy to see the stars and stripes, whose centennial anniversary those guns are now celebrating, planted by a hand so truly worthy to rally every American to its support."

Remarks were also made by the Rev. S. K. Lothrop, D. D., and the resolutions were unanimously adopted, all the members rising.

The President appointed Professor Lowell to write the Memoir of Mr. Quincy, and Dr. Holmes that of Mr. Motley, for the Society's "Proceedings."

On motion of Mr. George B. Emerson, it was
"*Voted*, That the commemorative proceedings of this meeting be printed."

F.

LIST OF HIS HONORARY TITLES.

THE following list of the societies of which Mr. Motley was a member is from a memorandum in his own handwriting, dated November, 1866.

Historical Society of Massachusetts.
   "   "   " Minnesota.
   "   "   " New York.
   "   "   " Rhode Island.
   "   "   " Maryland.
   "   "   " Tennessee.
   "   "   " New Jersey.
American Academy of Arts and Sciences.
American Philosophical Society, Philadelphia.
Doctor of Laws, New York University.
   "   "   " Harvard   "
   "   " Literature, New York University.
Royal Society of Antiquaries, England.
Doctor of Laws, Oxford University, England.
   "   "   " Cambridge   "   "
Athenæum Club, London.
Royal Academy of Arts and Sciences of Amsterdam.
Historical Society of Utrecht, Holland.
Historical Society of Leyden, Holland.
Doctor of Philosophy, University of Groningen.
Corresponding Member of French Institute ; Academy of Moral and Political Sciences.
Academy of Arts and Sciences of Petersburg.
Doctor of Laws, University of Leyden.

The last honorary title conferred upon him was that of Foreign Associate of the French Academy of Moral and Political Sciences.   This is the highest title the Academy can confer.

G.

POEMS BY W. W. STORY AND WILLIAM CULLEN BRYANT.

I CANNOT close this Memoir more appropriately than by appending the two following poetical tributes: —

IN MEMORIAM, — JOHN LOTHROP MOTLEY.

BY W. W. STORY.

Farewell, dear friend !   For us the grief and pain,
Who shall not see thy living face again ;
For us the sad yet noble memories
Of lofty thoughts, of upward-looking eyes,
Of warm affections, of a spirit bright
With glancing fancies and a radiant light,
That, flashing, threw around all common things
Heroic halos and imaginings ;
Nothing of this can fade while life shall last,
But brighten, with death's shadow o'er it cast.

For us the pain ; for thee the larger life,
The higher being, freed from earthly strife ;
Death hath but opened unto thee the door
Thy spirit knocked so strongly at before ;
And as a falcon from its cage set free,
Where it has pined and fluttered helplessly,
Longing to soar, and gazing at the sky
Where its strong wings their utmost flight may try,
So has thy soul, from out life's broken bars,
Sprung in a moment up beyond the stars,
Where all thy powers unfettered, unconfined,
Their native way in loftier regions find.

Ah, better thus, in one swift moment freed,
Than wounded, stricken, here to drag and bleed !

This was the fate we feared, but happy Death
Has swept thee from us, as a sudden breath
Wrings the ripe fruit from off the shaken bough, —
And ours the sorrow, thine the glory now !

How memory goes back, and lingering dwells
On the lost past, and its fond story tells !
When glad ambition fired thy radiant face,
And youth was thine, and hope, and manly grace,
And Life stood panting to begin its race ;
Thine eyes their summer lightning flashing out,
Thy brow with dark locks clustering thick about,
Thy sudden laugh from lips so sensitive,
Thy proud, quick gestures, all thy face alive, —
These, like a vision of the morning, rise
And brightly pass before my dreaming eyes.

And then again I see thee, when the breath
Of the great world's applause first stirred the wreath
That Fame upon thy head ungrudging placed ;
Modest and earnest, all thy spirit braced
To noble ends, and with a half excess
As of one running in great eagerness,
And leaning forward out beyond the poise
Of coward prudence, holding but as toys
The world's great favors, when it sought to stay
Thy impulsive spirit on its ardent way.

For thee no swerving to a private end ;
Stern in thy faith, that naught could break or bend,
Loving thy country, pledged to Freedom's cause,
Disdaining wrong, abhorrent of the laws
Expedience prompted with the tyrant's plea,
Wielding thy sword for Justice fearlessly, —
So brave, so true, that nothing could deter,
Nor friend, nor foe, thy ready blow for her.

Ah, noble spirit, whither hast thou fled ?
What doest thou amid the unnumbered dead ?
Oh, say not mid the dead, for what hast thou
Among the dead to do ?   No ! rather now,

If Faith and Hope are not a wild deceit,
The truly living thou hast gone to meet,
The noble spirits purged by death, whose eye
O'erpeers the brief bounds of mortality ;
And they behold thee rising there afar,
Serenely clear above Time's cloudy bar,
And greet thee as we greet a rising star.

IN MEMORY OF JOHN LOTHROP MOTLEY.

BY WILLIAM CULLEN BRYANT.

Sleep, Motley, with the great of ancient days,
    Who wrote for all the years that yet shall be.
Sleep with Herodotus, whose name and praise
    Have reached the isles of earth's remotest sea.
Sleep, while, defiant of the slow delays
    Of Time, thy glorious writings speak for thee
And in the answering heart of millions raise
    The generous zeal for Right and Liberty.
And should the days o'ertake us, when, at last,
    The silence that — ere yet a human pen
Had traced the slenderest record of the past —
    Hushed the primeval languages of men
Upon our English tongue its spell shall cast,
    Thy memory shall perish only then.

INDEX.